DECADES

The Bee Gees
in the 1970s

Andrew Môn Hughes, Grant Walters
& Mark Crohan

SONICBOND

sonicbondpublishing.com

Sonicbond Publishing Limited
www.sonicbondpublishing.co.uk
Email: info@sonicbondpublishing.co.uk

First Published in the United Kingdom 2023
First Published in the United States 2023

British Library Cataloguing in Publication Data:
A Catalogue record for this book is available from the British Library

ISBN 978-1-78952-179-5

Typeset in ITC Garamond & ITC Avant Garde
Printed and bound in England
Graphic design and typesetting: Full Moon Media

DECADES

The Bee Gees

in the 1970s

Andrew Môn Hughes, Grant Walters
& Mark Crohan

sonicbondpublishing.com

Dedicated to:

Jimmy Stevens

Manfred Baumann

Anneke Koremans

David English

Nel Nieuwpoort

Julie Barrett

Acknowledgements

The authors would collectively like to thank the following:
Stephen Lambe and Sonicbond Publishing for giving us the opportunity to take on this project. You surely have the patience of Job. Spencer Gibb, who has been a critical connection between the authors and his family's work, and a committed, ardent supporter of this entire project from start to finish.

Gerard Groux, Ric Holland, Frank Stiller, Reinhard Wenesch, and Minako Yoshida for their invaluable contributions and assistance with the picture section. Extra special thanks in this department to David Fedor for superbly photographing your memorabilia.

Marion Adriansen, Dick Ashby, Steve Barry, Melinda Bilyeu, Joe Brennan, Dennis Bryon, Hector Cook, Jessica Crohan, David English, Lesley Evans, Hazel Gibb, Justine Gibb, Gerard Groux, Milton Hammon, Beth Kujala, KittLarue, Jonathan Lea, David Leaf, Bernard Lupe, Lee Meadows, Vince Melouney, Mary Merrill, Jayne Henry Owens, Erling Paulsen, Andrew Sandoval, Malcolm Searles, Bob Stanley, Jane Stevens, Frank Stiller, Faye Ward, Blue Weaver, Peta Gibb Weber, Reinhard Wenesch, and Minako Yoshida, for their many heartfelt contributions and conversations along the way.

The 'Oh No' Group – Dan Box, Mark Byfield, Judy Farrar, Michelle Gibson, Ann Grootjans, Linda Keane-Bacon, Paul Mann, Darrin Mitchell, Richard O'Donoghue, and Ronnie Olsson for their friendship, banter and shared love of the Gibbs' music. This book series was written with all of you in our hearts.

Albhy Galuten and Karl Richardson for so many candid, helpful conversations in which their technical behind-the-scenes insight has breathed so much life into many aspects of this series.

Shindig!, Good Times, and *This Is Rock* magazines for positively reviewing the first book in the series, and likewise, Richie Unterberger for including it in his Top 25 (or so) Music History Books of 2021.

Edward Trayer and all at the *The Wishing Shelf Book Awards* – especially the reading groups – for their hard work and dedication. We thank you for reading and rating *Decades: The Bee Gees in the 1960s*, and we are greatly honoured to have been finalists in the 2021 awards.

David Fedor – *Bee Gees and Me* podcast; Sarah Stacey – *Gibbology: A Bee Gees Podcast*; Ben Montgomery – *Records Revisited Podcast*, and Jon Lamoreaux – *The Hustle Podcast*.

And last, but never least – Barry, Robin, and Maurice Gibb for their unfathomable talents that gifted the world with one of the greatest musical legacies of all time. Every word written here is dedicated to you with our utmost respect and admiration.

Authors' Note
This volume is the second in a series of four books in the 'Decades' series dedicated to The Bee Gees' lengthy career.

Thanks to ...

Andrew would like to thank: my wife Judy, for her love, patience, understanding and making my life so complete; Bella and Patch – our wonderful furry companions for the joy that they bring; my mother and father Enid and Mervyn for encouraging my love of music – the record player for Christmas in 1970 was the start of it all, but I guess the headphones a few years later showed that my tastes were changing; my sons Jonathan and Christopher, whose laughter is infectious, but usually at my expense. I love you all. Extra special thanks for extra special friends – Frank and Manuela Stiller.

Grant would like to thank: my wife Julie for her love and encouragement; my parents Gordon and Wendy, whose Bee Gees albums and turntable inspired a lifetime of listening; my brother Andrew for his enthusiasm and listening ear; Spencer Gibb for his friendship and argent innards; Quentin Harrison, Andy Healy, and all the talented scribes at *Albumism*; Walker Evans, Anne Evans, Susan Post, and the staff at *Columbus Underground* – the outlet that gave me my very first writing gig; Stacy Oliver-Sikorski who loves the written word as much as I do. Thanks also to David Wild, Juliana Hatfield, Lee DeWyze, Cat Geletka, Paul Stelzer, Sara Bucher Greer, Kenny Greer, Nevil Stephens, Stephen Johns, Simon Yee, Michael Gerbrandt, Joan Schmidt – all of whom have taken a special interest in our work. And cheers to the kind Bee Gees fans and music enthusiasts who have engaged with us.

Mark would like to thank: my three beautiful children, Bree, Edan, and Daina and their respective spouses, Dale, Michelle and James, for their continuing love and support. I would also like to send my love to my seven equally beautiful grandchildren Eliza, Ava, Archie, Darcy, Olivia, Poppy, and Billy. I also would like to thank Michael and Maxine Rankin for their research assistance. I dedicate my personal input to this tome to my five siblings Michael, Peter, Colin, Leo and Liz.

DECADES | The Bee Gees in the 1970s

Contents

Foreword

Having struggled at first with writing the foreword to the previous book in this series, I assumed that writing one about this particular era would be a walk in the park by comparison. As a lover of history, music, and the details of the recording process, I consider myself to be well-versed in the innovations, tricks, and technology that changed music as we know it. I also happen to know a lot about what the Brothers Gibb were doing at that time. So, what could go wrong?

Well, here we are – several dramatically different drafts later …

As far as The Bee Gees are concerned, I realised that discussing anything to do with recording studios, or trivia about hits, awards, or world records broken was redundant. That is exactly what this book covers, complete with quotes and interviews from people who were actually there.

In addition, writing about the personal journey of my family would be equally unnecessary. The subject is well covered, most recently in Frank Marshall's excellent HBO documentary *The Bee Gees: How Can You Mend A Broken Heart*. Also, the authors of this series already do an incredible job of implying the personal and creative pressures that came with The Bee Gees' incredible rise to success and fame across the 1970s.

It dawned on me that this introduction, instead of being a summary of what is already in this book, should be about what is *not*. I wanted to create a historical and cultural canvas. A backdrop for everything you are about to read. A primer for the decade and something to keep in the back of your mind as the story unfolds. Divided into separate yet sometimes overlapping sections, I will be focusing entirely on the United States – the place where The Bee Gees truly became musical icons for the ages. If you were to view the first book as a chronicle of the British or Australian 'dream', then you're about to discover that this next chapter is quintessentially American.

So, let's talk about America. A country that created modern music as we know it by suppressing the voices of Black culture, only to suffer the irony of having it shoved down their throats by a bunch of white dudes from England. The same place they had desperately fought to become independent from. The 1970s in America were a strange time. It would prove to be a decade of many steps forward followed by many more back. It was a time of solipsism and uncertainty. A time when the cultural revolutions of the 1960s could (and would) be tested to their limits. As both the harmony and violence of music festivals and mass protests faded away, the new decade faced many more many questions than answers. Would civil rights actually be respected? Would free love and sexual acceptance continue to be a central theme? Would children still be sent away to be killed or crippled in senseless wars? Would 'pop', 'rock' or 'R&B' music survive, or had it been a fad? 1970 alone saw the breakup of The Beatles, the premature deaths of Jimi Hendrix and Janis Joplin, and Marvin Gaye's sombre masterpiece *What's Going On?* fell largely on deaf ears.

Despite Gaye's commentary, it did appear that the start of the decade was heading in a promising direction. The war in Vietnam slowly came to an end, and the military draft was abolished. A landmark US Supreme Court decision was a major step forward not just for women's rights but for privacy overall, and Black people finally seemed to be more represented in the workplace, pop culture, and sports. Sounds great, right? Well, just as a seemingly routine burglary at the Watergate Complex would teach us, things can go downhill fast.

If there is something more 'American' than apple pie (which was probably German to begin with), then it must be the sheer determination and ability to fight against change. The passionate cries of the previous years had created numerous problems, and not just for people who didn't like marijuana or sandals, but for those who viewed them as an assault on capitalism. Peace and love are not profitable commodities, communal thinking erodes the upper class, independent companies with no intention of going public ultimately destroy corporate monopolies, and minorities working white collar jobs are a simple threat to decades of white privilege. The list goes on. A small but powerful group of politicians, religious organisations, and corporations had been working tirelessly behind the scenes on returning the country to a much more conservative era. The loud, progressive voices of the late 1960s were not remotely prepared for this quiet counter-revolution, and by the end of the decade, it had come very close to achieving its goal. It would have come much closer if money hadn't gotten in the way. This is after all an American story, and money almost always gets in the way.

Probably the last thing anyone was predicting at the time was economic uncertainty or instability. The post-war economy, partly due to military spending overseas, had been very good to America, yet by 1975 it was evident that things were not looking favourable. High taxation in many countries, notably the United Kingdom, was forcing companies and wealthy individuals to relocate elsewhere, naturally taking their money with them, while the looming OPEC crisis, amongst other things, was about to create a massive spike in the cost of living and unemployment. The future seemed bleak, but if anything was learned from the economic and cultural depression of Britain in the 1960s, it was that nothing brings people together more than an economy in distress. This drives us to the escapism of art, entertainment and the drowning of sorrows. This time around however, instead of the cries for change and the 'screw the man' mentality of the previous decade, people just wanted to party.

Which brings us to 'disco' – probably the most misunderstood musical genre of all time, as well as one of the most misappropriated uses of a word. Out of fairness, at the height of its cultural dominance, nobody could have ever predicted it would become a 'dirty word', but then the same could be said for 'liberal' or 'progressive'.

The origins of disco are pretty simple, but where it ended up is far more complex. The evolution of R&B and jazz into funk, combined with the smooth productions coming out of Philadelphia, had taken Black music to a new level. A level that made people want to dance. And by people, I mean *everyone*. All identities. This became the medicine needed to combat the depression of the world outside. This dancing often took place at a discothèque, which is a fancy French word for a bar with a DJ, and all facetiousness aside, this is how the genre got its name. On a musical side note, if you really want to dig into the origins of disco, listen to The Trammps. They are probably the fathers of true disco, and their aptly named 'Disco Inferno', later featured on the *Saturday Night Fever* soundtrack, is incredible.

At this point, *that* movie and its accompanying music should probably be discussed. In 1976, disco was still a relatively underground musical phenomenon, but it hadn't gone unnoticed that it was no longer confined to Black neighborhoods. This was a significant moment in post-segregation America because while white audiences had listened to Black music more openly throughout the 1960s, they generally did not spend time in Black clubs or bars, and vice-versa. More importantly, while Black Americans had been dancing at clubs for decades, white Americans had stayed clear – unsurprisingly as many majority politicians and churches had gone as far as to condemn cultural expression as 'demonic possession'. But eventually, they finally understood the escapism and release that dance could bring. A low-budget film, very much in the gritty style of the time, set out to not just document the culture of the growing weekend dance craze but also the causes behind it. *Saturday Night Fever* covers everything from economic turmoil to depression, sexism and racism. Amazingly, looking back, the original 'R'-rated version of the film even has a rape scene.

Nobody could have predicted what happened next. While audiences undoubtedly related to the themes of the film and its characters, what they truly embraced was the music, the choreography, and the idea that they, too, could live that life. With this in mind, the movie was re-edited and re-distributed with a 'PG' rating for a younger audience. Disco went national. John Travolta became a global star, and The Bee Gees headlined the biggest-selling album of all time.

As with any trend, everyone wanted a piece of the pie – and by 1979, just about anything was being labelled as 'disco', just to capitalise and make a few bucks. While many artists who were previously associated with other genres, were borrowing some themes and sounds, much of what was on the radio was not even disco. Behind the scenes, however, true disco was evolving, and in exactly the same place as it got its start: New York City. Studio 54 had become the unofficial headquarters, and its influence was felt in nightclubs all over the country. If you were an up-and-coming record producer, artist, or DJ and wanted to break into the disco scene, then you had to be welcome at Studio 54. Famous for its strict door policies (Nile Rodgers and Chic actually became known by writing a song about not being allowed in), the club set the standard for nightlife 'cool' that still exists today. Inside was a demonstration of what real disco had become. A melting pot of races, colours, ages, and sexual orientations, partying together and all wrapped up with a thick bow of flamboyant style. On any given night, you could stumble across regulars like Andy Warhol, Michael Jackson, Freddie Mercury, Grace Jones, Mick Jagger, or even Shirley MacLaine. The diversity of the celebrity patrons, along with the rapid growth of paparazzi culture, understandably gave Studio 54 plenty of media attention. However, it was the apparent display of cultural and sexual unity, combined with the astronomical success of 'that disco movie' that was the gift the conservative movement I mentioned earlier had been waiting for.

At the time, urban areas in America had many things in common. They were (and often still are) home to large, mostly working-class Black and Hispanic populations; and in the case of New York, Italian and Irish communities – all of whom felt very much disenfranchised.

The original *Saturday Night Fever* aside, take the time to watch *The Godfather*, *Mean Streets*, *Shaft*, *Superfly*, or absolutely any film by Melvin Van Peebles, and you will get an idea of what I'm talking about. These cities were also creative and artistic hubs, and over the years, there hasn't been a single defining moment in American culture that can't be traced back to them. I could write a list, but Motown-Detroit and Seattle-Grunge are good enough examples. Finally, urban America was somewhere that provided escape. Somewhere to follow big dreams or blend into the shadows. A place to re-invent yourself or find others who shared your views. This last point is particularly relevant because for decades, people had been moving from rural areas to escape the harsh and violent attitudes towards homosexuality. Cities were not necessarily safer places to be gay, but there was definitely less of a chance of someone being tied to the back of a tractor. By the 1970s, with comedians no longer being arrested for profanity and events like Stonewall in the rear-view mirror, New York had become openly proud of being 'liberal' and 'progressive' (I think by now you might see where this is going ...).

Based on a true story, one of the most significant films of the period was Sidney Lumet's *Dog Day Afternoon*. On the surface, it's a bank robbery movie starring Al Pacino that notably changed the general theme in movies that criminal acts are only performed by 'bad people'. Underneath, it's a human story of a gay man fighting to do the right thing for his partner – in this case, to finance their reassignment surgery, itself an almost unheard-of subject in 1975. The portrayal and direction are neither dramatic nor flamboyant and paint a matter-of-fact picture of normal, everyday life. It demands empathy and it very effectively forces the audience to put themselves in the character's shoes, regardless of their sexual orientation or whom they chose to love. It is not a 'coming out' story or one about the challenges and politics of being gay in America. Six Academy Award nominations later, including a win for Best Screenplay, there has never been a movie or TV show like it since, and we are only now, almost 50 years later, beginning to address these themes in mainstream media. In a world where entertainment success always dictates exploiting the same formula over and over, that fact alone encapsulates almost everything I'm writing about here.

Conservatives had now been handed a perfectly constructed racist and homophobic weapon to convince America that Black, brown and gay people were poisoning their children and morality. But since they couldn't say most of those things directly, it had to be implied. They needed a name, a code word, so to speak, that could summarise that sentiment and message. They finally had it: disco.

It worked. Fueled by the early days of opinion-based radio and television, megachurches, and a rejuvenated Ku Klux Klan had mostly abandoned white sheets and burning crosses in favour of business suits and political offices, a cultural crackdown began in a way not seen since Nazi Germany, complete with the public burning of 'inappropriate' materials. In this case, it just happened to be vinyl records as opposed to books. It was so effective that many people have forgotten about it or don't know it even happened. Radio stations became scared of what music to program, print media began to move away from covering certain subjects, and recording artists crept into the shadows to re-think their direction. Every successful publicity campaign needs a well-crafted package, and a catchy slogan alone would never be enough. After all, most of the people waving banners and chanting 'disco sucks!' had no idea what it even was. This campaign needed a face to go with the message, and any direct assault on Black or gay culture would, as the 1960s had proven, severely backfire. The solution was there the whole time. Standing right in front of them, on a sparkling silver platter adorned with multicoloured flooring and mirror balls, was a phenomenon bigger than disco itself. The biggest musical act in the world. Their faces were everywhere, from supermarket magazines and movie posters to the tail of their own airplane. Their songs were literally being played back-to-back on the radio, and their stadium tour was breaking records and driving young girls into a frenzy. While disco alone already had the perfect credentials to create a backlash, the real gift to conservatives was three white, straight, cisgender, and publicly apolitical superstars. The icing on the cake was that they weren't even American. And that brings us to The Bee Gees …

As I touched on in the previous book, The Bee Gees, often unwittingly, were both the creators of, and witnesses to, the many milestones that shaped the modern entertainment industry. As this book will show, this is the story of uncharted territory, with no roadmaps or preparedness for what's around the corner. In this case, it was a perfect storm. Now that we've covered some of the intricacies of disco, I'm going to drop a truth bomb: The Bee Gees were never really a disco act. Think about it. Name a disco song of theirs. It's pretty hard. Sure, 'You Should Be Dancing' or 'Boogie Child' might come close, but under scrutiny, that really has more to do with their titles. Even pre-*Saturday Night Fever*, those songs had elements of social commentary, and the latter was borderline tongue-in-cheek. If you think about it even further, some of their most memorable music from this era was what they had done best since they were children. Soulful, touching, and timeless ballads that always had their heart in great R&B. So why the blanket association with disco? Well, the first reason is a no-brainer: their association with a certain movie. Let's explore. Not a single person involved with *Fever* could have predicted the size of its success. When the album became the biggest selling of all time (more on that later), it wasn't by a small margin but by *millions* and *millions* of copies. One of the best explanations of this phenomenon came from my father when he said, 'People who didn't usually buy records bought that album'. It transcended music and became something that you just *had* to own. *Fever* not only blurred the lines of some musical genres (part of the reason that anything with a groove got labelled as 'disco'), but most significantly, it crossed racial lines, and this was something that had never happened before. Even though the 1960s had created unity of sorts between musical cultures, Black audiences, in general, did not typically buy 'non-Black' music – in part due to the intentionally divisive 'Black music charts' at the time. Record labels funnelled specific artists and singles directly to that audience, while mainstream top 40 or top ten charts still featured predominantly white artists in multiple genres. On the other hand, urban white kids were buying more and more records by Black artists, ironically for the same reasons – the Black chart and Black radio had become the coolest place to go to discover new music and underground trends. In fact, it was not uncommon for labels to send songs by white artists with an R&B flavour to Black radio before anywhere else. If it was a hit, then the artist's credibility improved, as did the chance of success on larger charts like the *Billboard* Hot 100. It didn't hurt the success of *Fever* that The Bee Gees had already passed this test numerous times, and by the end of 1976, they had gained a significant following with Black audiences. While 'crossing over', as it was called (yep, America was still shocked by desegregation …), was not a new thing, *Fever* proved that this, combined with visuals (film, and then music videos), could make unbelievable amounts of money. This became the precise formula for the explosive successes of Michael Jackson's *Thriller* and Prince's *Purple Rain* a few years later, with the former ultimately being the first album to break *Fever*'s sales record. The model was here to stay.

Back in uncharted territory – let's not forget that *Saturday Night Fever* was not really intended to be a disco or dance film. The new music contributed by the Gibbs (the most iconic dance scene in the film was set to 'You Should Be Dancing', a song from their previous LP, *Children Of The World)*, was not only very sophisticated but was used literally as a soundtrack. 'Stayin' Alive', a stomping, funky anthem infused with social themes, opens the film and firmly establishes *Fever*'s lead character Tony Manero's false bravado. 'How Deep Is Your Love' closes the movie with the appropriate reflection. Nothing disco here, just great and highly appropriate music. As the film took on a life of its own, nobody was ashamed of any association. In fact, quite the opposite. The careers of everyone involved had skyrocketed and besides, disco was cool. As an artist, I can tell you that you can call me anything you want if it makes more people pay attention to what I do.

The real point here though, is that for the general public, and ironically even some critics, it became incredibly easy and convenient to brand these brothers that way. Easy, because the truth was much harder to describe or sell. That The Bee Gees had actually become their own musical genre. From 1978 to the start of the next decade, there was virtually nothing on the radio they didn't have a hand in – and most things that weren't were heavily influenced by their sound.

As the first book in this series spelt out, the Gibb brothers always had very solid roots in R&B music. After all, these were the guys that wrote a song for Otis Redding with no initial intent to record it themselves, and if he hadn't tragically died, this book might not even exist. A significant portion of their early catalogue had been famously covered by Black artists, from Nina Simone to Al Green. With psychedelia and the British sound of the late 1960s now firmly in the past, there was a lot more freedom to tap into those roots and embrace that sound. In addition, the brothers' childhood influences, such as The Everly Brothers and other vocally oriented groups had provided them a love and understanding of folk, country, and Americana – styles evoked particularly well by Barry Gibb. Again, stripped of the trends and trappings of the previous decade, their work in the early 1970s showcased a lot more of those raw elements than had been immediately obvious earlier on. By 1975 however, under the guidance of the already legendary producer Arif Mardin, they had found the confidence to no longer just write but actually produce pure soul music. *Main Course* might be my favorite Bee Gees record. It covers just about every aspect of their musicology and serves as a magical soundtrack of their journey from Australia to Britain, to America. Wistful country and elements of rock combined with optimistic Philadelphia-inspired R&B. The set's closing track, 'Baby As You Turn Away' feels like a farewell to the Beatle-esque '60s and reminds you what makes them so special: their voices.

As performing artists, at least until 1979, The Bee Gees stayed sonically grounded in a veneer of R&B, their unmistakable falsetto vocals becoming a brand of its own. But behind the scenes, it was a very different story. They were no longer just writing songs for other artists or having their catalogue covered – they were putting their stamp on them. Along with Albhy Galuten and Karl Richardson, they had become a writing and production machine, developing hits for anyone in their path, most notably their younger brother. With Andy Gibb, himself an artist with a stronger connection to country music than his siblings, came the opportunity to truly blend their understanding of different musical styles. While still undeniably funky, Andy's music was sparser and grittier, allowing for those country-rock elements to bleed through. Carefully chosen musicians and guest players effectively solidified the sound of the Gibb/Galuten/Richardson production, and many other artists were about to get their hands on it, or at least attempt to emulate it. The Eagles (some of whose members coincidentally played on two of Andy's albums) took to Criteria Studios for their follow-up to *Hotel California*. With a significantly tighter sound, particularly on vocals, it's hard to listen to *The Long Run* and not think that the Gibb machine had not somehow influenced it, especially as we move into 1979, where that sound would reach new levels with The Bee Gees' own *Spirits Having Flown* album. Not only a production masterpiece, it also showcased a fairly dynamic shift in the brothers' songwriting. The falsettos were still there, but this was no longer a purist take on R&B; instead, it was rather a cinematic opera with its own distinct style. The bombastic 'Tragedy', with heavy, harmonised guitars and some of their thickest vocal productions yet, was about as far from disco as you could get. But nobody noticed, and if they did, they didn't care. The Gibbs had become a genre. It just didn't have a name.

By now, along with everything beginning to hit the fan with disco, it's not that hard to see the perfect storm I'd mentioned before brewing on the horizon. The Bee Gees' success was unprecedented in so many areas, but probably the most significant one was that it was entirely independent and 'in-house'. Robert Stigwood was their manager as well the owner of their record label and publishing company RSO, giving them creative freedom few other artists enjoyed. In addition to the development of this virtual radio takeover, Stigwood and RSO had produced the films *Saturday Night Fever* and *Grease*, along with almost every Broadway musical of the era. By the end of the decade, there was very little in American pop culture that wasn't connected to RSO in some way.

As with disco, these factors alone were more than enough to create a backlash, except nobody knew what a backlash was – let alone see it coming. Until this point, neither the industry nor the general public had much experience with media over-saturation and the repercussions from fame. Any opportunities for it to come close in the past had been thwarted by the break-up of a successful act, or the tragic death of a movie star, resulting in deification and martyrdom as opposed to victimisation and vilification.

So, there it was. Disco, The Bee Gees and the RSO Empire, and an underground conservative movement. All converging at the exact same moment and launching the 1980s into far more uncertainty than the decade before.

As the end of everything deserves an epitaph, I will leave you with the closing credits for this biopic. The Bee Gees did what they always did best. In what would become a recurring theme, they bounced back after devastation and turmoil, wrote more beautiful songs, and produced more hit records in the 1980s. Spoiler alert: There's a book about it coming …

As for disco, it ultimately got the last laugh, but not without casualties. Artists like Sylvester, Donna Summer, and Chic, just to name a few, should have enjoyed mega-stardom going into the '80s, although the latter, with the sublime productions of Nile Rodgers and Bernard Edwards, had a heavy hand in creating hip-hop. Others survived unscathed. Since they were both mentioned earlier and became cultural icons, it's with noting that Michael Jackson was a bonafide disco artist and Prince had a foot in the door in the late 1970s.

The evolution of 'true' disco would end up dictating music, fashion, and trends for decades to come – from the birth of hip-hop to the synthesiser programming of modern EDM. The UK and Europe neither abandoned the genre nor politicised it (although some did try), even going as far as to infuse it with punk, ska and other genres along the way. The 'second British Invasion' at American radio going into the 1980s consisted of anything from Wham! to Depeche Mode, to Eurythmics – diverse acts with no denial of their disco roots.

And America? Well, the jury's still out, but it's safe to say it's currently in violation of its probation and an arrest warrant is about to be issued

Also, I'd like to take a moment to apologise for my use of profanity at the end of the introduction to the previous book. It was crass, unnecessary, and totally uncalled for. I additionally wish to note that sections and early drafts of this foreword were penned in July 2022 in Thame, Oxfordshire, UK, in a room where Robin Gibb wrote a fuckload of hits.

Spencer Gibb
October 2022, Austin, Texas, USA

Prologue

Few artists in the entertainment industry can claim to have made a consistent impact across generations of listeners. However, those who are fortunate enough to have lengthy careers – be it Frank Sinatra, Dionne Warwick, or Paul McCartney – go through periods where their popularity waxes and wanes for one reason or another.

Ask any Bee Gees fan about their favourite songs or performances by the Gibbs and their opinion will more than likely be based on the era they remember most. For Australians of a certain age, it would be of the teenage brothers with Brylcreemed hair in matching waistcoats performing on their black-and-white television sets in the early 1960s. For baby boomers, it may be of the blossoming baroque pop-rockers during their first round of international success in the late 1960s when they climbed charts around the world with songs like 'New York Mining Disaster 1941', 'Massachusetts', and 'I've Gotta Get A Message To You'.

However, for the vast majority, The Bee Gees will be remembered for their nearly unparalleled popular dominance during the latter half of the 1970s as – albeit unfairly and inaccurately – the musical embodiment of the disco era.

Barry, Robin, and Maurice Gibb's ascent to the pop music stratosphere between 1975 and 1979 was far from swift. When the 1970s dawned, The Bee Gees, though they had become internationally famous, were, in fact, non-existent. After working arduously to achieve their childhood dreams of musical stardom, they nearly extinguished all they had accomplished, fracturing their brotherly and creative bond with a damaging combination of immaturity, ego, and exhaustion. In Britain, in particular, their sibling fury had played out on the front pages of the music press, usurping the energy they should have been investing in their craft.

When The Bee Gees reformed in August 1970 and began the long journey back to reclaiming their international success, it was the British punters who proved to be the most reluctant to forgive the brothers. Initially, the relaunch went perfectly. They charted two of their biggest hits in America almost immediately with 'Lonely Days' and 'How Can You Mend A Broken Heart'; amidst the country's post-1960s introspection, the pensive brothers working through the complex emotions of their reunion through their music was perfectly attuned.

Though the reception to their early-decade work in their homeland was tepid, they were still lauded in many other parts of the world as their chart singles and profitable concert tours continued to bourgeon.

But as the 1970s approached their midpoint, the Gibbs began to stagnate creatively – to the point where their planned follow-up to 1973's *Life In A Tin Can* – the rather aptly titled *A Kick In The Head Is Worth Eight In The Pants* – was outrightly rejected by Atlantic Records.

The Bee Gees' commercial appeal followed suit. The once reliable hitmakers were now just barely scraping the bottom of most of the world's album and singles charts. Their busy tour schedule also dwindled woefully, forcing them to perform around the club circuit in Northern England just to make ends meet. Before long, their label, Atlantic Records, was on the precipice of dropping them from their roster.

Luckily, the Gibbs still had staunch supporters in their camp: their manager Robert Stigwood and producer Arif Mardin, who was brought in to steer 1974's *Mr. Natural* into more contemporary territory, were unwavering in their belief of the brothers' potential to bounce back. Within a year, their collective diligence would pay off in the form of The Bee Gees' now classic opus, *Main Course* – returning them to both public and industry consciousness.

Main Course turned out to be just a catalyst for The Bee Gees' eventual vault to global superstardom in the latter part of the 1970s – in no small part as the result of their unwitting contributions to the soundtrack of the 1977 cultural juggernaut, *Saturday Night Fever*.

By 1979, the band that had begun the decade as a nonentity had become arguably the most popular music act in the world as they rewrote convention and broke boundaries.

That incredible story begins here …

1970

When the new decade began, The Bee Gees were no more – seemingly just one of many pop acts who had risen to fame in the 1960s and quickly faded after a few hits. While previously recorded Bee Gees material was to be released over the year, it was a front for a group that had expired. Personally and professionally, the brothers couldn't have been further apart. Once they'd been united as a single creative force with one shared dream to be successful, and now they were rather adamantly unwilling to go to one another for help finishing a song, to collaborate – or even just talk. Though they eventually came to realise they were artistically better as a threesome, they spent several months of 1970 creating independently. They each handled the time differently. The twins were the most productive by far, with Barry presumably less inclined to start a solo career.

Robin – still exultant following the success of his debut solo single 'Saved By The Bell' some months earlier – was now immersed in finishing his first solo album *Robin's Reign*. On 16 January, he released a third single: 'August October' b/w 'Give Me A Smile'. Though its immediate predecessor 'One Million Years' had flopped everywhere except Germany, greater things were expected from the waltz-like A-side 'August October'. Sadly, Robin's solo career had ostensibly peaked as the single stalled on the UK charts at number 45. It fared better elsewhere, proving popular in Germany, Denmark, and New Zealand: no doubt helped by his solo concerts at the end of January.

On 26 January Robin recorded four songs live at a session at London's BBC studios: 'Saved By The Bell', 'August October', 'Weekend', and 'Give Me A Smile'. They first aired on 30 January on *The Johnnie Walker Show*. All four recordings were later included on the 2015 3-CD set *Saved By The Bell: The Collected Works Of Robin Gibb 1968-1970*, along with interview segments with Brian Matthew, which appeared on BBC Transcription Service records for syndicated *Top Of The Pops* radio shows broadcast in overseas territories.

Having pre-recorded a performance of 'August October' for the 31 January broadcast of BBC 2 variety show *The Young Generation*, Robin flew to the US for an appearance on *The Andy Williams Show*. He then travelled to New Zealand for his only solo concert appearances during The Bee Gees' separation. His appearance at the *Redwood Music Festival* in Auckland – where he was billed as the special guest star on 31

January and 1 February – was less than successful. Fruit was thrown at the stage during both performances. At the first show, a tomato hit the unfortunate Robin before he'd sung a single note. His drummer Darrin recalled:

> I can assure you that a lot more was coming on stage than a tomato. There were bottles and cans and all sorts raining down on us. Robin was the first off the stage, very quickly followed by the rest of the band. Next day, same thing happened in spite of the increased security and the audience being pushed back about 20 feet with a no-go zone patrolled by German Shepherd dogs!

On 17 February, a new Robert Stigwood musical – *Sing A Rude Song*, featuring Maurice as Bernard Dillon – opened at London's Greenwich Theatre. The show began life in 1961 as Lord Ted Willis' idea for a musical biography of English music hall singer Marie Lloyd, who had risen to fame in the late 19th century. The original concept was based around the songs she was well known for performing, but the writers Caryl Brahms and Ned Sherrin had designs on introducing some of their own songs into the production. By 1962, the pair – having read two biographies and several books about the music hall era – produced the first draft of a script. They had meetings with elderly music hall artists, and they also met Marie Lloyd Jr., who had continued to sing her mother's songs in her own stage act.

Over the next few years, the script was developed further, and with the introduction of Australian-born composer Ron Grainer, the musical elements progressed. Grainer was then well known for writing television themes, with *Comedy Playhouse*, *That Was The Week That Was*, *Steptoe and Son*, and *Doctor Who* already under his belt.

In 1968 after the musical underwent a short-lived title change to *Hey! Cockie,* during auditions, Brahms and Sherrin sold a television version of what then became *Sing A Rude Song* to Yorkshire Television. Unfortunately, the transmitter mast at Emley Moor collapsed on 19 March 1969, and Brahms and Sherrin lost their production. Realising that 1970 was Marie Lloyd's centenary year, Brahms and Sherrin rushed to get the production to the stage. Auditions were held at the Greenwich Theatre: which had a tradition of music hall productions and a playhouse which had served Marie Lloyd well. As production costs rose, Robert Stigwood agreed to fund the show to the tune of £5,000.

Caryl Brahms' first choice to play Marie had always been English singer Georgia Brown, but she'd recently had a baby and was unavailable. Actress Millicent Martin (now better-known for playing Daphne's mother Gertrude Moon, on the US television sitcom *Frasier*) was named next, but delays led to her taking other jobs, and she was to appear at the Talk of the Town nightclub in Westminster when the show was planned to open. Keeping to the concept of a genuine East-Ender to play the part, it was offered to Barbara Windsor – best-known for her roles in several *Carry On* films – who loved the idea. She was no stranger to musicals, though her voice was untrained. What she did possess was a vibrant and cheeky nature, so true to the lady she was to play.

While Robert Stigwood was hoping The Bee Gees would reunite at some point, until they did, he needed to keep Maurice – the most insecure of the brothers – active and disciplined. Having a celebrity pop star in the cast of a stage musical would do no harm attracting an audience either and perhaps would broaden the show's appeal to younger patrons. Maurice recalled: 'I first saw the script in Robert Stigwood's office, and he asked if I would like to take it home and read it. Then the very next day, he asked me if I would like to play the part of Marie Lloyd's third husband Bernard Dillon'. Co-writer and director Ned Sherrin believed that 'Maurice came in in the first place simply because The Bee Gees had split up, and this was, I think, Stigwood's therapy for keeping Maurice interested: giving him something to do while the breakup was going on. I don't remember the ramifications of it, but I do remember that Maurice needed to be kept with something in his mind. So, I think that was the main reason for Robert investing in it'.

Never a confident solo singer, Maurice was required to sing just two solo songs in the show: 'Leave Me Here To Linger With The Ladies' and 'Tattenham Corner'. But he also had solo lines in two other numbers – 'Whoops Cockie! (Reprise)'/'We've Been And Gone And Done It', and 'Waiting For The Royal Train', which both featured leading lady Barbara Windsor.

On the show's opening night on 17 February, a pre-recorded performance of Barbara and Maurice performing 'We've Been And Gone And Done It' was shown on Thames Television's Today programme.

With the musical really being Windsor's show from beginning to the end, by all accounts, Maurice's performance didn't garner many plaudits from the critics. Maurice later said he didn't really enjoy the experience and had never worked as hard before.

Despite lukewarm reviews, the show's run at the Greenwich Theatre was an overwhelming success. 'People couldn't get in at the Greenwich; they were terribly keen to come', Sherrin remembered. 'We were playing to full houses all the time at Greenwich; it was absolutely packed. I don't think we had a spare seat at Greenwich, but then there was this long hang-about before it came to the West End'.

Also in February, the eponymous debut album by pop/rock outfit Tin Tin was released, bearing the credit 'Produced by Maurice Gibb' in quite large lettering on the front cover. The group included Australian duo Steve Kipner and Steve Groves. Maurice's connection to Kipner went back to their shared days in the Australian music scene, where Kipner was lead singer of Steve & The Board. Former Bee Gees drummer Colin Petersen and future Bee Gees drummer Geoff Bridgford had both been members of Steve & The Board. Bridgford was also briefly a member of Tin Tin before officially joining The Bee Gees in early 1971. Tin Tin were managed by Kipner's father Nat, who back in Australia, had co-managed The Bee Gees in 1966, and had run their record label Spin. Nat had also co-written several songs with Maurice. Studio Engineer Ric Holland recalled in his book *As I Heard It: In the UK Music Industry 1969 to 1979*, that Tin Tin's recording sessions were 'wedged in between Bee Gees and solo Gibb-brother recording dates. Sometimes Maurice came in to produce them, otherwise, Steve Kipner took control. There was never any continuity'.

Tin Tin's album followed their June 1969 single 'Only Ladies Play Croquet' b/w 'He Wants To Be A Star'. Maurice produced both tracks, playing harpsichord, bass, drums and Mellotron on the A-side, and bass and piano on the B-side. He also surfaced as a player on 'Spanish Shepherd' (Mellotron), 'Toast And Marmalade For Tea' (bass) and 'Manhattan Woman' (organ). When the album was released in the US in October, 'Come On Over Again' replaced 'Loves Her That Way', giving Maurice an additional bass credit. The album's second single, 'Toast And Marmalade For Tea' b/w 'Manhattan Woman', was released in the UK on 22 May. It became their first US single, released in December and becoming a hit there in 1971, peaking at number 20. On home ground in Australia, it fared even better, making the top ten. In a prudent marketing move, the Australian arm of Polydor opted to title the album after the hit single.

Former Bee Gees drummer Colin Petersen was also keeping busy, managing Irish singer/songwriter Jonathan Kelly, and producing his new single 'Make A Stranger Your Friend'. Proving that relations between Colin and Robin weren't strained – despite the latter's exit from The Bee Gees – Robin was invited to attend the IBC Studios recording session on 16 January and was photographed at the mixing desk with Colin. The session caused some friction between Robin and his new management, as Vic Lewis refused to allow Robin permission to participate in a 'super session' for the track organised by Colin. Press reports at the time showed a celebrity chorus, including Mick Taylor (The Rolling Stones), Klaus Voormann (Manfred Mann), Madeleine Bell (Blue Mink), Carl Wayne (The Move), Christine Holmes, Steve Rowland and Albert Hammond (all three from The Family Dogg), Jackie Lomax, Tony Ashton (Ashton, Gardner and Dyke), singer-songwriter Lesley Duncan, and actors/comedians Peter Sellers and Spike Milligan. The photo also shows another man – the only one of the group who is facing away from the camera with his hand cupped to his ear. When asked about Robin's participation, Jonathan Kelly said, 'I'm sure he came down and sang with us. I think that's very interesting because when he saw the photograph being taken, that's why he put his hand over his face. That's what happened, he's actually hiding! It would make sense that he was hiding from any photographer taking pictures'. To counter any controversy, Robin claimed he spent the remainder of the session 'sitting in the control room with Colin, commanding a view of the whole proceedings'. Certainly, there are photographs of the two sitting at the mixing desk, but others show Colin at the microphone, singing with the assembled celebrities.

Kelly's single was rush-released on 6 February, but it failed to break into the charts.

Robin's Reign was released in the UK in February 1970. Ideally, this would have happened much sooner – as in immediately following the single 'Saved By The Bell', which was a huge hit in summer 1969 – but the rest of the album had yet to be recorded. Indeed, the final tracks weren't completed until December.

Robert Stigwood's court action to prevent Robin from performing as a solo artist, had hindered progress. Robin's father, Hugh Gibb, attempted to have Robin made a ward of the court, as, at 20 years of age, he was still legally considered a minor. When these obstacles were finally cleared, he was able to proceed with his work plans. Robin was now under extreme pressure to get *Robin's Reign* out as quickly as possible. In hindsight, the album probably could have benefitted from a delayed release to allow Robin more time to smooth some of its rough edges.

Nonetheless, whilst the album disappointed some fans who had been brought up on a diet of Bee Gees releases, it served its purpose as a showcase for Robin's individuality which The Bee Gees' activities had constrained.

Robin's Reign – Robin Gibb (1970)

Personnel:

Robin Gibb: lead and backing vocals, acoustic guitar, organ, drum machine

Maurice Gibb: bass ('Mother And Jack'), piano ('Saved By The Bell')

Arranger/conductor: Zack Lawrence ('August October', 'Gone Gone Gone', 'The Worst Girl In This Town'); Kenny Clayton ('Down Came The Sun', 'Mother And Jack', 'Saved By The Bell', 'Farmer Ferdinand Hudson', 'Most Of My Life')

Musical director: Vic Lewis ('Give Me A Smile', 'Weekend')

Arranger: Kenny Clayton ('Give Me A Smile', 'Weekend')

Producer: Robin Gibb

Recorded between March 1969 and December 1969 at IBC Studios, London and Chappell Recording Studio, London

Release date: UK: February 1970, US: March 1970

Chart positions: West Germany: 19, Canada: 77

Any review of Robin Gibb's debut solo album must take into account his relative youth. He was barely 19 when he publicly announced on 19 March 1969 that he was leaving The Bee Gees, after which he immediately began recording this album. Having complained that his songs and vocals were being overlooked in The Bee Gees, he was under considerable pressure to produce a quality record. What's more, for the first time, he was writing and recording without his brothers' support and input.

The album has not aged well, though, in retrospect, it has attracted some avant-garde support. Despite having rather grandiose (and some might say pretentious) ideas, Robin was never a strong lyricist – perhaps due to his limited formal education, though he was quite well-read. On a song like 'Saved By The Bell' where the melody was strong, he got away with it, but those which were weaker melodically suffered even more.

Robin's initial recording process began with playing an elementary organ or guitar backing track, quite frequently with an electronic drum unit. With the basic instrumentation laid down, he would add his vocal – sometimes doubling it to give more strength. Without the support of his estranged brothers, he occasionally added a harmony or stacked numerous vocals. The demo would then be sent to an arranger to write an orchestral score. In a few instances, the initial demo recording would be retained, and the orchestra added.

Much of the album features a Rhythm Ace drum machine made by the Ace Tone company in Japan. The company was founded in 1960 by engineer and inventor Ikutaro Kakehashi, who later established the Roland Corporation: one of the world's premier manufacturers of electronic musical instruments. 'Saved By The Bell' has widely been recognised as the first major international chart hit that employed the technology: which was only a few years old at the time and was a rather remarkable innovation. It could play over a hundred rhythms, had 16 pre-set patterns, and four buttons that added separate sounds mimicking a cymbal, clave, cowbell and bass drum.

With the exception of the hit single 'Saved By The Bell', Robin produced the album with his new manager Vic Lewis: a British jazz guitarist and bandleader. Robin and Kenny Clayton co-produced 'Saved By The Bell'. Unbeknownst to brother Barry at the time, Maurice bridged the separation between him and his twin by playing piano on 'Saved By The Bell' and bass on 'Mother And Jack'.

In summary, it's an album that highlights Robin's quirky-and-sometimes-brilliant eccentricity but fails to rise above the mediocre.

The cover designed by Hamish Grimes – with its bold two-inch yellow lettering over a blue background – leaves no doubt that it's anything other than a Robin Gibb solo album. The album title appears below his name in marginally smaller lettering. Robin graces the front and back covers, dressed in a British military uniform that appears to be a mishmash of items gathered up for the photoshoot. The scarlet tunic is that of a Colonel on the Staff from the early 1900s. This rank was not attached to any regiment and was an administrative role within the Ministry of Defence. Navy blue tweed trousers with red lampasses (trouser stripes), and George boots complete the uniform. The accessories embellishing his outfit, which do not rightfully belong, are a maroon sash with two tassels normally worn by officers of the Foot Guards in full dress during ceremonial occasions, and an Albert helmet with a black and red horsehair plume, denoting it as being the headgear of the 3rd Dragoon Guards.

On the back cover, he wears the same uniform but sports a bearskin on his head. Without seeing both sides of the bearskin clearly, it is impossible to tell which regiment it is as the plume – or hackle, as it correctly named – is not visible. What can be determined is that it most definitely isn't the Coldstream Guards who wear a red hackle, or the Irish Guards who wear blue – both on the right. It could, therefore, be the Grenadier Guards who wear a white hackle, or the Welsh guards who have a green and white hackle – both on the left. The other possibility is the Scots Guards, who wear a bearskin without a hackle.

The photographs were taken by Robin's personal assistant, Ray Washbourne. In Austria, the sleeve varied – the title typeface was radically different, and the bearskin photo on both the front and back. In Japan, a 1968 Tony Gale photograph was used: showing Robin in contemplative mood, wearing a tweed jacket and smoking a cigarette.

'August October' (Robin Gibb)

Recorded at IBC Studios, London: 10 October 1969
Chart positions: Denmark: 3, New Zealand: 11, West Germany: 12, UK: 45
Released on 3 January 1970, this pretty waltz was the album's third single. The lyric hints at lost love. But like most Robin lyrics, detail is scant, and the melancholy comes through more from the voice and production style. Robin also recorded an Italian version ('Agosto Ottobre'), which was included on Rhino Records' excellent 3-CD set in 2015. The single's first pressing credited Anthony Browne as producer, while subsequent pressings corrected this to Robin Gibb.

Throughout the 1960s and 1970s, budget record labels would hire session musicians to re-record the hit songs of the day. These sounded very close to the originals but were offered at a much cheaper price. The songs had to be produced very quickly to be for sale at the same time as the hits they covered. In 1969 and 1970, Elton John supplemented his income this way – his voice appearing (anonymously) on several of these recordings, including 'August October' which was released on at least four different albums – *International Top 12* credited to The Tramps (Concert Hall SPS1315), *International Top 12* (Orange 30-6001), in Germany on *Love Grows And Other World Hits* (Fontana 6434009), and *Super Hits '70* (Maritim 47030FT).

'Gone, Gone, Gone' (Robin Gibb)

Recorded at IBC Studios, London: 10 October 1969
This is another desperately sad song, displaying the Robin trait of rhyming words without much concern about the lyrics actually making

sense. Intriguingly, the chorus only employs a pair of 'gone's, opposed to the three in the song title.

'The Worst Girl In This Town' (Robin Gibb)
Recorded at IBC Studios, London: 26 September 1969
The use of the then-new electronic drum unit is very evident in this lyrically interesting song, and serves as its driving force.

'Give Me A Smile' (Robin Gibb)
Recorded in London: December 1969
This was first released as the B-side to Robin's third single, 'August October'. His manager Vic Lewis was credited as musical director, and Kenny Clayton was acknowledged for the arrangement and conducting the orchestra. The song refers to a girl named Heather at one point, which appears to be because it was the closest word Robin could find that tentatively rhymed with 'pleasure'. The single's first pressing carries the credit 'Produced by Vic Lewis'. This was corrected to Robin Gibb on subsequent pressings.

'Down Came The Sun' (Robin Gibb)
Recorded in London: 1969
With a powerful chorus, this was one of the album's better tracks, and with an opening lyric mentioning the so the famous British naval commander Admiral Nelson, one could be excused for thinking this song might go to interesting places. Sadly, it doesn't, and soon resorts to rhyming couplets such as 'Boom goes the moon/We wonder why it happened so soon'. However, the engaging chorus does lift the song greatly.

'Mother And Jack' (Robin Gibb)
Recorded at Chappell Recording Studio, London: 10 March 1969
The B-side to 'Saved By The Bell' is a standout song in its own right. It's one of Robin's trademark story songs. Its protagonists receive a letter telling them their house is going to be pulled down, so they visit the emperor to see if he can help. Unfortunately, 'they got no answer'. The lyric is a lot of fun, and – depressing subject matter aside – the music is very upbeat, with the drum unit set on a calypso rhythm. The melody to a couple of lines required an extra syllable to fit the metre – 'Said he would think-ah, over his drink-ah' – but it works very well. Maurice's unmistakable bass-playing is heard on this track.

'Saved By The Bell' (Robin Gibb)
Recorded at Chappell Recording Studio, London: 10 March 1969
Chart positions: Denmark: 1, Ireland: 2, Netherlands: 2, New Zealand: 2, South Africa: 2, UK: 2, Yugoslavia: 2, West Germany: 3, Norway: 4, Australia: 9, Canada: 44

Robin's debut solo single had been released in June 1969, eight months before *Robin's Reign* arrived. He co-produced it with arranger Kenny Clayton. Though Robin was officially alienated from his brothers, Maurice played piano, organ and guitar, and added vocals: much to Barry's displeasure at the time. John Fiddy did the orchestral arrangement.

It's very Bee Gees-like, with similar production values, an infectious melody, and an irresistible chorus. Regrettably, the lyric is rather banal, but its commercial appeal is undeniable. It was the most successful song of Robin's solo career. To promote the single, he performed it on *Beat Club* in Germany, and on the BBC's flagship pop programme *Top Of The Pops*. The song was also a popular part of his solo concerts in the 2000s, and appeared on his 2005 *Live* solo album recorded with the Neue Philharmonie Frankfurt orchestra. It was also performed occasionally in post-reunion Bee Gees concerts. 'Saved By The Bell' and Robin's 1983 hit single 'Juliet' were the only two solo Gibb songs that The Bee Gees ever performed live.

'Weekend' (Robin Gibb)
Recorded in London: 1969

'Weekend' first appeared as the B-side to 'One Million Years' in November 1969. This recording is a slightly more upbeat ballad than the A-side. Sometimes the intrigue of Robin's songs was anticipating which rhyming word would be used. In this case, the words paired with 'weekend' were 'good friend' and 'send'. In Robin's view, it was the melody or the sentiment that was most important, and here it's sweet and quite endearing. The recording's musical director was his then-manager Vic Lewis, and arranger/conductor was Kenny Clayton.

'Farmer Ferdinand Hudson' (Robin Gibb)
Recorded in London: 1969

This a tragically-truncated version of a true Robin Gibb opus called 'Hudson's Fallen Wind' – which in its original 12-minute length is regarded as Robin's masterpiece. The prototype was the tale of a farmer who, following a terrible storm, was left with nothing. The lyric tells of the distress of his family and animals, and the devastation of his home and occupation. He died amidst the rubble the following morning.

While the condensed take on *Robin's Reign* (a meagre three minutes) is shallow compared to its parent version, it does contain the best lyrics the 19-year-old Robin had written up to that point.

'Lord Bless All' (Robin Gibb)
Recorded at IBC Studios, London: 10 October 1969
One of the last songs recorded for the album, 'Lord Bless All', is quite beautiful. Robin's voice is simply stunning. Without a standard verse/chorus structure, it's more like an Elizabethan Christmas carol. As such, it wouldn't have been out of place on Robin's 2006 album *My Favourite Christmas Carols*. It was entirely arranged and produced by Robin. He played organ, and double-tracked his lead vocal. Many Robin voice tracks created a convincing simulated choir of men and boys.

'Most Of My Life' (Robin Gibb)
Recorded in London: 1969
The album's final song is also its longest, coming in at 5:15. It's similar to 'Lord Bless All', essentially, with Robin's voice juxtaposed against a church-like organ. It's quite beautiful in its own way, the scant lyric telling of the loss of a woman.

'One Million Years' (Robin Gibb)
Recorded at IBC Studios, London: 26 September 1969
Chart positions: West Germany: 5, Austria: 8
Robin's second solo single is a disappointing affair. Though it made the top ten in West Germany and Austria, this was probably due to advance sales following its predecessor's success. The single was released in the UK on 28 November 1969: some five months after 'Saved By The Bell'. The song is painfully slow, and the lyrics are particularly weak, with Robin seemingly throwing in any rhyming word.

While the single was released in mono, a stereo mix was made for the Contour label's 1974 Bee Gees compilation *Gotta Get A Message To You*. However, the vocal was changed – most easily detectable in the second verse, with 'I will stand ...' on the stereo version and 'I shall stand ...' on the mono. Both versions – along with Robin's Italian version 'Un Milione De Ani' – finally appear together on the *Saved By The Bell: The Collected*

Works Of Robin Gibb 1968-1970 compilation released three years after Robin's death.

Though the song was omitted from the original *Robin's Reign* album in most territories, German pressings do include it as an additional closing track, mixed in mock stereo.

Robin's Reign – 2015 edition bonus songs

Following Robin's death in 2012, there was renewed interest in his solo catalogue – particularly his work during The Bee Gees' 15-month split of 1969-1970. Prior to the group's formal separation, Robin had announced his interest in recording solo. In August 1969 – following legal permission from Robert Stigwood to allow him to work on his own – he gave the UK media 11 song titles from his forthcoming album, which at that point was titled *All My Own Work* – 'Alexandria Good Time', 'The Flag I Flew Fell Over', 'I'll Herd My Sheep', 'The Man Most Likely To Be', 'Love Just Goes', 'Make Believe', 'I Was Your Used To Be', 'The Complete And Utter History', 'Seven Birds Are Singing', 'Sing A Song Of Sisters', and 'Beat The Drum'. Not one of those songs appeared on *Robin's Reign*, and most remained on the shelf until the 2015 release of *Saved By The Bell: The Collected Works Of Robin Gibb 1968-1970*. With the project being overseen by renowned music archivist Andrew Sandoval, the assembly was in good hands. The box set included 61 recordings on three CDs – Disc 1: *Robin's Reign … Plus*, Disc 2: *Sing Slowly Sisters – Sessions*, and Disc 3: *Robin's Rarities*.

It was an exceptional package of recordings from a little-known era of Robin's career. While most of the material was from his solo recording between March 1969 and April 1970, a few tracks were from 1968, and one from late-1970. All tracks – with the exception of those on *Robin's Reign* – were released for the first time on this set.

'Hudson's Fallen Wind' (Robin Gibb)
Recorded in London: 1969

This is an ambitious track, split into five sections, each separated by a brief silence. A beautiful orchestral introduction leads into Robin's dramatic opening narration. He strums acoustic guitar and sings – initially only with his trusty drum machine – and, partway through is joined by strings. This is where the story of the farming community begins. Strangely, it fades before it logically concludes.

The next section sounds familiar with the strange keyboard sound recognisable from 'Farmer Ferdinand Hudson': well-known from *Robin's Reign*. The following instrumental section mimics the storm to great effect, and portions are reminiscent of The Bee Gees' 1969 track 'Odessa'. The final part is 'Farmer Ferdinand Hudson' in its recognised form as it was released.

All in all, 'Hudson's Fallen Wind' is a grand and aspiring production. Had it been released at the time, it possibly could have taken Robin's career in a new direction. Regrettably, his management – and quite possibly his record company – didn't have enough confidence in it, preferring shorter, more-commercial songs. It's unfortunate that it wasn't heard until over four decades later.

'Alexandria Good Time' (Robin Gibb)
Recorded in London: March 1969

This was the original 'Saved By The Bell' B-side, but due to a technical malfunction, it was withdrawn. The handful of surviving singles have the track starting in the middle, playing to the end, with a few seconds of silence before the complete song is played. Why the rectification involved replacing 'Alexandria Good Time' with a totally different song – 'Mother And Jack' – is unknown, but the latter is a far better song. However, the slow-moving organ on the melody of 'Alexandria Good Time' is actually more characteristic of Robin's output at the time.

The World War I theme of 'Alexandria Good Time' is in line with two other songs of this period: 'Sing Slowly Sisters' and 'A Very Special Day'. There are historic references, one to the Boer War (1899 -1902), and the 20th century's shortest-serving British Prime Minister Andrew Bonar Law, who served in office for just 210 days in 1922 and 1923.

'Janice' (Robin Gibb)
Recorded in London: March 1969

A very early solo session, 'Janice', begins with a basic organ and Robin singing. It develops with the drum machine introduction and wordless multitracked backing vocals. Pizzicato violins add further interest in the middle section but are later replaced by a bowed string section. Despite Kenny Clayton's well-constructed arrangement, the recording still sounds unfinished. It has a better-than-average lyric for a Robin song of this period, but sadly – having a rather tedious and dull melody which runs for five and a half minutes, it didn't make the grade.

'Love Just Goes' (Robin Gibb)
Recorded in London: March 1969

Another track still seemingly in its embryonic stage, 'Love Just Grows' has a similar style and backing as 'Janice'. Again, the orchestral support adds greatly, and has quite a strong hook in the chorus.

'Goodbye Good World' (Demo) (Robin Gibb)
Recorded in London: 1969

Performed by Robin on guitar and vocal, this is quite a dark song, interspersed with some typically abstract lyrics. A version also exists on an acetate with a full arrangement sung by an unknown singer.

'Don't Go Away' (Demo) (Robin Gibb)
Recorded in London: February 1970

Another impossibly sad song of lost love – though this time delivered with a more-soulful feel than many of Robin's solo recordings. At over five minutes in length, it's probably too long, and certainly not 1970 single material. Robin does turn in a strong vocal, and his phrasing as he laments 'my woman' throughout is quite moving.

'Moon Anthem' (Robin Gibb)
Recorded at Chappell Recording Studio, London: 27 June 1969

Immediately following the announcement that Robin was leaving The Bee Gees, Stigwood litigation barred Robin from making solo recordings. As a way to work through this, his first two recordings – 'Moon Anthem' and 'Ghost Of Christmas Past' – were instrumentals and recorded under the pseudonym The Robin Gibb Orchestra and Chorus.

Given that Robin had no formal music training, Kenny Clayton warrants congratulations for his work here. Credited with the 43-piece orchestral and choral arrangement, his work is commendable, and particularly good, considering the arrangement would have probably been based on Robin's modest keyboard demos.

At more-than-five-minutes in length, 'Moon Anthem' is an intricate composition, written and recorded some weeks earlier, in anticipation of Neil Armstrong's first steps on the Moon on 21 July 1969. In the 19 June edition of *New Musical Express*, Robin called the song 'To Heaven And Back'.

The song itself is a very grand and somewhat pompous affair – perhaps a bit similar to The Bee Gees' *Odessa* instrumental 'International

Anthem'. It's like a film score that could have come from England's movie studios in the 1940s or 1950s. Gloriously portentous and patriotic, should the British ever land a person on the moon, this could be an appropriate song to mark the achievement.

'Ghost Of Christmas Past' (Robin Gibb)
Recorded at Chappell Recording Studio, London: 27 June 1969
Performed by The Robin Gibb Orchestra and Chorus

This is a fine piece of music. At 7:43 in length, it's another Robin Gibb epic. Again, arranged and conducted by Kenny Clayton, the melody hints at the influence of the hymn 'O God, Our Help In Ages Past'. 'Ghost Of Christmas Past' was possibly written and recorded for a television Christmas special that never eventuated.

As wonderful as this retrospective three-CD set was, it still omitted a number of tracks – including 'You're Going Away', 'Spread Your Wings', 'Lavender Water' and 'Midnight To Dawn'. The first version of 'You're Going Away' is similar to a number of Robin's demos of the era where he accompanied himself on organ alone. At this initial stage, it's played at an extremely slow tempo – probably dictated by Robin's basic keyboard abilities. Having developed the song a little more, he recorded it again later, accompanying himself on guitar.

'Spread Your Wings' begins with confident 12-string guitar, and a scat vocal – possibly an idea to be passed to an arranger for orchestra embellishment. It's an interesting narrative of a gold-digger girlfriend, and includes the bemusing couplet 'I found you in bed with your old friend/You pawned all my rings on the weekend'.

'Midnight To Dawn' also has Robin accompanying himself on guitar. The melody is quite upbeat, but it's just verse after verse, with no chorus to vary it. But it definitely had potential. Unusually for a demo, it fades out rather than coming to a natural end.

Robin wrote 'Lavender Water' with hopes of it being selected as the UK's entry for the 1970 Eurovision Song Contest, but it wasn't selected. Demos of it exist – one featuring a female vocalist, Lavender Farlane, and piano by Vic Lewis. The song chosen to represent the UK that year was 'Knock, Knock, Who's There?' by Mary Hopkin.

Maurice arranged and conducted the orchestra on 'Bye Bye, Blackbird' on former Beatle Ringo Starr's debut solo album *Sentimental Journey*, which was released in March. Maurice and Ringo lived very close to each other at the time and became friends. With their wives, Lulu and Maureen, they even made some fun home movies. One actually saw the light of day, appearing on a limited-edition video made available with Maurice's cooperation through The Bee Gees *Quarterly* fan club in February 1995, with proceeds going to charity. The two musicians had discussed the possibility of recording an avant-garde electronic album in early 1969. But only one track was recorded – on which Maurice spoke random words and phrases relating to synthesised sound – hence the title 'Modulating Maurice' – over Ringo's synthesiser instrumentation.

Also in March, the lead single from the soon-to-arrive *Cucumber Castle*, 'I.O.I.O.' was released. In the US, the record company chose 'If Only I Had My Mind On Something Else' instead. But following its failure to dent the charts (peaking at a miserable 92 on *Billboard*), they backtracked and rush-released 'I.O.I.O.' in April. But 'I.O.I.O.' didn't even equal its predecessor's performance – scraping the bottom of the chart at 98. But it wasn't all doom and gloom, as it became a top ten hit in Austria, Argentina, Belgium, Brazil, Denmark, The Netherlands, New Zealand and Spain.

The Marbles' final UK single – released on 20 March – was 'Breaking Up Is Hard To Do': a cover of Neil Sedaka's big 1962 hit. Its B-side was a fast horn-driven cover of The Bee Gees 1967 song 'I Can't See Nobody', which had already been released as the A-side of The Marbles' third single the previous year in the US and Germany, with the far more interesting Gibb composition 'Little Boy' on the flipside. While the English rock duo had achieved a top five hit in 1968 with their first record, 'Only One Woman', which was written and produced by The Bee Gees, their follow-up singles which were also Gibb songs, failed to reach the same heights. Possibly too closely associated with The Bee Gees, The Marbles had already split before 'Breaking Up Is Hard To Do' was released. The Marbles' self-titled album, including five of the seven Gibb songs they'd recorded was released shortly after, but strangely, not in the UK. It was reissued as *Rock Legends* in Australia in 1980. To date, the most worthy Marbles compilation is *The Marbles* – released in 2003 on the Repertoire label – which collects all their released output, including mono single mixes.

An article headlined 'Maurice Gibb Directing TV Series and Feature Movie' appeared in the 25 April edition of *New Musical Express*. Neither series nor movie came to fruition, but the reference to a dramatic film named *Bunker* – in which novice film director Maurice was to direct established actors Stanley Baker and Lionel Jeffries – was quite extraordinary. The report said the movie was 'a wartime story concerning five men who are trapped in a bunker. The title theme for the film is one of the items which Maurice has already recorded'. But Recorded Sound Studios engineer Ric Holland recalls things a little differently:

> We'd been hearing for months that he was to produce Richard Harris. Mo and Lulu had become friends with the actor after he'd appeared in a film *A Man Called Horse*. This set Maurice off on a Wild West theme. Next thing, he was recording a Western movie soundtrack-style theme which he originally called *Bunker*. He had some idea that his new pal Richard Harris was to create or appear in a western called *Bunker*. Gerry Shury did the arrangement, and Maurice played a 'Riders In The Sky'-type of guitar part, and later on retitled the composition 'Journey To The Misty Mountains'. He also recorded a song which he started with a spoken, down-home American accent, announcing: 'I can ride a horse'. You couldn't help but think that Mo was a bit of a fantasist.

American soul singer P. P. Arnold released the 'Bury Me Down By The River' b/w 'Give A Hand, Take A Hand' single on 17 October 1969, and continued to work with Barry Gibb as her producer in 1970. The three 1969 recording sessions had produced a further four songs – 'High And Windy Mountain', 'Let There Be Love', 'Piccaninny' and 'Turning Tide'. The first 1970 recordings were made at IBC in April, including two Blood, Sweat & Tears songs from their eponymous second album – 'You've Made Me So Very Happy' and 'Spinning Wheel' – which were big hits for them in the US. Two other songs – 'Happiness' and 'Born' – were originally written by Barry for his proposed solo album. A June session resulted in a second recording of 'Born' with a different arrangement. P. P. Arnold related how her collaboration began, in the sleeve notes to *The Turning Tide* – a retrospective release collecting her previously-unreleased material from the time:

> I was introduced to Barry Gibb by Jim Morris, who later became my husband, and Barry agreed to produce me and helped me to get a record deal. I was so happy and so excited about working with him, as I was a big Bee Gees fan and recorded 'To Love Somebody' on my second album *Kafunta*. Barry kept his word and helped me get a

record deal with his manager Robert Stigwood's RSO Records. Robert also became my business manager, and Jim became my personal manager. A lot of time went into rehearsing and learning the songs, and I was so happy when we were finally able to go to IBC Studios and start recording ... the recording sessions were all very uplifting, exciting and enjoyable. The songs and all of the Bill Shepherd arrangements were so beautiful, and I put my young heart and soul into every vocal and all the beautiful background vocal arrangements.

Barry was likewise enamoured with Arnold, saying, 'We made some beautiful records together and had some wonderful times together. This was the late-'60s and none of us knew where we were going. My brothers and I were experiencing a period of pain, not really speaking to each other, and I was looking to continue making music no matter what'.

However, the recordings remained on the shelf for over four and a half decades – some would say for good reason. Arnold lamented, 'Unfortunately, at the time, a lot of unexpected music industry politics came into play. And the recordings were never mixed and released. I was absolutely heartbroken'.

She elaborated on these events in her autobiography, *Angel Of The Morning*:

Andrew Oldham had a definite vision for me, Robert seemed less focused. I liked Robert, but we were from very different worlds. He was all business and had no real interest in where I came from or whether I was authentic or not. He was a very successful, very clever, elegant man. But I sometimes felt that he was being needlessly cruel towards me. Mostly he just wanted Barry to get back to the business of The Bee Gees – his cash cow – and I was getting in the way. He certainly wasn't giving me the managerial support I needed to get my record finished and Jim didn't have what it took what it took to keep the mercurial Barry Gibb on track. He tried at least, until one day the situation came to a head. Jim began to press Barry to get back to work on the album stressing amongst other things, the economics of the situation as he saw them. Accusing Jim of hustling him, Barry snapped. And that was it. Without any thoughts as to how this might affect me as an artist, the production was stopped. We'd spent nearly two years on the project and I had nothing to show for it. It was Immediate all over again. I'd been paid no advance and I'd stopped touring in order to get the record finished. It's still a mystery to me what actually happened, but I was told that Robert didn't think the tracks were commercial enough. I have no idea what the real reason that caused Barry and Jim to fall out. But the one thing was for sure, I was broke, and I had no idea what was going to happen next.

Eventually – on the 2017 heritage release *The Turning Tide* – eight of the recorded tracks were finally issued. They included the single tracks and all the other recorded songs except for 'Let There Be Love', one of the takes of 'Born' and 'Piccaninny'.

Arnold remembers:

We were back in the studio in November recording 'High And Windy Mountain', and 'Turning Tide', as well as a song I was definitely not happy with called 'Picaninny'. I felt Barry meant no harm – I put it down to simple foolish naivety as opposed to anything more insidious. And with all the uncertainty and problems surrounding the sessions, I didn't want to make any waves, so I recorded it. I shouldn't have done. I should have been stronger. I told myself that the lyric was being compassionate and empathetic about the civil rights revolution. But I still hated it. It had the racist slur that reminded me of a slave mammy singing to her child about the hard times ahead. As a Black American woman, it was a bad time for me to be singing the song. Barry was depressed and under pressure, and I seemed to be the recipient of this sad song, although I could hear Robin singing it. Perhaps Barry was missing Robin and was too stubborn to admit it. I wish that we'd had a conversation about it. We both should have opened up more.

In April, *Cucumber Castle* – the only Bee Gees album to not include Robin – was released. It had been some 13 months since he'd left and since their previous album, *Odessa* had been issued.

Cucumber Castle (1970)
Personnel:
Barry Gibb: vocals, guitar
Maurice Gibb: vocals, bass, guitar, piano, Mellotron
Colin Petersen: drums ('Then You Left Me', 'The Lord', 'I Was The Child', 'Bury Me Down By The River', 'My Thing', 'Don't Forget To Remember')
Terry Cox: drums ('If I Only Had My Mind On Something Else', 'I Lay Down

And Die', 'Sweetheart', 'The Chance Of Love', 'Turning Tide')
Geoff Bridgford: drums ('I.O.I.O.')
Vince Melouney: guitar ('I.O.I.O.')
P. P. Arnold: backing vocals ('Bury Me Down By The River')
Engineers: Philip Wade (IBC), Ric Holland (Recorded Sound)
Orchestral arrangements: Bill Shepherd
Producers: Robert Stigwood, The Bee Gees
Recorded between 7 May to mid-July 1969 at IBC Studios, London; 26-29
September 1969 at Recorded Sound Studios, London; 'I.O.I.O.' recorded 12
June 1968 and 8 October 1969 at IBC Studios, London
Release date: UK: April 1970, US: April 1970
Chart positions: Italy: 7, Australia: 10, West Germany: 36, Canada: 37, UK: 57,
US: 94

Cucumber Castle was recorded when the group were in great flux, personally and professionally. Robin had left on 19 March 1969 and was in a very public discourse with Barry. Fast fame, money, relationships, drugs and booze had strained the brothers' childhood bond to the point of breaking, and unchecked egos and immaturity nearly dissolved their professional careers. It was just three years since they'd launched themselves so successfully into the international arena after a long apprenticeship in Australia. It was a harrowing circumstance for everyone connected to them.

The album release was to be accompanied by a comedy television film of the same name. Two days into filming, Robert Stigwood fired drummer Colin Petersen. There are a couple of narratives explaining his dismissal – one being that he refused to act in the movie, and was told he was no longer needed. Another is that Stigwood became angry when Colin had questioned his conflict of interest as both The Bee Gees' manager and employer. Or perhaps it was a combination of both. In any case, Colin departed and sued The Bee Gees, in an attempt to prevent them using the group name without his inclusion. Needless to say, that effort failed. Colin remained bitter toward his former bandmates for a number of years; insisting he was owed royalties as part-owner of their moniker.

Despite all the drama and – no doubt – the pressure on the two remaining brothers to carry the group's obligations forward, *Cucumber Castle* is a solid album. With Robin gone, it allowed Barry and Maurice to delve into country music, which they both loved but Robin didn't, and four songs here are palpably flavoured as such. Though Robert Stigwood and the remaining Bee Gees share the production credit, it's likely Robert had more of a hands-off executive-producer role, and Barry and Maurice were in full control of the music – Barry takes vocal risks here that he hadn't on past Bee Gees efforts.

It's a different album from those they'd released prior and since. Barry takes the lead vocal on 11 songs, and he's in fine voice. The one song Maurice sings is a little disappointing. Furthermore, his vocal harmonies are only obvious in six songs. Yet his influence on the album is omnipresent: playing guitar, Mellotron, piano and bass in addition to his co-producer role.

Despite the trauma of the split, it perhaps for a time made Barry and Maurice's bond more secure, as Maurice was quoted as saying:

Since Robin left, Barry and I are a lot stronger, we're working much more together. We're having a ball. We can bring anyone we like into things. I did the majority of the backings anyway, even when Robin was with us, but there's more work for me now. I'm bringing me out more. I do six leads on the next album. Before, I think I only sang three all told. I write soft, and Barry keeps telling me to write harder music. I'm progressing more to the arranging side, and Barry is getting more, ideas-wise, he's freer with his words. At the moment, we'll go on as a two-piece, and if we find someone suitable to take Robin's place, we'll take him in. We've only seen two people. We're getting tapes from Wapping and Nottingham and Stoke and all over, but we want to get someone who can sing nice. We can take care of the hair and the clothes and all that. We're not looking for a copy of Robin, though.

Indeed – at one point, replacing Robin went beyond just talk, and upon a recommendation from Dave Dee, an English singer by the name of Peter Mason was identified as the man (or voice) for the job. Mason attended at least one *Cucumber Castle* session in 1969 after Barry selected him to replace Robin's voice in the vocal harmonies. Mason remembered singing on a tape of 'Don't Forget To Remember' and two other songs he later forgot the names of. Probably for the best, Stigwood – after some consideration – vetoed the idea of replacing Robin, and Mason was out. Mason couldn't hear himself on any of the completed *Cucumber Castle* songs.

Drums on the album are split between Colin Petersen, Terry Cox of folk-rock act Pentangle and Australian Geoff Bridgford. Cox was an excellent drummer, playing on many sessions for others. But his services were dispensed with due to his high pay rate which was set by the Musician's Union. Geoff Bridgford was then playing with Tin Tin, who Maurice was producing at the time. In studio engineer Ric Holland's book *As I Heard It: In the UK Music Industry 1969 to 1979*, he recalled Bridgford's elementary drum setup: 'Having seen and mic'ed up many drum kits since starting at the studio, I was very surprised at how small and economic Geoff Bridgford's kit was. It had only snare, single tom, hi-hat, crash cymbal and bass drum. It appeared dinky in comparison to other drummers' kits, but Geoff performed enough of what was required on it'. Holland remembers, 'Maurice brought in the first bowl-back guitar we'd seen: an Ovation. It was a Glen Campbell 6-string featuring a moulded synthetic body with a wood top and round sound hole. The distinctive metallic bowl-back sound became the vogue with acoustic players throughout the 1970s and '80s, but Maurice's really was a first. He also owned a Glen Campbell 12-string version'. The Bee Gees were to endorse Ovation guitars in press advertisements later in the year. Holland also noted that Maurice 'always overdubbed his bass: either a Hofner violin bass or a Rickenbacker bass. Both were brought in with him, and he recorded while seated in the producer's chair in the control room; he never played it live in the studio'.

Bee Gees recordings have always been admired for their wonderful orchestral accompaniments, and for many years, the man responsible was Bill Shepherd. He would come to the studio and be given rough mixes of the night's recordings. He'd take the tape home and prepare orchestral arrangements for overdubbing the next evening. Written parts for individual instruments had to be prepared quickly. Denmark Street copyist Gerry Shury wrote the parts out and delivered them to the studio in time for each session.

While Barry and Maurice seemed determined to continue as The Bee Gees, Robin's unique voice was truly missed on this album. His voice could sometimes take songs to places that Barry's voice couldn't. Lyrically, *Cucumber Castle* also lacks some of Robin's eccentricity, and as a result, the songs seem a little less abstract; perhaps more mundane at times.

Though recording finished in early-October 1969, the album wasn't released until April 1970. Despite the two striking hit singles 'Don't Forget To Remember' and 'I.O.I.O.', the album had a mixed chart response. While it was a top ten hit in Australia and parts of Europe, it failed in the world's two biggest record markets: the US and the UK.

The 55-minute television special wasn't screened until 26 December 1970, on BBC 2 in the UK, some eight months after the album was released. It was also screened on Australia's ABC network in early 1971.

The album was presented in a gatefold sleeve designed by Hamish Grimes. The front cover showed Barry and Maurice wearing chain mail and suits of armour. The typeface was an Old English style. The inner gatefold – with The Bee Gees now being just two – afforded each brother a panel. On the left-hand side, Barry – in character as Frederick the King of Cucumber – sits on a throne resplendent in a red doublet adorned with gold braid, matching gauntlets and ostentatious rings on most fingers. In his left hand, he holds a cucumber. The photograph chosen wasn't the best from the shoot, as Barry blinked while it was taken, his eyes were closed, and a hand holding a microphone appears in the top left-hand corner.

The right-hand gatefold panel shows Maurice as Marmaduke, the King of Jelly. He sits cross-legged with an exaggerated glum look on his face. He's wearing a brown-bodied doublet with red sleeves and a sash, red tights and calf-length boots of red suede. In his right hand, he holds a jelly on a plate. On the back cover, the brothers pose on a broad wooden staircase with ornately carved newels and balustrades, with a backdrop of wooden panels and leadlight windows. Barry sits on the stairs with an arm around Barnaby: his Pyrenean Mountain Dog. The photographs were all taken during the making of the television special, which was filmed at Robert Stigwood's house: The Old Barn, in Stanmore.

'If Only I Had My Mind On Something Else' (Barry Gibb, Maurice Gibb)
Recorded at Recorded Sound Studios, London: 8 October 1969
Chart position: US: 91
The album's opening song is a sweet ballad full of whimsy and romance. Barry took the lead vocal – as he did on all but one song on the album. It's not the most commercial song he ever wrote, but it does have a lingering melody. With Colin Petersen having been fired, Terry Cox played the drums.

It was released as a single in only the US, Canada, Australia and New Zealand – some eight months after the first single, 'Don't Forget To Remember'. Unlike its predecessor, it failed on the charts, only managing to scrape into the *Billboard* Hot 100 at 91. When the track appeared on the *Tales From The Brothers Gibb* box set in 1990, Barry's only comment was, 'If I'd only had my mind on something else'.

'I.O.I.O.' (Barry Gibb, Maurice Gibb)
Recorded at IBC Studios, London: 12 June 1968; Recorded Sound Studios, London: 8 October 1969
Chart positions: Austria: 2, Denmark: 3, New Zealand: 6, Spain: 6, New Zealand: 6, West Germany: 6, Argentina: 7, Brazil: 7, Belgium: 9, Netherlands: 9, Italy: 12, Australia; 14, UK: 49, US: 98

The album's oldest song was originally written during the *Idea* sessions in 1968. It was inspired by Barry's trip to Africa that year, which Maurice referred to as 'Barry's African jaunt'. It was the album's second single, but it's little known, despite being a more-than-reasonable hit in many parts of the world.

With a breezy tropical rhythm and a catchy chant, 'I.O.I.O.' (whatever it means) is quite memorable in its own way. Maurice later said it was never really finished, as it still had Barry's guide vocal on it. Engineer Ric Holland recalls Maurice playing congas and bass, and future Bee Gee Geoff Bridgford on drums at Recorded Sound Studios. The 'I.O.I.O.' chant is noteworthy as Maurice's only solo vocal on a Bee Gees' single A-side.

There are cover versions by actor Butch Patrick – best known as Eddie in the 1960s TV show *The Munsters* – and US boy band B3, whose 2002 cover hit number 4 in Germany: their biggest chart success. It was also a 2002 hit in South Africa for Kurt Darren – singing an adapted Afrikaans version called 'I.O. Meisie'.

'Then You Left Me' (Barry Gibb, Maurice Gibb)
Recorded at IBC Studios, London: July 1969

This is a pleasant ballad, with spoken-word drama at the beginning of each chorus. The primary hook is the repeated 'ba-by', which makes it particularly memorable. It's a great song, and the richness of Barry's vocal is a joy to hear. The track was the B-side of two singles: 'I.O.I.O.' in the US and Canada, and 'If Only I Had My Mind On Something Else' in Australia and New Zealand.

'The Lord' (Barry Gibb, Maurice Gibb)
Recorded at IBC Studios, London: July 1969

This is one of the strongest songs from a genuinely good album. It's a jaunty country number with a touch of gospel thrown in. It has a folksy, picked guitar introduction that switches to rhythmic strumming, joined by Maurice's lolloping bass. Barry launches into the lead vocal, before two tracks of Maurice – high and low – join in bold harmony in the chorus.

With the brothers brought up as Christians (they even went to a Catholic school for a short time in Australia), the lyric speaks of their beliefs, with the protagonist vowing, 'I'm gonna believe in the Lord'. It was performed in the *Cucumber Castle* television special, and the segment shows some great Barry and Maurice interactions. It's a lot of fun.

'The Lord' was one of the last sessions with drummer Colin Petersen before he was fired. It was released as the B-side of 'Don't Forget to Remember' in all territories except Canada.

'I Was The Child' (Barry Gibb, Maurice Gibb)
Recorded at IBC Studios, London: July 1969
This beautiful song is almost a companion piece to their 1968 classic 'First Of May', with the lyric speaking of lost childhood love and a broken heart. It's a dramatic, slow-ballad, and Barry's vocal – with a powerful chorus – is outstanding.

The song featured in the *Cucumber Castle* film but seemed out of place with its minor key; the song bears no relation to the loose plot, and there's no love interest in the film to match the song.

'I Lay Down And Die' (Barry Gibb, Maurice Gibb)
Recorded at IBC Studios, London: circa June 1969
According to Barry in a *New Musical Express* interview, 'I Lay Down And Die' was once proposed as the album title. As one of its strongest songs, it wouldn't have been a bad choice, but this was overridden by the cross-marketing plan of the *Cucumber Castle* television special.

It's totally compulsive listening, with a big powerful drum sound and once again, a fantastic Barry lead vocal. The dramatic finish finds him at the top of his natural range, and – quite simply put – it's awesome. The song was initially recorded using many backing vocals throughout but was only heard this way on the 'Don't Forget To Remember' B-side in Canada. The album mix left most of the vocals out.

'Sweetheart' (Barry Gibb, Maurice Gibb)
Recorded at Recorded Sound Studios, London: 26 September 1969
Maurice joins Barry in the wonderful chorus of this country-style commercial track. Released as the B-side to 'I.O.I.O.' in the UK, Europe,

Australia and New Zealand, it was melodically strong enough to be an A-side in its own right. Singer Engelbert Humperdinck thought so, and had a moderate hit with it, peaking at 22 in the UK, and 47 in the US.

'Bury Me Down By The River' (Barry Gibb, Maurice Gibb)
Recorded at IBC Studios, London: circa June 1969

This great country-inspired song could almost be the theme to a Western movie. It's an unusual Bee Gees song in that it has an audible female backing vocalist. It's also one of the few Gibb songs that they released after another artist had already released a cover of it. In this case, the artist was American-born singer P. P. Arnold – who had some late-1960s UK hit success, including 'The First Cut Is The Deepest'. It's her voice that can be heard on The Bee Gees' recording. Her single also had the Gibb song 'Give A Hand, Take A Hand', on the B-side and was also produced by Barry.

The song itself is excellent, with a soulful sound and a great Barry vocal. The recording was good enough to be considered for the album's lead single before being replaced by 'Don't Forget To Remember', but it remains a *Cucumber Castle* highlight.

'My Thing' (Barry Gibb, Maurice Gibb)
Recorded at IBC Studios, London: July 1969

'My Thing' is Maurice's only solo vocal on the album, and, regrettably, is its weakest song. One of five tracks from the album that were in the film, Maurice recorded it entirely alone, with no Barry backing vocals at all.

It has a light jazzy feel – perhaps just a bit of experimental fun, but it comes across as a very fragile composition. The song was dedicated to Maurice's Pyrenean Mountain Dog, Aston, who was evidently the 'dog lying under the table'. The silly line 'bowsie-wow-wowsie' didn't exactly help to elevate its integrity.

'The Chance Of Love' (Barry Gibb, Maurice Gibb)
Recorded at Recorded Sound Studios, London: 10 October 1969

The first of three robust closing ballads is a fine piano-led song. It has a particularly good Barry lead vocal, beginning softly but shifting into an emotive, raspy scream, which is very effective. At a little less than two and a half minutes, it's hardly an epic, and seems to end sooner than it should. Not that it's incomplete, but perhaps they didn't know how to develop it further. According to engineer Ric Holland, before recording Barry's vocal, he said, 'I haven't got any lyrics for this, so I'll sing whatever comes into my head' – which could partly explain the track's brevity.

'Turning Tide' (Barry Gibb, Maurice Gibb)
Recorded at Recorded Sound Studios, London: 25 September 1969
This is a guitar song with a beautiful melody and an uplifting chorus, which seems to stop too quickly. It appears to have originated in early 1968, appearing in copyright records as a Barry and Robin composition – indeed, recordings of it, including Robin, do exist. The song is the same, but oddly, the credit changed to Maurice over time.

'Don't Forget To Remember' (Barry Gibb, Maurice Gibb)
Recorded at IBC Studios, London: 7 May 1969
Chart positions: Denmark: 1, Ireland: 1, Netherlands: 1, New Zealand: 1, South Africa: 1, Norway: 2, Switzerland: 2, UK: 2, Belgium: 3, Austria: 8, West Germany: 9, Australia: 10, Spain: 27, Canada: 39, France: 42, US: 73
The final track on the album was the first single, although their respective release dates were several months apart. The single was a huge success globally, topping the charts in a number of countries and achieving top ten placement in many others. Its UK peak of 2 was ironic, as it matched Robin's achievement of reaching the same spot with his first solo single 'Saved By The Bell' some weeks earlier.

In 1990, Barry said sarcastically, 'I don't remember ... well, some of it maybe. We were all fighting about fame, and Maurice and I became The Everly Brothers, Robert Stigwood became *Jesus Christ Superstar*, Robin became solo, and chaos reigned. Time flies when you're having fun'.

A sentimental ballad, it has a rootsy timbre – a genre Barry and Maurice appreciated and were to revisit many times in the coming decades. But the record got some flak in the UK for being a rip-off of American country singer Jim Reeves. But Barry denied it was any such thing, saying it was a tribute to the late singer.

The group performed the song only occasionally – in a few shows of their 1975 North American tour (in a medley with 'Odessa') and on early dates of the 1989 European leg of the *One For All* tour. Following Maurice's sudden death in 2003, Barry and Robin sang the song as a tribute to him at a 2006 Diabetes Research Institute fundraising event in Florida. During this emotional performance, Barry took the first verse and Robin the second.

A number of extra songs were recorded during the album sessions – 'Who Knows What A Room Is' – a somewhat dreary song with a Barry lead vocal, in a similar style to 'Every Second, Every Minute', and 'The First Mistake I Made' from the next Bee Gees album *2 Years On*. Barry later said it was an attempted Beatles homage.

'Give A Hand, Take A Hand' was given to P. P. Arnold, who covered it in a style similar to this original recording. The Bee Gees resurrected the song for their 1974 album *Mr. Natural*. Arnold also recorded a version of 'High And Windy Mountain', which The Bee Gees recorded here as a fully-orchestrated mid-tempo country ballad with Barry on lead vocals.

'Every Morning, Every Night' began life as 'The Only Way', and is a slow plodding piano ballad. Maurice sings lead on 'Every Time I See You Smile'; Barry providing two spoken passages of what Bee Gees historian Joe Brennan described as 'greeting-card sentiments'.

'There Goes My Heart Again' was never fully developed, but the demo has a Barry lead vocal with rather exaggerated vibrato: perhaps a precursor to 'How Can You Mend A Broken Heart'. Barry and Maurice recorded 'One Bad Thing', which Barry later hijacked as a solo song.

With its catchy chorus, 'Twinky' is quite a fast-paced song about a girl, but it's nothing outstanding. It was later recorded by younger brother Andy in Australia in the mid-1970s.

One of the best unused songs is 'Go Tell Cheyenne', which has a great chugging feel, with Maurice on piano and Barry on rhythm guitar. The lead vocal is Barry, with Maurice and Billy Lawrie providing backing vocals and some beatbox-type percussive effects similar to those on 'Kitty Can' on the *Idea* album.

Engineer Ric Holland recalls 'Julia' as a 'Beatle-ish blues-rock groove with some brass'. The track featured Maurice on electric guitar. 'End Of My Song' was originally only identified on its tape box as 'Otis Redding demo' when it was written and recorded in 1967. It was possibly intended for Redding, but this never came to pass. Re-recorded here, Barry's vocal on this bluesy rocker is quite raucous.

'Railroad' (Maurice Gibb, Billy Lawrie)

Recorded at Recorded Sound Studios, London: 9 December 1969
Chart positions: Malaysia: 6, Singapore: 9
Maurice's debut solo single b/w 'I've Come Back' was released on 17 April 1970. Perhaps surprising some insiders, it was a strong commercial record. Co-written with his brother-in-law Billy Lawrie, the

song has a strong country feel, with the narrative of an ex-prisoner coming home. The song suits Maurice's voice, as he explained at the time: 'People have said that my single sounds like The Bee Gees. I sang the higher parts usually, and the other vocal parts I've added to 'Railroad' could be the others'.

Sometimes inclined to overproduce records, Maurice claimed that Lulu's advice was that the piano was too loud. Accordingly, he mixed the single no less than six times to please her.

The song's first British release on an LP was on the 1974 budget compilation *Gotta Get A Message To You*. It also appeared on the *Tales From The Brothers Gibb* and *Mythology* CD box sets. In the liner notes of the former, Maurice wrote, 'It was my first and last attempt at going solo', although he did release another solo single – 'Hold Her In Your Hand' – in 1984.

A promotional video for 'Railroad' was produced by Mike Mansfield, who also produced the *Cucumber Castle* television special. The opening scene was shot at London's Wandsworth Prison, and for the rest of the video, he's seen strolling down a stretch of railway line and exploring a disused signal box. A still from the video was used for a large front-page advertisement for the single in *New Musical Express* on 18 April. Maurice also performed the song on BBC 1's *Top Of The Pops* on 16 April and BBC 2's *The Young Generation* on 23 May.

Canadian Yves Lamoureux recorded a very nice version of the song for the 2003 Maurice Gibb tribute album *Everybody Clap*.

'I've Come Back' (Maurice Gibb, Billy Lawrie)
Recorded at Recorded Sound Studios, London: 9 December 1969

The 'Railroad' B-side is a slow and reasonable – if unexceptional – ballad. Bee Gees historian Joe Brennan noted it's far removed from the rigid verse/chorus structure that Barry preferred. In contrast to his twin brother, Maurice's lyrics (perhaps due to Billy Lawrie's influence) are all appropriate to the narrative, though, sadly, they don't lift the song greatly on this occasion.

Maurice always maintained that he never left The Bee Gees, but they left him. Essentially, he was correct. Robin walked out, frustrated his contributions weren't being respected, and Barry went solo when he felt Maurice wasn't concentrating on the group.

Endeavouring to keep Maurice busy during the split, Robert Stigwood employed him in the stage musical *Sing A Rude Song* for a short time.

But Maurice also kept himself busy in the studio, writing and recording his own songs and producing other artists.

Up to this point, Maurice had only written one song on a Bee Gees album: 'Where Are You' on the 1966 *Spicks And Specks* album. In 1970, at just 20 years of age, he was a creative yet uncertain young musician who really needed a collaborator to write with. That collaborator became Billy Lawrie – Maurice's then-brother-in-law. The two wrote and recorded together for the next two years. They also formed a production identity called Moby Productions – Moby being a portmanteau of Mo and Billy. They even created a logo in the shape of a whale á la Moby Dick.

Engineer Ric Holland remembers:

They'd come into the studio together, occasionally with hangers-on, day after day, evening after evening, Saturdays too. Billy idolised Maurice, tracked his every move and hung on his every word. Maurice being insecure, lavished the praise. He accommodated many of Billy's musical-or-otherwise ideas, and helped him achieve his ambitions. Billy was almost always around in the studio, and to say he was overenthusiastic would be an understatement. Mo's projects blended into each other, and an evening could be taken up with several acts being recorded, overdubbed or mixed. There was no strategy. Some recordings by this assortment of artists got released, most didn't. Nevertheless, it all went on and on.

The pair often employed members of Scottish band Stone The Crows – who were friends of Billy's – to assist with backing tracks. Holland recalls: 'Maurice would sit in the studio, sometimes stoned, and lay down a guitar or piano track, then overdub drums and bass guitar. He played everything by ear and was adept at creating bass lines on tracks'.

The pair were prolific writers, and although a number of their songs were released by other artists, none were commercially successful. Holland said of Maurice, 'He recorded further original material with various musicians providing accompaniment, but was hesitant over his solo work. He desired to be successful as an artist in his own right, but was also unsure of his songwriting, much of it written with Billy Lawrie. He'd also been used to supplementing the distinctive lead voices of his brothers Robin or Barry, and didn't reckon his own voice comparable to theirs'.

Maurice was recording songs for a solo album – as Barry and Robin were doing. At one point, the intended album title was *Journey To The Misty Mountains*, but was later changed to *The Loner*. Both were titles of songs he had written. But except for his 'Railroad'/'I've Come Back' single, and a limited edition four-song fan club EP, none of the tracks have been officially released.

For the sessions – from December 1969 to April 1970 – Maurice was supported by musicians including drummer Geoff Bridgford, guitarist Leslie Harvey of Stone the Crows, and – occasionally – on piano, Johnny Coleman: Lulu's arranger and pianist for a number of years. Holland recalled Maurice playing all other rhythm-track instruments, and they 'were embellished later with orchestrations by Gerry Shury. Gerry was chosen instead of Bill Shepherd, not only for variation, but Gerry gave Maurice the chance to take charge for a change. Cost was a factor, too, as Gerry, at the time, couldn't command large fees. Billy Lawrie was almost always in attendance, and gave Maurice constant encouragement bordering on idolisation. His sister Lulu attended some of the sessions for the single, and one evening during a mixdown'.

The release of *The Loner* was held back after the failure of the 'Railroad' single and was eventually cancelled altogether when The Bee Gees reformed in August. Interviewed by Nicky Horne on BBC Radio 1 two years later, Maurice appeared to have less-than-happy memories of the project: 'My solo LP is one thing that, well, to tell you the truth, I don't think it should be worth releasing, because I did it a while ago ... and I was under a great depression at the time when I did it, because I missed the boys very much. I just did it because I thought I had to do it'. Acetates exist of the full album, and from these, the assumed running order is as follows:

Side 1: 1. 'Journey To The Misty Mountains', 2. 'The Loner', 3. 'Please Lock Me Away', 4. 'I've Come Back', 5. 'Soldier Johnny', 6. 'She's The One You Love'

Side 2: 1. 'Railroad', 2. 'Laughing Child', 3. 'Something's Blowing', 4. 'Silly Little Girl', 5. 'Insight'

Most of the songs were co-written with Billy Lawrie, though the atmospheric instrumental 'Journey To The Misty Mountains' – complete with an intro featuring the sound of thunder – was credited solely to Maurice.

'The Loner' was a good strong song and worthy of being the title track. A year later, Maurice and Billy re-recorded it under the group name The Bloomfields: for the Richard Harris movie *Bloomfield*. With the exception of 'Railroad', 'Please Lock Me Away' is probably the most commercial song from the sessions. The somewhat murky production of 'Soldier Johnny' – a song with a good strong hook – doesn't fulfil its potential. Patrick Nankervis bettered the original with his cover version on the 2003 Maurice tribute album *Everybody Clap*. Nankervis' version featured Geoff Bridgford, who also played drums on Maurice's original recording.

Closing side one, the sessions' rockiest song, 'She's The One You Love' has an introduction reminiscent of The Supremes' 1966 hit 'You Keep Me Hangin' On'. A stronger, more-aggressive vocal from Maurice would have lifted this recording significantly.

Opening side two with the single 'Railroad' was a sensible choice. It leads into 'Laughing Child', which, while it's pleasant enough and suits Maurice's voice, is nothing outstanding. Little-known English singer Norman Hitchcock – who Maurice and Billy later produced – co-wrote 'Something's Blowing', which is partially based on an unpublished song by Hitchcock, who apart from being an aspiring singer, was an RSO staff writer. It's a fine track with a very nice orchestral arrangement from Gerry Shury. Maurice stretches his voice to the very limit of his upper register as the track fades out.

'Silly Little Girl' is a sweet and simple little love song, followed by the album closer 'Insight' – an instrumental that could almost be dismissed but for impressive brass and string arrangement. Almost like a theme to a James Bond film, it's a good recording in the end.

In 1976, four Maurice recordings from this period ('Laughing Child', Soldier Johnny', 'Something's Blowing' and 'Journey To The Misty Mountains') were released through the Netherlands-based *Bee Gees Information* fan club, thanks to one of the club's German helpers who owned an LP acetate. A limited-edition four-track EP (believed to be pressed as a limited run of only 200 copies) on the New Blood label was made available to fan club members only. It was the only release of the four songs. Bearing no title, the EP's picture sleeve states '*Bee Gees Information*' in large letters at the top, while below is a black and white photograph of Maurice overlaid with his name and the song titles. Understandably, considering its limited release, the disc has become a highly sought-after collectors' item.

Maurice and Billy wrote and recorded a number of other songs. Some of these – including 'Danny', 'Till I Try', 'Alabama', Give Me A Glass Of

Wine', 'Insight', and 'Touch And Understand Love' – have made it into the hands of some very fortunate collectors on extremely rare acetates. Others remain firmly locked in the vault – including 'Triangle', Going Where The Money Goes', 'Did You Receive My Letter, Susan?', 'It Takes A Man', 'Take It Easy, Greasy', 'Look At Me', 'I Fell Down', 'This Time', 'Number 3', and perhaps the most intriguing: 'A Man In The Wilderness'. Perhaps it was a coincidence, but *Man In The Wilderness* just happened to be the title of a film that Maurice's drinking buddy Richard Harris was making in 1970 (released in 1971).

Just three of the duo's songs were recorded and released by other artists in 1971: 'Touch And Understand Love' by Myrna March, 'Back To The People' by Bev Harrell, and 'Everybody Clap' by Lulu.

'Have You Heard The Word' by Steve Kipner and Steve Groves of Tin Tin, has become somewhat legendary since its recording on 6 August 1969. It was released as a single under the pseudonym The Fut on 1 May 1970, on the obscure Beacon label. There was no promotion, but it became sought-after based on the mistaken assumption that John Lennon wrote and sang on it. Lennon's assumed involvement came about during a Tin Tin recording session when Maurice – who was supposed to be producing – showed up after a trip to the hospital, having just broken his arm. Steve Groves claims the song began earlier in the day as a nice little composition by him and Steve Kipner called 'The Word'. Upon hearing the song, Maurice decreed it to be a real John Lennon number, and proceeded to play slide guitar using his plaster cast. Steve Kipner remembers: 'Maurice and Billy showed up with a bottle of Jack Daniels, and the engineer must have switched the tape on. They were singing in funny voices and talking like The Beatles. Maurice does quite a good Lennon, you know'.

With Maurice under the influence of painkillers and alcohol, the session went downhill, to the frustration of the two Steves. They abandoned the session, leaving Maurice alone with the bare-bones demo. Convinced in his state of inebriation that the song was very Beatle-like, he added his best John Lennon vocal impression. That's where the story should probably have ended, but Stone The Crows manager Mark London heard the finished tape and thought it was worthy of release. He spoke to Lionel Conway of Island Records, and persuaded him to take a chance with it, albeit via a subsidiary label. The B-side 'Futting' was a trumpet-led reggae instrumental that had no involvement whatsoever from Tin Tin or Maurice.

Maurice's Lennon impression was good enough to convince many that it was actually him, and so the legend of Lennon's involvement grew. When the single became unavailable, such was the demand that it started to appear on Beatles' bootleg albums – the first of which was *Have You Heard The Word* on the infamous CBM label (WEC 3624) in 1975, followed by many others over the years. Indeed, in the 1980s, demand was still high enough that a bootleg single of 'Have You Heard The Word' was produced on the Fut label – 7" bootlegs being a rarity. In May 1974, Abigail Music registered a US copyright of the song under Kipner and Groves, while the British equivalent PRS list it as Kipner, Groves and Billy Lawrie. In one final twist to the saga, Lennon's widow Yoko Ono also registered a US copyright under Lenono Music for John Lennon on 20 September 1985 – five years after his death – claiming the creation date was 1980: ten years after its 1970 release.

Sing A Rude Song (Original London cast album) (1970)

Personnel:
Vocals: Barbara Windsor, Denis Quilley, Maurice Gibb, The Company
Music direction and orchestration: Alfred Ralston
Production and additional orchestration: Maurice Gibb
Engineers: Mike Weighell, Ric Holland
Recorded on 3 and 4 April 1970 at Recorded Sound Studios, London
Release date: UK: May 1970
Side 1: 1. 'I'm In A Mood To Get My Teeth Into A Song' – Barbara Windsor, Denis Quilley, 2. 'That's What They Say' – The Company, 3. 'This Time It's Happiness' – Barbara Windsor, 4. 'Whoops Cockie!' – Barbara Windsor, Denis Quilley, 5. 'It Was Only A Friendly Kiss' – Barbara Windsor, 6. 'Whoops Cockie!' (Reprise)/'We've Been And Gone And Done It' – Barbara Windsor, Maurice Gibb, 7. 'Haven't The Words' – Denis Quilley
Side 2: 1. 'You Don't Know What It's Like To Fall In Love At Forty' – Barbara Windsor, 2. 'Waiting On The Off Chance' – The Company, 3. 'Waiting For The Royal Train' – The Company, Barbara Windsor, Maurice Gibb, 4. 'I'm Nobody In Particular' – Denis Quilley, 5. 'Wave Goodbye' – Denis Quilley, 6. 'Leave Me Here To Linger With The Ladies' – Maurice Gibb, 7. 'The One And Only' – Barbara Windsor, 8. 'Sing A Rude Song' – Barbara Windsor, The Company

One benefit of Maurice's involvement in the *Sing A Rude Song* musical was him being able to put his experience and talent to good use in producing the original cast album. It was recorded over two days in early April, and its release was timed to coincide with the musical's transfer to the Garrick Theatre in London's West End on 26 May. Music was by Ron Grainier and lyrics by Ned Sherrin and Caryl Brahms. Maurice had just one solo song on the album, 'Leave Me Here To Linger With The Ladies'. His other featured song in the show 'Tattenham Corner' was not included. He also duetted with Barbara Windsor on 'Whoops Cockie! (Reprise)'/'We've Been And Gone And Done It' and 'Waiting For The Royal Train'.

Engineer Ric Holland was not at all complimentary about the album:

Musically, the content of *Sing A Rude Song* could be considered barely-passable, to unlistenable. The lyrics were meant to be jocular, and the backing uplifting, but it would a long stretch of the imagination for them to be interpreted as such. Several weeks after the recording, mixes of the studio recordings were required. Maurice and (engineer) Mike (Weighell) could hardly contain their laughter. Not because the tunes or songs were funny or there was anything genuinely amusing, but because of the cheesy tackiness and awfulness of it all. Ultimately, Maurice was bashful and regretful about having been involved with the project.

Probably the best thing about the album was its cover art, designed by Hamish Grimes and Gustav Moody. The focal point is the round sepia photograph of Barbara Windsor and Maurice. It's bordered by a stylised red and orange Victorian/Edwardian *Sing A Rude Song* logo. A combination of pink, orange and red would normally be considered garish, but this is quite tastefully done. The design also transferred over to promotional flyers and posters.

Surprisingly for the show's backers and producers, it was not the hit they expected, and the reviews were not as positive as those for the original production at the Greenwich Theatre. Ned Sherrin tactfully commented that Maurice was not perhaps a natural stage performer: 'In retrospect, I think you could say that it wasn't quite his métier'. Maurice later agreed with that assessment. Sherrin concisely summed up the musical's life when he said, 'We had a triumphant house-full season at Greenwich. Then we languished, awaiting a West End home. By the time we came to the Garrick in May 1970, we competed with a heatwave, a general election, a World Cup, Wimbledon and a test match ... and lost'.

On 1 June, in an unusual bit of programme scheduling, Thames Television made a repeat broadcast of the *Frankie Howerd Meets The Bee Gees* special, which was first aired in 1968.

While Robin's departure from The Bee Gees is frequently discussed, it's occasionally overlooked that Barry, too, exited the group – in December 1969 – announcing he was pursuing a solo career. He released one single – 'I'll Kiss Your Memory' – with the intent to introduce an album he was in the process of writing and recording.

'I'll Kiss Your Memory' (Barry Gibb)
Recorded at IBC Studios, London: 15 and 20 February 1970

Barry's debut single was released on 5 June 1970. The slow country ode to lost love was romantic but something of a disappointment. In the liner notes of the 1990 *Tales From The Brothers Gibb* box set, Barry wrote: 'I think we've written a few good country songs in our time, although I'm not sure this is one of them'. Strings are very much to the fore in this sentimental ballad arranged by Bill Shepherd. At 4:26 in length, it was unusually long for a single.

The song's first appearance on an LP was on the Argentinian compilation album *Kitty Can* in 1973. Its first British LP release was on the Contour-label compilation *Gotta Get A Message To You*, and it also appeared on the *Rarities* compilation – part of a 17-LP German Polydor box set released in October 1983. The song's first release on CD was on the Japanese collection of Bee Gees and solo Gibb songs: *Rarities*, on the RSO label in 1989, followed in 1990 on the *Tales From The Brothers Gibb* box set.

A cover version by Jamaican reggae/ska artist Adina Edwards was released as a single on the Dynamic label in Jamaica in 1973. That recording was also included on her album *Don't Forget To Remember* along with covers of the title track and 'I've Gotta Get A Message To You'.

'This Time' (Barry Gibb)
Recorded at IBC Studios, London: 9 March 1970

This was the B-side of 'I'll Kiss Your Memory', and was a bit more optimistic and upbeat. However, it lacked the commercial edge expected. While 'This Time' has never appeared on a CD, it was on the compilation LPs *Rarities* and *Kitty Can* together with its A-side.

To promote his new single, Barry recorded three songs which would be broadcast on BBC Radio 1's *D.L.T. show* on 14 June, presented by DJ Dave Lee Travis. The songs were the two sides of the single, and a song called 'Happiness' which received the first of a limited number of official airings on the show. It was also included on BBC Transcription Service discs for syndicated broadcast by various global radio stations. Barry also appeared on *Top Of The Pops* in the UK, and on German television's *5-4-3-2-1 Hot And Sweet*. A large advertisement for the single appeared on the front page of the 6 June edition of *New Musical Express*.

While talk of The Bee Gees reuniting was circulating in the UK music press, Barry escaped the media by flying to Australia to host the televised *Go-Set* magazine Pop Poll Awards on 30 June. He presented the King of Pop crown to local singer Johnny Farnham, and also performed 'Words'. The Bee Gees won the Best International Group award.

According to Barry, the final realisation that The Bee Gees were finished came in the studio when recording the *Cucumber Castle* follow-up when he was told that Maurice was in Australia accompanying Lulu on a tour. Barry's memory was that he quietly took his guitar and walked out of the studio, recognising he now needed to concentrate on a solo career. Interestingly, his output during the split – compared to Robin and Maurice – was relatively modest. In retrospect, the previously driven-and-productive songwriter seemed genuinely stunned and saddened that it was finally over for The Bee Gees. Australian singer Ronnie Burns – who stayed with Barry at this time – recalled that Barry seemed somewhat depressed, morose, and preferred the isolation of his apartment with his future wife Linda to a recording studio. Certainly, the titles of several songs he wrote for his intended solo album seemed to reflect his introspective mood.

Barry's solo recordings began on 15 February and were spread over five sessions – the final being on 23 March. None of the musicians were credited, though future Bee Gees drummer Geoff Bridgford has said he played on them. One familiar person in the studio was Bee Gees' arranger Bill Shepherd, who undoubtedly played a big role in developing the songs.

The album was never officially named, but within the fan community, it's become known as *The Kid's No Good*. The only reference to this title can be found in the song 'Come Home Johnny Bridie' on The Bee Gees' 1973 album *Life In A Tin Can*.

Acetates of some tracks do exist, but nothing resembling a complete album has ever surfaced. However, the proposed running order is believed to have been the following:

Side 1: 1. 'Born', 2. 'One Bad Thing', 3. 'The Day Your Eyes Meet Mine', 4. 'Happiness', 5. 'Peace In My Mind', 6. 'Clyde O'Reilly'

Side 2: 1. 'I Just Want To Take Care Of You', 2. 'I'll Kiss Your Memory', 3. 'The Victim', 4. 'This Time', 5. 'What's It All About', 6. 'Mando Bay'

The strong opening cut 'Born' is a great R&B song with a good rough-edged Barry vocal. The song – with its female background vocals including American singer P. P. Arnold – has a real Ray Charles feel. Arnold herself recorded the song in June with some minor lyric changes.

'One Bad Thing' was the album's intended second single; the painfully slow ballad 'The Day Your Eyes Meet Mine' intended as its B-side. The slow but comparatively upbeat ballad 'Happiness' was a potential power ballad, but Barry was somewhat restrained from really launching into it. The track is supported nicely by Bill Shepherd's tasteful string arrangement. Barry also produced P. P. Arnold's 1970 cover of the song, which was eventually released in 2017 on her album *The Turning Tide*.

'Peace In My Mind' was another great ballad that deserves release, with nice orchestral work by Bill Shepherd. Fortunately, Shepherd's arrangements weren't wasted, as they were used on singer Katja Ebstein's German version, 'Frieden In Mir', on her 1971 album *Freunde*.

The side-one closer was to have been 'Clyde O'Reilly' – a song about a farmer – a surprising and uncanny parallel to Robin's 'Farmer Ferdinand Hudson'. Neither had happy endings.

This was one of Barry's songs of the era with a real country feel. At the time, he was quoted as saying, 'I love country music and I probably allowed a little more than I should have to influence me. But I do music that I enjoy, and hope that everyone else will enjoy it too. If you try to work for whatever everyone else wants, I think that you get lost'. American singer Roy Head covered the song in 1973.

Side two opener – the laid-back country ballad 'I Just Want To Take Care Of You' – is one of pleading melancholy, with Barry's own background vocals very evident. Responding to comments that 'I'll Kiss Your Memory' sounded very Bee Gees-like, Barry commented, 'It's not the same orchestra as we used with The Bee Gees, but Bill Shepherd is the only arranger I'll ever work with. I double-tracked my voice seven times, because I knew exactly how I wanted everything done'.

'The Victim' is an unusual song with a faster tempo than the previous few songs. The single B-side 'This Time' follows, and in contrast to most of the album, it's optimistic and appears to reflect Barry's determination to try again: 'This time it's gonna be different/This time

I'm gonna do things my way'. The upbeat tempo is matched by the confident chorus.

'What's It All About' is another laid-back country track, the lyric seems more akin to Barry McGuire's 1965 hit 'Eve Of Destruction'. The song could have worked quite nicely on the 1973 Bee Gees country-rock-influenced album *Life In A Tin Can*.

With guitar adding a tropically tinged atmosphere, mixed with a delightful string arrangement, the closing track sweeps the listener away to the fictional 'Mando Bay'. It's a beautiful, romantic, if a little sleepy, recording. The song was covered a year later by Peter Maffay who recorded versions in both English and German.

One of the best songs from Barry's solo sessions – with lush orchestral support by Bill Shepherd – was the ballad 'Moonlight'. Surprisingly, it didn't make the proposed album. But it was unexpectedly included on a 1971 Melbourne radio station Bee Gees special – the only time the song has been aired.

Sing Slowly Sisters – *Robin Gibb* (recorded for release, 1970; publicly issued for the first time in 2015)

Personnel:
Robin Gibb: vocals, guitar, organ, piano
Engineers: Ric Holland (Recorded Sound), John Pantry, Ted Sharp (IBC)
Orchestral arrangements: Kenny Clayton
Producers: Robin Gibb, Vic Lewis
Recorded between 1 January and 17 April 1970 at Recorded Sound Studios, London and IBC Studios, London

This was intended as Robin's second album. However, when the brothers reunited, it was agreed with management to cancel all planned solo releases in favour of the new Bee Gees product. The album – along with other Robin recordings from the period – was finally released in 2015 as part of the posthumous box set *Saved By The Bell: The Collected Works Of Robin Gibb 1968-1970*.

Robin began recording *Sing Slowly Sisters* just months after finishing his prior album *Robin's Reign*, and before it was released. Still estranged from his brothers, the final recording session for this album was 23 June. When The Bee Gees reformed in August, plans for releasing all three of the brothers' solo albums were shelved. While the running order is not confirmed, a comprehensive collection of the songs on a double-sided acetate has surfaced, and perhaps provides the biggest clue as to its likely assembly.

Side 1: 1. 'Sing Slowly Sisters', 2. 'Life', 3. 'C`est La Vie Au Revoir', 4. 'Everything Is How You See Me', 5. 'I´ve Been Hurt', 6. 'Irons In The Fire', 7. 'Cold Be My Days'

Side 2: 1. 'Avalanche', 2. 'The Flag That I Flew', 3. 'Return To Austria', 4. 'Make Believe', 5. 'All's Well That Ends Well', 6. 'A Very Special Day', 7. 'Sky West And Crooked'

The running times (not including gaps between tracks) are 26:36 for side one, and 23:19 for side two: a total of 49:55. For the era, this would have been a very long album.

'Sing Slowly Sisters' (Robin Gibb)
Recorded in London: January 1970

With a martial drum introduction, this is possibly the saddest song Robin ever wrote. While sad, slow Robin songs weren't unusual, this tells of the women who were left behind as their fathers, husbands and brothers marched off to World War I.

The BBC Radio 4 programme *Lost Albums* featured *Sing Slowly Sisters* on 19 May 2007, and Robin told presenter Pete Paphides, 'It was actually about the womenfolk. There was a kind of irony about the womenfolk in that the propaganda was to encourage men to go to war, that it was a noble thing to go and fight for your country, and if you didn't go, the women made you feel guilty. So, there's a sting in the tail of the support that women had for the men in World War I'. With Robin often accused of being a poor lyricist, here the words are thoughtful and appropriate.

In 2008, he wrote a song called 'Wing And A Prayer' (not the 1989 Bee Gees song of that title) that included two verses from 'Sing Slowly Sisters'. He made it available to fans via download from his website. It was released again in 2014 on his posthumous album *50 St. Catherine's Drive*, but with the revised title 'Wherever You Go' – to avoid confusion with The Bee Gees' song.

'Life' (Robin Gibb)
Recorded at Recorded Sound Studios, London: 17 April 1970

In complete contrast, 'Life' is very upbeat. A full-blown orchestra with brass section to the fore, drives the song along. The jovial melody masks the narrative of a husband whose wife leaves him.

'C'est La Vie, Au Revoir' (Robin Gibb)
Recorded in London: January 1970

The French title translates to 'That's life, goodbye'. It's another song about the end of a relationship, and again, the melody belies the storyline. The chorus opens with a rousing 'Hurrah, hurrah' – evocative of the popular American Civil War song 'When Johnny Comes Marching Home'. It almost implies relief that the relationship is over, before a more reserved and resigned 'C'est la vie, au revoir' brings it to a polite end.

'Everything Is How You See Me' (Robin Gibb)
Recorded in London: January 1970

Another upbeat number. Continuing with Robin's possibly-unintentional foray into the American Wild West, the magnificent introduction is reminiscent of the theme to the 1958 western movie *The Big Country* – attributable to orchestral arranger Vic Lewis.

'I've Been Hurt' (Robin Gibb)
Recorded at IBC Studios, London: 2 April 1970

The first of three songs recorded on 2 April features a beautiful backing by a string and woodwind octet arranged and conducted by Kenny Clayton. It's a sad and mournfully slow song, which at over four minutes, is probably a little too long.

'Irons In The Fire' (Robin Gibb)
Recorded at IBC Studios, London: 2 April 1970

The second song recorded on 2 April has a harpsichord and string quartet as accompaniment. It is pure baroque pop, although, in the booklet notes for *Saved By The Bell*, Bob Stanley noted that it 'sounded positively ancient; Regency maybe, or even pre-industrial – we picture Robin in a ruffled shirt, sitting at his harpsichord, a roaring fire in the corner'. Stalwart IBC engineers John Pantry and Ted Sharp oversaw the session. Both had worked with The Bee Gees previously, but the experimental nature explored here must have come as quite a surprise. Kenny Clayton's arrangement is quite outstanding.

'Cold Be My Days' (Robin Gibb)
Recorded at IBC Studios, London: 2 April 1970

The third 2 April track is a mini-epic, clocking in at over six minutes. It's another beautiful and tasteful Kenny Clayton harpsichord and string quartet arrangement. The song was written about the town Shipston-on-Stour in Warwickshire. In a BBC Radio 4 interview in May 2007, Robin said it refers to his youthful experiences riding horses with Barry. However, the lyric casts the song much further back in time with the reference to 'Gentlemen of leisure, please remove your hats, relax all spats'.

It is rather long, and it takes patience to get to grips with. It's a basic verse/chorus structure, so it would have benefitted enormously from a bridge or instrumental interlude to break it up, though that would have inevitably made it even longer.

A noteworthy lyric reference to The Isle of Man – the brothers' place of birth – comes in the line 'You can see Snaefell from Peel Castle tower'. Snaefell – at 2,034 feet above sea level – is the highest mountain on the Isle of Man, while the ancient castle in the small fishing port of Peel on the island's west coast dates back to the 11th century. The Gibb family even lived on Snaefell Road in Douglas in the early-1950s, and Robin owned a house in Peel in the 2000's.

'Avalanche' (Robin Gibb)
Recorded in London: 1970

'Avalanche' is a very sparse recording, consisting of just an acoustic guitar, a single drum and the vocal tracks. The opening lead vocal seems to push Robin's voice to the limits of his range, and he does sound a little strained. However, when a single harmony line is double-tracked and a wordless backing vocal is added, it pads it out nicely and sounds far more under control. Robin's supporting vocals are prominent.

In 2007, Robin co-wrote another song with the title 'Avalanche', with Peter-John Vettese. But that song bore little resemblance to this original. The new song appeared on Robin's excellent posthumous 2014 album *50 St. Catherine's Drive*.

'The Flag I Flew' (Robin Gibb)
Recorded at IBC Studios, London: 9 April 1970

In an August 1969 *New Musical Express* interview, Robin listed 'The Flag I Flew Fell Over' for his next album. Probably an error on the part of the reporter, it was eventually called 'The Flag I Flew'. The first chorus line actually says, 'The flag I flew, well it fell down around my shoulder'. It's another Robin song boldly stamped with his trademarks of sad and slow, and about lost love. The lush orchestral backing includes a beautiful French horn countermelody and accents.

'Return To Austria' (Demo) (Robin Gibb)
Recorded in London: February 1970

A demo of this song appeared on the *Saved By The Bell* set. The accompaniment is a slow organ part played by Robin as he seems to search for lyrics. His trusty drum machine joins in with a waltz rhythm five minutes into the eight-minute recording. Where the lyrics aren't forthcoming, he scats. Even in this early recording, the chorus is strong, and Robin's voice is quite beautiful at times.

It's interesting to hear how the song developed into its final form a couple of months later – a song about Austria would not be complete without Viennese waltz-style strings, so that's what it got. The master of such things – Johann Strauss – would have been pleased to have had such homage paid.

Somewhat predictably, it's another sad song of lost love with some nicely thought-out lyrics.

'It's Only Make Believe' (Robin Gibb)
Recorded at IBC Studios, London: 9 April 1970

This is not the 1958 Conway Twitty song that was popularised again by Glen Campbell in 1970. This is another slow, plodding recording; the lyric paraphrasing a Bible proverb at one point: 'To give is to receive'. There is no profound meaning to this: it's merely part of a convenient rhyming couplet. The lyric could also be a foil pointedly referring to the brothers' recent estrangement: 'I've never been alone before/It makes me feel so insecure/There's nowhere that I can turn'.

'All's Well That Ends Well' (Robin Gibb)
Recorded at IBC Studios, London: 9 April 1970

The lyric hints at lost love, like many of Robin's songs. But in this case, it's a little more resigned and philosophical. That said, those lines are brief, and the second half is instrumental, merely repeating the melody of the first. If the melody sounds familiar, it appears to be an adaptation of one of Robin's favourite Christmas carols: 'In The Bleak Midwinter'. Whether this was deliberate or a subconscious coincidence has never been discussed.

'A Very Special Day' (Robin Gibb)
Recorded at Recorded Sound Studios, London: 1 January 1970

Robin playing simple piano arpeggios are the only accompaniment here. He also sings the lead vocal, double-tracked harmonies and wordless backing vocals. The lyric is pretty ambiguous, about a soldier leaving to go to war – a theme somewhat consistent with the title track '*Sing Slowly Sisters*'. The reference to Irish playwright George Bernard Shaw is possibly a tad pretentious, but entirely in keeping with Robin's penchant for dropping historical characters and references into his songs.

'Sky West And Crooked' (Robin Gibb)
Recorded at Recorded Sound Studios, London: 1 January 1970

The term 'sky west and crooked' is West Country slang for someone who is 'not quite right in the head'. The song had nothing to do with the 1965 film of the same name starring Hayley Mills.

The arrangement is incredibly sparse, with just acoustic guitar. But by double and triple-tracking vocal harmonies, Robin weaves layers of wordless countermelodies. It's a remarkable work. The lyric includes the lines, 'I spent years as my father's apprentice/He was a dentist in East Derbyshire'. The very Englishness of this simple phrase epitomises Robin in this period as a well-to-do gentleman, albeit of a different age.

Related recordings

'Great Caesar's Ghost' (Robin Gibb)
Recorded in London: January or February 1970

This starts strongly with a fine orchestral introduction, and generally has a perfectly satisfactory and graceful waltz rhythm. But the lyric is simply bizarre and makes no sense at all. The title probably caused even more confusion for non-English speakers – with no bearing whatsoever to a ghost, let alone Caesar! To the unenlightened, the phrase was used as a euphemism in place of exclamations such as 'Good God' or similar (worse) expressions. It alludes to the Shakespeare play *Julius Caesar* in which the murdered Roman emperor's ghost appears to Brutus. It's best known as words spoken in frustration by Perry White – the editor of fictional newspaper *The Daily Planet* in the *Superman* radio program and comics of the 1940s and 1950s, and later the television series.

At one point, this song was mooted for possible release as a single.

'Engines Aeroplanes' (Robin Gibb)
Recorded at Recorded Sound Studios, London: 27 February 1970

A very fine, up-tempo and commercial song with country piano, this was considered for the B-side of Robin's intended fourth single, 'Great Caesar's

Ghost'. 'Engines Aeroplanes' wasn't entirely forgotten when The Bee Gees reunited and was apparently under consideration for the *Trafalgar* album in 1971, as Robin then re-recorded some vocal tracks for it.

'Anywhere I Hang My Hat' (Robin Gibb)
Recorded at Recorded Sound Studios, London: 17 April 1970
This is slightly more upbeat than many of Robin's songs from these sessions, and was also nicely arranged. However, the lyric remains typically abstract, and detracts from the finished product greatly.

'Loud And Clear' (Robin Gibb)
Recorded at Recorded Sound Studios, London: 17 April 1970
From the final sessions for the *Sing Slowly Sisters* album, 'Loud And Clear' has an identical melody to 'I've Been Hurt' from the same album. The lyrics are typically immaterial.

Over half a century later, it seems totally inevitable that The Bee Gees would reunite. But in the English autumn of 1969 – with Barry and Robin openly criticising each other in the UK music press – the chances appeared to be highly unlikely. Maurice – the self-proclaimed 'man in the middle' – was perhaps the bridge to reconciliation between the other two. Unlike Barry, he'd never stopped talking to Robin; even working on two songs on his first solo album. Fraternal siblings – coming from separate eggs – may not have the same uncanny connection as identical peers, but they do grow up alongside each other in the same environment, often hitting milestones at very similar times, and are perhaps more emotionally and psychologically bonded than regular siblings. Indeed, Robin and Maurice have told stories of transcending distance to feel each other's pain at times. As such, they naturally were the first to reunite creatively.

Their first collaboration was in June 1970, and over the next two months, they wrote over 14 songs together, before Barry joined them following Robin's offer of an olive branch. Of the 14 songs, only 'Distant Relationship' and 'I Can Laugh' progressed to The Bee Gees reunion album *2 Years On*, albeit with new titles and lyrics. 'Distant Relationship' became 'Sincere Relation', and 'I Can Laugh' was transformed into '2 Years On'. Curiously, as close as they obviously were, Robin and Maurice had rarely written together without Barry's involvement.

Barry's reintegration occurred in August 1970 after Robin visited him to suggest they put their discourse behind them and try again. Barry immediately accepted, asking Robin to assist him with a new song he was working on. That song became 'How Can You Mend A Broken Heart'. When Maurice joined them the next day, they all wrote 'Lonely Days': their first tri-part collaboration in 18 months. While they didn't know it then, they'd just written what would become the two biggest hits to date of their already stellar career.

While sibling tension may have been easing, business imperatives driven by the Robert Stigwood Group Ltd. – the parent company of RSO, which was going public – accelerated The Bee Gees' formal reunification. The group's long-time personal manager Dick Ashby recalled: 'As RSO was going public, and with their shares in the company, they were very much involved financially. Robert had to get each of them in one at a time to sign papers, discuss their new share deal and their new parts in the company. I think, once again, Stiggy has to be credited with it. He said to them, 'Look, we're going public … what a great thing it would be to launch the public company press-wise if you all came back together'. The Bee Gees official reconciliation was announced on 21 August, but their first television appearance wouldn't be until 31 October – on the first episode of a new London Weekend Television series called *Ev*, hosted by Kenny Everett.

With the group's future still uncertain at this point, Polydor re-released the 1969 double album *Odessa* as two separate LPs as part of the budget 99 series.

Sound Of Love

Release date: UK: July 1970
Side 1: 1 'Lamplight', 2. 'Sound Of Love', 3. 'Give Your Best', 4. 'Seven Seas Symphony', 5. 'With All Nations (International Anthem)'
Side 2: 1. 'I Laugh In Your Face', 2. 'Never Say Never Again', 3. 'First Of May', 4. 'The British Opera'

Polydor rather oddly reissued the second *Odessa* disc as the first part of their reissue effort. The first *Odessa* disc followed in October, as *Marley Purt Drive*. Polydor's German budget label Karussell issued *Sound Of Love* without its companion. The sleeve design was by Hamish & Gustav, who adopted a classy and tasteful approach with a decoupaged violet frame housing an early-period photograph of the brothers posing by a globe, against a blue/grey background.

With Barry's divorce from his first wife, Maureen finalised on 17 July, he and his girlfriend Linda Gray, wasted no time in making plans to get married. Just six and a half weeks later on 1 September – Barry's 24th birthday – the couple were married at Caxton Hall register office, London. Barry had met the former Miss Edinburgh during the taping of the BBC's *Top Of The Pops* in 1967. Their marriage would become one of show business's longest and most successful.

'One Bad Thing' (Barry Gibb)
Recorded at IBC Studios, London: 23 March 1970

'One Bad Thing' is a great, upbeat, poppy song, which was planned to be Barry's first solo single in the US and Canada, and the follow-up to his failed debut 'I'll Kiss Your Memory' in the UK and Europe with a scheduled release date of 2 October. Like Maurice and Robin's solo projects, the single was cancelled when The Bee Gees reunited.

Unfortunately, ATCO in Canada didn't get the memo, and pressed some copies. While most were destroyed, a few survive to this day, fetching huge sums on the collector's market.

The song's origin dates back to the previous year's *Cucumber Castle* sessions, when the song was credited to Barry and Maurice. But by the time Barry came to record it by himself, it had become a solo composition – in all likelihood, he'd been generous with sharing the credit when The Bee Gees existed as a recording entity, but probably didn't feel the need when the group had dissolved.

The song has been recorded by four different acts – New Horizon, The Freshmen, Ronnie Burns and Wildwood.

'The Day Your Eyes Meet Mine' (Barry Gibb)
Recorded at IBC Studios, London: 9 March 1970

Another song started back in 1969, with a shared Maurice credit that was subsequently dropped. It's a very measured, romantic ballad, planned as the B-side to Barry's second single, 'One Bad Thing'. Barry had also produced a version by Australian singer Samantha Sang, possibly to be the follow-up to her first single, 'The Love Of A Woman', which had just failed on the charts the previous year. Sadly, visa problems curtailed Sang's UK career, and she returned to Australia.

Barry told the media that American singer Andy Williams was also going to record the song, although it never materialised. While Barry's recording has never been released, Lou Reizner's recording of the song appeared on his eponymous album in 1971.

The second part of Polydor's single LP *Odessa* reissues appeared in October as *Marley Purt Drive*, in their budget-price 99 series.

Marley Purt Drive

Release date: UK: October 1970
Side 1: 1. 'Odessa (City On The Black Sea)', 2. 'You'll Never See My Face Again', 3. 'Black Diamond'
Side 2: 1. 'Marley Purt Drive', 2. 'Edison', 3. 'Melody Fair', 4. 'Suddenly', 5. 'Whisper Whisper'

The first *Odessa* disc was the second to be issued. Evidently, in Germany, sales of the first album *Sound Of Love* weren't sufficient to justify releasing the second instalment there. This album is, therefore, exclusive to the UK.

The sleeve design was a garish affair by Hamish & Gustav, with an indigo title strip across the top, and an orange background with a yellow road complete with white road markings in the cover's main body. This was overlaid with an *Odessa* promotional photograph of the brothers posing by a crudely-cropped ship's mast. The original photograph included drummer Colin Petersen, but he was omitted from the line-up as if to purposely deny him his legacy as part of the group. Petersen's departure had been acrimonious – not so much from the Gibb's perspective, but from Robert Stigwood's, and legal proceedings continued for a number of years before matters were concluded.

On 6 November, 'Lonely Days' – the much anticipated first single from the reunited trio – was released. The B-side was the equally strong 'Man For All Seasons' – both from the forthcoming new album *2 Years On*. The British media was generally receptive to the reunited Bee Gees, and they were welcomed back to the BBC's *Top Of The Pops* on 12 and 19 November. However, the single peaked at only 33 in the UK. Fortunately, it was a big hit around the world – particularly in the US, where it was number one on the *Cashbox* and *Record World* charts, and number three on *Billboard*. It was The Bee Gees' biggest hit there to that point.

A promotional film of the song was made, clearly designed to reaffirm the brother's reconciliation. The first scene shows Maurice sitting by a window playing a Fender Malibu acoustic guitar, followed by a second scene showing Barry leaving his apartment at 68 Eaton Square in London, and taking his dog Barnaby for a walk. The third scene depicts Robin looking at some of the awards The Bee Gees had won over the years and opening a patio door. At the end of each scene, each brother is seen getting into their car. Barry's is a Rolls Royce Silver Cloud III Drophead Coupe, Robin's a Mercedes 280SE, and Maurice's a Rolls Royce Silver Shadow. They drive off and meet up in the middle of a field, get out of their cars and make a three-handed handshake. It's at this point we notice a continuity error – where Robin got in the car on the left, but gets out on the right. They drive off into the distance as the song fades out.

On 9 November, they recorded four songs from the new album live at a BBC session – 'Alone Again', 'Every Second, Every Minute', 'Lonely Days' and 'Man For All Seasons'. These were broadcast on Radio 1's *D.L.T.* show presented by DJ Dave Lee Travis on 15 November.

On 20 November, Maurice's side project Tin Tin released their third single, 'Come On Over Again' b/w 'Back To Winona'. The hauntingly beautiful A-side was co-written by founding Tin Tin members Steve Kipner and Steve Groves with their drummer (and future Bee Gees member) Geoff Bridgford. The bassist was Carl Groszmann – a previous member of Steve & The Board in Australia, where he used the stage name Carl Keats.

The single was the first Moby Productions release, and the supporting 5 December full-page advertisement in the *New Musical Express* showed a spouting whale – to the casual observer, it appeared to be more about Maurice and Billy than Tin Tin.

In November 1970, The Bee Gees formally resurfaced as a trio with their new album *2 Years On*. The brothers later said that after an acrimonious 17-month split, their reunion was somewhat forced on them prematurely, due to structural changes within their management company, the Robert Stigwood Organisation.

2 Years On (1970)

Personnel:

Barry Gibb: vocals, guitar

Robin Gibb: vocals

Maurice Gibb: vocals, guitar, bass, piano, organ
Geoff Bridgford: drums
Alan Kendall: guitar
Orchestral arrangements: Bill Shepherd, Gerry Shury ('Sincere Relation', 'Lay It On Me')
Engineers: John Stewart (De Lane Lea), Lew Hahn (Atlantic)
Producers: Robert Stigwood, The Bee Gees
Recorded between 13 June 1970 and 5 October 1970 at De Lane Lea Studios, London
Release dates: US: October 1970, UK: November 1970
Chart positions: Australia: 22, Canada: 22, US: 32

When their reconciliation was announced, the brothers had already been working together for a short period, particularly Robin and Maurice. But their first writing and recording sessions were tentative and restrained as they rebuilt their working and personal relationships. Robin and Maurice had already written two songs that were included on *2 Years On*: a writing combination that hasn't appeared on any other Bee Gees' album.

When Barry joined in on the writing, the results were excellent – the first session producing two future top three singles: 'How Can You Mend A Broken Heart' and 'Lonely Days'. But for various reasons, the latter's release was delayed until the next album *Trafalgar* the following year. Other titles such as 'Alone Again', 'I'm Weeping', 'The First Mistake I Made' and 'Tell Me Why' seem to reflect the solemn emotions they were going through. Also, the album was somewhat rushed, with management encouraging them to get new Bee Gees product out, and to get out on the road.

The album's songwriting credits had a greater split than any other Bee Gees album except perhaps for their final album in 2001: *This Is Where I Came In*. *2 Years On* has aged well, as the overall quality is generally very good. It was reasonably popular in the US, making it to number 32, and it reached number 22 in Australia and Canada on the back of the success of the 'Lonely Days' single. But after witnessing their very public infighting over the previous 18 months, the British public didn't rush to embrace the reformed band.

Future Bee Gees band member Geoff Bridgford played drums on the album. He had already worked with Maurice and Barry on their solo projects, and he became a fully-fledged member of The Bee Gees in 1971.

The album cover – designed by Hamish & Gustav – has a simple white background with a broad grey-bordered photograph of the brothers in the centre. Barry is standing behind an ornate gilded table upon which stands an equally ornate clock – perhaps to imply the passing of time – while Robin is seated in a green velvet wing-back chair, with Maurice sporting splendid snakeskin boots, sitting cross-legged on the floor. This photo is duplicated on the back cover. The typeface used throughout is quite elaborate – in keeping with the rather-staid group photograph. Where it fails, is with credits on the UK edition, as the small print doesn't make for easy reading. The US edition took advantage of the additional gatefold sleeve space, and sensibly placed them alongside individual photos of each brother.

There were sleeve variations in Australia, New Zealand and Greece – all using a photo taken in what appears to be a clock repair shop with a man working away in the background. The choice of photo is puzzling in that only Maurice is looking directly at the camera; Robin appears distracted and Barry is in mid-guffaw. The only common theme carried on is a clock in the foreground. The Australian issue uses it in a similar manner to the British and American issues, with a plain frame around the photo but significantly larger. For some inexplicable reason, the photo is in a mirror image. The New Zealand issue orientates it correctly in a much larger version. The back cover of both uses the same image as other territories. The Greek edition also uses the mirrored photograph: taking up the entire front cover.

'2 Years On' (Robin Gibb, Maurice Gibb)
Recorded at De Lane Lea Studios, London: circa August/September 1970
As twins, Robin and Maurice seemed able to weather the group conflict a lot better than Robin and Barry did. Indeed, Maurice worked compatibly with the others during the split. The ability to work with Maurice first may have eased Robin into working with Barry again. Robin and Maurice were to write together again, but only outside The Bee Gees, teaming up for Robin's 1980s solo albums.

Beginning its life as a song called 'I Can Laugh', '2 Years On' was adapted to reflect the group's split, and the close-harmony a cappella introduction was added. Despite the title, the time frame of the actual split fell considerably short of two years. The song has typically abstract Robin lyrics, which appear to have nothing to do with the previous tumultuous 17 months, though the line 'The storm will break, but never me you'll see' might be telling. Speaking to Alan

Smith of the *New Musical Express* at the time, Maurice said, 'This is a song Robin got together himself. It's a kind of mass of ideas on which we did the backtrack a while ago, although he changed the lyrics in the studio'.

'Portrait Of Louise' (Barry Gibb)

Recorded at De Lane Lea Studios, London: 5 October 1970

If Barry was inspired by Dutch/English artist Sir Peter Lely's (Pieter van der Faes) famous 1671 painting *Portrait Of Louise*, then Louise the Duchess of Portsmouth (Louise Renée de Penancoët de Kéroualle) would have certainly been flattered to have such a fine song written about her. For Barry, it was 'simply a song about love, but the title doesn't come into the words at all. The idea of the words is that if you fall in love with a woman, you're not interested in what she's been. Musically it's a slight tribute to The Searchers – not a take-off, just a tribute. They had some beautiful sounds'.

Of Barry's four songs on the album, this is possibly the best. It's beautiful, with superb orchestral embellishments and outstanding chorus harmonies. A key change in the final chorus is a little contrived, but it works so well. The eight bass drum beats before the introduction are a bit unusual – possibly a count-in which would normally be left off the final recording – but it's a great song, with enough commercial appeal to have merited its release as a single.

'Man For All Seasons' (Barry Gibb, Robin Gibb, Maurice Gibb)

Recorded at De Lane Lea Studios, London: 20 August 1970

Recorded at the same session as 'Lonely Days', according to Robin, this is an archetypal Bee Gees song with Barry and Robin sharing the lead vocal. It was a sound that hadn't been heard in almost two years. A strong track, it demanded its own release as an A-side, but, unfortunately was relegated to the 'Lonely Days' B-side. When the group appeared on *The Andy Williams Show* in the US, and an Austrian show called *Wunsch Dir Was*, they performed both 'Lonely Days' and 'Man For All Seasons'.

Using film and book titles to inspire them, was a long-standing Gibb brothers songwriting trick, Robin saying in this case, 'It was a marvellous film title, and we thought it strange that nobody had ever written a song to fit'. The Oscar-winning film about 16th-century saint and philosopher Sir Thomas More had been released in 1966.

'Sincere Relation' (Robin Gibb, Maurice Gibb)
Recorded at De Lane Lea Studios, London: 13 June and circa August/September 1970

This started as a demo titled 'Distant Relationship'. Robin explained it was a tribute to his late father-in-law George Hullis, 'who was 60 when he died unexpectedly a while ago. He spent the last three days of his life at my house, and he told me he was going to die'. While it retained the original melody, the lyric changed significantly as it developed. Though its intentions were honourable, it's a slow and rather mundane song, which even the brilliant voice of Robin couldn't save.

'Back Home' (Barry Gibb, Robin Gibb, Maurice Gibb)
Recorded at De Lane Lea Studios, London: 18 August 1970

One of the better tracks of this uneven and somewhat tentative reunion album, 'Back Home' bounced off the turntable and was the rockiest Bee Gees recording since 'Idea' in 1968. Though credited to all three brothers, the song appeared to show a lot of Maurice's influence. It's too short to go anywhere, but it's a bit of fun. This song, 'Lonely Days' and 'Every Second, Every Minute' hinted that the group might evolve more confidently as a rock outfit. Sadly, this was not to be, as the next few albums tended towards a more ballad-focused sound.

The lyrics have a contemporary reference to the September 1970 aeroplane hijackings by the Popular Front for the Liberation of Palestine, and to the 36th President of the United States Lyndon B. Johnson, who earlier in the year had been replaced by Richard Nixon.

What's a bit unusual about 'Back Home' is that it has all three brothers singing in harmony throughout, with no one taking a lead vocal: certainly a rarity in their vast catalogue.

'The First Mistake I Made' (Barry Gibb)
Recorded at De Lane Lea Studios, London: 30 September 1970

This hidden gem is classic Barry Gibb, with an Americana feel, somewhat reminiscent of 'Marley Purt Drive' on *Odessa*, but capturing something closer to Jerry Jeff Walker's seminal 'Mr. Bojangles'. Barry explained: 'It's a story of someone who's gone through life and never knew his mother and father, and how everything he ever did in his life was the first mistake he made'.

In keeping with much of the album's material, it's rather melancholy, though American musician Phil Seymour did a convincing performance on the 1994 *Melody Fair* tribute album issued by Eggbert Records.

'Lonely Days' (Barry Gibb, Robin Gibb, Maurice Gibb)

Recorded at De Lane Lea Studios, London: 20 August 1970
Chart positions: Canada: 1, Brazil: 2, Denmark: 3, US: 3. Belgium: 7,
Australia: 8, New Zealand: 10, Austria: 15, Germany: 25, UK: 33, France: 48

Incredibly, many of the biggest Bee Gees hits have been written very quickly. Robin remembered that 'Lonely Days' was 'written on Addison Road in Holland Park in London, in the basement of Barry's place', with Barry adding that it 'was written in ten minutes. It was that quick. I was at the piano ten minutes'. The studio version plods a little, but it's had a good shelf life as a live favourite with a faster and voluminous chorus. Who would have thought it would still be bringing concert audiences to their feet, decades later?

It was a huge hit in the US, occupying the top slot in *Cashbox* and *Record World*. But *Billboard* has always been the gold standard of American music surveys, and the single achieved a slightly lower peak of 3 on that chart. 'Lonely Days' yielded The Bee Gees their first Gold single in the US, certified on 30 March 1971. It was the first of eight they'd receive over the next eight years.

Resurrected for Barry's 2021 solo album *Greenfields*, he was joined by the successful American country quartet Little Big Town. It's one of the high points of that set for sure, and though it doesn't stray too far from the original arrangement, it's a more lively and energetic performance.

'Alone Again' (Robin Gibb, Maurice Gibb)

Recorded at De Lane Lea Studios, London: 5 October 1970

A clear highlight of *2 Years On*, 'Alone Again' should have been a single. It was performed on television in the UK and was recorded for a BBC radio session, so they must have realised the song's strength at the time. But after 'Lonely Days', there were no further singles from the album.

Originally credited on the album to Robin and Maurice, on the US LP and ensuing CD it was credited to Robin alone.

'Alone Again' has plenty of Maurice instrumentation and vocal harmonies, but Barry's voice can't be heard. The concept of the reunion may be more in theory than practice in some aspects of *2 Years On*.

'Tell Me Why' (Barry Gibb)

Recorded at De Lane Lea Studios, London: 5 October 1970

This was written with Ray Charles in mind, just before a session, with the lights down. The song divides a lot of fans. To some, it's slow and doesn't really rise to a climax, and to others, it's very soulful. One wonders if Barry singing it with piano rather than guitar might have lifted it somewhat. It showcases one of Barry's earliest breathy vocals – a style he explored further with great success for the rest of his career – particularly on 'How Can You Mend A Broken Heart'. But much to his chagrin, he would also be mercilessly parodied for it.

On their 1972 album *Back Roads*, Kenny Rogers & The First Edition covered the song in a bluesy gospel style, which held even less appeal than the original for those who disparaged it in the first place. Of course, Barry was to work with Kenny Rogers 11 years later when he wrote and co-produced Rogers' 1983 album *Eyes That See in the Dark*.

'Lay It On Me' (Maurice Gibb)
Recorded at De Lane Lea Studios, London: 13 June 1970
Maurice was the brother who liked to rock out every now and again, and he was a big fan of swamp rock – a music genre created in the 1950s by young Cajuns and Creoles in the South Louisiana region. In particular, Maurice was a big fan of American singer-songwriter Tony Joe White – best known for his 1969 hit 'Polk Salad Annie'. Hence, the influence on this fun track is obvious.

For the next few years, 'Lay It On Me' became Maurice's signature song, his designated solo spot on their 1971 and 1974 tours, and a fan favourite. He proclaimed, 'This is a Maurice Gibb solo, backing and all! It's sort of swamp soul, and I recorded it at ten in the morning. I love the whole feel of it'.

'Every Second, Every Minute' (Barry Gibb)
Recorded at De Lane Lea Studios, London: 30 September 1970
A good rocking song with a strong Barry vocal, this was performed on the 1971 tour, and was very popular among fans. Barry told Alan Smith of the *New Musical Express*: 'This is another one of mine; a more-aggressive roll-on thing than some of the others I did. It was written for a film called *Melody* but was replaced by something else. I think it kind of builds'.

'I'm Weeping' (Robin Gibb)
Recorded at De Lane Lea Studios, London: 20 August and 29 September 1970
Another morose Robin song, and again it's more fact than fantasy. It's autobiographical to a degree with some poetic licence, telling of a poor upbringing, and how – now that he's reached adulthood – he revisits

the place he grew up only to find the house gone and everything else also changed. Robin recalled it as 'a song of mine I wrote on holiday in Madeira, and, as normal in my songs (I stick to a rule book!), I don't mention the title. I was thinking about my past'. The song is very slow, and while there's a gradual dynamic build-up, the tempo remains the same. The accompaniment by Bill Shepherd's orchestra and Maurice is beautifully sparse.

Having worked with Ringo Starr on his album *Sentimental Journey* earlier in the year, Maurice also claimed to have played piano on George Harrison's 'Isn't It A Pity' on his *All Things Must Pass* album released in November. But there are two versions of the song on the album – one the well-known seven-minute version, and the other a reprise titled 'Isn't It A Pity (Version Two)'. Phil Collins, who played on that album's 'Art Of Dying', claims he remembers Maurice being at the session, though no documentation to corroborate this has surfaced. The 2021 50th anniversary reissue of the album did fill in a few gaps, though – including confirming the presence of Eric Clapton, who at the time was under contract to Robert Stigwood, as was Maurice.

On 12 November, Robin seemingly randomly recorded two demos at Recorded Sound Studios in London. 'Why Not Cry Together' is a basic bare-bones demo with Robin accompanying himself on acoustic guitar. The lyric seems a little more thought-out than usual. The second song was 'After The Laughter'. It's not known whether these songs were for a specific project or he was simply laying down ideas for the next Bee Gees album. Neither song has surfaced on any Bee Gees or Robin Gibb album.

Inception/Nostalgia (1970)

Side 1: 1. 'In The Morning', 2. 'Like Nobody Else', 3. 'Daydream', 4. 'Lonely Winter', 5. 'You're The Reason', 6. 'Coalman'
Side 2: 1. 'Butterfly', 2. 'Storm', 3. 'Lum-De-Loo', 4. 'You're Nobody Till Somebody Loves You', 5. 'You Won't See Me', 6. 'The End'
Side 3: 1. 'I'll Know What To Do', 2. 'All By Myself', 3. 'Ticket To Ride', 4. 'I Love You Because', 5. 'Paperback Writer', 6. 'Somewhere'
Side 4: 1. 'The Twelfth Of Never', 2.'Forever', 3. 'Top Hat', 4. 'Hallelujah, I Love Her So', 5.'Terrible Way To Treat Your Baby', 6. 'Exit Stage Right'

Exactly how and why the *Inception/Nostalgia* compilation was conceived is unknown. Indeed, the brothers were unaware of its existence until

Maurice, Ringo Starr and their wives went on a skiing holiday to Switzerland, where Ringo chanced upon the album in a record shop. He commented he'd never seen that one before – and neither had Maurice! The material included was presumed to be under a licensing agreement between Polydor and Festival Records in Australia. But questions arise as to why Polydor in England didn't release it, or for that matter, Festival themselves. They probably weren't prepared to risk releasing an album of older material to an apparently unforgiving public in the UK.

Polydor released the double album on their budget imprints Karusell (Germany) and Triumph (France) without The Bee Gees' knowledge. It's a collection of unreleased tracks culled from the 1966 sessions at Ossie Byrne's St. Clair Studio in Sydney. It's a mixed bag of 24 original compositions and covers – effectively a follow-up to the 1968/1969 *Rare, Precious And Beautiful* album series. It was only available for a short time, but Polydor released it in Japan as *Inception And Nostalgia* in July 1972, following the group's successful first tour there in March. Many compilations appeared in later years, with various tracks from this album scattered amongst them. This original album was a highly sought-after, and due to its rarity, it was, for many years, an expensive set for collectors to acquire.

Having not toured since late 1968, The Bee Gees were now two musicians down in their performing line-up, and needed to recruit a lead guitarist and drummer. The successful guitar applicant was Alan Kendall, who recalls, 'I'd just finished a US tour with Toe Fat, who had been opening up for Eric Clapton's band Derek and the Dominos. Toe Fat had a couple of albums out but hadn't achieved much commercial success, so the management company let us go'. At various times, Toe Fat included keyboard player Ken Hensley and drummer Lee Kerslake – who both later joined Uriah Heep – and bassist John Glascock who later joined Jethro Tull. Kendall only played on the *Toe Fat II* album. The inner gatefold of The Bee Gees 1972 album *To Whom It May Concern* shows Kendall's guitar case leaning against his speakers, bearing the name Toe Fat. Kendall told Guitar Player magazine:

At that time, The Bee Gees were getting back together after a pretty contentious breakup, and were planning a ten-day US tour in support of a single they had out called 'Lonely Days'. Robin Turner of RSO called me and said The Bee Gees were looking for a guitar player who could also play bass, to which I replied, 'I would love to try out for the gig, but unfortunately, I can't play bass'. He then said, 'Just say you can play bass and come down for the audition'. As you can imagine, I was pretty nervous about this but desperately needed a gig and went along with it. Fortunately, I had a few days before the audition to do some woodshedding. The drummer – who was also auditioning that day – and myself went into the pub next door to the rehearsal hall, for a bit of Dutch courage and who should walk in but Maurice Gibb, with what looked like briefcase in his hand. 'Hey, you must be the drummer and guitar player. Let's have a drink before we start playing'. 'Hmm! This gig is looking pretty good already', I thought to myself. After a quick tipple, we strolled next door to the rehearsal place, and the next person I saw was Barry wearing a huge fur coat, talking to his very glamorous wife Linda while holding onto a large Afghan hound and smoking a huge spliff'. He walked over, said hello, shook our hands, and offered us a toke. 'Better and better', I thought, 'and we haven't even started playing any music!'. Maurice had been noodling about on his beloved Rickenbacker bass and doing a line check. Seemingly satisfied with things, he wandered over to where we were all chatting, and opened his briefcase, which turned out to be a portable bar!

Alan Kendall got the job as lead guitarist – a position he held throughout the decade and beyond. The drum seat was filled by Geoff Bridgford.

During a promotional trip to Germany, The Bee Gees recorded performances of 'Lonely Days' and 'Man For All Seasons' at the Rhein-Main-Halle in Wiesbaden. This was broadcast on *Wünsch Dir Was* presented by Dietmar Schönherr and Vivi Bach, on Austrian (ORF), German (ZDF) and Swiss (SRG) television networks on 19 December.

On Boxing Day (26 December), BBC TV finally screened the *Cucumber Castle* film. Filmed over 15 months prior, when the group were down to just Barry and Maurice, the 55-minute comedy had originally included drummer Colin Petersen, but after he was sacked, his scenes were re-shot. Inspired by the *Bee Gees' 1st* track 'Cucumber Castle', the idea to create the *Cucumber Castle* TV show had first been floated in late 1967. It was certainly no surprise that the brothers, who were cine-camera buffs – and had made endless home movies while growing up in Australia – were interested in being on screen themselves. It was originally intended to be a 13-part series but ultimately ended up being a single one-off special.

Apart from Barry in the role of Frederick the King of Cucumber, and Maurice as Marmaduke the King of Jelly, the supporting cast included Eleanor Bron as Lady Marjorie Pea, Pat Coombs as Sarah Troutsbottom, and Julian Orchard as Julian the Lord Chamberlain. Special guest stars were Frankie Howerd as the King, Lulu as the cook, Spike Milligan as the court jester, and Vincent Price as Count Bogsville.

Of the album's 12 songs, only 'The Lord', 'My Thing', 'I Was The Child', 'Then You Left Me' and 'Don't Forget To Remember' appeared in the TV special. Additional numbers included Lulu performing The Bee Gees song 'In The Morning' (which she'd recorded for her *New Routes* album) and Simon and Garfunkel's 'Mrs. Robinson'. Blind Faith – the supergroup co-managed by Robert Stigwood and comprising Steve Winwood, Eric Clapton, Ginger Baker, and Ric Grech – also made an appearance, playing the old Buddy Holly song 'Well All Right'.

The programme was topped and tailed with superb orchestral versions of 'Cucumber Castle', and a surprisingly up-tempo 'Holiday' arranged by Bill Shepherd. Sadly, the show was a ratings flop. But it seemed to be a good distraction, with Barry later saying, 'I think it was good that we did *Cucumber Castle*. It doesn't mean I think that *Cucumber Castle* was good, I just think it was good we did something really silly'.

By coincidence, later that same day, brothers made their final television appearance of the year on the centrepiece of London Weekend Television's Boxing Day schedule. *Holiday Showtime* was hosted by Maggie Fitzgibbon, and included guests Peter Cook, Les Dawson, Thora Hird, Max Jaffa, Arthur Lowe, Vincent Price, Hattie Jacques, Reg Varney, and special guests The Bee Gees who performed two songs from their new album, 'Alone Again' and 'Lonely Days'. Other musical guests on the show were jazz musicians Acker Bilk, Chris Barber and Kenny Ball.

Recorded on 15 December, it fell in the middle of a strike by the colour department at London Weekend Television, and so it was recorded in black and white.

1971

Following a short Christmas holiday with their families, the group returned to work, including rehearsals for their forthcoming US tour. The rehearsals were interrupted for an appearance on Saturday, 9 January, on *The Rolf Harris Show* on BBC 1. They performed their current single 'Lonely Days', which after a bright start following its release the previous November, stalled at 33 in the UK, regretfully rising no higher. Barry was openly disappointed with the UK sales, saying, 'That's not to say that I think 'Lonely Days' has had its day here. I'm still waiting for it to do better, and I'm not convinced it's going to drop away without a trace. Maybe the American success will revive some of the interest'.

In early 1971, Maurice got involved with creating advertising jingles. Recordings were almost always done with session musicians. One of the singers was Bob Saker: a well-known voice on television commercials at the time. Amongst his best-known character voices are the *Sugar Puffs* Honey Monster, and George the *Hofmeister* bear. Saker and his business partner Jack Winsley had connections with Robert Stigwood and his artists because their company, Winsak, rented offices from him at 67 Brook Street, London.

Jingles, in general, were created by dedicated jingle writers, light-music composers and mainstream arrangers. Occasionally, conventional songwriters composed the ads. For example, an ad for the carbonated health drink *Lucozade* was written and sung by UK singer-songwriter Albert Hammond, who also played piano on the recording. Radio or television commercials were usually of 30 seconds duration, though, for broadcast reasons, they actually needed to be exactly 28.5 seconds. This was to allow for tape roll-up and start-and-stop times when aired. They might be music only, or music with vocal or a spoken voice-over.

Maurice's first-known involvement with a commercial was for *Ultrabrite* toothpaste which was recorded in January 1971. He produced the jingle and Bob Saker sang.

Around the same time, Maurice was working with actor Richard Harris. Maurice, at the time, announced he'd be writing and performing the soundtrack to Harris' latest film *Bloomfield*, though there was some confusion, with denials from musical director Johnny Harris, who insisted he was contracted to score the picture and write two songs for it. He added that there would be four other songs in the film: one by Maurice Gibb. That song was 'The Loner', which Maurice and Billy Lawrie released as a single about a year later under the name The Bloomfields.

Eventually, Harris recorded an album's worth of material with Maurice, but the master tapes still languish on a shelf somewhere, and the material is unlikely to ever see the light of day.

Bob Saker was at one of the recording sessions at Nova Studios, and recalls: 'I remember going to a session with Richard Harris, and I remember being there, and he was pissed out of his head and he knocked a pint all over the desk. Gone! Goodnight!' ... 'I remember one song – 'Half of every dream is Mary, half of every dream is she...' – I remember that song'. His recollection is entirely correct, as the song 'Half Of Every Dream' surfaced as a Richard Harris B-side in 1972.

On 11 February, The Bee Gees began a short US tour supported by American gospel, soul and R&B vocal group The Staple Singers. Recalling the first show at the Palace Theatre in Albany, New York, Maurice was ecstatic:

When we did Albany, it was incredible. It was the first time we'd actually been on stage in two and a half years. And once you make one mistake, that's it, you just wait for the next one. Nothing is spontaneous on stage – everything is made to look spontaneous, but it's all carefully calculated. Robin forgot the lyrics in 'Really And Sincerely'. He used some from 'I Started A Joke'. So when we got to 'I Started A Joke', he just used the lyrics to 'Really And Sincerely' that he'd forgotten, and no one knew the difference. They think you've rewritten it for the stage.

The tour continued with shows at the Philharmonic Hall at the Lincoln Center in New York City, the Painters Mill Music Fair in Owlings Mills, Maryland, and the Auditorium Theatre in Chicago. Rehearsals at the Civic Auditorium in Santa Monica, California, on 19 February were interrupted following earth tremors – quite unnerving being just ten days after the devastating San Fernando earthquake. A concert planned for the following day at the Garden Auditorium in Vancouver, Canada, was cancelled. The tour concluded at the Paramount Theatre in Portland, Oregon, on 21 February. With the band backed by a 20-piece orchestra in full formal dress, the tour setlist was 'New York Mining Disaster 1941' (Overture), 'To Love Somebody', 'Really And Sincerely', 'Lay It On Me', 'Jingle Jangle', 'In The Morning'', Holiday', 'Every Second, Every Minute',

'I Can't See Nobody', 'Words', 'Portrait Of Louise', 'I Started A Joke', 'I've Gotta Get A Message To You', 'Lonely Days' and 'Massachusetts'.

The Stateside trip provided opportunities for several television appearances to promote the current single. On the popular *Andy Williams Show*, in addition to performing 'Lonely Days', they also performed the highly regarded B-side 'Man For All Seasons'. Over the next few weeks, they performed 'Lonely Days' on *The Tonight Show, Starring Johnny Carson*, *The Johnny Cash Show* and *The Ed Sullivan Show*. The final TV appearance of the trip was on ABC's late-night *Dick Cavett Show*, again performing 'Lonely Days', which had just peaked at number three on *Billboard*. It had entered the chart on 5 December and spent 14 weeks in the Hot 100. For seven of those weeks it was in the top ten. This achievement made 'Lonely Days' the best-selling Bee Gees single in the US to that point.

Recording of the new album commenced on 28 January, with drummer Geoff Bridgford who had toured with them in January, officially joining in March. In Australia in late 1966, the Australian-born Bridgford had replaced Colin Petersen as the drummer in Steve & The Board when Petersen left for the UK, where he joined The Bee Gees. Now – some two years after Petersen's departure from The Bee Gees – Bridgford was taking his place again. Bridgford originally travelled to the UK in March 1969 with Australian band The Groove, following their winning the *Hoadley's Battle of the Sounds* competition. Following a lack of UK success, the group disbanded. Bridgford quickly turned to session work, and joined another Australian ex-pat group Tin Tin, which included Steve Kipner: leader of his former group Steve & The Board. Having already worked with the Gibb brothers individually and collectively, Geoff was now officially a Bee Gee, and the Australian links to the group continued for the short term. At the time, the amicable Bridgford commented:

Naturally, I am very, very pleased. I sort of drifted into it … I was gigging around with Tin Tin, and at the same time I was doing a lot of session work for them, I played on all of their solo albums (including *Cucumber Castle*) while the breakup was in force. When they got back together again, I played on *2 Years On* and the single 'Lonely Days'. It just seemed natural that we should stick together for a tour, but I was very surprised when they asked me to become a member. I'd expected to be on sessions with them, but not as a fully-fledged Bee Gee. We all get on so well, it seems the natural thing to be joining them. I feel a bit guilty about leaving Tin Tin, but I am really happy for them.

On 26 March, New Horizon released a cover of Barry's song 'One Bad Thing'. It was one of four singles the group released between 1971 and 1973, each on a different label: Polydor, Bell, York and Decca. New Horizon was actually an identity of session singer Bob Saker, though on 'One Bad Thing' he duetted with British session singer Tony Burrows, who sang lead vocals on songs for several one-hit wonder acts – Edison Lighthouse's 'Love Grows (Where My Rosemary Goes)', White Plains' 'My Baby Loves Lovin'', The Pipkins' 'Gimme Dat Ding' and First Class' 'Beach Baby'. New Horizon recorded 'One Bad Thing' at Recorded Sound Studios with engineer Mike Weighell and assistant Ric Holland, with producer Jack Winsley.

Though Maurice wasn't directly involved, when the recording was complete, Bob and Jack played him the track, and he remarked, 'Barry will be pleased with that'. Engineer Ric Holland notes in his book *As I Heard It: In the UK Music Industry 1969 to 1979*, 'Curiously the producer was credited as Tony Burrows – I've no real idea why, but suspect something contractual or financial or both. Tony Burrows was frequently seen at the studio with Jack and Bob through 1970 and early 1971, and perhaps this production credit was a private arrangement. For sure, though, Jack Winsley produced'. The single was released on Bell Records in the UK and US but sank without trace.

April 1971 saw the release of four different projects with Gibb connections, and due essentially to their short record-store life spans, they quickly became collector's items. The first was Lou Reizner's eponymous album which included covers of Barry's 'Morning Of My Life', and of particular interest, 'The Day Your Eyes Meet Mine' – Reizner's inclusion of the obscure slow ballad was intriguing. The American-born Reizner was best-known as the producer of Rod Stewart's first two solo albums, the orchestral version of The Who's rock opera *Tommy*, and Rick Wakeman's *Journey To The Centre Of The Earth*. As an A&R executive, Reizner signed British progressive rock group Van der Graaf Generator, and arranged a US deal for David Bowie. He later worked with The Bee Gees on the soundtrack for the 1976 movie *All This And World War II*.

The second project was by Myrna March – a veteran, though little-known American country singer – who recorded the Gibb/Lawrie composition 'Touch And Understand Love'. Recorded at Starday-King Studio in Nashville, it was a single on two US labels – King and Agape. Though March continued in the music business, this was to be her final recording. The song was one of the first written by Maurice and Billy following The Bee Gees' split. They recorded it on 9 December 1969 at Recorded Sound Studios in London. Possibly intended for Maurice's solo album, the slow ballad found its way to Myrna March through a publishing company. For March's version, producer Hal Neely and arranger Bergen White closely shadowed the arrangement of Maurice's original demo.

On 16 April, Bev Harrell released a new Gibb/Lawrie song 'Back To The People' in the UK. Harrell was a popular Australian singer, best known for her 1967 hit 'What Am I Doing Here with You?'. The petite Adelaide-born songstress was subsequently voted Australia's Top Female Vocalist', and in 1969 travelled to the UK to expand her career. Despite the Australian connection, she had not met Maurice prior to the session. He produced and played on the recording. His wife Lulu sang backing vocals, and Geoff Bridgford played drums, with John Fiddy credited as arranger. Though the song was reasonably commercial, it did not chart. Maurice also produced the B-side 'Travellin' Easy' – written by Jack Winsley and Bob Saker – with both single sides credited to Winsak Productions. Harrell had previously released Robin's 'I Am The World' from The Bee Gees *Spicks And Specks* album as the B-side to her 1968 Australian single 'One Way Ticket'.

23 April saw the release of Lulu's single 'Everybody Clap' in the UK. Titled 'Everybody's Got To Clap' in some countries, it's one of the most commercial songs Maurice and Billy ever wrote. To ensure the record got the best backing band available, Maurice recruited the crème de la crème of UK musicians, including Leslie Harvey (Stone The Crows) on guitar, John Bonham (Led Zeppelin) on drums, and Jack Bruce (Cream) on bass. Billy Lawrie sang backing vocals for his sister and co-produced the track with Maurice. Despite being an infectious sing-along, and having a high-profile performance on *Top Of The Pops* on 29 April – when Maurice and Zoot Money (Dantalian's Chariot, Zoot Money's Big Roll Band) played acoustic guitars and Billy played bass – the single didn't chart. Backing vocals for this mimed performance were provided by five singers around a single microphone, and resident dance troupe Pan's People did their dance routine and handclaps. In the Netherlands, the B-side was a cover of The Bee Gees' 'Melody Fair' (not

produced by Maurice) from Lulu's then-current album of the same name. 'Everybody Clap' was included on the 1994 compilation From *Crayons To Perfume – The Best Of Lulu*. In 2003, the Maurice Gibb tribute album – appropriately titled *Everybody Clap* – included the song as its finale, with all the album contributors taking part.

Also, in April, The Bee Gees won the German pop magazine *Bravo*'s Silver Otto award. The coveted Golden Otto was won by Creedence Clearwater Revival, and the Bronze award by Deep Purple. It signified a change in the musical landscape since The Bee Gees had won the Golden Otto consecutively in 1968 and 1969 but also showed the German fan base's faithful dedication.

Melody

Release date: UK and US, May 1971
Side 1: 1. 'In The Morning' – The Bee Gees, 2. 'In The Morning (Reprise)' – Richard Hewson Orchestra, 3. 'Melody Fair' – The Bee Gees, 4. 'Melody Fair (Reprise)' – Richard Hewson Orchestra, 5. 'Spicks And Specks' – Richard Hewson Orchestra with children from Corona School 6. 'Romance Theme In F' – Richard Hewson Orchestra, 7. 'Give Your Best' – The Bee Gees
Side 2: 1. 'To Love Somebody' – The Bee Gees, 2. 'Working On It Night And Day' – Richard Hewson Orchestra with Barry Howard, 3. 'First Of May' – The Bee Gees, 4. 'First Of May (Reprise)' – Richard Hewson Orchestra, 5. 'Seaside Banjo' – Richard Hewson Orchestra, 6. 'Teachers Chase' – Richard Hewson Orchestra, 7. 'Teach Your Children' – Crosby, Stills, Nash & Young

The soundtrack album for the movie *Melody* was notable for the inclusion of a new version of 'In The Morning', which was used in the film's main title sequence. While the new version was retitled 'Morning Of My Life', it retained its original title on the album.

Beginning its UK celluloid life under the title *S.W.A.L.K.* – an acronym for a message that British schoolchildren traditionally wrote on the envelopes of love letters – standing for 'sealed with a loving kiss' – it was changed to *Melody* for global release, but not before some albums were released with the original title.

The young stars of the 1968 film *Oliver!* – Mark Lester as Daniel Latimer and Jack Wild as Tom Ornshaw – were reunited in *Melody*, joined by newcomer Tracy Hyde in the role of Melody. Other notable actors included Roy Kinnear and Kate Jones as Melody's parents, Keith Barron and Sheila Staefel as Daniel's parents, and John Gorman (of The

Scaffold) as the Boys' Brigade Captain. In brief, it's a sweet romantic story told from the perspective of the children. It's a film where adults play only supporting roles. Despite the star power of Lester and Wild, fresh from huge success with *Oliver!*, the film flopped in Britain and the US. Intriguingly, the film and its accompanying soundtrack became a big hit in Japan, topping the album charts and spawning two hit singles for The Bee Gees in the shape of 'In The Morning' and 'Melody Fair'. The film was also very successful in Argentina, Mexico, Chile, and was a modest success in South Africa.

For collectors, the album artwork variations were a dream come true, with the UK issuing two sleeves – one as *S.W.A.L.K.* and the other as *Melody*. France also had two titles and likewise two sleeves: *Mercredi Après Midi* and *22 Les Prof ...!* The US, Argentina and Taiwan all had greatly varying covers. In Japan, the album was again issued in two different gatefold sleeves.

Destined to become a genuine Bee Gees classic, 'How Can You Mend A Broken Heart' was released as a single in the UK on 28 May 1971, and in the US the following month. Some thought it was The Bee Gees covering a mid-century pop standard, which is testament to its classic quality. Based on what was popular in the US in 1971, it's no surprise it was such a huge success. The single topped the *Billboard, Cashbox* and *Record World* charts in the US, and was number one in Canada and Malaysia. It was promoted well on British television, with appearances on *Top Of The Pops* on 3 June, and *Whittaker's World Of Music*, on which the group also performed 'I've Gotta Get A Message To You'. But the single's UK TV promotion didn't translate into record sales – it simply didn't resonate with the British audience. Still, with the biggest record-buying market in the world on their side, this was to be an extremely important single for the group.

Also, on 28 May, another cover version of 'One Bad Thing' was released in the UK, this time by The Freshmen. The group was formed in 1962 in Larne, County Antrim, Northern Ireland, and were among the most popular Irish showbands of the 1960s and 1970s. They specialised in complex vocal harmonies and supported The Beach Boys on their 1967 tour of Ireland.

On 24 June, 'Moonlight' – a beautiful Barry Gibb ballad – was released as the B-side of American crooner Jerry Vale's single 'Which Way You Goin' Girl' in the US. It also appeared on his 1971 album *I Don't Know*

How To Love Her. The song was originally from the 1970 sessions for Barry's unreleased album.

In late June, Maurice booked a Friday session at Island Studios in London for a new project – Alamow – a duo comprising Maurice and The Hollies' lead singer Allan Clarke. According to the session engineer Ric Holland, 'They'd co-written a song 'Maureen', which sounded reminiscent of The Hollies' 'Jennifer Eccles' era. Mo fancied doing the recording at Island Studios in Basing Street. Island had a cool, trendy reputation, and it was understandable that artists and producers wanted to work there or at least try it'. Allan and Maurice played guitars with the session drummer and cut a rough vocal track. Holland remembers:

> Maurice had also booked a West Indian steel band to add atmosphere because he and Allan reckoned the song would be enhanced by the cheery sound of steel drums. The players were okay, but the steel drums were manky, out of tune and devoid of the resonance and ringing that would normally be expected. I couldn't get a clean sound out of them. The band were mic'ed-up in stereo, as there were plenty of tracks available on the 16-track tape, and the sound was just about acceptable.

The duo reconvened the following Wednesday at the newly renamed Nova Sound Studios near Marble Arch (formerly known as Recorded Sound Studios). Ric continues: 'Allan and Maurice took to the studio to do the vocals, Allan singing lead in his distinctive voice. Overdubbing complete, we did a rough mix which one of Maurice's cohorts took to Command Studios to have 7" acetates cut for Allan, Mo and me'. Following the final mixing, the recording and the Clarke/Gibb partnership became nothing more than a fading memory for the people involved. A commercial release was never mentioned.

On 9 July, The Bee Gees and their entourage arrived in Sydney for their first Australian tour since leaving in early 1967. The tour was considered by several concert promoters, but all but one felt The Bee Gees to be too high a risk to take on at the time. The promoters who took a chance – Ron Blackmore, Paul Dainty and David Trew – were ultimately well rewarded for their faith.

The support act for the tour was popular singer Russell Morris, who was well known for his hits 'The Real Thing', 'Part Three Into Paper Walls', 'Rachel' and 'Mr. America'. The tour visited all of Australia's state capitals except Darwin in the Northern Territory. Beginning at the Festival Hall in Brisbane on 10 July, The Bee Gees were accompanied by a 16-piece orchestra conducted by Bill Shepherd. At the next concert – in Sydney – they received a rapturous response from the audience. *Go-Set* magazine reported, 'The applause was deafening almost ten minutes after The Bee Gees had left the theatre and were on their way to their hotel!'.

The Canberra Theatre followed, where according to *Go-Set*, 'The crowd leapt from their seats and yelled for more. Canberrites have rarely been known to show such overwhelming enthusiasm for a visiting act of any sort'.

After a day off, it was a short trip across the water to Australia's island state of Tasmania for a show at Hobart's Moorilla Estate. The next day it was back to the mainland and Melbourne's Festival Hall for a show that was filmed for TV broadcast. Further shows – in Adelaide and at Perth's Beatty Park Aquatic Centre on 17 July – concluded the Australian tour.

After a few days' rest, they flew to New Zealand for two concerts – Auckland on 23 July, and Wellington on 25 July – both in the north island, unfortunately for south islanders.

Soundblast magazine said, 'The Bee Gees 1971 tour was one of the very few Australian sell-out successes. The promoters' faith had been justified, prompting further Antipodean tours over the next three years.

Barry had personally gifted the song 'One Bad Thing' to popular Australian singer Ronnie Burns while he was a house guest of Barry's in London in mid-1970. Burns – who had already had two successful singles with Gibb songs in 1967 – released his cover in July on Festival Records in Australia only. Though it received good airplay, it failed to make the charts. It later appeared on Ronnie's 1972 album *We've Only Just Begun*. In 1971, Sydney group Wildwood also released 'One Bad Thing' in Australia and New Zealand, on the Banner and Interfusion labels, respectively.

On 27 August, The Bee Gees began a 24-concert tour to promote their soon-to-be-released album *Trafalgar*. Starting with a single show in Canada at the Place des Nations amphitheatre in Montréal, the tour continued in the US, where they played 23 shows across 16 states in 34 days. The tour concluded on 3 October at the Keil Auditorium, St. Louis, Missouri. The tour support act was Tin Tin, who were following up the success of their single 'Toast And Marmalade For Tea', which had been a US top 20 hit earlier in the year.

During their New York stopover, The Bee Gees pre-recorded an appearance on the top-rating NBC chat show *The Tonight Show Starring Johnny Carson*, performing their recent US hits 'How Can You Mend A Broken Heart' and 'Lonely Days'. The show was broadcast a few days later, on 9 September.

Trafalgar (1971)

Personnel:
Barry Gibb: vocals, guitar
Robin Gibb: vocals
Maurice Gibb: vocals, bass, piano, Mellotron, guitar, organ, drums
Geoff Bridgford: drums
Alan Kendall: lead guitar
Engineer: Bryan Scott
Orchestral arrangements: Bill Shepherd
Producers: Robert Stigwood, The Bee Gees
Recorded between 28 January and 7 April 1971 at IBC Studios, London
Release dates: US: September 1971, UK: November 1971
Chart positions: Australia: 8, Spain: 9, Canada: 17, US: 34, Japan: 57

Barely two months after finishing *2 Years On* and touring Australia and the US, The Bee Gees were back in the studio recording the follow-up *Trafalgar*. No doubt, under pressure to consolidate the success of 'Lonely Days' and regain their pre-split position as a pre-eminent group, the brothers responded well and produced a strong album. Despite *Trafalgar* being an excellent set, the sheer amount of ballads seemed to demonstrate a level of confusion over where the group thought they should be in the marketplace. Despite the high quality of the songs, their maudlin style would soon become a millstone around their creative necks. The Bee Gees were quickly being labelled as a pop-ballad group. Part of their identity crisis might have stemmed from their formula working well in the US – a market that had afforded them a respectable amount of success for the first part of their career, but certainly not on the frenetic level they experienced in the UK and Europe. After the pervasive social, political and financial turmoil the US endured in the late-1960s, their culture had become much more introspective, and the music industry followed. So, while The Bee Gees were still healing from their own internal strife, their emotional reflections on lonely days and broken hearts were perfect themes for their Stateside audience.

Following their tentative first steps to reunite for the *2 Years On* album, the brothers were working confidently together again. Barry and Robin were particularly prolific, with five collaborations on *Trafalgar*. However, only one of the 12 songs here received the hitherto standard B., R. & M. Gibb credit. This album has three Barry solo compositions, so he was continuing to write alone as well. Vocally, it was all becoming very familiar, with Barry and Robin handling all the lead vocals except for the two Maurice-led songs – 'Trafalgar' and 'It's Just The Way'. Maurice continued his multi-instrumentalist role, playing bass, piano, organ and Mellotron.

The year 1971 also saw the rise to prominence of the singer-songwriter era, with meaningful introspective lyrics becoming more important to listeners and critics. On *Trafalgar*, the Gibb brothers failed to meet the challenge of putting more thought into their lyrics. While there were exceptions, their continued use of abstract or simple verbiage in too many songs was to have an impact on their credibility as mature songwriters. Their flair for melody and song structure was not in doubt, but their ability to make their words coherent, was. This had long-term implications, as, at times, despite their eminent singles-chart success, The Bee Gees struggled to rise above the pop artist label throughout their career, and so many of their albums were overlooked as classic contributions to music.

That said, *Trafalgar* is still a solid work, and produced their biggest US chart hit to that point, with 'How Can You Mend A Broken Heart'. Following that single's success in many world markets, the album was very popular in Australia, Italy, Spain and Canada. In the US, it reached 34 on *Billboard*.

Following the contributions of Geoff Bridgford and Alan Kendall as session musicians on the previous albums, they were credited for their input in the album liner notes. Incorrectly spelt as 'Jeoff' on the original vinyl and CD sleeve notes, it was to be Bridgford's only credited appearance on a Bee Gees album as an official member of the group.

In August 1996, Mobile Fidelity Sound Labs (MFSL) issued a special audiophile edition of *Trafalgar*. The album was remastered in a process called half-speed mastering, where the sound recording was transferred to disc while the cutting lathe moved at half-speed. The album was remastered from the original analogue two-track master tape, without compression and with minimal equalization. The recording was pressed on 200-gram *SuperVinyl*, which was more durable than regular vinyl, and had lower surface noise. It was packaged in a heavy cardboard sleeve with an inner cardboard stiffener and a special plastic liner. All MFSL releases were numbered limited editions with the number embossed in gold on the back cover. At the same time, MFSL issued a 24-carat-gold CD with stunning sound quality.

Trafalgar was the second Bee Gees album (after *Odessa*) to be included in Robert Dimery's book *1001 Albums You Must Hear Before You Die*.

The album artwork was overseen by Hamish Grimes – formerly of Hamish & Gustav. The cover painting was by renowned maritime artist Nicholas Pocock (1740 – 1821). He painted a number of scenes depicting the Battle of Trafalgar a decisive naval battle fought off Cape Trafalgar on the south coast of Spain during the Napoleonic Wars. The British fleet under Horatio Nelson defeated the combined fleets of France and Spain, which were attempting to clear the way for Napoleon's projected British invasion. The album cover painting is titled 'The Battle of Trafalgar, 21 October 1805: End of the Action'. It was created in 1807, and is housed at the National Maritime Museum in Greenwich. The album was in a gatefold sleeve, and the painting covers both the front and back. The inner gatefold photograph was by Roger Brown, and is a pastiche of the Arthur William Devis painting 'The Death of Nelson' (1805). The photo shows Barry as Lord Nelson, and in positions relative to those in the original painting, Geoff as Captain Thomas Hardy, Maurice as ship's surgeon William Beatty (In the painting, he feels Nelson's pulse, or lack thereof, and is about to pronounce him dead), and Robin as the Reverend Alexander Scott, Nelson's chaplain (rubbing his chest to relieve the pain). Maurice recalled there was 'a great deal of giggling about Nelson's purported last words 'Kiss me, Hardy' and who was kissing who during the photo shoot'.

Another figure visible on the US edition but blacked out on the UK cover is father Hugh Gibb. Hugh's part in the picture was unplanned, according to road manager Tom Kennedy: 'He was just there at the time … [The photo shoot] was actually done on a barge on the Thames. The photographer needed someone, and thought, 'Hugh will do''.

The tableau is littered with humorous additions, such as Geoff reading a copy of British children's comic *The Beezer*, and a pile of other comics under Maurice's foot. There's a bottle of Coke on the shelf, and a modern stethoscope at Barry's feet.

'How Can You Mend A Broken Heart' (Barry Gibb, Robin Gibb)

Recorded at IBC Studios, London: 28 January 1971

Chart positions: Canada: 1, Malaysia: 1, US: 1, Chile: 2, Australia: 2, New Zealand: 6, South Africa: 7, Netherlands: 16, Belgium: 21, Italy: 24

The opening track was also its first single, and could not have been a stronger choice. Released on 28 May 1971, the B-side was 'Country Woman', written by Maurice.

'How Can You Mend A Broken Heart' is a sensational song with a beautiful lyric, great harmonies and an eminently-memorable melody. In summary, it's a very well-crafted pop classic. According to Barry and Robin, it was written the previous year on the same day as 'Lonely Days' and was the first song the previously bickering sibling pair wrote together following their reunification. The delay in releasing it has never been explained, but it's thought that it was first offered to US crooner Andy Williams. While Williams did record a wonderful version of it for his 1971 album *You've Got A Friend*, it wasn't released as a single. Barry has also said the song's influence goes back to Skeeter Davis' 1962 hit 'The End Of The World' – a song the teenage Bee Gees sang on Australian television.

In 1972, 'How Can You Mend A Broken Heart' was nominated for the Grammy for Best Pop Performance by a Duo or Group with Vocal. The other nominees were Sonny & Cher for 'All I Ever Need Is You', Three Dog Night for 'Joy To The World' and the London cast for *Jesus Christ Superstar*. The Carpenters were the winners with their eponymous album. It was the first of many Bee Gees Grammy nominations.

Perhaps almost as well known as The Bee Gees original, is soul-legend Al Green's classic cover from his 1972 album *Let's Stay Together* – and it was released as a single in France in 1978. That version gained exposure on the soundtracks of *Good Will Hunting* (1997), *The Virgin Suicides* (1999), *Notting Hill* (1999) and *The Book of Eli* (2010). In 2008, Green's version was remixed as a duet with Joss Stone for the film adaptation of *Sex And The City*: her vocal being added to the track.

In 2002, Barry sang backing vocals on Canadian crooner Michael Bublé's version of the song on his debut album. That version reached 22 on the US *Billboard* Adult Contemporary chart. Other notable versions were recorded by Johnny Mathis, Cher, Teddy Pendergrass, Julio Iglesias, Barry Manilow and jazz singer-pianist Diana Krall.

Barry and Sheryl Crow duetted on the song on his 2021 album *Greenfields*. This is probably best described as lounge music.

'Israel' (Barry Gibb)

Recorded at IBC Studios, London: 6 April 1971
Chart position: Netherlands: 22
In May 1972, 'Israel' was released as a single in Belgium, the Netherlands and Portugal.

Barry told Richie Yorke of the *New Musical Express* in November 1971: 'I wrote this as a tribute; a dedication to the country. The whole lyric was ad-libbed, as no words were written down. I just sang what came into my head after I got the tune'. It's a great song, sung with a lot of passion, but possibly let down a little by extolling the virtues of the 'beautiful sand' a little too much.

'The Greatest Man In the World' (Barry Gibb)

Recorded at IBC Studios, London: 6 April 1971
A pleasant-enough song, but perhaps not as good as Barry thought it to be at the time: 'To me, it's very romantic, the best love song I've ever written'. It's tediously slow and the hook line 'I'd be the greatest man in the world 'cause I can say I got the greatest girl' is romantic but not particularly memorable. In an interview on the Australian tour promoting the album, Maurice was generous with his praise of Barry, saying it was 'the best song he's written all year'.

'It's Just The Way' (Maurice Gibb)

Recorded at IBC Studios, London: 7 April 1971
The first of two Maurice songs on the album is a jaunty little number, nicely arranged and executed. Typical of Maurice's style, it seems to be from the everything-but-the-kitchen-sink school of record production – not quite at the level of Phil Spector's Wall of Sound, but Maurice certainly wasn't afraid of using everything available to him. It's a simple four-chord trick pretty much all the way through, but it works so well – even in the instrumental break, which is merely a boosted rhythm guitar track. This was most certainly Maurice's best solo songwriting effort to this point.

'Remembering' (Barry Gibb, Robin Gibb)

Recorded at IBC Studios, London: circa February/March 1971
The first of the album's two broken-hearted love songs, in which the wife leaves the protagonist, and he lives in hope of her returning someday. Robin claimed the song was his personal tribute to Roy Orbison, and

comparisons to his 'In Dreams' can certainly be made with the style of the introduction. However, for many, the song is just too overwrought.

'Somebody Stop The Music' (Barry Gibb, Maurice Gibb)
Recorded at IBC Studios, London: circa February/March 1971

Barry admitted that this was 'a bit weird, a mixture of two songs' – similar to the likes of The Moody Blues' 'Question' and The Beatles' 'A Day In The Life', which both started as two songs. The division point within 'Somebody Stop The Music' is clearly defined as being immediately after the second chorus, where it suddenly turns into a bluesy boogie-woogie.

'Trafalgar' (Maurice Gibb)
Recorded at IBC Studios, London: 15 February and 7 April 1971

Maurice's second song here was one of which he was quite-rightly immensely proud. He sang, and played every instrument, including drums. Despite the album cover, and the opening lines 'I rolled into the smoke/ And there I lost my hope', it's not about the Battle of Trafalgar. Maurice explained, 'It's a song about a very lonely guy who lives in London and spends a lot of his time feeding the pigeons in Trafalgar Square'.

'Don't Wanna Live Inside Myself' (Barry Gibb)
Recorded at IBC Studios, London: 7 April 1971
Chart positions: Canada: 29, Netherlands: 29, US: 53

The album's second single was only released in Canada, Japan, the Netherlands, Portugal, Spain and the US. 'How Can You Mend A Broken Heart' proved to be a hard act to follow. The new single met with mediocre chart placings, with a best showing of 29 in the Netherlands, while it didn't even break the top 50 in the US. At the time, it was Barry's favourite song on the album: 'I don't know if it reflects me or not. Maybe I was in a bad mood when I wrote it'. The song wasn't in the live set until the 1975 US tour when it took on a different life with Robin singing the 'I have seen the jaded tiger' part. A prominent organ also really lifted it.

'When Do I' (Barry Gibb, Robin Gibb)
Recorded at IBC Studios, London: 28 January 1971

Sung throughout by Robin, 'When Do I' sees him utilising many facets of his versatile vocal range and timbres. His lower register is as impressive as the high, which saw far more use. He throws in a probably inadvertent triplet on the word 'losing' in the second verse and the use of an almost staccato style and melisma in the chorus add colour. It's a very sweet song.

'When Do I' was also covered by Peter Maffay in the German language. The song is not literally translated, and it became the title track of his 1971 album *Du Bist Wie Ein Lied*. Nothing particularly remarkable in that, but the album is interesting to fans and collectors as he also recorded two otherwise unreleased Gibb songs in German for the album, 'Mando Bay', a song scheduled for Barry's unreleased solo album, *The Kid's No Good* in 1970 and 'If I Were the Sky' (as 'Ich Bin Dein Freund'), an out-take from the *Trafalgar* sessions. It became even more interesting when, in 1973, the album was issued in the UK, South Africa and Venezuela with the lyrics in English.

'Dearest' (Barry Gibb, Robin Gibb)
Recorded at IBC Studios, London: 23 March 1971

The sentimental 'Dearest' is a heartbreaking ballad that pushes melodrama to its limits. Barry and Robin share the lead vocal in this slow tearjerker that one critic described as 'so pathetically sad that it comes across as a parody'. The song was also the B-side of the 'Israel' single in Belgium and the Netherlands.

'Lion In Winter' (Barry Gibb, Robin Gibb)
Recorded at IBC Studios, London: circa February/March 1971

The Lion in Winter was a 1968 British-American historical drama film set around Christmas 1183 – about political and personal turmoil among the royal family of Henry II of England. This has absolutely nothing whatsoever to do with the song 'Lion in Winter', as Barry explained to Richie Yorke of the *New Musical Express* in November 1971 that it's 'about a young guy in show business'. But it does seem likely that the movie inspired the song title.

The bass drum pattern played eight times in the introduction is way too long. It goes on for 34 seconds – an eighth of the four-minute song. A couple of passes would have been ample before the guitar and vocal comes in.

The song begins quietly with Barry taking the first verse, and then comes Robin with the chorus. It begins well enough, but very soon, you're wondering who's strangling him! It's a *Marmite* moment – you either love it or hate it! Reminiscent of parts of 'I Can't See Nobody' and the later 'Method To My Madness' on the *Life In A Tin Can* album, let's just say that's it's not his best effort. On the bright side, Barry's aggressive vocal later in the song grabs it by the collar and lifts it substantially.

Released as the B-side to the 'Israel' single in Portugal.

'Walking Back To Waterloo' (Barry Gibb, Robin Gibb)
Recorded at IBC Studios, London: 29 March 1971

This closes the album with a spectacular flourish, and appears to tip its hat to the album cover's Napoleonic war theme. The introduction of sparse descending piano octaves sets the scene perfectly for the melodramatic verses – the first by Robin and the second by Barry, which are passionately delivered. All three brothers sing in powerful unison on the chorus melody, and the backing vocals are in three-part harmony. The orchestral arrangement lifts to an incredible climax before bringing the song and album to an apt conclusion.

Related Songs

'Country Woman' (Maurice Gibb)
Recorded at IBC Studios, London: 6 April 1971

Barry and Robin shared the writing credits on 'How Can You Mend A Broken Heart' but Maurice had the B-side, 'Country Woman' to himself. In terms of the mechanical royalties paid for the sales of the single, which were significant, Maurice actually made more money than his brothers!

Although he hadn't written many songs alone, he saw his current style as his 'Country, or swamp music period. Really a warmup to much better songs'. He joked, 'Johnny Cash, you have nothing to worry about'.

It's a lively song, quite like much of the material on his unreleased solo album, *The Loner*, on which he collaborated with Billy Lawrie. All things considered, it is not unreasonable to assume that this song was an uncredited collaborative effort; Billy has since revealed he wrote lyrics for several of Maurice's compositions of this era.

A number of session outtakes that didn't make the final cut were very strong songs. The wonderfully idiosyncratic 'If I Were The Sky' was a Barry and Robin composition, and has Robin's wonderful, eccentric lyrics all over it. With a Robin lead vocal, it was one of the earliest Barry and Robin co-writes after the reformation. German singer Peter Maffay recorded it as 'Ich Bin Dein Freund' for his second album *Du Bist Wie Ein Lied* in 1971. He also recorded it with the original English lyric for the album's South African edition, *It's You I Want To Live With*.

Barry's 'Irresponsible, Unreliable, Indispensable Blues' is a classic 12-bar blues with a similar feel to 'Road To Alaska' which followed on the 1972 album *To Whom It May Concern*. The demo also identifies it as 'The Lumberjack Song' – a reference to the opening line, 'Born to the son of a lumberjack'. All three brothers wrote 'God's Good Grace', which features a Robin solo vocal. The opening piano notes are precognitive of their hit 'Run To Me' from the following year. Robin's excellent and unusually up-tempo 'Engines Aeroplanes' from his unreleased *Sing Slowly Sisters* was also re-recorded for *Trafalgar*.

Though unlikely to have been recorded for *Trafalgar*, the sessions produced 'Ellan Vannin' – often referred to as the alternative national anthem of the Isle Of Man – the actual anthem being 'O Land Of Our Birth' or 'O Halloo Nyn Ghooie' in the Manx language. The brothers always held the island of their birth in high regard.

Beginning life as an 1854 poem by Eliza Craven Green, it was later set to music by J. Townsend or F. H. Townsend, depending on the reference source. The Bee Gees version is very short, with just the first verse and chorus. It's mainly sung in unison, with occasional harmonies, an organ and a simple string arrangement. They re-recorded the song in 1998 to benefit a Manx charity, and performed it at six of their *One Night Only* concerts in 1998/1999.

Maurice – always one to keep himself busy – penned two more advertising jingles in October. Both were for confectionery products – the chocolate manufacturer *Cadbury*, and *Spangles*; a brand of boiled sweets manufactured by Mars Ltd. in the UK from 1950 to the early-1980s.

In late 1971, Barry Gibb put aside his usual perfectionism to release three delightful recordings to the British-based *Barry Gibb Fan Club*. Accompanying himself on acoustic guitar, the recordings were included on a 1971 EP on the Lyntone label, issued to fan-club members only. The pressing run is believed to have been just 200 discs, and it's now become a highly sought-after collectable.

'King Kathy' (Barry Gibb)

With a spoken introduction and some rehearsal strums, this is – in Barry's words – 'the story of a horse'. It's a sad tale about a racehorse who dies – very unusual subject matter for Barry.

'I Can Bring Love' (Barry Gibb)

Another spoken introduction with more practice strums. This very beautiful ballad has an extra verse which was later dropped for the version that appeared on the next Bee Gees album.

'Summer Ends' (Barry Gibb)

With a length of 4:46, this is the longest song of the three on this EP, and probably needs more development than the other two. Still, it's a nice, slightly meandering ballad of a broken heart and the last days of summer. In 1972, the little-known American vocal trio, Company, included their cover of the song on their only album.

In December, The Bee Gees US label Atlantic issued the Barry ballad 'Don't Wanna Live Inside Myself' as the follow-up to 'How Can You Mend A Broken Heart'. Edited from 5:24 to 3:50 (by removing the last verse and chorus), the single didn't break into the top 50. Perhaps the B-side – the potent 'Walking Back To Waterloo' – might have been a better choice.

Astral Taxi, the second and final album by Maurice's Australian protégés Tin Tin, was released in December. It was produced by Billy Lawrie, with Maurice named as executive producer. Group members Steve Kipner, Steve Groves and Johnny Vallins wrote most of the songs, and two were written with Billy Lawrie. Kipner, Groves and Vallins all went on to successful songwriting careers – Kipner in particular, writing hits including 'Hard Habit To Break' for Chicago, 'Physical' for Olivia Newton-John, and 'Genie In A Bottle' for Christina Aguilera. However, Tin Tin's 'Is That The Way' – the chosen single from *Astral Taxi* – failed to break into the charts.

Before the year was out, three more Bee Gees singles – all from years passed – were released in some countries with some success. In the Netherlands, 'When The Swallows Fly' from the 1968 album *Idea* reached 18. 'Give Your Best' from the 1969 album *Odessa* was the B-side.

In Japan, 'Melody Fair' and 'In The Morning' were released as singles – older songs from the recent film soundtrack *Melody*, which had been very successful there. Both singles sold well, and Japan was fast becoming one of The Bee Gees' most supportive fan bases.

The year's final Gibb-related release was Katja Ebstein's German cover version of Barry's 'Peace In My Mind', which was written during

The Bee Gees' estrangement. Ebstein has represented Germany at the Eurovision Song Contest, and is the most successful performer to have taken part without ever winning – being placed in the top three every year she performed: 1970, 1971 and 1980.

Her version of 'Peace In My Mind' was not literally translated and appeared as 'Frieden In Mir'. It was recorded at IBC Studios in London with arranger Bill Shepherd. It appeared on her United Artists album *Freunde*. It was originally released in a gatefold sleeve, accompanied by an eight-page lyric booklet. The reissue was in a single sleeve with a slightly different cover photograph.

1972

Work began early in the new year for The Bee Gees, with a recording session at IBC Studios on 3 January. They recorded two songs on that day, 'Paper Mache. Cabbages And Kings' which would appear on their next album later in the year, and 'Passport' which didn't make the grade. Notably, this was Geoff Bridgford's final recording session with The Bee Gees.

In between Bee Gees recordings and touring, Maurice continued to work with his brother-in-law Billy Lawrie on a number of projects. The first to see release in 1972 was 'The Loner', by The Bloomfields, which was released as a single on 7 January. The song was originally written for Maurice's solo album in 1970, but following the failure of his debut single 'Railroad' and the reformation of The Bee Gees, the album was shelved. The Bloomfields weren't a bona fide group, it was just a convenient moniker for Maurice and Billy.

The song was used as the theme song to a new Richard Harris film titled *Bloomfield* – released in the United States as *The Hero*. The record, which was not a hit, was released in the UK on Pye and in the US on Capitol and featured a song called 'Homing In On the Next Trade Wind' by the British country rock band Heads, Hands and Feet on the B-side. Both songs were also featured on the movie soundtrack albums for *Bloomfield*, released in January, and *The Hero*, released in September.

In view that it had been six months since The Bee Gees had a charting single with 'How Can You Mend a Broken Heart', a new single was required. Gone were the days of the late 1960s when a Bee Gees album could quickly produce two or three hit singles. At this point in their career, they had to be satisfied with one. The new single to keep The Bee Gees in the public eye was 'My World'.

'My World' (Barry Gibb, Robin Gibb)
Recorded at IBC Studios, London: 13 October 1971
Chart positions: Hong Kong: 1, Italy: 1, Australia: 3, Spain: 4, Brazil: 5, Argentina: 6, Denmark: 8, Netherlands: 9, New Zealand: 9, Canada: 11, Ireland: 14, Belgium: 15, UK: 16, US: 16, Japan: 27, West Germany: 41
'My World' was released on 14 January 1972 in between the *Trafalgar* and *To Whom It May Concern* albums. Whilst it was a non-album single, it was later included on the compilations *Best Of Bee Gees, Volume 2* and *Tales From The Brothers Gibb: A History In Song 1967-1990*.

The song has a basic verse/chorus form, with the first and second verses sung by Robin,repeated as the third, sung by Barry, and the fourth returning to Robin. All three sing the chorus and repeats at the end, with a key change up before Barry ad-libs through the fade. Robin remembers it as 'one rollicking little jaunt that me and the lads came up with in downtown Birmingham, England, whilst doing a television show called *The Golden Shot* – the ensuing result being that it went on to be a huge top 20 hit in the UK and the US, that left the three of us drooling with pleasure'.

While you can't deny the recording's appeal and the pure power of the harmonies, the lyric of the chorus, in particular, is banal and repetitive. The Gibbs were slowly falling into the trap where they believed their unique sibling harmonies would lift every song. It did this time, but only just.

The music video showed the group in a recording studio, and an engineer's hand is seen twiddling the knobs every now and again. Barry was flitting between being bearded and clean-shaven between albums and appears here with no facial hair. This was drummer Geoff Bridgford's only appearance in a Bee Gees promotional film clip.

They appeared on *Top Of The Pops* promoting the single no less than three times – the first on 13 February (the day before the single's release), performing a live vocal over the backing track. This performance was repeated on the 3 and 24 February programmes. An appearance on *The Golden Shot* on 23 January seemed appropriate, as that's where the song was created in the first place. The good promotion reaped its rewards, and the single peaked at 16 in the UK, as it did in the US. It made the top ten in numerous territories, notably topping the charts in Italy following a promotional visit and two late-February concerts, and in Hong Kong, where The Bee Gees visited on their Far East tour later in 1972.

'On Time' (Maurice Gibb)

Recorded at IBC Studios, London: 21 October 1971

This was the 'My World' B-side. Maurice remembers it as a song he 'wrote in '71 in Maryland, US, during my swamp period'. He performed it in a solo slot on concert tours of Japan and Australia in 1972, only to revert back to 'Lay It On Me' in 1974.

'On Time' was re-recorded for the 1984 film *A Breed Apart* (starring Rutger Hauer, Kathleen Turner, Powers Booth and Donald Pleasance).

Maurice wrote the entire film score, but it's never been made available as a soundtrack album.

In 2003, UK band Trafficker did a wonderful powerhouse cover of 'On Time' for the international tribute CD to Maurice Gibb: *Everybody Clap*. The intro and outro featured parts of a telephone answering machine message from Maurice.

Barry's eldest son Stephen Gibb also did a fine cover of it as his solo spot on Barry's *Mythology* tour in 2013.

On 28 January, The Bee Gees began their second Australian tour. While their previously adopted homeland had been overlooked for tours during their golden period of 1967-1969, this was the second tour there in less than seven months. For their North American concerts, the group were accompanied by a 40-piece orchestra. But for the Australian tour, it was reduced to a more economical 16-piece ensemble. Much to the delight of their concert promoters (Ron Blackmore, Paul Dainty and David Trew), the group played to capacity houses, with additional concerts added in Brisbane and Melbourne, as the first shows sold out within a day. The second Melbourne concert was filmed and screened shortly after on ABC television. Reviewing the show for the top-selling music magazine *Go-Set*, Stephen Maclean reported, 'They were brilliant! The huge crowd (at the Sydney Showground there were 20,000, according to 2SM), and so was their response. It seems that everybody loves The Bee Gees'. Considering Australia's relatively small population of 13,200,000 at that time, it was one of the highest for record sales per capita in the world. So, despite the long distances involved, touring there made commercial sense. The tour consisted of eight sold-out concerts across four states.

Young English singer Norman Hitchcock made his vinyl debut with the single 'Just Another Minute' b/w 'One Wheel On My Wagon' on 4 February 1972. He worked in the RSO publishing department. A songwriter himself, he suggested that 'Just Another Minute' might be good for Lulu to record, though Maurice wasn't convinced. But English singer Peter Denyer released it as a single on 29 September 1972. Sometimes it's not what you know, but who you know that's important, and with all the elements already in place, Maurice felt Noman should record the song himself, and offered to produce the record. A short-term Polydor recording contract was quickly drawn up, and he recorded both songs with Maurice at IBC in November 1971. Billy Lawrie and Alan Kendall also played on the track, with Gerry Shury arranging.

In February, The Bee Gees travelled to the Netherlands to take part in an annual gala sponsored by local record companies. The *Grand Gala du Disque* was held at the Concertgebouw in Amsterdam and was presented by Willem Duys and Mies Bouwman. The entire show was broadcast live, beginning on 25 February. But the show ran overtime significantly, and The Bee Gees' actually appeared in the early morning of 26 February. The Brass United Orchestra – conducted by Rogier van Otterloo – accompanied artists including Gene Pitney, Gilbert O'Sullivan, Peret, Lenny Kuhr, Roy Black, Middle Of The Road, Charles Aznavour, Hildegard Knef, Ivan Rebroff, Helen Reddy, The New Seekers, Rod McKuen, Labi Siffre, The Beach Boys and Johnny Cash. The Bee Gees were the penultimate international act to appear, performing a short set comprising 'New York Mining Disaster 1941', 'Words', 'My World', 'Massachusetts' and 'Lonely Days'. An unauthorised three-CD set of the entire four-hour show is known to exist.

On 28 February, the group flew to Rome for television engagements. They performed 'My World' and 'Lonely Days' on *Teatro 10*, and 'Massachusetts', 'New York Mining Disaster 1941', 'Words', 'I Started A Joke', Lonely Days', 'My World' and the closing portion of 'Odessa' on a 20-minute programme called *Special Bee Gees*, which was broadcast on 20 September. They played two concerts during their visit to Italy, the first at the 8,000 capacity Palazzo dello Sport in Bologna on 1 March, and the second in Rome the following day, also at a venue called Palazzo dello Sport.

Following the Rome shows, drummer Geoff Bridgford resigned. 'My last concert was at the Pallazzo dello Sports in Rome. It was a wild concert – almost a riot with chairs being thrown about'. Bridgford conceded that being with The Bee Gees had been everything he'd aspired to. 'They were successful, having two huge records in the States. I was staying at the best places, like the Waldorf Astoria, and getting well-paid. But looking back, I can see it was unsettling but an important time for both myself and the brothers. We were young, successful, famous, wealthy and fully involved in the early '70s music business of sex, drugs and rock 'n' roll'. However, at just over 18 months since the group had reformed, Geoff admitted some tension was still present between the brothers:

They were still getting used to being back together after the breakup and at the same time achieving greater success than they had before.

And with that came more, new and different business and personal concerns that subtly affected the situation. I had been going through some problems with my marriage, and there was an extreme amount of substance abuse which was taking its toll on everyone in its own way. As you do in life, I simply found it was time to move on; time to make a change ... Robert Stigwood called me in to try and convince me to stay, because they had another tour all planned. Whilst I was with The Bee Gees, I was on a weekly retainer and a substantially larger wage when on tour, but I was never included into The Bee Gees' royalty situation. However, when I was leaving the band, Robert did get together with me to offer a royalty deal at the time. But I'd made up my mind ... The Bee Gees are one of the most popular bands of our time, and back then, in 1970, '71 and '72, it was a great experience to be a part of it. There were some magical moments in the studio and performing live. It was a highly creative transitional period for The Bee Gees and myself, and some great songs came out of that time.

Following Bridgford's departure, highly respected Australian session drummer Chris Karan took the drum stool for the next tour. Like Bridgford, Karan was born in Melbourne, but his musical background had been in jazz bands, and he'd migrated to the UK in 1962.

The Bee Gees arrived in Hong Kong to crowd scenes reminiscent of their early German tours, as police tried to restrain enthusiastic teenage fans. The audience response at the 19 March concert was equally fervent, as local newspaper *The Star* reported: 'After more than six months of negotiations, The Bee Gees – the darlings of the pop fans – came, saw and conquered a 16,000-strong audience of screaming fans'. Another Hong Kong newspaper – *The Standard* – was equally ebullient in their praise of the show at the Government Football Stadium in Sokonpo: 'Memories of those hazy, crazy days of the '60s and Beatlemania were revived last night when The Bee Gees – by sheer professional talent – captivated and won the 16,000 fans at the stadium'. This was the largest audience to ever attend a pop concert in Hong Kong up to that point.

After Hong Kong, The Bee Gees toured Japan for the first time. Like Australia, Japan had one of the biggest record-selling statistics per capita in the world. It remained a profitable and loyal market for the group for the rest of their career, and they toured there several times.

On 22 March, The Bee Gees held a press conference at Tokyo's Hilton Hotel, where Polydor Japan presented them with Gold records awards for the *Melody* soundtrack album. The Japanese tour was short, but every concert had a capacity audience. The first was at Kokaido Hall in Shibuya – a special ward of Tokyo – on 23 March. The next day, they performed at Tokyo's legendary Nippon Budokan. The final two concerts – on 25/26 March – were at the Osaka Festival Hall. The setlist was similar to the Australian tour, but with one notable addition – at the request of Polydor Japan, they included 'Melody Fair', which had been a big hit due to the popularity of the *Melody* movie.

The tour continued to Kuala Lumpur in Malaysia, where they played two concerts at the Stadium Negara (on 30/31 March), and then on to Singapore at the National Theatre on 1 April. To get around Singapore's then-strict no-long-hair rules, the touring party was granted special 48-hour passes. The tour's final concert was on 2 April at Seneghan Stadium, Jakarta, Indonesia. Initially scheduled to play at a 10,000-seat indoor venue, the itinerary was changed to a 60,000-seat outdoor stadium. Just before going onstage, it rained heavily! Their long-time personal manager Dick Ashby recalled:

Obviously, there was a lot of tension going on through the day, with me trying to get the fee up. Then about an hour before the show was due to start, there was a torrential downpour of rain, so all the equipment had to be bunged under the stage – total disaster. By this time, all the people were coming in, including the Prime Minister of Indonesia, who was in the royal box. I worked it out in the end that the final call was 38,000 people in the stadium. Anyway, tour manager Tom Kennedy came to me and said, 'Look, I'm scared of the group going on. It's wet – a guitar has only got to touch something and someone will get electrocuted!'. So, I went back to the hotel with this in mind and said, 'We're not going on!'. The promoter's wife burst into tears, saying, 'You must go on, the royal family is there'. So, in the end, the promoter says to me, 'Right, well if the support group goes on and they don't get killed, will you go on?'. What could I say to that?

The support act from Bali, played and survived, so The Bee Gees had no option, and took to the stage. The audience was manic, and the music was largely drowned out by the din of the crowd. The Gibbs later claimed that armed soldiers prevented them from leaving the stage, though the promoter claimed they were just providing security. Maurice recalled, 'All our people told us we would be electrocuted. The system was really bad, so we were a bit worried about that. We thought we might do an acoustic set, but no, they didn't want that. Eventually, it calmed down, and we did go on, but it was crazy. That was the wildest place I think I've ever worked'.

Returning to the UK after the tour, The Bee Gees began work in earnest for the next album, working quickly to complete it. Four sessions (10, 12, 17 and 21 April) produced the goods, plus the extra tracks 'It's All Wrong' and 'I Lay Down And Sleep', which didn't make the final cut.

Back to the grind of being pop stars and keeping themselves in the public eye, The Bee Gees appeared on a television variety show presented by Jimmy Tarbuck – *Tarbuck's Luck* – which aired on BBC 1 on 22 April.

Irish actor and singer Richard Harris released his latest single 'Turning Back The Pages' in April. But it's the B-side 'Half Of Every Dream' which is of more interest, as Maurice was the arranger and producer. He'd spoken of working on an album with Harris on several occasions, but this is the only known recording to surface from any of the sessions. The single was only released in a few territories. In the US and Canada, it was released on ABC/Dunhill, and in Portugal on Probe.

'Half Of Every Dream' has appeared on two CDs, both released on the Raven label in Australia. The first was the 2005 double CD reissue of Harris' albums *My Boy* (1971) and *Slides* (1972) where it appeared as a bonus track on the *Slides* CD. The second was as the penultimate track on the 2008 compilation, *The Anthology 1968-1974: Man Of Words, Man Of Music*.

Another of Maurice's side projects was with Liverpudlian singer-songwriter Jimmy Stevens. Recalling in his memoir, Jimmy said he 'was summoned to London to RSO in Brook Street, and was booked into a nice hotel. The next day, I went to the office and met John Davies and Mike Snow; also Sam Mortimer from the publishing department, and I signed up with them. Some days later, I was sent to a studio to get my songs down. In the RSO office, I met Maurice Gibb of The Bee Gees. We became good friends and drinking buddies. Maurice decided to be my record producer for his Moby Productions company, to be released on the Atlantic label. I could hardly believe that me – a lad from Garston – was recording on the same label as Ray Charles, Aretha Franklin and

The Drifters'. Maurice decided to record the album at Morgan Studios, as he wasn't happy using IBC at the time.

The album was recorded in two sessions – the first in April, on which the musicians included Bee Gees guitarist Alan Kendall, and Led Zeppelin drummer John Bonham, who, for contractual reasons, couldn't be credited on the album, so he appeared as Gemini: his zodiac sign. At the recording session, Jimmy played the piano and sang at the same time – the results are very good, giving a very spontaneous live feel to the finished record. Maurice, in his role of producer, supervised the session and dubbed his bass part later.

Jimmy recalls that at the second session, in May, 'we had Peter Frampton on guitar, Mike Kellie originally from Spooky Tooth on drums, and then Mo would dub on his bass. I did 'Girl From Denver', 'Paid My Dues', and out of the blue came an amazing version of 'Bye Bye Love'. I'd never done it like that before. I was amazed with it myself!'.

The first songs released were the single 'Don't Freak Me Out' b/w 'Tears (Behind My Eyes)' on 21 July. Just three weeks later, on 11 August, a second single was released featuring the incredible rendition of the Everly Brothers' hit 'Bye Bye Love'. The B-side this time was the lolloping 'Paid My Dues'. The album – titled *Don't Freak Me Out* in the UK – followed in early September.

Jimmy appeared on BBC 2's *The Old Grey Whistle Test* on 19 September, performing 'Girl From Denver' and 'Tears (Behind My Eyes)'. On 9 October, he recorded 'Happy Birthday Sam', 'Allerton Towers', 'Paid My Dues' and 'Tears (Behind My Eyes)' for BBC Radio 1's *Top Gear* programme presented by John Peel, which was broadcast on 19 October and repeated on 9 November.

In May, a 40-minute Bee Gees TV special was broadcast on NCRV in the Netherlands. Made there earlier in the year, it included scenes filmed in Roode Steen (also known as Kaasmarkt – cheese market), and de Waag (weigh house) in Hoorn in the northwest of the country.

On 10 June, a prime-time Saturday night TV audience witnessed the first episode of a short-lived new London Weekend Television series called *2Gs And The Pop People*. 2Gs referred to the dance troupe The Second Generation. The Bee Gees performed 'Morning Of My Life' and 'Walking Back To Waterloo'.

On 7 June, the now-classic Bee Gees song 'Run To Me' was released as the first single from their forthcoming album. To promote it, they made two studio appearances on BBC 1's *Top Of The Pops* (on 13 July and 3

August). One was repeated on the show's 10 August episode. Also, a promotional film clip featuring a heavily-blonded Barry was released to television around the world. 'Run To Me' became The Bee Gees' last big hit in the major markets for three years.

Four tracks from the forthcoming album *To Whom It May Concern* were played on BBC Radio 1's *Jimmy Young Show* on 24 July. They were touted as BBC-session recordings but were in fact, mono mixes of 'Alive', 'Bad Bad Dreams', 'Never Been Alone' and 'Run To Me' made at IBC by engineers Damon Lyon-Shaw and Richard Manwaring. The only significant difference in any of the mixes was 'Never Been Alone', lacking its orchestral accompaniment.

Around September, there were three work-in-progress albums for Decca subsidiary York Records, which was linked to Yorkshire Television. The artists were Peter Ransome, Mike Berry and Bob Saker. Berry's album *Drift Away* and Saker's *They've Taken Back My Number* credited Maurice on bass. Ransome's album did not. Engineer Ric Holland said, 'credits printed on the back of Mike Berry's, Peter Ransome's and Bob Saker's York LPs are all identical and that is not right. It would've come about because somebody at York Records did not care enough to research and collate the correct details. Both Mike's and Peter's albums were recorded at Nova Sound Studios; only Bob's was compiled from sessions at Nova and at other studios (Audio International and Olympic). Musician details are wrong, too – for instance, Maurice Gibb didn't play on anything. Maurice would've heard the version of his song 'On Time', but wasn't involved with the recording. John Fiddy – bass player and arranger on the sessions – told me shortly before his death that he had never even met Maurice Gibb'.

It's a difficult call – maybe Ric Holland and John Fiddy didn't witness Maurice playing on the albums, but that's not to say that he didn't – there has to be a reason for him to be mentioned in the credits, after all.

Instrumental contributions to recordings are far more difficult to confirm than vocals, but Maurice had a quite distinct playing style and sound and with some intent listening, some tracks on the Mike Berry and Bob Saker albums do have that familiar feel about them.

Even before *To Whom It May Concern* was released, The Bee Gees were back in the studio recording their next album. But this time – possibly in search of a different vibe and some West Coast inspiration – they relocated to California for a few months. They began work on their next opus *Life In A Tin Can,* at the Record Plant in Los Angeles.

With most of the work completed, arranger Johnny Pate and a 14-piece orchestral group added the final touches to 'Saw A New Morning', 'I Don't Wanna Be The One', 'Living In Chicago' and 'Method To My Madness' before the mix-down.

A couple of days later, Robin had an unexpected call which led him to leave the sessions for a while – his first child Spencer was born on 21 September: four weeks earlier than expected. Robin recalled, 'Everything had been arranged months in advance so that I could be near when the baby was born'. But Spencer – who grew into a talented and unique artist like his father – had other ideas. Robin reminisced: 'I went off to America, and the next thing I knew, there was a call to say I was a dad'. The proud new father rushed home to meet his son – named Spencer in honour of Robin's hero Sir Winston Spencer Churchill, with the middle name David as a tribute to Molly's late brother. 'Molly and I have been longing for a baby. I feel as though I'm living on cloud nine'.

Norman Hitchcock's second single, 'Baby Come On Home' b/w '(Have You Seen My) Angelina' was released on 6 October. The songs were again written by Hitchcock, and recorded in January at IBC with Maurice and Billy as producers. Maurice also played bass, with Billy on backing vocals, Allan Kendall on guitar, and Geoff Bridgford on drums. Another short-term contract was made, but this time with RCA Victor.

In 1978, Hitchcock reinvented himself under the significantly cooler stage name of Gene Farrow. He released the album *Move Your Body* which included sleeve notes stating, 'Gene Farrow's recording career began when he joined the Robert Stigwood Organisation on leaving school. He had already started writing songs and while at RSO, met up with Maurice Gibb of The Bee Gees, who immediately saw the potential of Gene as a recording artist. Maurice cut some of his songs, and the result of this collaboration was two singles featuring Gene as both writer and artist'. Farrow's album had no Gibb involvement, though the single titled 'Hey, You Should Be Dancing' did raise eyebrows. The album spawned no less than five singles, two of which – 'Don't Stop Now' and 'Move Your Body' – were minor UK hits resulting in two *Top Of The Pops* appearances.

The new Bee Gees album *To Whom It May Concern* was released in October. It continued the personal and melodic sound of its immediate predecessors. Respected Bee Gees historian Joe Brennan described it as 'a farewell to the old Bee Gees'.

To Whom It May Concern (1972)

Personnel:
Barry Gibb: vocals, guitar
Robin Gibb: vocals
Maurice Gibb: vocals, bass, guitar, piano, organ, Mellotron, harpsichord, mandolin, Moog synthesiser
Alan Kendall: guitar
Clem Cattini: drums
Geoff Bridgford: drums ('Paper Mache, Cabbages And Kings', 'Alive')
Orchestral arrangements: Bill Shepherd
Engineers: Mike Claydon, Damon Lyon-Shaw, Richard Manwaring, Andy Knight
Moog synthesiser engineer: Mike Vickers
Recorded between 21 October 1971 and 21 April 1972 at IBC Studios, London; 'We Lost The Road' recorded January 1971 at IBC Studios, London
Release dates: UK and US: October 1972
Chart positions: Spain: 6, Italy: 10, Australia: 13, US: 35, Canada: 50, Japan: 53

While still having hits with the likes of 'My World' and 'Run To Me' when *To Whom It May Concern* was released, the band were quickly losing their overall direction, and seemingly, their spark. Stephen Holden's *Rolling Stone* review summed it up quite succinctly when he said The Bee Gees now occupied 'a very limited territory of pop music', dealing mainly in ballads of 'momentary pathos', and that the album was 'headphone mood music that makes no demands beyond a superficial emotional surrender to its perfumed atmosphere of pink frosting and glitter'. By their own later admission, the group – once known for their unique creativity – had become a 'ballad band'. Following 'How Can You Mend A Broken Heart' and 'My World', the Gibbs had fallen into the trap of thinking that that was what the public wanted from them. Maurice later said that at this point in their career, they didn't know who their audience was: hence the album title.

Despite its apparent lack of risk and creativity, the album is a diverse collection, and has some excellent songs, including the hit single 'Run To Me', and 'Sea Of Smiling Faces': a signature Bee Gees song if ever there was one. They also venture into some good rock music with 'Road To Alaska' and 'Bad, Bad Dreams'.

For a number of people who had contributed to Bee Gees or Gibb solo projects over the years, it was their final appearance on a Bee Gees album. Musical arranger and orchestra leader Bill Shepherd first worked with them in Australia in 1965 and had played an integral role in all their albums since 1967. Drummer Geoff Bridgford who had been working with the brothers since 1970, left the band during the album's recording. British session drummer Clem Cattini took his place for the remainder of the sessions, while Chris Karan played drums on the following tour. The album was also the final appearance for engineer Mike Claydon, who had also worked on most of their albums since 1967.

The Bee Gees' flair for melody and melancholy was still very evident, they were still popular with their devoted core fan base, and continued to have successful tours in North America, Australia and the Far East. When *To Whom It May Concern* was released in October 1972, it received mixed reviews. The group's album-chart success was waning, and the album only reached 35 in the US. In the UK, it was their third consecutive album to fail to chart. On the back of some minor success for the single 'Alive' in Australia, the album sold quite well there, and it was also successful in Italy and Spain.

A change was needed – so was inspiration! The Gibb brothers had become too comfortable in writing and recording material they liked. They weren't taking risks. But recording outside the UK with different musicians might be a start. They would also need to set aside a decent amount of time for it rather than finding time between touring. They also needed a producer who would challenge them and bring out the best in them!

The album was attractively packaged, with the three cover photos taken on the Japanese tour. The back photo was from their early years in Australia, taken on the set of the popular weekly pop show *Bandstand*. It was the inner gatefold which set the album apart. It featured pop-up caricatures of the brothers against a background of associates as the orchestra. The pop-up idea was a novelty for sure, but it wasn't the first time such a device had been employed in an album cover. That honour went to Jethro Tull's 1969 LP *Stand Up*.

The Bee Gees associates were represented by cartoon bodies but actual photographs of their heads. The line-up, from left to right in the back row, are Chris Cooke (Maurice and Lulu's assistant), John Davidson (RSO head of publishing), Ahmet Ertegun (head of Atlantic Records), Peter Brown (director of RSO in New York), Beryl Vertue (Frankie Howerd's manager), Frankie Howerd (British comedian and actor), Robert Stigwood (Bee Gees manager), Rik and John Gunnell (RSO). In the front row, are Linda Gibb (Barry's wife), Lulu, Molly Gibb (Robin's wife), Ruby Bard (RSO booking agent), Mike Housego (RSO head of publishing), Tom Kennedy (Bee Gees road manager), Ray Washbourne (Robin's personal assistant), David Shaw (Robert Stigwood's business partner and accountant) and John Taylor (RSO office manager). Lurking behind the speakers and mixer is Dick Ashby (Bee Gees' personal manager), and the man behind the speaker stack in the bottom right is Ray Cane (RSO). The conductor is Bill Shepherd, Chris Karan, who played on the Japanese tour, is on drums, and the guitarist is Alan Kendall. Hugh Gibb completes the picture, manning the lights.

Some copies of the UK LP omitted 'Run To Me', and a sticker was added to the sleeve to note this.

'Run To Me' (Barry Gibb, Robin Gibb, Maurice Gibb)

Recorded at IBC Studios, London: 12 April 1972
Chart positions: Brazil: 2, Australia: 3, South Africa: 3, Italy: 5, Canada: 6, New Zealand: 6, Ireland: 7, Spain; 8, UK: 9, Argentina: 10, Denmark: 10, US: 16, Netherlands: 28, France: 85

Written at Robert Stigwood's house in Beverly Hills, 'Run To Me' brings together so many great Bee Gees trademarks in what is quite simply a perfect three-minute pop song. The lyric has a familiar pop ballad theme where the narrator longs to be noticed by a broken-hearted girl. Barry and Robin trade vocals on the verses and choruses, and the ubiquitous three-part harmony is astonishingly good. Bill Shepherd's orchestral arrangement is tastefully combined with some nice drum fills from Clem Cattini, which really brings the song to a rousing conclusion.

The single was well-promoted through music paper advertising, TV appearances on both sides of the Atlantic, and a simple promotional film when a personal appearance was not possible. It performed very well globally, peaking at number nine in the UK, and 16 in the US. A perennial fan favourite worldwide, the song remained in the live setlist for the duration of their career.

Among the many covers of this fine song was the 1985 duet by Barry Manilow and Dionne Warwick. Beautifully produced by Manilow, it broke into the British top 100, peaking at 86. In 2007, Robin's eldest son Spencer recorded 'Run To Me' as his contribution to an assortment of songs by children of well-known artists titled *A Song For My Father*. Featuring the unique (and, sadly, rarely heard) voice (and guitar) of Spencer Gibb, this was the first recording of a Bee Gees song by one of their children.

Barry included a version of 'Run To Me' on his successful 2021 album *Greenfields* – a duet with Brandi Carlile. Barry is in fine form on the first verse, but things take a dive when Carlile begins the vocal gymnastics the song really does not call for.

'We Lost The Road' (Barry Gibb, Robin Gibb)
Recorded at IBC Studios, London: 28 January 1971

This song is a remnant from the *Trafalgar* sessions, with Barry originally singing all the verses. During its hibernation, the second and third verses swapped places. The lead vocals were re-recorded for the album, with Barry taking the first verse, and Robin the second and third. The strong three-part chorus harmonies are superb, but the song itself is not strong enough to lift it to above average.

It's pure conjecture, but in line with the album title seeking an audience, could 'We Lost The Road' be an expression of the group's feelings and frustrations about their career at this point?

In 1971, a cover version was released by a German group called Horizon, of whom little is known. The song was a single A-side, predating The Bee Gees version by a year. The B-side was 'We Can Make It Together', written by German pop star Peter Maffay and his producer Michael Kunze. The link to this recording and the three Bee Gees songs Maffay covered in 1971 appears to be a deal brokered by Bill Shepherd and The Bee Gees' publishing company.

'Never Been Alone' (Robin Gibb)
Recorded at IBC Studios, London: 10 April 1972

This sweet contemplative song by Robin opens with acoustic guitars and subtle oboe accents. Strings are added on the second verse, and low-key horns later in the song. Simply put, it's beautiful.

'Paper Mache, Cabbages And Kings' (Barry Gibb, Robin Gibb, Maurice Gibb)
Recorded at IBC, London: 3 January 1972

This nonsense song befitting its odd title, is just a bit of fun. It's essentially broken into three parts. The first is a jaunty little segment with Maurice taking both piano and mandolin, giving an almost *Zorba The Greek* feel. The second part is slow, with Barry and Robin earnestly singing about having their hearts broken as if they were made of fragile paper mache. The third part repeats the first verse before a stanza with the lines 'Jimmy had a bomb and the bomb went bang/Jimmy was everywhere' repeats until the fade-out.

Many years after its release, it was revealed the 'Jimmy' referred to was Jimmy Stevens who Maurice produced, and he also supported The Bee Gees on a number of their tours in 1972/73.

The song was the B-side of the single 'Alive', however, in Denmark they preferred 'Paper Mache, Cabbages and Kings' and it reached number 8 on the Danish radio play charts.

'I Can Bring Love' (Barry Gibb)
Recorded at IBC Studios, London: 10 April 1972
This first appeared on the extremely rare Barry Gibb Fan Club EP in 1971. That version was a simple single-take live performance with Barry accompanying himself on acoustic guitar. That makes this the second older song dusted down for the album. The arrangement retains the song's original simplicity, adding the most subtle of embellishments to make it into a proper production.

'I Held A Party' (Barry Gibb, Robin Gibb, Maurice Gibb)
Recorded at IBC Studios, London: 17 April 1972
This is almost a throwback to *Bee Gees 1st* – a story song so-favoured by Robin, harpsichord à la 'Turn Of The Century', and the almost-Gregorian droning is an echo of 'Every Christian Lion Hearted Man Will Show You'. The song is in waltz time – rock 'n' roll it ain't! This is probably not where The Bee Gees should have been in the marketplace in 1972, but retrospectively examining the album, it epitomises the all-round quirkiness of it which makes it so beloved by some fans.

It's a tale of a party host who doesn't receive any guests. His assumed manservant/butler Birkworth remains stoic and suggests the guests might have simply been delayed. With the realisation that nobody is going to turn up, the host drinks a little too much, and he and Birkworth sleep through the night. The closing line, 'I never knew him so well' could imply a number of things, but most likely that they were friends above being simply master and servant.

The opening chords of the instrumental section are uncannily similar to the theme from *The Persuaders!* – an action/comedy series starring Tony Curtis and Roger Moore, which was broadcast weekly in the UK from 17 September 1971 to 25 February 1972.

'Please Don't Turn Out The Lights' (Barry Gibb, Robin Gibb, Maurice Gibb)

Recorded at IBC Studios, London: 12 April 1972

Behind the somewhat abstract lyric, lies a beautiful soul sound. The song is almost gospel in the way the harmonies are used. Robin's lead vocal intro is great, but it's the vocal harmonies with the brothers' beautiful, unassailable and unique sibling sound that make the song a little different. It finishes all too quickly.

In 2017, eight children of Lesley, Barry, Robin, Maurice and Andy Gibb released a tribute CD titled *Please Don't Turn Out The Lights,* including songs of all four brothers. Naming themselves The Gibb Collective, each child covered a song or songs – usually deep cuts as opposed to hits. For this song, Barry's son Stephen, Robin's son Spencer, Maurice's children Adam and Samantha, and Andy's daughter Peta, combined beautifully to produce a scintillating cover.

'Sea Of Smiling Faces' (Barry Gibb, Robin Gibb, Maurice Gibb)

Recorded at IBC Studios, London on 17 April 1972

The Bee Gees have always had a big following in Japan, touring there extensively in 1972, 1973 and 1974. This track was released as a single there in the wake of the group's first visit.

It comes across as a genuine expression of appreciation for their concert audiences – the only time a group really sees and interacts with their fans. This becomes a personal experience, and is understood by the lines, 'Will you smile and tell the world about me/Can there be no doubt about me/I was your friend' and 'The look in your eyes, to see your smile'.

There's a beautiful string introduction arranged by Bill Shepherd, individual verses by Barry and Robin, with both voices on the third verse à la 'Massachusetts', and a compelling chorus with all three brothers. It's the model Bee Gees song and sound of the period and has always been a big fan favourite.

'Bad Bad Dreams' (Barry Gibb, Robin Gibb, Maurice Gibb)

Recorded at IBC Studios, London: 12 April 1972

Recorded on the same day as the gentle 'Please Don't Turn Out The Lights', 'Bad Bad Dreams' could not be a bigger contrast! It was probably the most raucous Bee Gees song recorded up to that point.

121

The electric guitar rock sound was quite a departure from what most people expected. Guitarist Alan Kendall gets an opportunity to cut loose with a solo, and a bold and brash horn section is a tip of the hat to the early Chicago sound.

'You Know It's For You' (Maurice Gibb)
Recorded at IBC Studios, London: 12 June 1971
This is Maurice's featured lead vocal on the album. It's a medium-tempo number on which plays acoustic guitar, electric piano and a range of Mellotron sounds. The song suits Maurice's understated vocal style nicely.

'Alive' (Barry Gibb, Maurice Gibb)
Recorded at IBC Studios, London: 21 October 1971
Chart positions: Netherlands: 17, Canada: 28, US: 34, Australia: 45
Whilst Barry says this is one of the songs 'we don't remember writing', Maurice said it was actually written backstage prior to an appearance on *The Tonight Show Starring Johnny Carson*. It's a classy, well-written song with a fine Barry lead vocal. Released as the album's second single on 10 November 1972, it received UK TV promotion with an appearance on *Top Of The Pops* on 30 November. Further promotion followed in the Netherlands on *Top Pop*, and in the US, but despite this, it only performed moderately on the charts.

'Road To Alaska' (Barry Gibb, Robin Gibb, Maurice Gibb)
Recorded at IBC Studios, London: 21 April 1972
A great rock track, this time a 12-bar blues style with Robin on lead vocal, and lead guitarist Alan Kendall getting another opportunity to solo. Released as the B-side of 'Run To Me', it made a good strong song coupling for those adventurous enough to flip the record over. 'Road To Alaska' was performed during some concerts in 1974/75, and on the PBS TV show *Soundstage* in 1975.

'Sweet Song Of Summer' (Barry Gibb, Robin Gibb, Maurice Gibb)
Recorded at IBC Studios, London: 17 April 1972
This was The Bee Gees' first opportunity to use the Moog modular synthesiser, which was gaining popularity in the music industry. The synth intro introduces the verse melody, utilising different octaves

and the portamento effect of sliding between notes. The lyric has no discernible verse/chorus form and is incredibly brief for a five-minute song. The instrumental section begins with Maurice playing octaves on bass, then the Moog while Robin throws in some odd wailing for good effect. It's all a bit too experimental to be overtly successful. One reviewer went so far as to call it 'abuse of a Moog synthesiser'.

Mike Vickers, formerly of Manfred Mann, was credited as the engineer on the track, although it was more a case of knowing how to create specific sounds with the Moog which looked extremely complicated with all its various modules, and interconnecting cables looking like an old-fashioned telephone exchange. He remembered the session 'was all very informal and relaxed. There were loads of other keyboards lying around, they were all around the walls, so they would use what they felt like trying. It was there ready for them. I was only there for a very short time and went home. I have a feeling they made the song up on the spot. That may not be right, but I seem to recall there was something like that going on. I think they were reacting to some extent to what we were doing'.

Having only completed work on the *Life In A Tin Can* album a few weeks previously, still in Los Angeles, the group returned to the Record Plant to record what was effectively their third album of the year. These recordings became the legendary unreleased album *A Kick In The Head Is Worth Eight In the Pants*. Recorded in October with largely undocumented personnel, the songs were 'Elisa', 'Wouldn't I Be Someone', 'A Lonely Violin', Losers And Lovers', 'Home Again Rivers', Harry's Gate', 'Rocky L.A.', 'Castles In The Air', 'Where Is Your Sister?' and 'It Doesn't Matter Much To Me'. Arranger Jimmy Haskell added orchestral embellishments to a number of tracks at two sessions in November.

The set saw their songwriting seemingly more unified than it had been since 1969. Whether this was actually the case is a matter for debate, as there do appear to be songs stylistically attributable to individual brothers.

A few weeks after the release of *To Whom It May Concern*, the second single extracted was 'Alive'. Released on 4 November in the US, it was The Bee Gees' final single on ATCO, following Robert Stigwood forming his own label RSO Records a few months later. Similarly, in the UK, the 10 November release was their last single on Polydor during this era.

The single received some positive reviews in the US, with *Billboard* calling the A-side a 'dynamite, driving ballad', and *Cashbox* describing it as a 'fine selection in traditional Bee Gees fashion'. That description was quite apt, as 'Alive' was indeed another standard piano ballad. However, it was to be their last such single for 20 years.

For their final concert appearance of the year, they took a break from sessions at The Record Plant, to appear at The Ultimate ROQ Concert/ Festival at the Los Angeles Memorial Coliseum on 25 November. The open-air concert had an incredible line-up, including Sly and The Family Stone, Stevie Wonder, The Eagles, Chuck Berry and more. The new Los Angeles radio station KROQ hosted the event, which attracted a crowd of 32,848 excited music fans who paid $3 for tickets. All proceeds were donated to the United Free Clinics of Southern California, which offered treatment for drug addiction. The station touted the event as not only the greatest show in the history of Los Angeles, but as a way of thanking the city for welcoming KROQ to the airwaves. The headline act was to be Sly Stone, who was flying in directly from his Madison Square Garden concert. But the concert was fraught with problems from the very beginning, with a two-and-a-half-hour delay meaning Sly Stone didn't get on stage until after 2 a.m. Los Angeles city codes prohibited the playing of live music after 2:00 a.m., but a special dispensation allowed him to stay on until 2:30 a.m. The time issue was the least of the LAPD's concerns, as they made more than 400 drug arrests at the concert.

It was a memorable show for The Bee Gees, but for the wrong reasons. Yoko Ono had called the station to explain why she and John Lennon couldn't be there in person, and to lend their support. Rather than save the message for a natural break in proceedings, a DJ walked on stage when The Bee Gees were actually in the middle of a song and took over the microphone to make the announcement. Their road manager at the time – Tom Kennedy – remembers: 'KROQ – that was a fiasco – it was completely unprofessional! This DJ came out and literally had a Walkman and played this message from Yoko Ono – you couldn't hear a thing'. The group walked off in disgust but were persuaded to give it another try. 'They did finish their songs, but the whole show degenerated at that point, and as I was going through the tunnel with their equipment, the riot police were coming down. It was just so badly organised'. The event was filmed, and portions were broadcast in July 1974 as *The Coliseum Concert*, including The Bee Gees songs 'Alive', 'I Started A Joke' and 'Lonely Days'.

Buoyant after the group's first tour of Japan earlier in the year, Polydor Japan were eager for a return visit. Keen to keep The Bee Gees in the public eye, in November, they released 'Sea Of Smiling Faces' b/w 'Please Don't Turn Out The Lights' as a single. While it was a moderate hit there, it wasn't released anywhere else as a single.

In November, *The Jimmy Young Show* on BBC Radio One broadcast an exclusive mix of 'Sea Of Smiling Faces'. Again, in lieu of making a new recording in the true spirit of a BBC session, this was merely an IBC mono mix of the album version, omitting the orchestra. Mixes of 'Alive' and the original 1967 version of 'Massachusetts' were made at the same time, both with orchestra removed, but neither was broadcast.

Having been a Bee Gee for just one televised concert in 1969, sister Lesley had quietly disappeared from the limelight and moved back to Australia to raise her family. But in 1972, she was asked to duet with Australian country singer Ian B. MacLeod on his *Restless* album. They sang three songs together – 'Rings Of Gold', 'Keep On Smiling' and – most interestingly, a cover version of The Bee Gees' 'Give Your Best' from their 1969 album, *Odessa*.

The album was only ever released in Australia, initially on the Troubadour label in 1972. The back cover of the album features a photograph of Lesley and introduces her as the 'sister of the world-famous Bee Gees'. Subsequent issues with different back covers were issued on the Festival label in 1974 and later on Bunyip.

Easy-listening group Company, comprising David Stuart, Jack Moran and Joe Croyle, recorded 'Summer Ends' on their eponymous (and only) album in 1972. It was a song Barry wrote for his 1970 solo album and released on his fan club EP in 1971. It was good that the song saw a broader release, but the interpretation took the term 'easy-listening' to the extreme, and to describe it as pedestrian would be being kind. For discophiles, probably the most interesting thing about it was the record label – Playboy Records (part of Hugh Hefner's Playboy Enterprises) – which featured the iconic rabbit-in-a-bow-tie logo.

1973

Years later, The Bee Gees were to look back on 1973 and 1974 as unsuccessful and directionless. They didn't know who their audience was any more, or what their audience wanted from them. In one documentary, Maurice referred to the group as being in a 'dead zone'. In 2021, Barry mentioned that following their official 1970 reunification, it actually took four years for them to really learn to work and write together again. Interim drummer Geoff Bridgford has since hinted that in his short period as a Bee Gee, there was a strong undercurrent of unresolved tension amongst the three siblings.

Despite achieving immediate success following their reformation, the chart triumphs of 'Lonely Days' and 'How Can You Mend A Broken Heart' possibly only papered over existing cracks in their complex interpersonal relationships. Perhaps, in retrospect, these years back on the road (albeit with families in tow) – just like they were back in the early Australian days – were exactly what the group needed. Perhaps they really needed to feel the hunger again. Time would tell.

However directionless and inconsistent they might have been, success is relative. Compared to their golden years of 1967-69, and in the immediate two years following the group's reformation in 1970, maybe things didn't seem so rosy. But compared to many artists, they still scored some good chart hits in Australia, New Zealand, Japan and the Far East. This continued chart success also allowed them to tour those countries and the US very successfully, and certainly funded their continued recording ventures. With an extensive tour schedule and growing families, they had less time to work with other artists. As such, most side projects and solo projects stopped. When not touring or with family, they focussed on Bee Gees projects.

The first documented activity of 1973 was a session in London on 8 January. They recorded 'King And Country', 'Life Am I Wasting My Time?', 'Jesus In Heaven' and 'Dear Mr. Kissinger'. Quite why they recorded them is not known, as it's assumed the ten songs recorded in Los Angeles. the previous October would have made an album in their own right. However, the songs were added to the ends of the two stereo master tapes for *A Kick In The Head Is Worth Eight In The Pants* – 'Dear Mr. Kissinger' and 'Jesus In Heaven' to the end of side one, and 'King And Country' and 'Life, Am I Wasting My Time?' to the end of side two.

The 19 January single 'Crystal Bay' by British actor Steve Hodson – best known for playing Steve Ross in Yorkshire Television's *Follyfoot* – was Maurice and Billy Lawrie's final songwriting collaboration.

Hodson came to record the disc by pure luck. He told *Look In* magazine: 'I was just walking down the corridor in the office block, when some guy comes out of an office and says, 'Hey Steve, would you like to make a record?'. He didn't even ask me if I could sing!'. It turned out that the man represented York Records, 'So they sent me down to London to make the recording. I'd never dreamed of making a record before. I had done a bit of singing at drama school, but nothing special – just the sort of thing that all drama students have to do'. Of the finished record, he said, 'I thought it was worse than what I know I can do'.

Fiachra Trench arranged the song, and the track is noted as a Winsak production, so it was most likely produced by Jack Winsley. The record was issued in a black-and-white picture sleeve (quite unusual for a UK single in 1973) showing Steve sitting on the gate to Follyfoot Farm.

19 January 1973 also saw the US release of The Bee Gees' latest album *Life In A Tin Can*. It was issued six weeks later, on 1 March in the UK. *Rolling Stone* anointed the album with faint praise, saying it was 'vaguely pleasant and certainly innocuous enough to fit right in with the prevalent '70s soft-rock ambience'.

Life In A Tin Can (1973)

Personnel:
Barry Gibb: vocals, guitar
Robin Gibb: vocals
Maurice Gibb: vocals, bass, guitar, Mellotron, organ, electric piano
Alan Kendall: guitar
Sneaky Pete Kleinow: pedal steel ('South Dakota Morning', 'Come Home Johnny Bridie')
Tommy Morgan: harmonica ('South Dakota Morning', 'My Life Has Been A Song')
Jerome Richardson: flute ('Living In Chicago')
Ric Grech: violin, bass ('While I Play')
Jane Getz: piano ('Come Home Johnny Bridie')
Jim Keltner: drums
Orchestral arrangements: Johnny Pate
Engineers: Mike Stone, Chuck Leary
Producers: The Bee Gees

Recorded in September 1972 at The Record Plant, Los Angeles
Release dates: US: 19 January 1973, UK: 1 March 1973
Chart positions: Italy: 10, Australia: 19, Canada: 54, US: 69

Life In A Tin Can is an inherently different Bee Gees album in many
ways, and there are a number of firsts associated with this relatively
little-known release. It was the first to be issued on Robert Stigwod's
RSO label, which within five years, would be one of the most successful
record companies in the world. It was also the first album where The
Bee Gees were officially credited as the sole producers. In actuality,
they'd been uncredited co-producers of their records, probably since
their Australian days. It was also the first time they'd recorded an album
in Los Angeles. But with all the firsts, the album also marked a stark
reduction in record sales. Immediately on hearing it, it was obviously
quite different with a greater country-rock/Americana feel. In retrospect,
it's easier to see that the brothers were lacking direction and inspiration.

It's the shortest Bee Gees album ever, with only eight tracks and a
playing time of little over 32 minutes – extraordinary considering what
prodigious songwriters the brothers had always been. Four of the songs
were written by Barry alone; the rest by all three brothers. At this point,
there was no Bee Gees band behind them – only guitarist Alan Kendall,
who had been with them for two years. The rest of the work was
done by session musicians, including legendary drummer Jim Keltner,
'Sneaky' Pete Kleinow of The Flying Burrito Brothers on pedal steel, and
bassist Ric Grech – formerly of Blind Faith, Ginger Baker's Air Force and
Traffic – incorrectly noted as 'Rik' in the album credits. Robin having to
leave the sessions suddenly when his son Spencer was born a month
early, on 21 September 1972, would not have helped. Though he was
gone for only a week, what impact did that have? Perhaps it's also a bit
strange that Barry and Maurice wrote no songs together in his absence.

Maurice told *Billboard* that the band had moved from London to Los
Angeles because, 'We're going to attempt a concept album that's a major
departure from our usual Bee Gees trademarks. And if that doesn't work
out, we'll do something else'.

A concept album never surfaced, but what did was a collection
of songs of varying quality ranging from the excellent 'Saw A New
Morning' to the somewhat tedious 'My Life Has Been A Song'. Other
tracks like 'While I Play', 'South Dakota Morning' and 'Come Home
Johnny Bridie' are all great country rock, but overall, the album is

too short and lacks spark, with overblown arrangements and some unnecessarily long songs. Vocally, they sound great, with Barry taking the lead on three songs, with vocals shared with Robin on the other five. There were no solo Robin or Maurice vocals on this album, which was unusual.

When 'Saw A New Morning' inexplicably failed as a single, the album was doomed to follow. *Life In A Tin Can* only reached 69 on the US charts, and failed to chart in the UK and Germany completely. On the bright side, the album reached 10 in Italy, possibly aided by the previous year's concerts in Bologna and Rome. But it sold a comparatively miserable 175,000 copies worldwide. Bizarrely, the now-defunct *Record World* magazine awarded *Life In A Tin Can* 'Album of the Year'. Nearly 50 years later, the album is a serious fan favourite, as it showcases the group's rarely-heard country rock side.

The album was presented in an elaborate gatefold sleeve. The designer was John Youssi, who worked on many album covers in the early-to-mid-1970s. These days he's best known as an illustrator for pinball machines.

The front cover perfectly grasps the concept of *Life In A Tin Can* and shows the top of a drink can with the group's name and album title embossed, and the ring-pull hole die cut to reveal a photograph of The Bee Gees inside. The photograph of the brothers was taken by Ed Caraeff at a photo shoot on 22 October 1972 in Los Angeles. Caraeff's work is included in the permanent collection of The Rock and Roll Hall of Fame and has been featured on hundreds of albums and on the covers of numerous magazines, world-wide. His ground-breaking chance photo of Jimi Hendrix burning his guitar on-stage at the Monterey Pop Festival in 1967 is widely considered to be one of the most iconic rock photos of all time and is the only photo ever to appear twice on the cover of *Rolling Stone* magazine. Caraeff would go on to work extensively with The Bee Gees in the mid to late 1970s.

The back cover is a grainy photograph of an exploded drink can, by Marc Hauser – known for photographs of celebrities like Woody Allen, John Belushi, Eric Clapton, Cindy Crawford, Mick Jagger, Michael Jordan, Sophia Loren, Oprah, Dolly Parton and Dennis Rodman. He also took the cover picture for John Mellencamp's *Scarecrow* album.

The inner gatefold uses Hauser's photograph as its base upon which David Larkham, founder of Tepee Graphics created a rather chaotic yet captivating collage. Larkham is an award-winning art director, illustrator and designer. His career includes service as Elton John's long-time art

director, and he's also had a hand in album packaging and concert
publicity for Paul McCartney, David Bowie, Bob Dylan, The Rolling
Stones, Genesis, The Beach Boys and many more.

'Saw A New Morning' (Barry, Robin Gibb, Maurice Gibb)

Recorded at The Record Plant, Los Angeles: September 1972
Chart positions: Hong Kong: 1, Italy: 20, Australia: 38, US: 94

Sometimes it's hard to figure out why a single would not be a hit.
Certainly, 'Saw A New Morning' – released in March 1973 – seemed
strong enough. In fact, it was considered to be the best Bee Gees
single in some years. Sounding like nothing they'd done before, a
great introduction, interesting narrative and a powerful chorus with the
Gibbs in full vocal attack, makes this a very commanding song, with
Barry and Robin alternating verse leads. It should have been a winner
– but it wasn't!

With its reference to a prison escape and a 'snubnose' revolver, it does
have a distinctly American feel, which may have been a distraction for
audiences in some territories. Barely breaking into the US top 100, and
not even making the chart in most of Europe, it was a minor hit in Canada
and Australia. Its solitary success was in Hong Kong, where it topped the
chart, but you can't feed the family based on sales in Hong Kong.

'I Don't Wanna Be The One' (Barry Gibb)

Recorded at The Record Plant, Los Angeles: September 1972

In contrast to the strong opener, this could have been on any of their
previous two or three albums. It's pleasant enough, but with its sad
refrains and surrounding melancholy, there's no progression from what
they'd previously done. As nice as it is, you get the feeling it's the sort of
romantic song Barry could write in his sleep.

'South Dakota Morning' (Barry Gibb)

Recorded at The Record Plant, Los Angeles: September 1972

This is a beautiful ode to the expansive, sparsely populated mid-Western
US state. Had Barry even been there? He hadn't been to Massachusetts
when he wrote that classic! When all is said and done, it doesn't really
matter because Barry could write beautiful country or bluegrass songs
with ease. It's a pretty song, given a boost by guest musicians 'Sneaky
Pete' Kleinow of the Flying Burrito Brothers on pedal steel, and famed
session musician Tommy Morgan on harmonica. But it's puzzling why

they brought 'Sneaky' Pete in, as their resident guitarist Alan Kendall was a competent pedal steel player himself.

It's interesting to note that for the first verse, Barry's guitar is in the right channel, and Maurice's in the left. Listening to each channel separately shows Barry's strength as a good solid rhythm player, using open tuning, while Maurice was a more adept instrumentalist, playing a more-intricate picked part with conventional tuning.

It's been speculated that the song was inspired by the Black Hills flood: the most damaging flood in South Dakota history. Fifteen inches of rain fell on 9 and 10 June 1972, causing severe flooding resulting in 238 deaths and 3,057 injuries. Over 1,335 homes and 5,000 cars were destroyed. Given the Gibbs' penchant to draw their subject matter from tragedies à la 'New York Mining Disaster 1941', this seems entirely plausible.

'Living In Chicago' (Barry Gibb, Robin Gibb, Maurice Gibb)
Recorded at The Record Plant, Los Angeles: September 1972
This is the album's longest song, at a whopping 5:41! It was previewed in a shorter form on *The Tonight Show Starring Johnny Carson* on 9 November 1972 – more than two months prior to the album's US release. The song plods a little but has a good vocal showing from Robin and Barry, and the harmonies are very strong. It's a nice arrangement when it starts to get going with Jerome Richardson's flute solo, but the minute of outro strikes as overkill.

The lyric is typically Gibb-abstract, with a somewhat limp chorus of 'If you're living in Chicago, you're alone/If you're living in Chicago, it's your home'.

In a question-and-answer session during the recording of the *Soundstage* show in Chicago in 1975, an audience member asked, 'Do you really feel that if you're living in Chicago, you're alone?' with Barry replying, 'We wrote 'Living In Chicago' while we were in L.A.'. He couldn't elaborate any further. In summary, it appears it's a strong song about nothing.

'While I Play' (Barry Gibb)
Recorded at The Record Plant, Los Angeles: September 1972
Once again, country influences are to the fore on this song sung by Barry. Ric Grech adds slick violin licks on this fun recording which is one of the stronger tracks on an uneven album. The strange sound heard at 0:32 has always mystified fans – it's a note played on a Clavinet through a wah-wah pedal.

'My Life Has Been A Song' (Barry Gibb, Robin Gibb, Maurice Gibb)

Recorded at The Record Plant, Los Angeles: September 1972

This features a nice lead vocal by Robin, but in a similar vein to another song on the album, 'I Don't Wanna Be The One'; the song could have easily fitted on any of the group's previous two or three albums.

It was possibly, the weakest track on the album, but it's not a bad song by any stretch of the imagination. It stands as a good example of how their songwriting was stagnating. The song was also the B-side of the ill-fated 'Saw A New Morning' single.

'Come Home Johnny Bridie' (Barry Gibb)

Recorded at The Record Plant, Los Angeles: September 1972

This screamed out to be a single, but it never happened. The closest it got was as a flexi-disc giveaway with the May 1973 edition of the Brazilian magazine *Geracao Pop*.

The session players brought in to enhance the track really do make a difference: Sneaky Pete's pedal steel is just great and it was good to have a proper piano player in there in the form of Jane Getz too. Maurice could never have got close to doing what she did.

The line 'The kid's no good' appears in this song – it is purportedly the intended title of Barry's unreleased solo album from 1970.

'Method To My Madness' (Barry Gibb, Robin Gibb, Maurice Gibb)

Recorded at The Record Plant, Los Angeles: September 1972

This is a great song, but somewhat flawed, with strained vocal performances by both Barry and Robin. Barry's normally perfect delivery slips a cog twice as he strains to reach the high notes, and in the bridge where Robin flies off into a strangulated solo that was just way over the top! It would have been wise to have dropped the key a couple of notches to get it just right. Having said that, it has a certain charm as it stands, and it's a great album closer!

It's worthy of a very concentrated listen to pick up on the backing vocal counter-melody – it's so strong it could have made a great song in its own right.

While covers of Gibb songs were decreasing at the time, an interesting one did surface in January. Veteran American singer Roy Head – best known for his 1965 smash hit 'Treat Her Right' (which was only denied the top spot in the US by The Beatles' 'Yesterday') somehow came across Barry's song 'Clyde O'Reily' – originally intended for his unreleased 1970 solo album *The Kid's No Good*. Head successfully crossed over to country music in the early-1970s, and his version of 'Clyde O'Riley' was the B-side to his single 'Carol' which was released on 20 January 1973 on TMI Records in the US. TMI was a small label connected with the Trans Maximus Inc. recording studio in Memphis, which was run by famed Stax Records house guitarist Steve Cropper, who produced the record.

Between the US and UK releases of *Life In A Tin Can*, The Bee Gees made their first UK concert appearance since 1969's televised show at The Talk of the Town when sister Lesley took Robin's place. The sold-out concert with The London Symphony Orchestra at London's Royal Festival Hall on 19 February was a great success. The support act was former Zombies singer Colin Blunstone. The concert was to celebrate the formation of RSO records, which officially launched on 1 March with the release of *Life In A Tin Can*. The concert is also notable for being the first for new drummer Dennis Bryon, formerly of Amen Corner.

The concert setlist was: 'New York Mining Disaster 1941', 'To Love Somebody', 'Really And Sincerely', 'Lay It On Me', 'Saw A New Morning', 'I Can`t See Nobody', 'Words', 'Morning Of My Life', 'Don`t Forget To Remember', 'Wouldn`t I Be Someone', 'I Started A Joke', 'My World', 'Alive', 'Run To Me', 'How Can You Mend A Broken Heart', 'I`ve Gotta Get A Message To You', 'Massachusetts' and 'Lonely Days'.

On 6 January, *Melody Maker* reported that The Bee Gees were planning a live album, possibly recorded at this concert, but that as they already had an abundance of material to release, it wouldn't be available until 1974. Sadly, the live album never materialised, and it's unclear whether the concert was recorded. If it does exist, it would be a magnificent document of the group in concert with an orchestra.

On 23 February, Jimmy Stevens released his third Maurice-produced single, 'High Heel Blues' b/w 'Tailpieces' in the UK. Neither song was on the Don't Freak Me Out album. In the US, the single was released to coincide with his support slot on the forthcoming Bee Gees tour.

Setting off for a North American tour in support of their new album, the entourage departed London's Heathrow airport on 23 February. Barry, Linda, Robin, Maurice, their father Hugh and younger brother Andy flew in style in first class, while guitarist Alan Kendall, drummer

Dennis Bryon, conductor Glyn Hale and support act Jimmy Stevens were forced to slum it in the cheap seats. Also in tow were personal manager Dick Ashby, road manager Tom Kennedy and Robin's assistant Ray Washbourne.

The tour opened with two dates in Canada – the first show at the O'Keefe Centre in Toronto on 25 February. A concert at the Forum Concert Bowl in Montreal followed on the next night. On 27 February in Montreal, they performed an acoustic version of 'Living In Chicago', and sang live vocals over backing tracks of 'Saw A New Morning' and 'Run To Me' on the TV show *Musical Friends*.

After a couple of days off from the tour – during which they appeared live on *Good Morning America* – the tour resumed on 3 March at the Capital Theater in Passaic. Two consecutive nights at the Philharmonic Hall at the Lincoln Centre in New York followed. After the second show, as it was Andy Gibb's 15th birthday, Jimmy Stevens recalled, 'We took him to the local club. Alan Kendall and I got up and backed Andy as he sang Bee Gees songs. He sounded just like Barry – you couldn't tell the difference, and he was only 15'. Jimmy also remembered the night in Birmingham, Alabama, on 16 March when 'I had a great gig, and I was just doing my last song 'Hey, Jude'. The Bee Gees, from behind the curtains, joined in the 'Nah, nah, nahs' with me! It sounded better than The Beatles. The crowd went wild'.

After a few more shows, a four-day break allowed the tour to flip over to the West Coast. Though there was some time to relax and recharge their batteries, there was still work to be done. On 27 March, they recorded their first appearance as guest hosts on the popular late-night music show *The Midnight Special*. From the tour itinerary, the plan was to perform an acoustic version of 'Living In Chicago' and three songs with live vocals over backing tracks to be chosen from: 'To Love Somebody', 'Massachusetts', 'Lonely Days', 'Alive', 'Run To Me' and 'Saw A New Morning'.

When the show was broadcast on 6 April, they actually performed 'To Love Somebody', 'Lonely Days', 'Saw A New Morning', and a medley comprising 'New York Mining Disaster 1941', 'I Started A Joke', and 'How Can You Mend A Broken Heart'. The Bee Gees were the show's hosts and their guests were Gladys Knight, Johnny Nash, Skeeter Davis, and Jerry Lee Lewis, with whom they performed 'Money'.

The Bee Gees' blend of music and lively repartee struck a chord with the audience, and the show reported its highest ratings ever. The show producers were understandably pleased, and The Bee Gees were asked back to host three more shows. No other act did as many guest-host appearances.

On 28 March, they appeared on *The Tonight Show, Starring Johnny Carson*. Introduced by Johnny, he gave their following night's concert in Santa Monica a plug, and they performed live versions of the new song 'Wouldn't I Be Someone' in all its full-length glory, and a bombastic rendition of their current single 'Saw A New Morning'. The booking for this show was made very late on in the schedule and does not even appear in the tour itinerary. It required The Bee Gees conductor for the tour, Glyn Hale, to re-write the usual orchestral score to create unique arrangements on the flight to Los Angeles as the show's resident musicians, the Doc Severinson Big Band was predominantly brass and saxophones, and didn't include any strings. In the interview that followed, Maurice revealed that 'Wouldn't I Be Someone' was from a new album scheduled for release in mid-July.

Concerts followed in Santa Barbara, Seattle, and the final show at the Paramount Theatre in Portland, Oregon, on 1 April. The tour party departed the US the next day and returned to London.

On 30 March, the single 'Saw A New Morning' was released in the UK. *Billboard* magazine's review noted the now-very-obvious Bee Gees 'distinct vocal blend' and the backing instrumentation that 'sounds like a symphonic orchestra'. The other influential US trade magazine *Cashbox* wrote, 'The accent is on melody and three-part harmony, as Robin, Barry and Maurice prove that they're still one of the finest vocal groups around'. Promotion in the US was good, with their high-profile appearances on *The Tonight Show Starring Johnny Carson* and *The Midnight Special*. But despite this, the single only reached 94 on *Billboard*, and didn't chart in the UK at all. Hints in later years indicated that the newly-formed RSO Records might have had distribution problems, which hindered the single's chart success.

In some countries, the single's picture sleeve included former Bee Gees drummer Geoff Bridgford. France was one of the guilty countries, using a group photo showing a beardless Barry. Italy used the same photograph but were savvy enough to realise that Bridgford had left the group the year before. But figuring that Barry was the one with the leonine mane and beard, they left Geoff in and airbrushed Barry out!

On their return to Britain in April, Lulu asked Maurice for a divorce. After marrying very young in 1969 – Lulu was 20 and Maurice was

19 – it had been a turbulent three and a half years. Speaking of their marriage years later on an episode of *Piers Morgan's Life Stories*, Lulu said, 'We thought we were king and queen of the world and were fabulous'. Of Maurice's growing alcoholism, Lulu said, 'The drinking was a part of it, but we shouldn't have got married in the first place – we should have just had a romance. I decided it had to end. He didn't want it to end, and it hurt him. I totally loved and adored him, but in love with him? I was probably in love with love'.

In April, the music press reported that in June, The Bee Gees would embark on their first UK tour in four years. The tour was initially touted to be 11 concerts, but four further dates were added a few weeks later. The support act was to be Jimmy Stevens again and the 15-piece Westminster Symphonia conducted by Glyn Hale was to provide the orchestral backing for The Bee Gees. In addition, they were to appear at the Royal Command Performance at London's Royal Festival Hall on the day after the final tour concert.

A full-page advertisement appeared in the *New Musical Express* on 26 May – a little late considering the tour was to commence on 4 June with a show at the Guildhall in Preston. On 9 June, it was revealed that the tour's first five dates had been cancelled – the *New Musical Express* stating that the 'reason for the postponement is that drummer Dennis Bryon dislocated a shoulder, and it was impossible to replace him, as rehearsals had already been completed, and immediately prior to the scheduled opening, The Bee Gees were taping a TV special (*The Midnight Special*) in Los Angeles'. A revised advertisement appeared in that week's music papers but to no avail. All of the shows – except for the final performance at the London Palladium – were cancelled. The Bee Gee's personal manager Dick Ashby told *Melody Maker*: 'I admit some of the ticket sales for the early dates were not as good as they could have been, and the group is perhaps not as popular in Britain as they once were, but they were quite willing to play to non-capacity audiences'.

The alarming aspect – when correlated with the decline of their record sales – is how out of sync with the era's musical trends The Bee Gees were. The tour venues were all in large towns or cities, and the venues weren't particularly big. The smallest venue was the 1,514-capacity Princess Theatre in Torquay, and the largest was the Liverpool Philharmonic Hall which could accommodate 2,600.

The tour itinerary was littered with other promotion, including the 15 June taping of the BBC Radio *Top Twelve Show* at Studio B7 at

Broadcasting House in Portland Place, London: a mere stone's throw from IBC Studios. With the show's format requiring guest artists to nominate the favourite songs its interesting to note the brothers' initial song choices. Robin chose 'Breaking Up Is Hard To Do' (Neil Sedaka), 'It's Over' (Roy Orbison), 'Amos Moses' (Jerry Reed), 'Strawberry Fields Forever' (The Beatles) and 'Betcha By Golly, Wow' (The Stylistics). Barry chose 'Vincent' (Don McLean), 'Harvest' (Neil Young), 'Long Cool Woman In A Black Dress' (The Hollies), 'Jealous Guy' (John Lennon) and 'Without You' (Harry Nilsson), while Maurice plumped for 'Superstition' (Stevie Wonder), 'Use Me' (Bill Withers), 'Good Vibrations' (The Beach Boys), 'Stay With Me' (Lorraine Ellison) and 'Layla' (Derek and the Dominos).

The following day, in what appeared to be a rather bizarre engagement, The Bee Gees attended the opening of the Stanmore Old People's Home. This was organised by Robert Stigwood, who lived locally at a house called The Old Barn. The brothers were told to arrive with acoustic guitars, and have a small speech and a few songs prepared, including 'The Wild Rover'.

A promotional film for their new single 'Wouldn't I Be Someone' was made on the afternoon of 19 June, and that same evening a BBC Radio session was taped at Aeolian Hall in Bond Street, London. The recordings sound remarkably similar to the released versions of the songs, but they were most definitely new recordings. Glyn Hale conducted the orchestra, which was added to the newly recorded rhythm tracks, and then The Bee Gees added the final vocals.

The only remaining concert of the UK tour was the 24 June show at the London Palladium. Jane Coulson's 7 July *New Musical Express* review was positive yet ironically prophetic: 'Sunday Night at the London Palladium with The Bee Gees sounds rather like an event packed with blue-rinsed mums and hosted by Bruce Forsyth, but the Gibb brothers quickly proved they are not ready to be put out to the pasture of the nightclub circuit just yet'. However, in less than a year, that is precisely what they would be doing.

At the Palladium show, support act Jimmy Stevens fell victim to a road-crew prank. Road manager Tom Kennedy recalled: 'We actually wired an alarm clock under his piano above the pickup mic. When he was halfway through a love song, the alarm went off. But being the trooper that he was, he carried on'.

Sadly, the Royal Command Performance scheduled for the following day, was cancelled. This was to have been at the Royal Festival Hall on the south bank of the River Thames, in the presence of Her Royal Highness Princess Anne. The order of artist appearance was to be John Denver, Nina Simone, The Guess Who, Jose Feliciano, The Bee Gees, and Paul McCartney and Wings. The intention was for the concert to be televised for worldwide distribution and recorded for an album for RCA. The Bee Gees had a 15-minute time slot, and were to be backed by a 25-piece orchestra conducted by Glyn Hale. The suggested setlist was 'New York Mining Disaster 1941', 'I've Gotta Get A Message To You', followed by an acoustic segment consisting of 'Morning Of My Life', 'Don't Forget To Remember', 'Living In Chicago', a short version of 'Wouldn't I Be Someone' and 'Massachusetts'.

On 22 June, RSO released 'Wouldn't I Be Someone' as the lead single from the next album. While it failed in the bigger record markets, *Cashbox* said the song 'continues in the same warm and sincere Bee Gee style that has produced hit after hit for this super talented family of stars'. *Billboard* praised the song as having 'many melodic and lyrical hooks'. The group promoted the single on *Top Of The Pops* on 6 July, in what was to be their last in-person British TV appearance until December 1981 on *The Parkinson Show*.

'Wouldn't I Be Someone' (Barry Gibb, Robin Gibb, Maurice Gibb)

Recorded at The Record Plant, Los Angeles: October 1972
Chart positions: Hong Kong: 1, Italy: 17, Australia: 52, US: 115

Though it wasn't intended to be, 'Wouldn't I Be Someone' became a non-album single. It's a good, slow ballad with strong hooks. Perhaps it was too slow, as it failed to chart in most territories, though it was number one in Hong Kong, bolstered by the group's concert appearances.

Some years later, Robin said (somewhat sarcastically, one would suspect), 'This is truly one of those songs that would be sacrilege to describe! For to do so would take away from that special relationship that has been created between the track and the listener'. It's difficult to disagree, but 'that special relationship' generally manifested itself as an overwhelming sense of wonderment – what on earth was it about?!

The wonderful string outro and Alan Kendall's guitar solo – which was intended for *A Kick In The Head* – was faded out for the single. But the full-length version was released on the American and Canadian editions of *Best Of Bee Gees, Volume 2*, and in the 1990 box set *Tales From The Brothers Gibb*.

A promotional film exists showing the band performing the song. The brothers are in profile, close up, and occasionally in mirror-image as if playing their guitars left-handed. Barry is actually left-handed but has always played his guitar right-handed. New drummer Dennis Bryon and guitarist Alan Kendall also got a good share of screen time.

'Elisa' (Barry Gibb, Robin Gibb, Maurice Gibb)
Recorded at The Record Plant, Los Angeles: October 1972

'Elisa' was the B-side to 'Wouldn't I Be Someone' everywhere except Germany. The ballad is notable for being the only Bee Gees song to feature solo lead vocals by all three brothers.

It was another track scheduled for *A Kick In The Head*, and appeared on the *Tales From The Brothers Gibb* box set. However, its first album release was on the British budget compilation *Gotta Get A Message To You* in 1974, and its subsequent reissue in 1978.

'King And Country' (Barry Gibb, Robin Gibb, Maurice Gibb)
Recorded at IBC Studios, London: 8 January 1973

For many years most Bee Gees fans were unaware of this track as it was originally only released as the B-side to 'Wouldn't I Be Someone' in Germany. Barry said the song 'came out of one of my solo sessions. I think it's about Vietnam; too long and too slow'. He is a little harsh on himself here, as it's not a bad song, though it requires a bit of listener patience before it gets going.

Due to its appearance on bootlegs, many believed it to be from the *Kick In The Head* sessions, although it was actually recorded three months later than what was intended to be the album and was recorded in London, not Los Angeles.

Its first album appearance was on the 1982 Germany-only compilation *Bee Gees Greatest Volume 1 – 1967-1974*. Both releases were in an edited version, and it was only on the 1990 box set *Tales From The Brothers Gibb* box that the full-length version finally saw the light of day. It was worth the wait, and it's only on hearing this that you realise how brutally short the edit was.

Also on 22 June, The Bee Gees' second appearance on *The Midnight Special* aired in the US. As guest hosts again, the other acts were Wilson Pickett, The Steve Miller Band, Jimmie Spheeris and Maxine Weldon. This time The Bee Gees performed 'I've Gotta Get A Message To You' and 'Run To Me'. They also performed a bluesy version of 'Hey Jude' with Wilson Pickett and reprised one of their childhood standards, 'Alexander's Ragtime Band'.

Singer Graham Bonnet – formerly of The Marbles (who had success with the Gibb brothers' song 'Only One Woman' in 1968) – rekindled his friendship with Maurice in the spring of 1973, and they began working together. Graham had decided to record a Neil Sedaka song. He told Steve Wright (author of Graham's biography *Behind The Shades*): 'All of his comeback stuff was great; such a young voice. I was thinking of recording a song from his new album, which I loved. So, Maurice and I recorded 'Trying To Say Goodbye'. As this was going on, Graham got to meet Neil. Maurice knew him and invited him to a session. 'I was singing, and he opened the door. This little face looked around and said, 'Hello?'. Neil hung around while I did the vocal and was very impressed. He was giving me the thumbs up when I did the takes'.

Looking for a suitable B-side, Graham settled on The Bee Gees' 'Castles In The Air' from their unreleased album *A Kick In The Head Is Worth Eight In The Pants*. Session musicians played on the song, which left Graham free to concentrate on his vocal performance. With the single in the can, Graham's manager Marian Massey negotiated a one-off single deal with RCA Records. Issued on 29 June, (although promo copies of the single said 15 June), there was absolutely no advertising for the record. Nobody at RCA showed the slightest interest – they didn't even organise any promotional photographs. Bonnet's superb version of 'Castles In The Air' was issued on CD as a bonus track on the 2016 album *Back Row In The Stalls*.

While Graham was struggling to find his feet, the career of his actress girlfriend Adrienne Posta was blossoming. She was busy working on the movie *Percy's Progress*, and in between filming she was working with Maurice and Billy Lawrie, cutting the Neil Sedaka song 'Love Will Keep Us Together' on which Graham played bass and guitar. She was signed to DJM records for a one-off single. Adrienne suggested recording Graham's song 'Dog Song' with 'Express Yourself' on the flipside. Therefore, her Moby Productions version of 'Love Will Keep Us Together' didn't see the light of day. Following Maurice and Lulu's separation and eventual divorce, Maurice ceased collaborating with Billy.

Barely a month after recording the last song for *Life In A Tin Can* – and some months before it was even released – The Bee Gees were back at The Record Plant in L.A. recording their next album. They later said they weren't dedicating enough time to their albums at this point – fitting in sessions when they could in between touring. The result of these new sessions was to be the infamous unreleased album *A Kick In The Head Is Worth Eight In The Pants*. Originally intended for release in July 1973 (as Maurice revealed to Johnny Carson earlier in the year), legend has it their US label declined to release it due to considering it not commercial enough. Release plans were far enough advanced for it to have been assigned a catalogue number for the US (SO871), but when the single 'Wouldn't I Be Someone' failed to chart, the album was canned. What's more likely is that Atlantic Records head Ahmet Ertegun and Robert Stigwood agreed there were no hits on the album. They'd worked together for years and had formed a good business relationship. Following the relative failure of the previous two Bee Gees albums, they couldn't afford another misstep.

Whilst the complete album has never been officially released, bootlegs of it do exist. However, all of these erroneously include 14 songs rather than the ten that made up the album. The four additional tracks were recorded in January 1973 in London, and were appended onto the 2-track masters. The actual album track listing was scheduled to have been:
Side 1: 1. 'Elisa', 2. 'Wouldn't I Be Someone', 3. 'A Lonely Violin', 4. 'Losers And Lovers', 5. Home Again Rivers'
Side 2: 1. 'Harry's Gate', 2. 'Rocky L.A.', 3. 'Castles In The Air', 4. 'Where Is Your Sister', 5. 'It Doesn't Matter Much To Me'

However, with 14 songs to choose from, some substitutions might have been made for the final selection had the album been released.

Listening to the recordings now, one might agree with Ertegun and Stigwood that the proposed album contained no hits, but that doesn't necessarily make it a bad album. It's probably a stronger set of songs than *Life In A Tin Can*, and certainly makes for far more interesting listening.

The gentle ballad 'Elisa' opened side one, followed by the more-forceful single 'Wouldn't I Be Someone'. 'A Lonely Violin' is another nice piano ballad with a beautiful fluid solo violin. Though The Bee Gees version of the song remains unreleased, a version by Percy Sledge appeared on his albums *Shining Through The Rain* (US and Japan 2004) and *My Old Friend The Blues* (Europe 2009).

Stepping up a gear, 'Losers And Lovers' is a good up-tempo song with a Barry-and-Robin vocal over a lively gypsy accompaniment, while 'Home Again Rivers' is a country ballad with Robin on lead vocal. When

Barry and Maurice join in singing at the end, the result is wonderful. The existence of a double-sided acetate containing these two songs, may suggest that they were being considered for release as a single.

Side two opens with the ballad 'Harry's Gate', which Barry said 'was about a gate we used to swing on when we were kids'. It's all very nostalgic, with the lyric 'Back in 1958, we used to swing on Harry's gate' – this was the year that the Gibb family left Manchester and emigrated to Australia – but could this just be a convenient rhyming couplet? When they later sing 'Back in 1964, we used to knock on Harry's door', it reinforces this theory. Let's call it poetic licence – but it's nice to have the picture in your mind's eye. The song then segues into 'Rocky L.A.' which is a great little rocker repeating much of the lyric from 'Harry's Gate'.

'Castles In The Air' opens with piano and has a Barry vocal, while Robin takes on the choruses with a flamboyant orchestral backing. Thirty seconds of this has been legally released – on the 1978 publishing promo album rather long-windedly titled *Stigwood Music, Brothers Gibb Music and Unichappell Music proudly present the words and music of Maurice Gibb/Barry Gibb/Robin Gibb*. The album included 30 seconds each of 50 Gibb brothers' songs, with a view to other artists covering them.

'Where Is Your Sister' follows – it's a simple song with some beautiful acoustic guitar and Barry's best soft vocal delivery.

The final song on the planned album was to be 'It Doesn't Matter Much To Me'. This original version saw an unexpected release on the 1974 UK-only budget label compilation *Gotta Get A Message To You*. Whether this was intentional or an error is not known, but it has made this LP an essential part of a complete Bee Gees collection, as this version has never been made available elsewhere.

'Dear Mr. Kissinger' is the only overtly political song The Bee Gees ever recorded. It was extremely topical in respect of America's involvement in the Vietnam War at the time, asking, 'Would you send a man like Nixon to the front?'. Barry kicks into a convincingly serious tone for the lines 'Let us gather all together in the land/We'll surround the Vatican City hand in hand'.

'Jesus In Heaven' appears to be a direct plea to Jesus for help to survive, but then states 'I will not pray for you/I wasn't born to'. That point aside, it's a great vehicle for the brothers' unison singing.

'Life, Am I Wasting My Time' starts out with a great full-force vocal from Barry, before slowing down to a different, slower melody, with Robin utilising a rare raw vocal sound.

As for the brothers' opinion of *A Kick In The Head Is Worth Eight In The Pants* – they were inclined to criticise it, dismissing it as a poor album. For Barry, it was 'some nice music, but just totally mainstream pop. They were downers, written about ourselves and things like that ... it was definitely a wrong direction'. When he was asked about the album in a 2021 internet chat with fans, he said they 'were all smoking too much weed at the time'.

Whilst a change of musical direction was soon to follow, this final piece of the old Bee Gees remains as a fine collection of songs which deserves a wider audience.

When the brothers were told that the record company had rejected the album, it was a watershed moment in their career. Fortunately, their ever-faithful manager Robert Stigwood hadn't given up on them, though he recognised they needed to be revitalised; to be challenged. Historically the Gibb brothers worked better when challenged; when their backs were against the wall. This episode was no different. But they needed a producer – someone experienced who could command their respect, and inspire and challenge them. Stigwood and the savvy and powerful Ahmet Ertegun put their heads together and came up with a gem of an idea – an idea that, within a few short years, would make music history.

That idea was the recruitment of famed record producer Arif Mardin. While initially, the brothers were a bit annoyed they could no longer produce themselves, the choice of Mardin – a multi-Grammy winner who had produced Hall and Oates, Aretha Franklin, Dionne Warwick, Donny Hathaway and Roberta Flack, to name just a few – could not be faulted.

In August, RSO released a new compilation album, *Best Of Bee Gees, Volume 2*. It's not unreasonable to assume it might have been rushed to market to replace the cancelled *A Kick In The Head* album.

Best Of Bee Gees, Volume 2 (1973)

Release date: UK and US: August 1973
Side 1: 1. 'How Can You Mend A Broken Heart', 2. 'I.O.I.O.', 3. 'Don't Wanna Live Inside Myself', 4. 'Melody Fair', 5. 'My World', 6. 'Let There Be Love', 7. 'Saved By The Bell'.
Side 2: 1. 'Lonely Days', 2. 'Morning Of My Life', 3. 'Don't Forget To Remember', 4. 'And The Sun Will Shine', 5. Run To Me', 6. 'Man For All Seasons', 7. 'Alive'

In the UK, the *Best Of Bee Gees, Volume 2* compilation contained 14 songs. Except for 'Man For All Seasons', every track had been released as a single somewhere in the world. Notable by its absence, however, was 'Saw A New Morning' from *Life In A Tin Can*.

The compilation saw the first album inclusion of their most recent significant hit, 'My World', and conveniently included the 1971 recording of 'Morning Of My Life', which had previously only been available on the *Melody* movie soundtrack.

The North American compilation included the full-length version of 'Wouldn't I Be Someone' (from *A Kick In The Head*), and re-sequenced the tracks:
Side 1: 1. 'Wouldn't I Be Someone', 2. 'I.O.I.O.', 3. 'My World', 4. 'Saved By The Bell', 5. 'Don't Forget To Remember', 6. 'And The Sun Will Shine', 7. 'Run To Me', 8. 'Man For All Seasons'
Side 2: 1. 'How Can You Mend A Broken Heart', 2. 'Don't Wanna Live Inside Myself', 3. 'Melody Fair', 4. 'Let There Be Love', 5. 'Lonely Days', 6. 'Morning Of My Life', 7. 'Alive'

The front cover of the LP featured a group photograph from the same photoshoot with Ed Caraeff that had been commissioned to provide the front cover photo for their *Life In A Tin Can* album released earlier that year, despite the fact that nothing from that album appeared on this compilation.

The rear of the sleeve featured a still photograph by Allan James from the 'Run To Me' promo film. What isn't immediately apparent is that the photograph is a mirror image. The giveaway is that the curved portion of a grand piano body is always on the right-hand side, though here it's on the left. The back cover also features complimentary notes from British lyricist Tim Rice.

The interesting compilation album *Massachusetts* appeared on Polydor's budget Contour label in August 1973.

Massachusetts (1973)
Release date: UK: August 1973
Side 1: 1. 'Massachusetts', 2. 'Tomorrow Tomorrow', 3. 'Sir Geoffrey Saved The World', 4. 'Sinking Ships', 5. 'Sweetheart', 6. 'The Singer Sang His Song'
Side 2: 1. 'New York Mining Disaster 1941', 2. 'Lamplight', 3. 'On Time', 4. 'Barker Of The U.F.O.', 5. 'Close Another Door', 6. 'The Lord'

In an obvious attempt to include at least a couple of recognisable songs for casual buyers, both sides open with hit singles – 'Massachusetts' and 'New York Mining Disaster 1941', respectively. Where this set comes into its own is in the non-album tracks that hadn't appeared on LP previously. The single A-side 'Tomorrow Tomorrow' and B-sides 'Barker Of The U.F.O.', 'Sir Geoffrey Saved The World', 'Sinking Ships', 'The Singer Sang His Song' and 'On Time', all made their first appearance on a British album here, padded out with four rather random choices. Though the album was not an exhaustive B-side collection, it was a worthwhile release.

Though initial sales were slow, Massachusetts gained momentum over the next several years – no doubt riding on the coattails of the group's late-1970s re-emergence with the hits 'Jive Talkin'', 'You Should Be Dancing' and the *Saturday Night Fever* soundtrack. It eventually sold very well – the British Phonographic Industry certifying it silver in February 1978. Surging again with the success of the *Spirits Having Flown* album, it went one better in April 1979, achieving Gold status.

The album cover photographs, both front and back, were taken on the March 1972 tour of Japan. The front cover shows the brothers dressed smartly in full-flight performance – Maurice playing his Rickenbacker 4001 bass, Robin characteristically with his hand to his ear, and Barry playing a Gibson J-200 acoustic guitar. The group name is in huge, bold white letters on a dark background. The back cover was a well-thought-out marketing tool, showing four full-price albums that were in print on Polydor at the time: *Best Of Bee Gees, 2 Years On, Trafalgar* and *To Whom It May Concern*.

The album sold well enough to warrant reissue, not once, but twice – and much to the delight of collectors worldwide, with different sleeves. The 1978 reissue cover art featured a photograph taken during the medley portion of their rehearsal for the American TV show *The Midnight Special* on 10 October 1975, bordered in blue with a stylish graphic logo in the top right-hand corner.

The second reissue was in 1983. The featured photograph was not particularly striking, being taken from their 6 April 1973 appearance on *The Midnight Special*. The photograph was bordered in red with a bold orange logo.

On 10 August, The Bee Gees were guest hosts of *The Midnight Special* for the third time. Hosting the 'Best Of British Special', the other guests were The Hollies, Herman's Hermits, Wayne Fontana and the Mindbenders, The Searchers, Billy J. Kramer and the Dakotas, and Gerry and the Pacemakers. With such a packed show, The Bee Gees performed only 'New York Mining Disaster 1941', 'Turn Of The Century' and 'I Can't See Nobody' – notably all from their 1967 *Bee Gees 1st* album. While The Bee Gees technically came after the British Invasion, they also performed an excellent acoustic medley of the Beatles songs 'If I Fell', 'I Need You', 'I'll Be Back' and 'She Loves You' with just Barry on guitar.

From a young age, the youngest Gibb brother Andy had designs on becoming a pop star. Barry bought him his first guitar when he turned 12. Learning to play, Andy began performing at small clubs on the island of Ibiza, where he was living with his parents. Feeling unsettled there, Hugh and Barbara moved back to the Isle of Man, and Andy became involved with the local island music scene. Maurice took an interest and decided it would be good experience for Andy to record a couple of songs, so he and Andy flew to London to do this. On 23 August, Andy recorded two songs at Nova Studios with Maurice as producer. The first song was 'My Father Is A Rebel': written by Maurice, especially for Andy. It's a typical country rock song as favoured by Maurice at that time, with an American Civil War theme. Andy's voice sounds very mature for one so young. The second song, 'Windows Of My World' is a much more mellow piece. Taking the style into account, it's likely this was one of Andy's first songwriting attempts, possibly in collaboration with Maurice.

Setting off on tour again, a crowd of enthusiastic fans greeted The Bee Gees in Tokyo on 30 August for their second visit to Japan. *The Best Of Bee Gees, Volume 2* album was released there to coincide with the tour, with the incentive of the first 20,000 copies coming with an exclusive poster of the group from an appearance on *The Midnight Special*. The opening act was again Jimmy Stevens, who also saw the release of his new single 'Paid My Dues' b/w 'Bye Bye Love' mid-tour on 10 September.

The first show was on Barry's 27th birthday – 1 September – at Tokyo's Shinjuku Kosei Nenkin Hall. It was the tour's only concert to include 'Living In Chicago' in the set. Following concerts in Fukuoka, Okayama, Nagoya, Osaka, Kyoto and Shizuoka, they returned to the Tokyo venue for two concerts on 14 and 15 September. The second of these was an afternoon show filmed for Japanese television's *Love Sounds Special*, and was broadcast on 27 September. After the concert, the entourage flew to their next stop: Hong Kong. Unfortunately, heavy rain forced the postponement of the scheduled 16 and 17 September shows at the Government Football Stadium, which were rescheduled for 29 and 30 September.

On a further stop in the Far East, Maurice happened upon an Australian band called Crimson performing at the Hilton Hotel in Kuala Lumpur. The group comprised Carmel Chayne (vocals), Kelvin Monaghan (guitar, saxophone, flute), Greg Cull (keyboards), Kenny Leroy (bass) and Wayne Bonner (drums). Monaghan recalled: 'Maurice heard us playing. He loved the music, loved the band and loved the whole concept of what we were doing. He said, 'I'd love to take you over to England and record, as I love this music". Monaghan thought it was just talk, but 'three weeks later, Chris Cooke turned up at the Hilton with tickets and said, 'Well, we're off!'. We nearly fell over'. Cooke was the director of Maurice's production company, and he recalls that 'Moby Productions were looking for acts to record, and we thought they were a good possibility'.

On 14 September, another episode of *The Midnight Special,* including The Bee Gees, aired in the US. Hosted by Curtis Mayfield, the other guests were Jim Croce, Gladys Knight & The Pips, Natural Four, Wilson Pickett, Helen Reddy, Sly and the Family Stone, and War. The Bee Gees played 'Lonely Days' and 'Run To Me'.

Then on 12 October, they made their fifth appearance on the show in six months, again as guest hosts. The guests for this episode were extremely diverse, ranging from rock 'n' roll legend Chuck Berry to progressive rock giants King Crimson, with soul singer Barbara Mason and rock organist Lee Michaels also in the mix. Performing 'Massachusetts', Lay It On Me', 'Alive' and 'Alone Again', The Bee Gees also resurrected another song from their childhood repertoire: 'Bye Bye Blackbird'. But the show highlight was Chuck Berry performing 'Reelin' And Rockin'' and 'Johnny B. Goode', joined by the brothers who danced and sang along and even attempted Berry's trademark duck walk.

23 November saw yet another appearance on *The Midnight Special,* but this was a little different as it was recorded in London. Hosted by Peter Noone, the guests were all British acts – Herman's Hermits, Electric Light Orchestra, David Essex, Manfred Mann's Earth Band, Gilbert O'Sullivan and Robin Trower. The Bee Gees performed just two songs on this episode – 'Bad Bad Dreams' from *To Whom It May Concern*, and 'I Don't Wanna Be The One' from *Life In A Tin Can.* Strangely, their performance was filmed on 15 October at the base of Nelson's Column in *Trafalgar* Square. Bearing in mind the songs

performed were deep cuts, would it have been too obvious to include Maurice singing 'Trafalgar'?

Soon after returning from the Far East, Jimmy Stevens recalled, 'Maurice and I did some recordings with little Jimmy McCulloch (Stone The Crows), Paul Jones (Manfred Mann) on mouth organ, Pete Willsher on steel guitar and Mike Kellie (Spooky Tooth) on drums. We got some tracks from it, but they were never released'. Others included in the sessions were Alan Kendall (guitar), Zoot Money (keyboards), and Maurice, as usual, played bass. Gerry Shury arranged and conducted the strings. The intention was for Maurice to produce another album. The recorded songs included three of Jimmy's – 'Sinner' (recorded in New York with Alan Kendall and some of his American friends), 'Yoko' and 'The Band' – and covers of 'Tennessee', 'Fiddler's Tramp' and 'Maggie May'.

DJ John Peel had championed Jimmy's album and booked him to record another session for his BBC radio show *Top Gear*. On 21 November, he recorded four new songs – 'Won't You Be My Yoko', 'Please Don't Let It Be', 'Thank You For Being A Woman' and 'Lola': first broadcast on 6 December, and repeated on 3 January 1974.

After a bust-up with Roger Forrester (later Eric Clapton's manager), RSO cancelled Jimmy's contract before the end of the year. The recordings remain unreleased, though Jimmy did make some CD-R copies which he sold at gigs in the Liverpool area in the early-2000s under the stage name Summertime.

Without a doubt, Barry's finest production to date was his first child Stephen Thadeus Crompton Gibb – born 1 December, weighing 5lbs, 8ozs. Stephen was to become a musician himself, playing guitar for The Bee Gees at their *One Night Only* concerts in 1998 and 1999, and at Barry's solo shows and on his records post-Maurice and Robin's deaths. Stephen also wrote with Barry on projects, including Barbra Streisand's excellent 2005 album *Guilty Pleasures,* and Barry's 2016 solo album *In The Now.*

Maurice's former Moby Productions partner Billy Lawrie released his only album *Ship Imagination,* in December. It contained the song 'Freedom', which they co-wrote with Stone The Crows guitarist Leslie Harvey. It's possible this song and recording date back to 1971. Musicians included Harvey's bandmates Maggie Bell on backing vocals (credited as Mags Maglint), and guitarist Jimmy McCullough (credited as Jimmy McAnonymous). Lulu sang backing vocals. Oddly, no bassist was credited, but it was Maurice.

1974

Following Stephen's birth in December, Barry and Linda moved to the Isle of Man in the Irish Sea. Settling in Douglas – the capital and largest town – they were also close to Barry's parents and brother Andy who had also moved back there to live. Maurice also moved there following his separation from Lulu. It was a shift not entirely due to sentiment but with a more practical issue – Britain's expensive early-1970s tax situation. Barry explained: 'We were all born on the Isle of Man, which helps us enormously if we live there, taxwise. The Labour government in England had raised the taxes to something like 83% on the pound, which was terrifying to anybody who was actually making good money'.

Most of January was spent in the studio finishing the next album *Mr. Natural* under the experienced control of their new producer Arif Mardin. At first, a little put out by Mardin replacing them as producers, the brothers quickly realised his work was wonderful. Mardin soon became a mentor for the trio, and they affectionately referred to him as Uncle Arif. Recording for the new album had begun on 14 November 1973, eventually encompassing three studios in two countries: IBC and Command in London, and Atlantic in New York. The brothers would later lament that they were still not devoting enough time to recording, but rather fitting in recording sessions between tours and television appearances.

Once the recording sessions had finished, the group prepared for their next US tour. Their live act was changed slightly for this tour. They still used an orchestra, but the first half was just The Bee Gees and their band. The set included four new songs from the forthcoming album – 'Down The Road', '*Mr. Natural*', 'Heavy Breathing' and 'Give A Hand, Take A Hand' – and their sound had a considerably rockier one than before.

Arriving in London in January, Maurice's discovery, Crimson, were put up in serviced apartments in Abbey Road, and they were soon in a recording studio with Moby Productions director Chris Cooke at the helm: 'Moby had used Morgan Studios, and we had a relationship with them, and it fell to me to oversee the recordings'. For Crimson guitarist Kelvin Monaghan, it was a musical dream come true: 'We walked into the studio where Rick Wakeman was mixing *Journey To The Centre Of The Earth*, and we used his engineer and his gear. Keith Emerson was recording there; in fact, everybody who was anybody was recording there. Yes had just finished *Tales From Topographic Oceans*. All that sort of stuff has been done, and suddenly we found ourselves in this whirlwind scene in London'. After recording a few songs, the band began gigging, appearing at The Speakeasy. But by this time, Crimson felt a name change was in order due to possible confusion with King Crimson, so they decided on the name Soliloquy. More gigs followed at venues, including The Marquee in Wardour Street and the Windsor Castle pub in Brixton. Maurice lent the band his Rolls Royce so they could arrive in style.

Maurice was going through some personal problems at the time, so it was Chris Cooke via Moby that funded the pressing of an EP containing three tracks recorded at Morgan Studios – on side one, 'Alive To Die', and 'Father Moonshine'; on side two, 'Asian Ways' and 'Lady Tarantula'. The label Lyntone pressed a run of 50 copies (LYN 2867), which appeared as the only record on the Moby Productions, Ltd. label and bore the address and telephone number of RSO at 67 Brook Street, London.

Hedley Leyton, who worked for Polydor's A&R department, saw a couple of Soliloquy shows at The Speakeasy and he took the marketing department to see the band, trying to steer the label towards signing them: 'I did not push that hard, as, if I had got a positive reaction from the marketing guys who came along, it might have played out a bit differently' – there was also interest from EMI and Mushroom Records, but nothing translated into the offer of a contract'.

Then the political climate had an impact. Monaghan recalled: 'Right in the middle of this, the energy crisis hit. London pretty much shut down at 10 p.m., which is why I wrote the song 'Three Day Week'. It was the most depressing period of time, as TV was closing down at 10 p.m., shops and businesses were only open for three days as there was no oil or petrol, and there was no vinyl for records. Polydor told me that they weren't pressing records at this time, so they couldn't really sign us'.

Soliloquy continued to perform, and even recorded a few more tracks – at The Workhouse: Manfred Mann's studio on the Old Kent Road – and it was suggested that they tour in Europe until the energy crisis blew over.

Before launching their new US tour, The Bee Gees promoted their next single 'Mr. Natural' which was to be released the following week, on *The Mike Douglas Show* on 25 February. Following an interview with the host, the group also performed their 1967 hit, 'Massachusetts'.

The new single, 'Mr. Natural' b/w 'It Doesn't Matter Much To Me', was released in the UK four weeks later, on 29 March.

The US tour commenced on 4 March at the Philharmonic Hall in New York City, with the final show at the Valley Forge Music Fair in Philadelphia on 28 March. At the tour's penultimate show – at Nashville's Municipal Auditorium – legendary singer Roy Orbison watched the concert and visited the group backstage to congratulate them and tell them he was recording 'Words' on his next album.

The set took on a radically different format to those of previous tours, as the group opened with a rock set: the band comprising Alan Kendall, Dennis Bryon and Geoff Westley. After a short interval, they returned for the second half, performing their hits backed by an orchestra.

They opened the concerts with a punchy rock version of 'In My Own Time' (from *Bee Gees 1st*) and closed with a raunchy extended version of the new album's 'Heavy Breathing'. It wasn't uncommon for this song to extend to ten minutes or more at some shows. The 12-bar rocker 'Road To Alaska' (from *To Whom It May Concern*) was another deep cut included in the set. The group seemed more inclined to rock their audiences than croon to them as they'd perhaps done before. Guitarist Alan Kendall and new drummer Dennis Bryon were eager participants for the new sound.

The new keyboard player and musical director for 1974 was classically trained conductor/arranger Geoff Westley. He listed the instruments he played as keyboards, flute and a 'short white stick with cork handle'. As conductor for another Stigwood project – *Jesus Christ Superstar* – Westley's employment with The Bee Gees was always going to be an interim arrangement.

The concert setlist was: 'In My Own Time', 'Road To Alaska', 'Don't Wanna Live Inside Myself', 'Marley Purt Drive', 'Down The Road', 'Give A Hand, Take A Hand' and 'World'. After a short intermission, the group returned with an orchestra for the show's second half – 'Let There Be Love', 'Mr. Natural', 'And The Sun Will Shine', 'I Can't See Nobody', 'Run To Me', 'Morning Of My Life', 'Alexander's Ragtime Band', 'To Love Somebody', 'How Can You Mend A Broken Heart', 'Words', 'I've Gotta Get A Message To You', 'Massachusetts', 'Lonely Days' and 'Heavy Breathing'.

An unspecified concert from the tour was recorded for the syndicated radio show *The King Biscuit Flower Hour*. A half-page *Rolling Stone* advertisement showed that the hour-long broadcast on 28 March would be split between The Bee Gees and Brownsville Station, and that the broadcast would be available in quadraphonic sound. The Bee Gees segment included 'Don't Wanna Live Inside Myself', 'Give A Hand, Take A Hand', 'World', 'Let There Be Love', 'Mr. Natural', 'How Can You Mend A Broken Heart', 'Words', 'Massachusetts' and 'Lonely Days'.

Following the short but successful US tour, The Bee Gees returned to the UK to promote the new album. At this point, the UK seemingly had yet to forgive the brothers for the very public sibling discourse of 1969, their worldwide hit 'Lonely Days' hadn't broken into the top 30, and 'How Can You Mend A Broken Heart' hadn't charted at all. 'Run To Me' in 1972 was their only single to break into the UK top ten.

Due to this distinct lack of interest from the British public, the 1974 UK tour was not at concert halls and theatres but at smaller clubs. One particular week-long booking at The Batley Variety Club near Leeds commenced on 28 April and was a turning point in The Bee Gees legend. Performing as a nightclub act with the jangling of tableware in the background took the brothers back to their early days of struggling in Australia, playing at RSLs and other clubs. Barry recalled the time: 'We were back doing the Northern clubs. We realised we'd come full circle and we were back doing clubs again. It was the most horrible sinking feeling'. Their shows at this point – as they had back in Australia – even included a small comedy routine, which one reviewer commented was 'so super-kitsch that the audience were baffled rather than amused'. Another week's residency commenced on 12 May at the Golden Garter in Wythenshawe (a mere ten-minute drive from the brothers' childhood stomping ground of Chorlton-cum-Hardy), and another at the Fiesta Club in Sheffield commencing on 19 May. The final week's residency at Bailey's Club in Liverpool, due to begin on 9 June, was cancelled. This truly was rock bottom.

The nightclub dates were something of an epiphany for the brothers. Robin said, 'We've come to this, and we just walked out of that club and we never looked back. We said that is never ever going to happen to this group. We knew we've got so much more to offer'.

These were Barry's thoughts:

This is it. We've hit bottom. We are has-beens. We have to get back up there. It has to happen. We'd lost the will to write great songs. We had the talent, but the inspiration was gone. We decided right then we were going to do it, and honestly, it took us five years to get to know one another again. There is nothing worse on Earth than being in the pop wilderness. It's like being an exile. And the other artists treat you like crap, saying things like, 'Hey, I didn't know you were still together'. It's then you realise they haven't thought of you for years. It's all ego. This whole business is ego.

One positive thing did come from the Batley appearances: Maurice met his future wife, Yvonne Spenceley, who worked at a neighbouring steak house. The two would marry the following year.

Fortunately, with the new album already in the can and final production work being completed by Mardin back in Los Angeles, the fight back to success had already begun, if just tentatively, at this stage.

Mr. Natural (1974)

Personnel:
Barry Gibb: vocals, guitar
Robin Gibb: vocals
Maurice Gibb: vocals, bass, Mellotron, organ
Alan Kendall: guitar
Dennis Bryon: drums, percussion
Geoff Westley: piano, keyboards
Phil Bodner: clarinet ('Charade')
Horn and string arrangements: Arif Mardin
Engineers: Damon Lyon-Shaw (IBC), Andy Knight (IBC); Alan Lucas (Command); Gene Paul (Atlantic)
Producer: Arif Mardin
Recorded between 14 November 1973 and 28 January 1974 at IBC Studios, London; Command Studios, London and Atlantic Recording Studios, New York
Release dates: US: May 1974, UK: July 1974
Chart positions: Australia: 20, US: 178

Mr. Natural – an album Robin later described as 'transitional' – was the first of three Bee Gees albums to be produced or co-produced by legendary R&B producer Arif Mardin. Manager Robert Stigwood paired the group with Mardin following the rejection of A Kick In The Head Is Worth Eight In The Pants. The Gibbs were stunned, as it was the first time a record company had rejected one of their albums. The slight of being allocated a producer to lift their game must have been eased by the nomination of Mardin, as the Gibb brothers had long been R&B aficionados and were well aware of his industry status. Mardin encouraged them to stretch themselves and be innovative. Maurice said simply, 'Arif was brilliant; full of ideas'.

As a result, *Mr. Natural* is an album of good strong material. In some ways, it's quite similar to their earlier albums, as it has a good mix of ballads, pop and up-tempo songs. The big difference was the up-tempo songs had a real rock/R&B feel. *Mr. Natural* was possibly the most guitar-orientated Bee Gees album since 1968's *Horizontal*. For the first time, guitarist Alan Kendall was joined by drummer Dennis Bryon. They worked together in the band for the next six years. Though the R&B was not as evident here as it would be on ensuing albums, Mardin began to entice the brothers' love of Black music from them. Both the band and producer were looking for a new Bee Gees sound. Mardin later wrote, promoting the album: 'It brings The Bee Gees' sound and identification into today's vein. While there are fresher and newer techniques used, the group still retains their individuality'.

Vocally it's excellent, with Barry taking the lead six times, and sharing the lead with Robin on the five other songs. For the second time in succession, there were no solo Robin or Maurice vocals. Barry's vocals on the rockier material are particularly strong, and the first hint of what would be become their trademark sound over the next few years – their falsetto singing – can be heard, albeit as background on at least one track. They also seemed to be writing together a lot more than on the previous album – with one solo Barry composition, three by Barry and Robin, one by Barry and Maurice, and the remaining six by all three.

Though the critics received it positively, *Mr. Natural* wasn't the hit that was anticipated, and when the first single 'Mr. Natural' died, so did the album. But it was very successful in Australia, where on the back of a sell-out tour, the single and the album sold very well. Retrospectively, Maurice commented on the album's failure to chart: 'We simply were not devoting enough time to our albums. We recorded *Mr. Natural* while on tour. Every time we had a few days off, we'd be shooting back to New York to do a few tracks. When we finally finished, we knew we could do better work'.

Despite the overall song strength, *Mr. Natural* remains one of The Bee Gees' most obscure albums. Though the brothers rarely mentioned it, it remains a strong fan favourite.

The cover photographs were taken by Frank Moscati at the Corner Bistro, 331 West 4th Street, Greenwich Village, New York, and showed a happy middle-aged man staring out of the large window. He wears a suit and trilby hat, and cups his face in his hands while holding a fat cigar stub in his left hand. This, we must assume, is *Mr. Natural*. The bistro window is illuminated with a large neon sign with the group's name and the album title. The back cover is taken from the exact same viewpoint, but evidently a while later, and shows a slightly dishevelled *Mr. Natural* with a partially-consumed beer in front of him, in the process of being ejected by a stern-looking waiter.

In a 2021 interview, Barry admitted he was still mystified by the meaning of the front cover, as it had no connection to the title song whatsoever. He also made the point that until 1979's *Spirits Having Flown*, The Bee Gees had little control over their album covers.

'Charade' (Barry Gibb, Robin Gibb)
Recorded at IBC Studios, London: 20 December 1973
Chart positions: Chile: 7, US: 103

The opening track is a radical departure from the previous album *Life In A Tin Can*, and being the most mellow song they'd recorded to this point, caught the seasoned Bee Gees fan a little off guard. With its shimmering electric piano and Barry's almost whispered vocals, it was less than the required dynamic opening track to launch into the new album. For opening-track-dynamic comparisons, go to their next album *Main Course*.

'Charade' is as beautiful and complex a piece as they'd written or recorded to this point. It's also possibly the biggest piece of schmaltz they'd ever recorded and doesn't really represent the album at all. Any track that has since been described as smooth jazz – with a celestial clarinet solo – should not open any rock/pop group's break-back album. When it released as a single in some markets, the contrast between the A-side and the raucous B-side – the thumping 'Heavy Breathing' – was stark.

But for all that disparagement, it is quite a classy song, with Arif Mardin's string arrangement making it float along. The clarinet solo played by Phil Bodner is pretty slick, fluidly played and with a melody that beautifully complements the song. Maurice once referred to it as 'The song for making love'.

Barry recommended the song to his protégé, Australian singer, Samantha Sang, who recorded it for her *Emotion* album in 1978.

'Throw A Penny' (Barry Gibb, Robin Gibb)
Recorded at IBC Studios, London: 17 December 1973 and 5 January 1974
'Throw A Penny' was the album's second single in the US, Canada, Japan and New Zealand. It was a good, but not perfect, choice to follow 'Mr. Natural'. It was a more typical Bee Gees ballad with a strong hook-laden chorus. The album version has a slow middle section which was brutally edited out of the single (taking it from 4:49 to 3:32), but it does make it flow better.

'Down The Road' (Barry Gibb, Robin Gibb)
Recorded at IBC Studios, London: November 1973
The album really gets going with this excellent rocker – a huge, missed opportunity for a single, though it remained in concert setlists until 1976. It's got everything! It's the full-voiced rock song fans had waited years to hear. Barry sings full-force throughout, with Robin doubling in places. Maurice joins in on the chorus and must be given credit for pipping Barry to the post with singing in falsetto – Maurice's high harmonies are quite simply stunning on this track! Dennis Bryon's drumming and Maurice's bass – complete with slides – drive the song, and the horn stabs are dynamic. Full of great lines, 'Ain't no heavy Mister Leather gonna paddle my butt anywhere' must surely be the peak of their lyrical prowess! The track was a precursor to the more-upbeat rock songs 'Nights On Broadway' and 'Wind Of Change', which would follow within a year.

Barry Gibb is perhaps best known these days for his falsetto singing and his ballads. But this recording proves he was an excellent rock singer if required, and it's one aspect of the group that perhaps we deserved to hear more of over the years.

The stereo mix is useful in illustrating how the song would have sounded without the horn section, by merely fading out the left channel, which also contains a rather funky clavinet played by Geoff Westley.

'Voices' (Barry Gibb, Robin Gibb, Maurice Gibb)
Recorded at IBC Studios, London: 5 January 1974
The pace of the album is slowed right down with 'Voices', which has a slightly unconventional structure in that it has very short verses and a much longer chorus.

The purity of Robin's voice is striking from the opening line of the first verse on which he is accompanied by Barry's simply strummed acoustic guitar. Robin sings the first two lines in the verses and Barry takes over for the folksy 'Doo da dee doo doo' parts. The chorus is all Barry, singing in syncopation, stressing almost every syllable.

As with 'Method To My Madness' on *Life In A Tin Can*, there's a strong backing vocal countermelody. Though 'Nights On Broadway' is usually credited for being the debut of Barry's hitherto-unheard falsetto, it's clearly evident in the enduring fadeout heard on 'Voices'.

This was The Bee Gees final session at IBC Studios.

'Give A Hand, Take A Hand' (Barry Gibb, Maurice Gibb)

Recorded at Atlantic Recording Studios, New York: 21 January 1974

Upon inspection of the record labels, this song is conspicuous with its stand-out publishing date of 1969: five years earlier than the album's other songs. The credit to Barry and Maurice indicates it was written during the split period, which begins to make more sense.

In fact, when The Bee Gees were just Barry and Maurice, they recorded the song, but never released it.

However, P.P. Arnold, who had supplied backing vocals to a few songs on the *Cucumber Castle* album, issued it as the B-side to her single 'Bury Me Down By The River', also penned by Barry and Maurice. This made it one of the relatively few Bee Gees songs that was released by another artist before The Bee Gees' own version was released, albeit some five years later. The Bee Gees version is over a minute longer than the P.P. Arnold version and is a far more dramatic piece.

This new version of 'Give A Hand, Take A Hand' was one of just two tracks on the *Mr Natural* album recorded at Atlantic Recording Studios in New York, and it is very different stylistically to the original 1969 recording, being much slower and given an almost gospel feel rather than country blues, although Alan Kendall puts in some nice touches on tremolo guitar. Arif Mardin's production is far more sophisticated, with far more dynamic elements present.

The popular American gospel, soul and R&B singing group The Staple Singers – who supported The Bee Gees on their 1971 US tour – recorded this song that same year, including it on their *The Staple Swingers* album.

'Dogs' (Barry Gibb, Robin Gibb)

Recorded at IBC Studios, London: 18 December 1973

Side two opens with this rock ballad, with Geoff Westley (who doubled as tour orchestra leader at the time) giving his best shot at Elton John piano playing. It's a strong song despite its unfathomable lyric, and was actually planned to be the first single.

Canadian duo, D.O.M. comprising Steve Barry and Yves Lamoureux brought the song up to date with their version which appeared on the 2002 album *Ordinary People ... Living Ordinary Lives – An International Tribute To The Bee Gees.*

'Mr Natural' (Barry Gibb, Robin Gibb)
Recorded at Command Studios, London: 8 January 1974
Chart positions: Australia: 11, US: 93

The album title track was one of just two tracks recorded at Command Studios in London. It's a good representative track as it combines the feel of the powerful rockers and the sweet ballads with the by-now-familiar vocal lead sharing between Barry and Robin.

Where the inspiration for the title came from is not clear, but there was a counterculture comic book character called Mr. Natural, created and drawn by artist Robert Crumb. It is interesting to note that in 1973 a pornographic film called *Up In Flames* was made, featuring Mr. Natural and another pair of comic strip characters, The Fabulous Furry Freak Brothers.

While the single failed in the major markets, on the back of a very successful tour, it was a big hit in Australia, charting as high as number 4 in some states. In 2019, Whyte Horses, a psychedelic pop band from Manchester, recorded a fine cover of the song with guest vocalist La Roux (Elly Jackson) on their album *Hard Times.*

'Lost In Your Love' (Barry Gibb)
Recorded at Atlantic Recording Studios, New York: 28 January 1974

'Lost In Your Love' is Barry's song all the way, working as closely as he can with a soul gospel style. It starts quietly with piano but builds slowly with the addition of organ, bass and drums. The vocal becomes more intense and passionate and almost becomes ad-libbed at the climatic finale. It's a good strong ballad. Musical pundits over the years have speculated what the late Joe Cocker could have done with this song had he been given the chance.

'I Can't Let You Go' (Barry Gibb, Robin Gibb, Maurice Gibb)
Recorded at IBC Studios, London: November 1973

Written in Los Angeles but recorded at IBC Studios in London, 'I Can't Let You Go' was another song which was representative of the overall rockier sound of the *Mr. Natural* album. Melodically sound, with a slow start, it builds strongly. The track features Barry on powerful lead vocals with Robin complementing in parts. A sensible flip-side choice for the 'Throw A Penny' single, it's also a great album track.

'Heavy Breathing' (Barry Gibb, Robin Gibb)
Recorded at IBC Studios, London: 14 November 1973

Another song written in Los Angeles but recorded in London. A great rock number with a stomping electric band and horn section would not have been out of place on an early Chicago album. Barry surprises by not singing the chorus again after the final verse, instead panting 'I'm so, so tired' while Alan Kendall cuts loose on a muted guitar solo into the fade – not the case in concert, however, as the song was the encore closer, and dependent on how the show had gone and audience reaction it could go into an extended jam lasting up to fifteen minutes!

'Had A Lot Of Love Last Night' (Barry Gibb, Robin Gibb, Maurice Gibb)
Recorded at Command Studios, London: January 1974

To close the substantially rockier-than-average Bee Gees album, the Gibb brothers reverted to more familiar territory with a much gentler song. Recorded at Command Studios in London, it's smothered in angelic harmonies, with Barry giving the verses a dramatic reading over Geoff Westley's piano and Arif Mardin's tasteful string arrangement. It's not the album's best song, but it showed off the group's versatility as songwriters and performers.

Related Recordings
It Doesn't Matter Much To Me (Barry Gibb, Robin Gibb, Maurice Gibb)
Recorded at IBC Studios, London: 4 January 1974

Originally a song recorded in 1972 for the rejected *A Kick In The Head* album, this second version was recorded some 15 months later in January 1974. This version seems a little faster, with significantly more backing vocals and an altogether bolder arrangement. Robin really pushes himself on this song, especially the ad-libs at the end, which could really be considered the first lead falsetto vocal on a Bee Gees record.

It was originally released as the B-side to the 'Mr. Natural' single. This recording saw its' first release on an LP on the German-only release

Bee Gees Greatest Volume 1 – 1967-1974 but even then, it remained an obscurity until it saw broader release when it was eventually issued on CD on the *Tales From The Brothers Gibb* box set in 1990.

In the album notes from that box set, Barry dismissed it as 'not a very good song', although acknowledging the 'good vocal by Robin'.

Robin and Molly had cause for celebration when their daughter Melissa Jane was born at 5:00 a.m. on 17 June. Newspaper reports dubbed the new baby 'Little Miss Natural' as a nod to the album.

In August, Polydor's Contour imprint issued a second budget collection along similar lines to 1973's *Massachusetts*, under the slightly incomplete title *Gotta Get A Message To You*. Again, the formula of hit singles to open each side was employed, with the title track on side one, and 'World' on side two.

Gotta Get A Message To You (1974)

Side 1: 1. 'I've Gotta Get A Message To You', 2. 'Elisa', 3. 'Road To Alaska', 4. 'My Life Has Been A Song', 5. 'Jumbo', 6. 'I Am The World'
Side 2: 1. 'World', 2. 'Railroad', 3. 'One Million Years', 4. 'I'll Kiss Your Memory', 5. 'It Doesn't Matter Much To Me', 6. 'Paper Mache, Cabbages And Kings'
Release date: UK: August 1974

This album is notable for a number of reasons – the first being the different mix of 'I've Gotta Get A Message To You'; up to that point, unavailable in Britain. What appears here is the stereo mix previously issued on the American ATCO versions of *Idea* and *Best Of Bee Gees*.

'Elisa' the flipside of 'Wouldn't I Be Someone', the single A-side 'Jumbo', and solo efforts by all three brothers – Maurice's 'Railroad', Robin's 'One Million Years', and Barry's 'I'll Kiss Your Memory' – all made their first British LP appearances on this compilation.

For a budget LP issued so long ago, *Gotta Get A Message To You* still remains an essential part of any Bee Gees collection, as it contains the original 1972 version of 'It Doesn't Matter Much To Me' unavailable elsewhere to this day. Originally intended for *A Kick In The Head*, the take included here was quite different to the one released as the B-side of the 'Mr. Natural' single.

A stereo mix of 'One Million Years' was also prepared specifically for this LP, and it features a different lead vocal. This mix was exclusive to

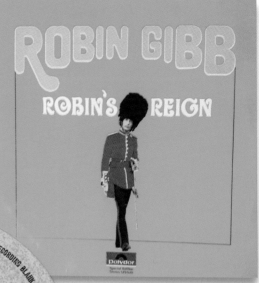

Right: Austrian edition of *Robin's Reign*. (Polydor)

Left: Single-sided four-track acetate with songs from Robin's *Sing Slowly Sisters* album, including an unreleased instrumental version of the title track.

Right: German record club edition of *Songs Of Cucumber Castle*. (Polydor)

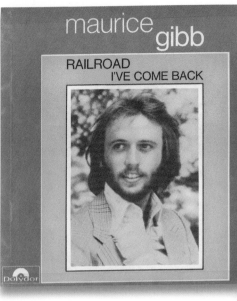

Left: French edition of Maurice's solo single 'Railroad'. *(Polydor)*

Right: Theatre programme for Sing A Rude Song in which Maurice performed alongside Barbara Windsor.

Left: 1976 fan club EP featuring four songs from Maurice's unreleased solo album, *The Loner. (New Blood)*

Right: Barry Gibb Fan Club EP. *(Lyntone)*

Left and below: Sheet music and withdrawn Canadian edition of Barry's proposed solo single, 'One Bad Thing'. *(ATCO)*

Left: Greek edition of *2 Years On. (Polydor)*

Right: 1971 US tour programme.

Left: 1971 Australian tour programme.

Right: UK edition of the *Melody* soundtrack album under its original title, *S.W.A.L.K. (Polydor)*

Left: 'Maureen' by Alamow – a collaboration between Maurice, and Allan Clarke of The Hollies.

Right: Malaysian edition of *Trafalgar. (Apache)*

Left: 1972 Japanse tour programme.

Right: Venezuelan edition of
To Whom It May Concern.
(Polydor)

Above: Australian edition of *To Whom It May Concern* had no pop-ups in the gatefold. *(Spin)*

Right: Malaysian edition of *Life In Tin Can*.

Left: Concert programme from 19 February 1973 at the Royal Festival Hall, London.

Right: German edition of 'Wouldn't I Be Someone'. These tracks were intended for the album *A Kick In The Head Is Worth Eight In The Pants*, which was never released.

Left: Maurice managed the group Soliloquy – their EP was the only record pressed on the Moby Productions label. (*Lyntone*)

Right: 1974 Australian tour programme.

Left: Robert Stigwood Organisation sticker with a rare Bee Gees logo from 1974.

Above: Russian edition of *Main Course,* released on four different coloured vinyl LPs. *(Melodyia)*

Above: Bee Gees belt buckle. *(Image Factory)*

Right: 1975 US tour programme.

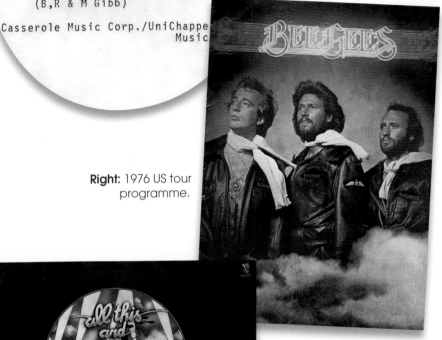

```
        SIDE TWO
      THE BEE GEES

1."Subway" (B,R & M Gibb)  4:23
2."Love Me" (B,R, & M Gibb) 3:58
3."Boogie Child" (B,R & M Gibb)
                           4:11
4."The Restless Years"(B,R & M Gibb)
                           3:18

5."Children Of The World"  3:07
  (B,R & M Gibb)

Casserole Music Corp./UniChappe
                         Music
```

Left: *Children Of The World* acetate with 'The Restless Years' – the original title for 'The Way It Was'.

Right: 1976 US tour programme.

Left: UK edition of *All This And World War II* which features The Bee Gees singing three Beatles songs.

Right: Israeli single LP edition of *Saturday Night Fever*. (*RSO*)

Left: Coloured vinyl editions of *Saturday Night Fever* from Australia (grey), South Africa (orange) and the UK (red). (*RSO*)

ORIGINAL MUSIC FROM THE MOVIE WRITTEN BY BARRY, ROBIN AND MAURICE GIBB
FROM THE ROBERT STIGWOOD PRODUCTION

BEE GEES
STAYIN' ALIVE
NIGHT FEVER
MORE THAN A WOMAN
YOU SHOULD BE DANCING

YVONNE ELLIMAN
IF I CAN'T HAVE YOU

SPECIAL DISCO VERSION

Right: Special five-track *Saturday Night Fever* promo 12" featuring a unique extended mix of 'Stayin' Alive'. (*RSO*)

Left: UK pink vinyl edition of *Sgt. Pepper's Lonely Hearts Club Band.* (A & M)

Right: French edition of Barry's 'A Day In The Life' with a non-album version of 'Sgt. Pepper's Hearts Club Band' on the B-side. (RSO)

Left: Italian edition of Barry's 'A Day In The Life' with a non-album version of 'Nowhere Man' on the B-side. (RSO)

Right: Robin introduces his son, Spencer, and daughter, Melissa, to Oscar the Grouch on *Sesame Street. (Children's Television Workshop)*

Left: French edition of *Sesame Street Fever. (Polydor)*

Right: Special 50 track publisher's promotional album, including a 30-second clip of 'Castles In The Air' from the unreleased album, *A Kick In The Head Is Worth Eight In The Pants. (RSO)*

Above: Three Bee Gees Jigsaw Puzzles. *(EMMC)*

Right: Bee Gees-branded AM/FM radio ...

Left: ... and record player. *(Vanity Fair)*

Right: Bee Gees lunchbox and flask. *(Thermos)*

Left: Toy guitar. *(EMMC)*

Right: *Sgt. Pepper's Lonely Hearts Club Band* bubble gum cards. *(Donrus)*

Left: US *Spirits Having Flown* picture disc. *(RSO)*

Right: 1979 *Spirits* tour pass.

Left: Official Bee Gees Fan Club record - *A Personal Message From The Bee Gees*. *(EMMC)*

this album, until it surfaced in 2015 on *Saved By The Bell: The Collected Works Of Robin Gibb.*

The balance includes 'I Am The World' (the B-side of their first international single, 'Spicks And Specks'), and the album tracks 'Road To Alaska', 'Paper Mache, Cabbages And Kings' and 'My Life Has Been A Song'.

Like its predecessor *Massachusetts, Gotta Get A Message To You* was also certified Silver in the UK, in March 1979.

Album cover designer Jack Levy chose a photograph from the Ed Caraeff session that spawned the photos for *Life In A Tin Can* and *Best Of Bee Gees, Volume 2*. In all actuality, this is the most striking of the photographs from the session to be used. The back cover shows three full-price Bee Gees albums available on Polydor and RSO, including the most recent release, *Mr. Natural.*

The compilation was reissued only once, in 1978, with a new catalogue number and new artwork. This time the cover photo was from their 20 December 1976 concert at The Forum in Los Angeles during the recording of the *Here At Last ... Bee Gees ... Live* album. The performance shot shows an atmospheric layer of dry ice flooded with pink lighting – a theme carried through to the album logo.

Following the failure of the 'Mr. Natural' single, 'Throw A Penny' was released in the US and Canada in June.

The group commenced their most extensive tour yet of Canada in Halifax, Nova Scotia, on 21 August. They played to sold-out houses all over Canada, finishing at the Centennial Concert Hall in Winnipeg, Manitoba, on 31 August. After the concert, the group went to Eaton's Warehouse for a party to celebrate Barry's birthday. Although it started a few hours early, the party went on until 2.00 a.m., by which time his birthday had actually arrived.

After a short break, the group appeared again on *The Tonight Show Starring Johnny Carson* on 11 September, before flying to Honolulu for a one-off concert on 13 September. From Honolulu, they flew directly to Christchurch to commence their Australasian tour. In New Zealand and Australia, the release of the 'Mr. Natural' single had been delayed to coincide with the tour. In Australia, that delay would prove very beneficial, as the single performed well there.

Following successful shows in Christchurch and Auckland in New Zealand, the touring party – which included Barry's wife Linda, their son Stephen and Yvonne Spenceley (who was experiencing her first time in the celebrity spotlight as Maurice's fiancé) – flew to Australia for what was to be their most successful tour there yet. Due to strong ticket sales, extra concerts were added in most states. There were two extra concerts in Melbourne, taking the total of sell-out shows there to four.

The support band for the tour was Mr. George, and as a late addition to the schedule, Soliloquy. As their UK work visas were expiring, Soliloquy had decided to return to Australia, and as Maurice still represented the band, it made sense for them to open The Bee Gees concerts. After the tour ended, Soliloquy remained in Australia. Used to working up to six nights a week, the band were lucky to get one or two gigs a week playing in small pubs in Melbourne, so it was inevitable that some band members called it quits and the band faded into obscurity.

Andy Gibb had only just arrived in Australia himself, accompanied by drummer John Stringer and lead guitarist John Alderson, who were members of his group Melody Fayre. Andy had formed Melody Fayre in the Isle of Man earlier in the year, and the group had played over 60 shows there. The three had travelled to Australia on the back of Barry's encouragement. Andy later recalled: 'Australia is a great training ground because you can be the biggest name in Australia, and without outside help, you will not get heard outside of Australia – that's just the way it is. So, you can make a lot of mistakes there, and there are also very tough audiences there. You can become the biggest name in Australia and never get heard until you leave to do something elsewhere'.

Stringer remembered:

Once we realised this fella's the brother of The Bee Gees, and he's not got a half bad voice – once we started getting the practising together and the playing together – we sounded good. We thought we did sound good, we could go somewhere. It was an opportunity not to be missed ... we stayed the first week or ten days in the Town House – the best hotel you could stay in – on the same floor as The Bee Gees. We felt important because we were on exactly the same footing as The Bee Gees. We went everywhere with them. I mean, when they went to the concerts in the evening, we joined in the entourage. They had a limousine for us as well, and we thought this is tremendous.

After the concerts, the boys would return to the hotel with them. Alderson recalled: 'We sat there ... on the floor, and they were just singing around us, with Barry on the guitar, and I just sort of sat there in awe. It was lovely to be party to that, to just sit and watch famous people just jamming. They were always jamming. They used to have some right sing-songs'.

While in Sydney, Maurice joined Andy in the recording studio, on organ. Andy had been signed by Kevin Jacobsen and Col Joye's ATA label, and was recording what was intended as his first single 'To A Girl'. The 16-year-old Andy was credited with writing the ballad, but as John Stringer recalls, Andy needed assistance with the melody, so Maurice and John Alderson may warrant credit as co-writers. Andy made his first television appearance, performing the song live on *The Ernie Sigley Show* in Melbourne. The arrangement bore little resemblance to the recording made at the time – which included rather long instrumental sections. The introduction alone was 30 seconds long, and there was a slow, rather uninspiring guitar solo between the first chorus and second verse, which lasted 27 seconds, which really didn't make it radio-friendly. From verse three onwards, it improved, with a cello and organ added. The single – b/w 'Walking Alone' – was never released. It would have made a pleasant album track.

Of course, the management of Andy by Col Joye and his brother Kevin Jacobsen, who had guided The Bee Gees twelve years earlier, was no coincidence. All parties had maintained a strong friendship and trust with each other. To the reassurance of his older brothers and also Andy's parents, Andy would be well mentored during his time in Australia.

As with their 1971 and 1972 concerts, The Bee Gees were backed by a 20-piece orchestra, and the final Melbourne show on 3 October was filmed for a one-hour television special. With colour television having just been launched in Australia, Melbourne's Channel 7 made a significant financial outlay – committing to filming in the countryside at Yarra Glen, an hour's drive from Melbourne. The footage included Robin and Maurice riding horses, and Barry driving a horse and cart. This was interspersed with concert footage for the TV special, and one reviewer wrote, 'With the aid of brilliant television production and direction, The Bee Gees stamped themselves in that one programme as masters in their field. They played, sang and clowned their way through all their hits. And when the visual action slowed, outdoor shots of the group were delicately cut in'. With the televised concert edited to include the outdoor scenes, the programme screened the dynamic 'Spicks And Specks' (switched to concert opener from its actual setlist placing as the first song of the encore), 'Road To Alaska', 'Mr. Natural', 'And The Sun Will Shine', 'I Can't See Nobody', 'Run To Me', 'Lay It On Me', 'In The Morning', 'Alexander's Ragtime Band', 'To Love Somebody', 'I Started A Joke', 'How Can You Mend A Broken Heart', 'Words', 'I've Gotta Get A Message To You', 'Massachusetts' and 'Lonely Days'. While this made for a good one-hour special for the masses, the complete unedited concert, with deep cuts 'In My Own Time', 'Marley Purt Drive', 'Down The Road', 'World', and a very long version of 'Heavy Breathing', really excites, showing The Bee Gees as a superbly-cohesive live unit.

When the group left Australia after the final concert at the W.A.C.A. Oval in Perth on 7 October, their new album was at number 20 on the Australia charts, and the 'Mr. Natural' single was in the top ten in some states.

The group then flew to Manilla for the first show of the tour's Far East leg (which took in the Philippines, Hong Kong, Malaysia and Japan), on which they performed 20 concerts. The Hong Kong show on 16 October was filmed for a local TV special.

Visiting Japan for the third consecutive year was testimony to the group's huge market there. Comprising 15 concerts, the tour commenced with a sell-out Tokyo show on 19 October. The schedule for the rest of the Japanese leg was particularly tight. One example of the strict timetable was the concert at Shizuoka (about 74 kilometres from Tokyo). The entourage travelled there from Tokyo on the midday bullet train, played the evening show at the Sunpu Kaikan Hall and returned to Tokyo on the bullet train that evening. The final show was at the Hokkaido Kosei Nenkin Kaikanu in Sapporo.

Following the Japanese tour, the group flew to Anchorage, Alaska, for their final concert of the year, on 10 November. It had been a long two-month tour covering eight countries.

After the Alaskan concert, the individual band members returned to their respective homes to celebrate Christmas and to rest and recuperate before starting work on their next album. Barry and Maurice returned to the Isle Of Man, where they both had homes, and Robin to England.

Whilst significant chart success continued to evade The Bee Gees in 1974, random covers of Gibb brothers' songs continued unabated. Nigel Olsson's, cover of 'Only One Woman', released on 1 November was a little different.

The record actually featured the entire Elton John band – Nigel Olsson on drums and lead vocals, Davey Johnstone on guitars, Dee Murray on bass, Ray Cooper on percussion, and Elton John himself on piano. Written by Barry, Robin and Maurice, 'Only One Woman' was originally recorded and became a UK top-five hit for The Marbles in 1968. Olsson's cover reached just number 58 in the UK and number 91 on the US *Billboard* chart.

Despite the relative failure of *Mr. Natural*, the brothers were more excited about recording than they'd been for years. Their new producer Arif Mardin had given them confidence in themselves again. They knew they could do better work and were willing to take risks and extend themselves.

They were about to record what became one of their most important albums. While they were still making good money on tours, they urgently needed a big hit record in the important markets. The pressure was on.

Before they left to record their new album, one of the changes required and recognised, was the recruitment of a permanent keyboard player to replace Geoff Westley, who had returned to his role as conductor for the *Jesus Christ, Superstar* stage show.

Drummer Dennis Bryon suggested Derek 'Blue' Weaver – an old friend who had played with him in the groups Brother John and The Witnesses, Amen Corner and Fair Weather. Weaver – born 11 March 1947 in Cardiff, Wales – had more recently been in Strawbs – with whom he scored two big hits, 'Lay Down' and 'Part Of The Union' – he replaced Rick Wakeman, who had gone on to join progressive rock supremos, Yes – and then Mott The Hoople with whom he toured the US with Queen as the support band. Weaver by now had built up a fine reputation as a session player which also had quite lucrative, and he was reluctant to give that up. He recalled:

Ever since Dennis was with The Bee Gees, he would always say to me, 'Let me have a word with them and see if we can get you in as a keyboard player'. It was Dennis who was always contacting me saying, 'Oh, come on, let's get a band together'. I think they all most probably said, 'Let's get a band together, let's get rid of the orchestra, let's try to do something a bit different'. So, Dennis kept phoning me and saying, 'Let's do something'. Well, at that time I was playing with Mott The Hoople and also doing a lot of sessions. I was having a great time with a pop band and doing lots of session work and playing with lots of different people.

As a result of Dennis's persistence, Blue was persuaded to meet with the group. 'I went over to the Isle of Man', he recalled, 'and stayed with Barry for the weekend – went over on Friday night and came back on the Sunday night'.

Weaver remembers the 'meeting' was more a social gathering of friends than an audition with Barry playing guitar and singing, with discussions about songs and arrangements:

As I'm leaving, Hughie and Barbara, everybody's around ... they're all there, and we'd all had a good drink and a meal and a laugh. I'm walking out the door, and Barry says, 'Here! I haven't heard you play piano yet!'. I was actually putting my bags in the car, and I said, 'Oh, do you have a piano?'. They had this old thing in the back – it was all out of tune – I can't even remember what I played. I mean, they knew I could play, I suppose. I rattled out a quick tune on the piano, and they said, 'Fine, can you come to Miami next month?'.

As informally as that, Blue Weaver was in The Bee Gees band. With hindsight, he admitted it was an easy decision to make:

When I joined, I think it was the lowest ebb that the three brothers had been. I'd actually heard *Mr. Natural* as well, and I thought that was great, and there were elements in that that I obviously felt we could take further. I think we were all optimistic. We were going off to Miami to make an album in the winter; we were going to stay at 461 Ocean Boulevard – you know, Eric [Clapton] had had a massive hit from that. We were going with Arif, you know, it was all looking positive. There had never really been any problem with The Bee Gees – I mean, they were always capable of writing songs.

1975

To the disappointment of everyone involved, *Mr. Natural* had failed to end The Bee Gees' nearly three-year commercial slump – a veritable eternity in the industry at the time. The album performed poorly in almost every market, and none of the singles generated much radio or retail interest. While partnering with Arif Mardin resulted in some of their most sonically cohesive and engaging material in recent memory, it was clear their musical approach was no longer clicking in a public sense.

By the end of 1974, the top brass at Atlantic had also become more concerned about the group's dwindling appeal. In the 2020 *How Can You Mend A Broken Heart* documentary, Barry remembered: 'They were about to drop us. We had to adopt a new sound. We had to adopt a new attitude'. Unwilling to give up on his proteges, Robert Stigwood advocated for another chance to get them back on track. That meant starting from scratch – including their working environment. The most popular narrative is that it was RSO labelmate Eric Clapton who urged the Gibbs to escape Britain for sunny Miami, where he'd written and recorded his first studio album in four years – *461 Ocean Boulevard* – a year prior. The title was the address of a waterfront house that then-RSO Records President Bill Oakes rented for him in the Golden Beach neighbourhood. The result was an unqualified comeback for Clapton, yielding his first US number one album and single – a cover of Bob Marley's 'I Shot The Sheriff'. Others claim Stigwood led the charge, alleging Clapton wouldn't have been so generous with his encouragement as he'd been quite bitter about Stigwood's close relationship with them. Regardless of who did the nudging, the Gibbs and their partners – along with Alan Kendall, Dennis Bryon and Blue Weaver – were on a plane to Florida on 1 January for a fresh start.

The burgeoning Miami music scene was gaining national influence, significantly propelled by the local independent label TK Records. It was founded by record producer and executive Henry Stone and singer Steve Alaimo (who coincidentally recorded the original 1963 version of 'Every Day I Have To Cry', which The Bee Gees later covered for their sixth Australian single). TK's roster – which included artists like George McCrae, The Hues Corporation, and KC and the Sunshine Band – was responsible for a number of early American disco hits. The Bee Gees weren't strangers to Black music. Even their early Australian recordings had soul earmarks, which they refined more obviously for their later productions like 'To Love Somebody', 'I Can't See Nobody', and 'The Change Is Made'. Black artists like Nina Simone, Al Green, P. P. Arnold, and The Staple Singers had enthusiastically covered Bee Gees songs. But to connect to a contemporary mid-1970s audience, the Gibbs would need more than the theatrical ballads that had been their ticket into the limelight.

Another important ingredient was booking time at Criteria Studios – a renowned facility that had been in business about as long as the Gibbs had been singing. Florida transplant Maxwell 'Mack' Emerman opened the studio in 1958 from funds he'd saved working for his father as a candy delivery man during the day and as a sound engineer at local clubs at night. Seven years later, the studio's first big chart success helped put it on the map – soul icon James Brown booked it to record what became his 1965 King Records hit 'I Got You (I Feel Good)'. By 1970, Criteria Studios' reputation had attracted many artists – especially R&B/soul acts like Brook Benton, 'Wicked' Wilson Pickett, and Betty Wright. Karl Richardson, The Bee Gees' eventual engineer-turned-co-producer, worked at Criteria Studios in the early 1970s when Atlantic began regularly using it as a secondary home for many of its heavy-hitting New York-based artists. Karl told the authors in a 2022 interview: 'They booked our Studio B from 3:00 p.m. on until the wee hours – you know, whenever they went home. We could use the studio for other purposes in the morning, for things like transfers, quick sessions, voice-overs – whatever we did'.

By 1973, Criteria Studios had added a third studio, with prime albums by Derek and the Dominos, Aretha Franklin, The Allman Brothers, and Grand Funk Railroad among their list of productions. Karl also moved up in the ranks as things got busier: 'We had done some Delaney & Bonnie records, and some Aretha, and Lulu. As I was working my way up from being a disc-mastering engineer to an assistant engineer and finally a full-blown engineer, I'd gotten my hands on a number of Atlantic artists'.

A long line of big Atlantic talent and their prolific producers were more than eager to flock to Miami, especially when the harsher New York winters hit. Criteria Studios soon gained the nickname 'Atlantic South'. Karl said, 'Their production staff was Arif Mardin, Tom Dowd, and Jerry Wexler, and they all had vacation homes in Miami Beach. So, I would go and hang out with Jerry and fix his stereo at his house – you know, whatever. They became normal folks just cruising in and around the studio all the time'. Karl's entry into The Bee Gees camp happened one day while he and Arif were working on another project:

> Arif was brilliant, you know. He was an arranger, and he was gifted and had great ears. And I was working on an album with Average White Band – half was cut in New York, and half was done at Criteria Studios in Studio B. And Arif goes, 'Wait till you see the group I'm bringing in. They sing like angels'. And I said, 'Who's that?'. He says, 'It's The Bee Gees'. I said, 'Oh, I know who they are. They've been around a few blocks!' [*laughs*] So, me being aware of pop music at the time, I said, 'Yeah, sure, I'd love to work with them!'

The Gibbs and their entourage quickly became enamoured with their new surroundings. The sunshine and warm climate was an easy comparison to what they'd experienced living and working in Australia, especially the years they spent in Redcliffe, Queensland. Karl recalled: 'They had all this inspiration coming down to Florida – you know, hanging out on the beach – it was a very changing environment'.

All good vibes notwithstanding, The Bee Gees were saddled with a tremendous amount of pressure to craft a hit album. Sessions for what became *Main Course* began on 6 January. Karl affirmed:

> They came into the studio, and it was obvious to me at about day one-and-a-half that Barry Gibb was the leader of the pack. I mean, he was the creator. They all had input into the records, but you could tell that Barry was the driver. That sound of the three brothers together ... I would put them on one microphone – in cardioid, of all things, which meant that the vocals were on the side of the mic. Usually, it would be facing whoever sang the lead part, if, let's say, they were doing three-part harmony. So, on something like 'Nights On Broadway', it would be duelling vocals.

Karl also remembers that some of Criteria Studios' technology was novel to the Gibbs and the band, and it heightened the excitement: 'We all hit it off right away. Everyone was really enthusiastic. I was giving them stereo mixes in the headphones, and I don't think they'd really heard [that] before. When I'd cue them up, they'd say, 'Wow! Can you hear that? Yeah! I can hear everything!'. Everybody got a charge out of being there'.

Despite all the new and interesting elements at play, the first few days were reportedly a bit of a struggle. The initial batch of songs written in the first two weeks of January were all Barry and Robin co-writes that were more reminiscent of their past than representative of the forward-thinking sound they desperately needed to change their fortunes. Blue Weaver recalled the first track recorded 'was a sort of ploddy ballad called 'Was It All In Vain?'. I always remember the first line, because in the house where we were staying – in 461 Ocean Boulevard – the dining table, above it was a chandelier, and I think Barry must've got the opening lyric; he must've been sitting there, looked up, and the first line was 'As I gaze into the chandelier', or 'My chandelier', or something, which I think, a day or two later, I read and changed it to 'As I gaze into my can of beer'. The song wasn't developed beyond the first session, and Blue feels that 'They'll think it wasn't important because it wasn't worthy. But it was important to me, because it was my introduction to The Bee Gees. Nobody's ever heard that, so, obviously it *was* all in vain. We knew after a couple of days because then we started getting better ideas'.

Two ballads followed – 'Your Love Will Save The World', which was eventually dropped from the project, and 'Country Lanes', which survived the final cut without further apparent tinkering. They also recorded an early version of 'Wind Of Change', which was reportedly vastly different from the fast, gritty iteration that made the final cut of the album. At Blue Weaver's request, there was even an effort to resurrect 'Only One Woman', the hit the brothers had penned for their friends The Marbles in 1968. 'I just said, 'Barry, I've never heard you sing this'. We did a fair bit of work, but it was never released. I love that song with Graham Bonnet singing it'.

In the 1979 book *Bee Gees: The Authorised Biography*, Linda Gibb recalled the shaky start: 'They were in the studio putting some tracks down. Dick [Ashby] and Tom [Kennedy] and I were the onlookers, and we were looking at each other, thinking, 'This isn't what's happening now. They've got to write something more up-tempo''. Atlantic head Ahmet Ertegun and Robert Stigwood were also concerned. In the book, Stigwood confessed: 'When they started, I didn't like a lot of the tracks. I flew down to Miami and told them I wanted to scrap a lot of the things they'd done and I'd like them to start again. I would swallow the costs – not to worry – but to really open their ears and find out in contemporary terms what was going on'.

The brothers justifiably had cold feet about all the stylistic changes being asked of them. Barry: 'We've always been capable of writing [R&B] music, but we were too scared of having the confidence that we could play it as good or better than others. I think the main lesson we learned from Arif was that the music has to be vibrant. It has to have some magic about it'. On 10 January, Arif paused the sessions, suggesting the Gibbs take a break and listen to current pop artists as inspiration for the next group of songs they would write. The brief hiatus paid off in dividends. Ten days later, they returned with the dynamic 'Nights On Broadway' (its original working title, 'All The Lights On Broadway', was changed at Ahmet Ertegun's insistence the song needed to be more 'adult', according to Barry). It was fresher and more innovative than what they'd been working on up to that point. Whatever reservations they'd had about finding their funk had vanished.

'Nights On Broadway' is most famously touted as the track that prompted the discovery of Barry's falsetto voice. Arif Mardin recalled in a 2001 interview with *The Light Millennium*: 'During the recording of the album, I asked Barry to take his vocal up one octave. The poor man said, 'If I take it up one octave, I'm going to shout and it's going to be terrible'. He softened up a little bit, and that's how their falsetto was born'. In 2001, Barry told *Mojo*: 'Arif said to me, 'Can you scream?'. I said, 'Under certain circumstances'. He said, 'Can you scream in tune?'. I said, 'Well, I'll try!''. It should be noted that Barry, Robin, and Maurice had all contributed falsetto vocals to their recordings prior to 1975. It had been employed more subtly as far back as 1967 on 'Please Read Me', then 'Let There Be Love' and 'Melody Fair' – and certainly on the *Mr. Natural* tracks 'Dogs' and 'Voices'. But it was Robin who had taken the first leap with an actual falsetto lead on the outro of 'It Doesn't Matter Much To Me', recorded in 1972. But Barry's purposeful ad-libs on the closing of 'Nights On Broadway' were a historic – and permanent – addition to The Bee Gees' sonic identity.

Blue Weaver's lifelong training and keyboard work brought an invaluable complexity and depth to the *Main Course* arrangements. His experimentation with synthesisers added interesting textures to the classic instruments the rest of the band were playing. The synth bass on 'Nights On Broadway' is particularly effective. Blue's studio contributions over the next few years would help shape not just The Bee Gees' sound, but the way they composed music – often without much-deserved credit. Though there were real strings for sweetening on many tracks they recorded moving forward, the group's previous reliance on a full orchestra as scaffolding for their melodies was, with a few exceptions, all but gone.

The team continued to build on the momentum of 'Nights On Broadway', spending long hours in Studio C while they built an additional eight songs over the next month. A few days after 'Nights On Broadway', they recorded 'Come On Over' – a balmy ballad that was a clear country-rock crossover. By 30 January, five more new songs were in some state of completion: 'Jive Talkin'', 'Songbird', 'Fanny (Be Tender With My Love)', 'All This Making Love', and 'Edge Of The Universe'. A revamped take of 'Wind Of Change' was recorded on 17 February.

Another new element introduced to the *Main Course* sessions was the click track. Since the band were mostly recording as a live ensemble, Arif Mardin used the click to keep everyone on tempo. In his 2015 autobiography *You Should Be Dancing: My Life With The Bee Gees*, Dennis Bryon remembered: 'It's an electronic beat generated by who knows what. The click was set to a fixed tempo and pumped through the [head]phones'. Dennis recalls it first being used on the recording of 'All This Making Love', and that it was 'obnoxious'. But it tightened the arrangements and perfected the precise grooves Arif was seeking.

In a matter of weeks, the brothers' songwriting and creative direction had made a remarkable about-face, finding a note-perfect midpoint between their melancholic pop sensibilities and R&B aspiration. Arif Mardin had figured out how to push the Gibbs in exactly all the right places and translate everything into actionable terms. But it's important to acknowledge how vastly crucial the brothers' raw talent and accumulated experience were to *Main Course*'s conception, as past analyses have sometimes implied that Mardin had unearthed a trio of dilettantes and expertly transformed them into savvy artists. The Bee Gees had always had the ability to make an album like *Main Course* – they just needed the right environment and encouragement to buy into their own competency.

On 21 February, the album sessions were completed with what became the closing track, 'Baby As You Turn Away'. The tapes travelled back to Atlantic in New York with Arif Mardin, who added strings and horns to some tracks, Joe Farrell's saxophone solo and Ray Barretto's congas to 'Wind Of Change', and Don Brooks' harmonica to 'Songbird'.

The band returned to the Isle of Man, taking a break in March. In April, they began rehearsals for a North American tour, which was scheduled to run from May to September. They set up in the restaurant of the Douglas Bay Hotel, which was shuttered during the winter months when tourism in the area was low.

Everyone's feeling that the album had evolved into something special seemed unanimous, but 'Jive Talkin'' especially had created a significant amount of excitement in the studio, and it emerged as the front-runner for the set's lead single. Robert Stigwood strongly agreed, but apparently, not everyone was convinced. According to Maurice, 'We were over the moon about 'Jive Talkin'', but when we played it to people at the record company, they didn't want it … Stigwood was fighting with them, telling them they were mad and it was a guaranteed number one single, and we were getting secret phone calls from the record company asking us if we could talk him out of it'.

'Nights On Broadway' was allegedly what Atlantic wanted to put out first. Eventually, Robert and the group won the argument, and on 8 May, RSO issued 'Jive Talkin'' as the appetiser to *Main Course*. Three weeks later, the single entered the US *Billboard* Hot 100 chart at number 87. On 9 August, it became their second American number one hit.

On 21 May, Robert Stigwood threw the group a 20th anniversary party in New York City at the Promenade Café in the Rockefeller Center – presumably commemorating the year Barbara Gibb reportedly discovered the brothers singing together for the first time in their Chorlton-cum-Hardy family home. Ahmet Ertegun and Average White Band were among the guests. Three days later – with 'Jive Talkin'' gaining traction and the tour imminently starting – *Main Course* was released in the US. It was a major moment of truth for The Bee Gees and their new sound in the world's largest record market.

Main Course (1975)

Personnel:
Barry Gibb: vocals, rhythm guitar
Robin Gibb: vocals
Maurice Gibb: vocals, bass, rhythm guitar
Dennis Bryon: drums, percussion
Alan Kendall: lead guitar, pedal steel
Blue Weaver: keyboards, synthesisers
Joe Farrell: tenor sax ('Wind Of Change')
Don Brooks: harmonica ('Songbird')
Ray Barretto: congas ('Wind Of Change')

Strings, horns, woodwind arrangements: Arif Mardin
Concertmaster: Gene Orloff
Producer: Arif Mardin
Engineers: Karl Richardson (Criteria Studios); Lew Hahn (Atlantic Recording Studios)
Recorded between 6 January 1975 and 21 February 1975 at Criteria Studios, Miami and Atlantic Recording Studios, New York
Release dates: UK: June 1975, US: 24 May 1975
Chart positions: Canada: 1, Spain: 8, US: 14, Australia: 29, West Germany: 29, New Zealand: 36

Often considered to be The Bee Gees' finest album, *Main Course* was a novel showcase for the R&B ground they broke in the studio that also retained the warmth and emotion that had made their music singularly special, to begin with. Reviews were generally favourable, tipping their hat to Arif Mardin's production talents and the brothers' infallible singing. There was a small contingent that were dismissive, insisting The Bee Gees had flagrantly appropriated the Black artists they'd claimed to admire. *Rolling Stone's* not-so-subtly backhanded review was among them, but it did concede the group had done so 'with remarkable flair'.

With *Main Course* being such a critical album, Robert Stigwood wanted to make an impact with it on record store racks. Having a distinctive cover was of paramount importance. To this end, he approached the California-based design firm Pacific Eye and Ear with a view to creating something special. Founding the company in 1972, Ernie Cefalu served as creative director. During the golden age of album cover art, the company became the premier source of designs, logos, lettering, and packaging. Between 1972 and 1986, they created 189 covers for acts, including Aerosmith, Alice Cooper, Black Sabbath, and The Marshall Tucker Band. Cefalu's most iconic work is without a doubt The Rolling Stones's lips-and-tongue logo, which first appeared on their 1971 album *Sticky Fingers*. Cefalu recalled: 'At the beginning of April 1975, I was contacted by The Bee Gees' manager, and my friend, Robert Stigwood, with whom I had worked on the very first *Jesus Christ Superstar* stage tour. Robert and I had worked really well together in the past, so calling me in, as he put It, was 'a real no-brainer call!'. He was deeply involved with the Brothers Gibb, and he went on to explain why this new album *Main Course* was so critical'.

The album artwork comprised four main parts: the new and soon-to-be-iconic Bee Gees logo, a nude woman bathing in a spoon, and a stream of weaving decorative ribbon that pulls the eye around the components – all set against a floral background. As wholesome as The Bee Gees' image had always been, the cover seemed a little risqué, but few, if any, realised the subtle use of the spoon as a drug reference.

Cefalu said, 'Robert always said that the *Jesus Christ Superstar* logo was one of his all-time favourites. He was also a huge fan of Pacific Eye and Ear. He wanted me to create a unique, ownable logo using their name that would represent the disco era for the band'. He proudly states that he 'created a really cool lettering logo – one of my best ever'. The package became complete when Cefalu 'worked with artist Drew Struzan, to marry my logo to a highly-memorable album cover illustration. Both the logo, [and] Drew's illustration of 'Beauty in a Coke Spoon', quickly became iconic symbols synonymous with the disco craze'. The floral background pattern varied in colour slightly in various territories: the UK and US covers were printed in olive green and light blue, while West Germany opted for emerald green and grey. In Greece, the cover dispensed with the pattern altogether and used a solid green background.

The album was The Bee Gees' first to include printed lyrics, and the insert was also a useful indicator of the pressing's country of origin, with olive green being used in the UK, whilst white was chosen in North America. In the Netherlands, it was a bright turquoise, and in Germany, a stark black. The small group photo on the lyric insert was taken by Ed Caraeff during a two-day shoot at his house in Coldwater Canyon, California.

Commercially, the set accomplished exactly what everyone hoped it would, which was to return The Bee Gees to public favour. It became their first US top 20 album since 1969. It remained on *Billboard*'s Top LPs & Tape chart for 74 weeks through December 1976. It was the first Bee Gees album since *Best Of Bee Gees* to be certified Gold by the RIAA in the US. In Canada, it topped the charts and was certified Double Platinum. Despite 'Jive Talkin'' being a top five hit in the UK, *Main Course* failed to chart there.

The omitted track 'Your Love Will Save the World' was recorded and released by American soul singer Percy Sledge (best known for his 1966 soul classic 'When A Man Loves A Woman') on his 1994 album *Blue Night*. A completed Bee Gees version from 1975 does exist with

Robin and Barry alternating lead vocals. Their version is streets ahead of Sledge's cover, and it's unfortunate it wasn't ever released officially.

Though *Main Course* has been reissued on LP, cassette, and CD several times over the years, a deluxe treatment with bonus material for which fans have been longing has never surfaced. In the summer 2020, Capitol/UMG did remaster and reissue the set on vinyl, which was offered on standard black – and what was fancifully touted as 'whitewater'-coloured (translucent white) – vinyl with the original artwork and lyric insert.

Main Course also reignited broader interest in the Gibbs as contemporary songwriters, with a number of established artists rushing to cover songs from the album and having success with various singles – among them were Olivia Newton-John, Candi Staton, Rufus featuring Chaka Khan, and The Seekers.

'Nights On Broadway' (Barry Gibb, Robin Gibb, Maurice Gibb)

Recorded at Criteria Studios, Miami: 20 and 30 January 1975
Chart positions: Canada: 2, US: 7, Netherlands: 8, New Zealand: 14, Belgium: 15, West Germany: 17, Australia: 67

The opening track marked a critical turning point for the group during the recording sessions. After struggling to write through a contemporary lens for the first few weeks of their Miami sojourn, the Gibbs minted a track that was to change their entire musical approach forever. 'Nights On Broadway' is arguably one of their greatest sonic achievements, capturing a perfect collision of their harmonic and melodic strengths. Blue Weaver's expert work on acoustic piano and synthesiser offered enormous depth to the arrangement. Dennis Bryon's steady drumming has been often underrated, but it's so essential to the cohesive movement of this and so many other Bee Gees songs of that period.

Another hallmark is the song's beautiful slow middle section. The production team had reportedly cut it from the mix early on, but at Robert Stigwood's insistence, it was reattached – with great difficulty, as it involved splicing the multitrack recording that had already been completed. Radio stations did receive a promotional single with the section edited out (which chopped the song down by nearly two minutes), perhaps an acknowledgement that the full-length version might be a gamble for radio programmers.

While much has been made of Barry's vocal innovation on the track, Maurice also played a key role in the 'Nights On Broadway' story. It was well known that he frequently sang the highest parts of their harmonies, but he also had the ability to match the tone of Barry's falsetto. The subject has caused some gentle argument among fans over the years, but it was he, not Barry, who sang the 'Blamin' it all' ad libs in live performances during that period when Barry employed his natural voice to support the main melody line. The recording from the 20 December 1976 Los Angeles Forum concert on the *Children Of The World* tour, captured for 1977's *Here At Last ... Bee Gees ... Live* album, serves as the best example.

The single became The Bee Gees' second consecutive top ten hit in North America, solidifying *Main Course*'s success. It was a puzzling non-charting flop in the UK, which was odd after 'Jive Talkin'' had done relatively well there. American R&B singer Candi Staton covered 'Nights On Broadway' on her 1977 album *Music Speaks Louder Than Words*, and it became a top 20 *Billboard* R&B hit. It was the only version of the song to chart in the UK, where it reached number 6.

In 2003, the song was resurrected with comically-altered lyrics as the theme to the recurring *Saturday Night Live* comedy sketch 'The Barry Gibb Talk Show', which featured cast member Jimmy Fallon and singer-songwriter Justin Timberlake as exaggerated caricatures of Barry and Robin hosting heated conversations with political dignitaries, media figures, and celebrities. Fallon and Timberlake are both self-proclaimed Bee Gees fans. Barry, who claimed that the gag initially upset him because it mischaracterised him and Robin, appeared at the end of the '... Talk Show' sketch that aired on the 21 December 2013 episode of *SNL*, adding his infamous falsetto lines to the closing theme alongside Fallon and Timberlake. It was the final time the sketch was performed, most likely out of respect for Robin's passing the previous year.

'Jive Talkin'' (Barry Gibb, Robin Gibb, Maurice Gibb)

Recorded at Criteria Studios, Miami: 30 January and 2 February 1975
Chart positions: Canada: 1, US: 1, New Zealand: 4, Ireland: 5, UK: 5, Italy: 8, Australia: 14, Netherlands: 23, West Germany: 23, Belgium: 24

'Jive Talkin'' has become one of the group's most enduring hits, yet it seems to be underappreciated for how ahead of its time it was. White pop groups generally weren't fashioning tracks this slick in 1975, and the Gibbs must have surprised themselves when the irresistibly funky syncopated percussion and chugging guitars started to come together. It sounded like nothing they had written or recorded before – not even the catchiest songs on *Mr. Natural* were this playful and sexy. Barry had used his breathy voice on previous songs – like 'Don't Wanna Live Inside Myself' and 'Charade' – but it had never been employed with such overt flirtation. All things considered, 'Jive Talkin'' was a gutsy wager as the album's first single for a group whose livelihood hung in the balance.

The origin of the song's unmistakable intro is one of Barry's most frequently spun stories, although some disparate variations have been told over the years. The preferred narrative is that concrete sections of the Julia Tuttle Causeway, the road which bridges Miami Beach to Miami proper across Biscayne Bay, created a compelling 'chunka-chunka' rhythm under the tyres of the Jeep he drove between 461 Ocean Boulevard and Criteria Studios every day (although that route would take a driver *very* unnecessarily far south). Karl Richardson, however, has said it was originally heard during a limousine ride on Broad Causeway along 125th Street, which, geographically, would make more sense. Barry's wife Linda is sometimes credited with inspiring the song title by allegedly suggesting to Barry that the sound was the 'drive talking'. Alan Kendall replicated the effect with his electric guitar, recalling in a 2019 interview: 'We were in the studio and Arif said, 'Can you do chicken pickin'?' I didn't really know what that was, so I just played this one note and muted it and thought it sounded like a chicken: 'tick-a-tick-*cah*-tick-a-tick-*cah*!'. Mixed with Barry's rhythm guitar, it really worked'.

The other long-standing story is that the lyric was originally written with the Gibbs equating the term 'jive' with the jazz dance originated by Black Americans in the 1930s – thus, an early version of the refrain was apparently 'It's just your jive talkin'/You dance with your eyes'. One of Arif Mardin's many lessons for his sibling students during the sessions was to clue them in on the term 'jive''s more modern definition as slang for 'bullshit', which gradually evolved the lyric, as evidenced by an early working tape. The official lines 'Love talkin' is all very fine, yeah/Jive talkin' just isn't a crime/And if there's somebody you love till you die', replaced the earlier 'Your night walkin' is all very fine, yeah/Love stalkin', it wasn't your crime/And when you're out walkin' with some other guy'.

Blue Weaver's prog rock acumen brought synthesisers prominently into the mix – an element that many mainstream pop outfits artists hadn't yet explored to a great extent. The doubling of Blue's synth bass and Maurice's electric bass on 'Jive Talkin'' was an innovation at the time, adding even more texture to the gabby interplay of the guitars, vocals, and rhythm section.

Though everyone in the Gibb camp was certain 'Jive Talkin'' would be a hit, The Bee Gees' lack of commercial clout posed a problem in convincing radio stations to give the new track a chance. Another well-worn yarn that has hung around over the years is that RSO pushed out 7" promotional copies to all US radio stations with blank labels, forcing them to listen to it without knowing who it was. That has since been disproven, though. Apparently, however, there *were* unmarked tapes of the song handed to a select few programmers and critics to gauge their initial reaction to it. Whatever the strategy was, it worked fairly quickly. Ten weeks after first entering the *Billboard* Hot 100, The Bee Gees had a US number one single for the first time in four years.

In the UK, positive response was just as swift, and in response to the blossoming hit, the BBC asked for a filmed performance for inclusion on *Top Of The Pops* – the first time The Bee Gees had appeared on the programme since performing 'Wouldn't I Be Someone' live in the studio on 6 July 1973. The request caught the group and management short. At home with his brothers on the Isle of Man, Barry took the initiative and popped into Terry Clough's Kelly Records shop in Douglas, and asked if he could borrow a guitar for the filming that was to take place at the local venue, Palace Lido. While the facility's daily rent of £25.00 was acceptable, Terry recalls the group and the BBC production team asking for 'More light, more light', as the Lido stage equipment was woefully inadequate. The less-than-ideal result was aired on 10 July. Afterwards, the BBC conceded that the video quality was not good enough – especially with 'Jive Talkin'' moving quickly up the charts. The Bee Gees were soon invited to the BBC *Top Of The Pops* studio in London to do the job properly. The re-shot video aired on 24 July and 7 August.

'Jive Talkin''s popularity was renewed two years later when it was included on the *Saturday Night Fever* soundtrack. In June 1987, it was covered and released as a single by UK music collaborative Boogie Box High, the founder of which was Andros Georgiou – a second cousin to British singer-songwriter and former Wham! front man George Michael, who had been commissioned to sing it. His vocal was never credited because of contractual issues with his label, Epic Records. In the end, it didn't matter as the public knew full well who they were hearing, and the revamped version returned the song to the UK top ten.

Popular American R&B band Rufus (featuring Chaka Khan) covered 'Jive Talkin'' on their eponymous album in November 1975. The single reached 35 on *Billboard*'s R&B chart in early 1976. *Rufus Featuring Chaka Khan* was the best-selling American R&B LP that year.

The song was a staple of The Bee Gees' concert setlist for the rest of their career, and has appeared on countless greatest hits compilations and all three of the live albums in their catalogue.

Barry included his own remake of 'Jive Talkin'' on his 2021 bluegrass-inspired album *Greenfields*, where he was joined by Jay Buchanan of American rock band Rival Sons, and country music singer Miranda Lambert. That version falls somewhere between pop and country but loses some of its original efficacy through a slower tempo. It would have been interesting to keep it at its normal clip with a rootsier rhythm section.

'Wind Of Change' (Barry Gibb, Robin Gibb)
Recorded at Criteria Studios, Miami: 17 February 1975

In some ways, 'Wind Of Change' feels like a preamble to 'Stayin' Alive' with its lyrical references to New York City and survival on the streets. Released as the B-side to 'Jive Talkin'', it drives the urban brassiness of 'Nights On Broadway' a few steps further in intensity. The track's tone and subject matter raised a few eyebrows among critics at the time, with *Rolling Stone*'s Stephen Holden rebuking the brothers for daring 'to pretend to speak for New York Black experience'.

Beginning life early in the album sessions, it's unclear if the song's musical and lyrical structure evolved from the original version, but it's certain that the tempo was increased from the initially slow take to the soulful driving speed we are familiar with.

Multi-instrumentalist Joe Farrell supplied the short, but searing saxophone solo after the first chorus. He was a respected session player who was well known to Arif Mardin, having played on projects with Mose Allison, The Band, George Benson, Chick Corea, and Aretha Franklin.

The song was used as the theme for a recurring Hockey Night in Canada featurette titled *Showdown*, which aired on the country's CBC network in the late 1970s and early 1980s.

'Wind Of Change' was incorporated into the 1976 tour setlist and subsequently included on the *Here At Last ... Bee Gees ... Live* album.

'Songbird' (Barry Gibb, Robin Gibb, Maurice Gibb, Blue Weaver)

Recorded at Criteria Studios, Miami: 30 January 1975

After three dynamic opening tracks – possibly the best introductory sequence on a Bee Gees album ever – the pace slows markedly with the beautiful ballad 'Songbird'. In *The Ultimate Biography of The Bee Gees: Tales of the Brothers Gibb*, Blue Weaver claimed to have had 'most of that melody for a long time, since just after The Strawbs. One night, I was just sitting at the piano and playing that, and Barry walked past and said, 'Oh, that's nice', and started humming along, came up with a melody, and then he sang the word 'songbird'. He's very quick, and usually, the first things out of his mouth end up actually being part of the lyric and usually the hook'.

This was the first non-Gibb songwriting credit to appear on a Bee Gees album since Vince Melouney's composition 'Such A Shame' was included on *Idea* in 1968.

The harmonica of American blues harp player Don Brooks – who had previously played on projects by Yoko Ono, Waylon Jennings, Jerry Jeff Walker, and Don McLean – is featured prominently from the second verse.

American singer Jimmy Ruffin recorded a version of 'Songbird' for his 1980 album *Sunrise*, which was entirely written and produced by Robin and Blue.

'Fanny (Be Tender With My Love)' (Barry Gibb, Robin Gibb, Maurice Gibb)

Recorded at Criteria Studios, Miami: 30 January, 17 and 19 February 1975

Chart positions: Canada: 2, New Zealand: 7, US: 12, Belgium: 29, West Germany: 42, Australia: 61

In the 1990 *Tales From The Brothers Gibb* box set liner notes, Maurice quipped: 'Without a doubt one of the best R&B songs we ever wrote. I love Arif Mardin's production and his understanding from three brothers who love R&B'.

The track is certainly one of the album's finest moments. Recorded after 'Nights On Broadway' had revealed the contrasting power of Barry's falsetto, this song was the first attempt to weave it into a main melody. Robin's falsetto can also be heard across the two key changes near the end. The complex ribboning of the voices here is infinitely impressive, and the blend is sometimes so smooth it's hard to discern who is singing which line. Blue Weaver admitted that the escalating melody and key changes were more than a subtle nod to Hall and Oates' 1973 single 'She's Gone' from their *Abandoned Luncheonette* album – also produced by Arif Mardin.

'Fanny ...' is one of just a few of The Bee Gees' major hits that they never performed live. In 2001, Maurice alluded to the reason in an interview with *Billboard*: 'We all love that one, but it's just a bitch to sing'. In the same article, he claims legendary producer Quincy Jones told him it was one of his favourite R&B songs of all time.

As the album's third single, 'Fanny ...' continued their high-charting trend in North America, but the song didn't find an audience in Britain. The fact that its protagonist's name also has a sexual connotation in Commonwealth slang (for the unenlightened, it is used as a vulgar reference to female genitalia) may have hurt its chances of being taken seriously in those markets. However, she was indeed a real person – a housekeeper named Fanny Cummings who worked at 461 Ocean Boulevard, and later for Robin and his family and at the Gibbs' Middle Ear Studios.

The song was covered multiple times in the late 1970s by Australian singer Gino Cunico, US singer, actress and RSO labelmate Linda Clifford, Canadian singer Carl Graves, and soul singer Bill Fredericks who in 1977 released the album *Love With You*, which was comprised almost entirely of Bee Gees remakes.

'All This Making Love' (Barry Gibb, Robin Gibb)
Recorded at Criteria Studios, Miami: 30 January 1975

An exasperated romp begins side two of *Main Course*. Barry once described the lyric as a play-by-play of the mechanics of sexual intercourse. His and Robin's alternating lead vocals are interspersed with comical sound effects, including a voice that gasps and then yelps 'Wave goodbye!', and a rather guttural growling tiger. All hilarity aside, it's a solid, engaging track with Blue Weaver's playful piano line and Alan Kendall's distorted guitar punching through the mix.

'Country Lanes' (Barry Gibb, Robin Gibb)
Recorded at Criteria Studios, Miami: 7 January 1975

Robin's spotlight moment on *Main Course* seems to be the only track preserved from the rejected batch of ballads from early in the album's recording sessions. Even though 'Country Lanes' is a characteristically 'old' Bee Gees composition, Blue Weaver's soulful piano and Dennis Bryon's deliberate drum rhythm give it some freshness.

In all markets, it was the B-side of 'Fanny (Be Tender with My Love)'.

Australian folk group The Seekers recorded a rather good version for their 1976 album *Giving And Taking*, featuring a lead vocal by Louisa Wisseling. That recording was produced by John Farrar, whose connection to The Bee Gees went back to their shared Australian days. Farrar maintained an indirect relationship with the Gibbs over the years as principal writer and producer for close family friend Olivia Newton-John.

'Come On Over' (Barry Gibb, Robin Gibb)
Recorded at Criteria Studios, Miami: 23 January 1975

The Gibbs had written and recorded a number of country tracks prior to 1975, so they seemed well-positioned to capitalise on the country-pop crossover trend that was emerging in the American music scene at the time. Robin and Barry again used their contrasting lead vocals in call-and-answer fashion on the verses and chorus. Alan Kendall's pedal steel adds effective texture to the rhythm section.

Olivia Newton-John released a cover version in early 1976, and it served as the title track from her seventh studio album of the same name. It reached 23 on the *Billboard* Hot 100 and was top five on the magazine's country singles chart.

'Edge Of The Universe' (Barry Gibb, Robin Gibb)
Recorded at Criteria Studios, Miami: 30 January 1975

In 1990, Barry described this song as 'a humorous flight of fancy about an alien and his pet dog. Baffling really'. The lyric is somewhere between abstract and absurd – perhaps as a specific backward nod to the fantastical subject matter of their 1967 track 'Barker Of The U.F.O.'. Nonetheless, it was certainly reminiscent of the weird characters and stories they wrote in the late 1960s. Blue Weaver's wheezy synthesisers add to the whimsy.

If the records kept of the *Main Course* sessions are correct, 'Edge Of The Universe' rounded out a rather ambitious studio day on 30 January 1975 when they also recorded at least a good portion of 'Jive Talkin'', 'Songbird', 'All This Making Love', and 'Fanny (Be Tender with My Love)'.

This track was the B-side to 'Nights On Broadway', although a new live version surfaced two years later as the only single from *Here at Last ... Bee Gees ... Live.*

'Baby As You Turn Away' (Barry Gibb, Robin Gibb, Maurice Gibb)

Recorded at Criteria Studios, Miami: 21 February 1975

The closing and last-recorded track is a mellifluous acoustic guitar-driven ballad that seemed custom-made to ensure Barry's falsetto had an opportunity to stretch to a full and complete lead. Maurice and Barry – in their natural registers – seem to be sharing the main vocal line on the choruses. For many fans, the track is a hidden gem among other more oft-discussed songs that could have easily been a single.

Michelle Phillips – formerly of American folk outfit The Mamas & The Papas – included her version of the song on her only solo album, 1977's *Victim Of Romance*. Welsh singer Tom Jones revamped it on his 1979 studio effort *Do You Take This Man*. Both are awkwardly plodding next to the subtle richness of the original.

On 30 May, a 40-city tour began at Hara Arena in Trotwood, Ohio (a suburb of Dayton). With the album not yet making a dent at retail, attendance at the first shows was understandably low. Things gradually improved by the time they played a 7 July show at Wollman Rink in New York's Central Park. *Variety*'s Fred Kirby remarked in his concert review that they 'seemed to more than half fill the 8,000-seat rink'.

The setlist contained five of the ten *Main Course* songs, three tracks from *Mr. Natural*, and a mix of familiar older tunes with a few interesting outliers: 'I've Gotta Get A Message To You', 'Edge Of The Universe', 'Come On Over', 'Don't Wanna Live Inside Myself', 'Words', 'Throw A Penny', 'Down The Road'; a medley of 'New York Mining Disaster 1941'/'Run To Me'/'Don't Forget To Remember'/'Odessa'/'Holiday'/'I Can't See Nobody'; 'How Can You Mend A Broken Heart', 'Jive Talkin'', 'Road To Alaska', 'To Love Somebody', 'Massachusetts', 'I Started A Joke', 'Nights On Broadway', 'Wind Of Change', 'Lonely Days', and 'Heavy Breathing'.

RSO labelmates Revelation (a New York-bred soul quartet who had signed with Robert Stigwood the year before) supported The Bee Gees for most of the tour.

On 11 July – en route to playing two dates at Milwaukee's Summerfest music festival – the group stopped in Chicago to record an instalment of *Soundstage*, a live concert television series broadcast by the city's Public Broadcasting Service affiliate, WTTW. In addition to many of the tour songs, the Gibbs offered quick takes of 'Lollipop', 'Happy Birthday

Sweet Sixteen', 'Bye Bye Love', and 'Alexander's Ragtime Band', which they would have sung in their early club days in Australia. They performed a new, slower blues-hued rendition of 'To Love Somebody', which featured a guest vocal by fellow RSO singer Yvonne Elliman. It's unknown if adding her was impromptu, but it seems like it was at least quickly planned, as Elliman can be seen reading lyrics written on her hand while singing the second verse incorrectly. The audience's reaction to the opening chug of 'Jive Talkin'' was particularly enthusiastic – by that time, the single had climbed into the US top 30.

As the tour and *Main Course* picked up steam, The Bee Gees were booked in between concerts on *The Mike Douglas Show* on 21 August (playing 'Jive Talkin'' and 'Nights On Broadway'), and *The Tonight Show Starring Johnny Carson* on 2 September ('Jive Talkin''). The tour concluded on 6 September at the Paramount Theatre in Seattle. The next day, they headed north to begin a 25-stop Canadian leg at Memorial Arena in Victoria, British Columbia.

On 12 September, the group quickly returned to California for their first appearance on *The Midnight Special* since 1973, playing 'Jive Talkin'', 'Nights On Broadway', and 'To Love Somebody', with Australian singer Helen Reddy. The Bee Gees and Reddy had last been on TV together in 1965 on *Bandstand* in Australia.

Overseas, 17-year-old Andy Gibb performed 'Words And Music', a rather good ballad he had written about a year earlier, on the 7 September episode of *Countdown* – a popular Sunday-evening music showcase on the Australian Broadcast Network. In August, he'd joined a new band – Zenta – with guitarist Rick Alford, bassist Paddy Lelliot, singer Glen Greenhalgh, and drummer Trevor Norton. Yet it would seem that Col Joye and Kevin Jacobsen were actively grooming Andy to be a solo artist rather than a frontman. By the end of the year, a hefty batch of new Andy songs – written since his arrival in Australia – were recorded at ATA Studios in Sydney, without his band mates: 'Take A Hold Of Yourself', 'Westfield Mansions', 'Turn Me On', 'You've Got To Live Your Life', 'Too Many People', 'Mister Mover', 'Blackbush City Lost', 'Gone With The Wind', 'Flowing Rivers', and 'In The End'. During these sessions, Andy also recorded 'Twinky', an unreleased Barry and Maurice song written during the group's breakup period. 'In The End' and 'Flowing Rivers' eventually surfaced (albeit with updated arrangements) on Andy's debut RSO album two years later. The latter had a fourth verse at this stage. In August, 'Words And Music' was released as a single (with the rocker 'Westfield Mansions' on the B-side) on the ATA label. It dented the lower region of the Australian singles chart in early 1976, reaching higher positions in some localities. It also cracked the New Zealand top 30. Though the result was only a minor hit, there was certainly enough momentum to prompt Joye and Jacobsen to invest more time in Andy's development over the next several months.

On 4 October – the same day The Bee Gees concluded their Canadian tour at The Forum in Halifax, Nova Scotia – 'Nights On Broadway' entered the *Billboard* Hot 100 just a few weeks after its release. It peaked at seven the week of 10 December, confirming the group's triumphant resurgence as hitmakers – at least in North America. The single did surprisingly less well in other parts of the world where they'd had frequent support over the years.

They were invited back to *The Midnight Special* on 10 October to reprise their rising hit, in addition to performing 'Wind Of Change' and an altered version of their tour medley: 'New York Mining Disaster 1941'/'Run To Me'/'World'/'Holiday'/'I Can't See Nobody', ending with 'How Can You Mend A Broken Heart'.

With the tour finished, the band returned to the UK. In mid-October, Maurice and Yvonne Spenceley announced their engagement – now that marriage was a possibility after his divorce from Lulu became final on 21 August. They decided to make it official in short order and were wed at a small ceremony at the Haywards Heath Register Office in West Sussex on 17 October. Barry was best man, attending on crutches and in a cast after having fallen on the steps of his house and breaking his ankle.

Yvonne Elliman's appearance with The Bee Gees at the Chicago *Soundstage* concert had reportedly opened the door for Barry to write songs for her forthcoming album. Elliman wasn't to release another LP until 1977, but she did record The Bee Gees song 'Love Me' in 1976.

In late 1975, the group were asked to sing six songs for the forthcoming feature film *All This And World War II*. Recording their vocals at Olympic Studios in London, they were already very familiar with the material, as the songs in the movie were all written by The Beatles. Ultimately, only three of The Bee Gees' tracks were included on the soundtrack, which was issued to coincide with the movie launch in October 1976.

In late November and early December, the group embarked on a short promotional tour of Europe, holding press parties in Paris, Milan, Hamburg, Copenhagen and Amsterdam – hoping to boost *Main Course* sales in time for the release of the album's third single 'Fanny (Be Tender With My Love)' at the start of the new year.

Everyone took a much-deserved break for the rest of the year. The icing on the cake was receiving their first Golden Reel Award (for *Main Course*) from AMPEX – an American electronics corporation that manufactured recording media and machines. To qualify, the award-winning album had to have been recorded and mixed solely on AMPEX tape products and also achieve Gold-record certification (at least 500,000 units at the time) from the Recording Industry Association of America (RIAA). AMPEX would also make a donation of $1,000 to a charity of the artist's choice. The Bee Gees opted to route the funds to The Children's Health Council.

Main Course was a desperately needed commercial and artistic refreshment. The group had restored their value at radio and retail, which no doubt encouraged the Atlantic Records brass to recant any remaining considerations they had of ousting The Bee Gees from the label. However, their relationship with Atlantic still came to a distressing end, just as the Gibbs were eager to return to the studio to record the follow-up album in early 1976. The plan was to continue working with producer Arif Mardin, but RSO's decision to end its US distribution deal with Atlantic at the end of 1975 – in favour of syncing with Polydor – resulted in Mardin being contractually unavailable to participate. It was an unimaginable disaster – Arif's expert direction and integration with the band had just started to pay off in all the ways they'd hoped. What now?

1976

Understandably, the Gibbs were deflated by the forced discontinuation of their working relationship with Arif Mardin, though they remained in close contact with him over the years and were to be reunited in 1986.

So, The Bee Gees were charged with the daunting task of making a follow-up to their first commercially successful album in years. The stakes were still high. They quickly searched for a new producer, travelling to Los Angeles in early January to try their hand with production veteran Richard Perry, who had helmed an impressive string of hit albums for Harry Nilsson, Barbra Streisand, Carly Simon, and Art Garfunkel – all eminent artists with era-defining voices. But any hope the group had of finding a good fit with Perry was soon dashed, and within a few days, they abandoned the little work they did with him. Albhy Galuten recalled in a 2021 interview with the authors: 'When I asked Barry what happened in L.A. with Richard Perry, he said, 'He was into this humiliation training stuff. It was too weird'. Richard was doing EST. I don't know if you've ever heard of it, but it was kind of like Scientology – you know, one of those things that wasn't quite a religion, but something like it'.

For context, EST training was a series of large-group self-help workshops designed by American author and lecturer Werner Erhard, driven by the idea that they would 'transform one's ability to experience living so that the situations one had been trying to change or had been putting up with, clear up just in the process of life itself'. It had several supporters in the entertainment industry, including John Denver and Diana Ross. Others criticised it as being cult-like and manipulative. 'But, anyway, Barry's interpretation of what Richard Perry was doing was humiliation training [*laughs*]. And I guess, you know, Richard is famous for not being present – for saying, 'Okay, great! Let's do it', and then disappearing and being on the phone for two hours'.

After the close, almost parental connection Arif Mardin had with the Gibbs, Perry's laissez-faire approach simply wasn't going to work. Karl Richardson recalled in the 2020 documentary *The Bee Gees: How Can You Mend A Broken Heart*: 'I got a call from Barry and he said, 'I want my studio time back and I wanna work with you''.

On 5 January, the group returned to Miami and went back to Criteria Studios three days later to record the new album as their own producers for the first time. As the Gibbs, Dennis Bryon, Blue Weaver, Alan Kendall, and Karl Richardson began work on the first track, it became evident there was something missing. Karl explained in the *Broken Heart* documentary: 'I'm in the control room. I said to Dennis the drummer, 'You know, that pattern you're playing right now is just a little too busy'. He said, 'Well, what do you mean?'. I said, 'I can't get into specifics about the note values'. I didn't have a technical term for the open-and-closed hi-hat or any of that stuff. So apparently, you know, I needed a communicator'. Karl, who had a deep pool of contacts from his years of work as a local engineer, reached out to prolific session player and producer Albhy Galuten to potentially fill the gap. Albhy recollected in late 2021:

I was in England working with a pub band named Bees Make Honey. It was my first independent production. I'd produced a couple of things for Atlantic Records – Jesse Ed Davis, Jo Mama, and some records for Dr. John. During the last mix, I got a call from Karl, and he says, 'What are you doing?', and I said, 'Well, I'm back on a plane first thing in the morning to Miami'. He says, 'Well, The Bee Gees are here and they really need a producer. I can do the engineering stuff, and Barry knows what he wants, but doesn't know how to describe it to anybody. We need some sort of a translator'.

Albhy had also played synth on Eric Clapton's *461 Ocean Boulevard*, and worked on sessions with Aretha Franklin, George McCrae, The Eagles, and Rod Stewart. Like the Gibbs, he had an ingrained love of soul music, and brought a good amount of experience of working with artists who landed in pop/R&B crossover territory.

Landing in Miami after his UK stint, Albhy 'got off the plane and went right to the studio, and they were tracking 'You Should Be Dancing'. And, you know, I gave them a couple of comments about it, and they liked it. I said, 'Well, okay, I'm kind of tired', and they said, 'Okay, well, we'll see you tomorrow'. And that's when we started working together'.

Albhy's formal education from the Berklee College of Music in Boston gave The Bee Gees the ability to render their abstract musical ideas into tangible products on tape. He proved to be invaluable as an arranger and occasional co-composer as the work progressed. In a matter of months, of course, their fledgling relationship blossomed into one of the industry's most successful production teams.

When Albhy was brought into the fold, the Gibbs were in a good place creatively and had a clear vision of what they wanted their next album to sound like. He claims they just needed some help operationalising what they were imagining in their heads:

> They'd made a record with Arif, and they had a leader and they knew what they were doing. He was like, 'Well, you do this and you do that'. And then they said, 'Okay, we can do it ourselves. Richard Perry didn't work, we don't need a producer'. But they really didn't have production experience. They didn't know how to manage tapes or tracks or even how to think about arrangements. I mean, obviously, they thought about arrangements – Barry had great ideas for string and horn lines. They knew all this stuff, but they really didn't have the experience. Being a producer is putting all the pieces together, so I think what happened when I came on is it was sort of a sense of relief for the brothers. They could still be creative and could still have the final say. It was all a collaboration.

While the sessions were ramping up, the release of 'Fanny (Be Tender With My Love)', backed with 'Country Lanes', as the third and final *Main Course* single added to their public and critical acclaim. It was released in the UK on 23 January, with the US release delayed until February. The single's momentum in North America certainly built excitement for the new album scheduled for later in the year.

By the end of January, three tracks constructed for the forthcoming *Children Of The World* album were in some state of completion: 'You Should Be Dancing', which was being groomed meticulously to be the first single, 'Love So Right', and 'Subway'. The following month, they recorded an early version of 'You Stepped Into My Life' before Robin and Maurice took a hiatus to return to the UK. On 23 February, Yvonne Gibb gave birth to her and Maurice's first child, Adam Andrew, born at Pembury Hospital, Tonbridge, Kent.

The exact dates of the younger brothers' departure and return are unknown, but their absence can be somewhat tracked in how the documented session work for *Children Of The World* unfolded throughout March. With Barry remaining in Miami to mix 'You Should Be Dancing' with Albhy and Karl, it's plausible the time they spent as a trio laid the groundwork for the three of them to emerge as The Bee Gees' chief production unit – and to set the stage for them working on other artists' projects starting later in the year.

Barry spent the time without his brothers to add specific touches to the album and pursuing a few extracurricular activities while he was at it. Crosby, Stills, Nash & Young alumnus Stephen Stills and session percussionist Joe Lala – who were working in an adjacent Criteria Studios studio – had already added percussion to 'You Should Be Dancing'. Barry and Stills enjoyed the collaboration enough to co-write the song 'Walk Before You Run', which reportedly didn't develop beyond a jam. Stills also played bass on Barry's new country track, 'Rest Your Love On Me', which was further tweaked and finished a few months later, but not released until late 1978.

At the end of February, a new song – 'The Restless Years' (the working title for what would become 'The Way It Was') – had been minted with Blue Weaver's piano to the fore, and bass from George 'Chocolate' Perry – a session veteran certainly familiar to Karl who had played on many records from the TK Records stable in the early 1970s. In early March, Barry wrote an additional track – titled 'The Feel' – but no formal recording is known to exist.

With Robin and Maurice returning to the studio by the end of March, the group worked on 'Lovers' before moving the entire operation in April and May to Morin Heights, Québec, Canada, to finish recording and mixing. As foreign nationals working in the United States, the Gibbs and their band members were faced with income restrictions – and with significant tax issues in play that made returning to the UK for professional purposes a tough premise, the relocation north seemed like the best option.

The *Children Of The World* sessions continued until at least 26 May, with most of the remaining songs having been finished earlier in the month: 'Boogie Child', 'Can't Keep A Good Man Down', and 'Children Of The World'. A few additional weeks were dedicated to tweaking and final mixes in preparation for an early fall release. Afterwards, the entire group took a break and returned to the UK.

Over in Australia, younger brother Andy continued to write new songs in the first half of 1976, and another bunch were taped with producer Col Joye. In June, their progress was interrupted by Robert Stigwood and Barry calling Andy to the US to record a debut album as part of the RSO stable. Although it was never officially announced, there were almost certainly plans to issue a full Andy Gibb set on Joye's ATA label later in the year. An advance single was scheduled and pressed: a cover of Ray Stevens' 'Can't Stop Dancin'', which became better known as a top 20 hit for American pop duo Captain & Tennille in the spring of 1977. But with Andy's impending departure for Miami, the single was withdrawn. Three songs from the sessions – 'To A Girl', 'Walkin' Alone', and 'Take A Hold Of Yourself' – remain unreleased. The rest – 'Come Home For The Winter', 'Let It Be Me', and 'Starlight' – were to be re-recorded for the new album after Andy arrived in the US. Before moving overseas, Andy married his long-time girlfriend Kim Reeder at the Wayside chapel in Potts Point, Sydney, on 11 July. Their marriage would be short and turbulent, mired by a multitude of incidents and issues that Andy would encounter as he became the next Gibb family success story.

During The Bee Gees' summer hiatus, their former guitarist Vince Melouney visited Barry on the Isle of Man. The pair wrote two songs – 'Let It Ride' and 'Morning Rain' – both of which could be described as country-esque. Though not professionally recorded in a studio, good-quality audio of the tracks does exist on a cassette owned by Vince. He has long been hopeful the tracks could be developed and released, and also to have The Bee Gees' former drummer Colin Petersen add tambourine to the mix. Vince's account of the writing session adds to the chorus of people who endorse Barry as a quick and masterful writer, which he described to the authors in late 2021:

I was living in London and had been working on some songs; some ideas that I had. However, I was getting quite frustrated. I was mainly having trouble with the lyrics, so I gave Barry a call, thinking maybe he can give me a few ideas. Barry and his wife Linda were living in the Isle of Man, and he said, 'Come over, let's have a listen'. Barry and I went into the living room, and I played him my songs that I had recorded on my little cassette recorder. 'Stop it there, let me hear that again', he said. 'I get a title first, then I write the song from there'. So, he got the title 'Morning Rain', and then he wrote the lyrics – he just sat there and just wrote it. It was all over in 15 minutes. He picked up his guitar – a beautiful J-200 acoustic Gibson. I had another one of Barry's guitars, but I can't remember what it was. I put in a clean cassette, and we recorded 'Morning Rain' on the first take, and it sounded really, really good. He said, 'Play me some more of your songs'. He found another piece there he liked that he could work with, and he called it 'Let It Ride'. He started to write the words, and then he got stumped – he was looking for something, but he couldn't find it. At that moment, the phone rang and he picked it up and answered. He wasn't there long. He said 'goodbye', put the phone down, picked up the pen and finished the song. Maybe the person on the line had said something that inspired him. We then recorded 'Let It Ride', and that again turned out really well. It was really great to see him again after all those years – and despite all his recent success, he was just the same as the last time I'd seen him.

On 21 June, 'You Should Be Dancing' (backed with the up-tempo urban R&B anthem 'Subway') was released as the first single from *Children Of The World* in the UK. The US issue followed on 16 July. The fine polishing of the track at different points across five months in the studio paid off as it raced up the US and UK charts. It was a powerful affirmation that The Bee Gees' *Main Course* rebound was no accident.

They made no live appearances performing their new hit until near the end of the year. But it was featured on BBC 1's *Top Of The Pops* three times over the next two months – first played over the end credits of the 29 July broadcast, and then on 12 and 26 August behind routines by the show's dance troupe, Ruby Flipper. Stateside, 'You Should Be Dancing' appeared in an *American Bandstand* dance montage segment on 11 September – a week after the single hit number one in *Billboard*.

Rather intriguingly, on the same broadcast, breakout actor and singer John Travolta was featured performing his new single 'Whenever I'm Away From You', and in his interview with Dick Clark, announced he'd been cast in the yet-to-be-named *Saturday Night Fever*: 'I'll get to dance in a film in January, and it's gonna be hot! It's about discotheques themselves, so I'll be, like, king of the discos!'. Of course, the film was still several months away from even being on The Bee Gees' radar, but the fact that 'You Should Be Dancing' and Walter Murphy's 'A Fifth Of Beethoven' were both included in this particular episode and eventually became part of the *Fever* soundtrack was perhaps more than coincidental. Travolta is known to have used 'You Should Be Dancing' in his dance rehearsals for the film, so it's possible that was the catalyst.

On 13 September, The Bee Gees' 14th studio album, *Children Of The World*, was released in the US and UK.

Children Of The World (1976)
Personnel:
Barry Gibb: vocals, rhythm guitar
Robin Gibb: vocals
Maurice Gibb: vocals, bass
Alan Kendall: lead guitar
Blue Weaver: piano, keyboards, ARP and Moog synthesisers

Dennis Bryon: drums
Joe Lala: percussion
Gary Brown: saxophones
Stephen Stills: percussion ('You Should Be Dancing')
George 'Chocolate' Perry: bass ('Subway', 'The Way It Was')
Horns: The Boneroo Horns – Peter Graves, Whit Sidener, Kenny Faulk, Neil
Bonsanti, Bill Purse
Engineers: Karl Richardson, John Blanch, Ed Marshal (Criteria Studios), Nick
Balgona (Le Studio)
Producers: The Bee Gees, Karl Richardson, Albhy Galuten
Recorded between 19 January and 30 March 1976 at Criteria Studios,
Miami, and 2 April to 26 May at Le Studio, Morin Heights, Québec
Release dates: UK and US: 13 September 1976
Chart positions: Canada: 3, New Zealand: 6, Italy: 7, US: 8, Australia: 16,
Norway: 16, Sweden: 22, West Germany: 36, Sweden: 36

The newly forged Bee Gees/Albhy Galuten/Karl Richardson production team nudged the group into further experimentation with the R&B scaffolding they'd developed recording *Main Course*. *Children Of The World* is a love letter to Philadelphia soul (the brothers readily identified groups like The Stylistics and The Delfonics as important influences), fused with the Black and Latin flavours of the Miami music scene that surrounded the album's making. The Gibbs were firmly in the driver's seat as producers for virtually the first time, which was critical in shaping their evolving sound. It wasn't only current and confident – it propelled the group to pop music's cutting edge, which is quite remarkable considering the state of their career just a year earlier.

Early working titles for the album included *Pacer* and *Response*. The set took nearly five months to record – the longest they'd spent continually assembling a record up to that point. The album brought the instrumental players' strengths front and centre, focusing on the sonic unity they wrapped around the songs. They weren't just playing on the tracks – they were actively involved in moulding the record's character. The chemistry they'd built during the creation of *Main Course* became more potent for its follow-up, and it was clear everyone was excited to express themselves. Barry told *Circus* magazine in early 1977:

Right now, it's a very vibrant band, and the songs are pouring out. In the old days, we took three or four weeks to cut an album, and now we're taking three months. It makes a hell of a difference, especially when you're in there with the right people. The band – Dennis Bryon, Alan Kendall and Blue Weaver – are more like Bee Gees than side musicians; these guys have been with us for years. On *Children Of The World*, everyone gets a cut, not just a wage.

They also found different ways to use Barry's falsetto – employing it as the sole lead on four tracks and threading it across the entire album in varying layers and bursts. While his voice had always been one of the driving forces behind their sound, it had become an even more versatile commodity over the past year. Albhy: 'I always thought of [Barry] having two voices – he has the forceful voice, and then he has the innocent, sweet, vibrato-y voice. He had – particularly with his falsetto – more control over his voice than anybody I've ever worked with'. Even Barry's natural tenor voice had transformed significantly in a short amount of time – compare the richness and depth it achieves on *Children Of The World* to what it sounds like on *Life In A Tin Can* just three years earlier. It's rather staggering.

The album's first sessions took place in Criteria's Studio C. While the studio was one of the country's best, Albhy remembers there were still enough technological limitations at the time to require everyone's cooperation in the process, as he explained in a 2021 interview with the authors:

> During those days, there was no computerised mixing. When we would mix a record and you had to have cues, you'd have to have everyone grabbing a fader. Karl and I would do the tricky moves – the crossfades and the phase in-and-outs. And then it would be, 'Okay Alan, when we get to the verse, press this button and press that button'. So, you know, it was definitely a team effort. In some ways, when you had to mix by hand, every mix was like a performance. It was more live. It wasn't like today when you can fine-tune it and remove all the errors. There was always some unpredictability in terms of how those came out.

When the sessions moved to Québec in April, the team was inspired by the beauty of Morin Heights, set against the province's picturesque Laurentian Mountains. But the change of scenery offered even more unexpected – and at times comical – layers. Albhy: 'We mixed the album at Andre Perry's studio (Le Studio). Beautiful studio. It was lovely. I think they had Studer machines – they weren't what we were used to, but they were great. It was in the spring, and we would keep the studio door open – not the control room, but the studio had a door to the outside. It was on this beautiful lake. And I remember this one time a peacock came wandering in, and we were like, 'What the *fuck*?!'".

The songs are a solid batch, and the arrangements feel less rigid than their predecessors, with fatter percussion, bright horns, and a liberal smear of synthesiser – Blue Weaver's keyboard skills were invaluable to the equation. There's a visceral degree of fun and experimentation that subsequent Bee Gees albums never recaptured to quite the same degree. In the grander kingdom of their catalogue, it's one of their more overlooked works. And while it's not widely regarded as a classic like *Main Course*, *Children Of The World*'s R&B/soul sensibility does hold up rather well all these years later. The songs could easily be covered by a current artist in those genres and sound as contemporary and infectious as they did in 1976. Albhy emphasises how important the brothers' cohesion was in confidently exploring new territory at the time: 'They were very much three brothers then. As we moved into the *Saturday Night Fever* era, it became more of the Barry show'.

Children Of The World scored the group their second hit album in a row and was their first US top ten entry since *Best Of Bee Gees* in 1969. It was the first Bee Gees set to be certified Platinum by the RIAA. In the UK, however, it was their second consecutive album to miss the chart, which was somewhat odd since both *Main Course* and *Children Of The World* had produced top five hits there. But since both sets' follow-up singles failed to make any impact in that market, there didn't seem to be much to fuel the sale of the albums once they reached shop shelves.

In America, The Bee Gees were doing more than racking up chart numbers – their songs were beginning to lead a major shift in the pop landscape. The danceable R&B that had long been a staple of underground clubs in cities like New York and Philadelphia was now becoming mainstream and accessible to a wider audience.

The front cover artwork is an atmospheric vignette of the brothers wearing flying suits of the Royal Flying Corps – the air arm of the British Army before and during World War I, until it merged with the Royal Naval Air Service on 1 April 1918 to form the Royal Air Force. The photograph was taken by Ed Caraeff, who first worked with The Bee Gees on the *Life In A Tin Can* cover shoot three years earlier.

Reportedly, the uniforms had been supplied by then-RSO Records executive David English.

With white scarves blowing in the wind (à la the lead character in the *Biggles* books) and Robin sporting a large Capricorn medallion, the image was ripe for parody. The comedy pop group The Hee Bee Gee Bees – Angus Deayton, Michael Fenton Stevens, and Philip Pope – did exactly that in 1980. For added comic effect, the cover of their single 'Meaningless Songs (In Very High Voices)' pictured them in the same pose but holding hair dryers to achieve the Gibbs' windswept look. The song was quite an impressive send-up of the Gibbs' falsetto harmonies and earned The Hee Bee Gee Bees a number two hit in Australia.

The logo that first appeared on the *Main Course* cover was used again here, and illustrator Tom Nikosey was responsible for the overall cover design and typeface. In a 2021 interview, Barry said the cover was the first one on which they had any input in terms of its look and feel.

On 8 May 2020, Capitol/UMe reissued *Children Of The World* on both black and limited-edition 'sunshine yellow' vinyl.

'You Should Be Dancing' (Barry Gibb, Robin Gibb, Maurice Gibb)

Recorded at Criteria Studios, Miami: 19 January, 1 and 8 February 1976, and Le Studio, Morin Heights, Québec: 6 May 1976
Chart positions: Canada: 1, US: 1, Ireland: 4, Italy: 5, UK: 5, Sweden: 8, New Zealand: 10, Norway: 11, Australia: 15, Netherlands: 12, West Germany: 16, Belgium: 20, France: 24

With its deliberate 123-bpm pulse, this is probably the most stereotypically disco track The Bee Gees ever recorded. It's a pure shot of adrenaline, fuelled by falsetto ad-libs and yelps – the new voice Barry cultivated in the *Main Course* sessions is at full throttle here, and its power and dexterity are impressive.

The lyric is somewhat nonsensical, perhaps by design. But it doesn't matter much, as the real spotlight is on the tight rhythm section, horns and synths. At least some of Barry's lead vocal was allegedly captured with him lying on the studio floor while the drums and bass played so he could more tangibly feel the vibration.

The appeal of the track's electric, layered atmosphere solidified the Gibbs' resurrection as chart movers, and validated the new production team's skill as record makers. Released in the summer of 1976 as the album's first single, it reached number one on the US *Billboard* Hot 100 and Dance Club Play charts and climbed to the top five in the UK and on the *Billboard* Hot Soul Singles surveys. In Canada, it became The Bee Gees' sixth *RPM* chart-topper.

Stephen Stills and Joe Lala were at Criteria Studios working on Stills' *Illegal Stills* album and his collaboration with Neil Young, *Long May You Run*. Albhy Galuten recalled in 2021:

> It seemed kind of stiff. It's sort of like they were doing early disco – it was just a four-on-the-floor bass drum – you know, *'boom-boom-boom-boom'*. The feel was kind of boring; it didn't really have any lope to it. So, I thought we should put some percussion on it; some Latin percussion. Next door was Stephen Stills, and Joe Lala was working with him. Joe was a great percussionist. We had them come in – and again, we had limited tracks – and play together. Stephen played timbales and Joe played congas, and then they'd both play shaker. And the agogo bells go *'tong-tee-kah-dong, tong-tee-kah-dong'*! We ended up with, I think, about six different instruments on three different takes, or maybe eight different instruments on four different takes. Ultimately, we bounced them all together, and suddenly the whole record just felt much better. It was really groovin'.

However, Albhy says not everyone was so keen on the rhythmic enhancement:

> You have the breakdown where it goes just to percussion, and then the vocals come in. And the record company was like, 'You shouldn't do that. That won't work for a single, and radio stations won't play it'. Karl and I said, 'Well, on the radio, there'll be all this compression limiting, which will bring the volume up. It'll sound *fantastic*'. And, of course, they didn't believe us. So, we went into Sterling Sound in New York and we mastered it and made a version that would sound like it would on the radio. We played it for (RSO President) Al Coury and those guys, and when it got to the percussion breakdown, it was *right* in your face. They said, 'Okay, we'll leave it in. You're right'.

Another important component that required some extra finagling was Alan Kendall's mid-song guitar solo. According to Albhy:

We were still on one 16 ... or maybe it was a 24-track, but we were still using single tapes. So, you didn't have lots of tracks – it wasn't like you could have the drums on four tracks, and eight tracks of vocals. You could do a couple of tracks and bounce them. If I remember correctly, we had done ... I think it was 13 guitar solos for that little eight-bar. None of them were quite right, and so I put together from all of those tracks, punching in and out and crossfading. I mean, you didn't have Pro Tools then, so you couldn't sample them all and move them in time. It was a matter of saying, 'Here are all the pieces of the puzzle, and let's put them together'. And it ended up being a very nice guitar solo.

While The Bee Gees camp clearly sensed the song was something special, they perhaps didn't predict it becoming a cultural phenomenon, especially among the LGBTQ+ community in America. In that context, 'You Should Be Dancing' wasn't just a hit; it was a statement of celebration and liberation. Former resident Studio 54 DJ – and owner of The Gallery night club in New York – Nicky Siano, explained in the 2020 *Broken Heart* documentary:

At the clubs, it *exploded* – not just, 'Oh, well, I heard that record and I really liked it'. It was three times a night at any club that you went to. There was a whole industry that was built around this clubbing thing. *Billboard* started a chart that was a dance music chart. This billion-dollar industry was being built way before The Bee Gees. A lot of people don't realise disco started in the gay and the Black community. People don't understand what it was like back then for gay people. There was a law in New York that did not allow people of the same sex to dance together in a place that had a liquor license. And then the law changed, and that allowed me to open my club.

Along with 'Jive Talkin'', 'You Should Be Dancing' was included on the *Saturday Night Fever* soundtrack, but it was also prominently featured in the film, leading many to (incorrectly) remember it as being written along with the other original songs from those sessions.

At least a few dozen covers of the song have appeared over the years – most notably those by American R&B singer Donnie Elbert, British pop/rock band The Beautiful South, jazz instrumentalist Lionel Hampton, and London-based club DJ Blockster. US alt-rock stalwarts Foo Fighters (as their alter-egos The Dee Gees, which reflected lead singer Dave Grohl's initials) paid tribute to The Bee Gees in July 2021 by including 'You Should Be Dancing' on the Record Store Day limited-vinyl release album *Hail Satin*. Side one was exclusively covers of Gibb songs (including 'Night Fever', 'Tragedy', 'More Than A Woman' and Andy's 'Shadow Dancing'). Side two consisted of five live versions of Foo Fighters originals.

In 1993, the Gibbs themselves recorded a new version of 'You Should Be Dancing' under the alternate title 'Decadance'. It was a bonus on some of the singles from their *Size Isn't Everything* album and was a hidden track on some international pressings of that album.

'You Stepped Into My Life' (Barry Gibb, Robin Gibb, Maurice Gibb)
Recorded at Criteria Studios, Miami: 3 February 1976, and Le Studio, Morin Heights, Québec: 7 May 1976
The Gibbs expanded their exploration of R&B/funk textures with the more-tricky strut tempo and wah-wah guitars of 'You Stepped Into My Life'. It was the B-side of the 'Love So Right' single. Both tracks served as a double A-side in the UK and Scandinavia.

Albhy remembers playing piano on the track 'as an orchestral element more than a part'.

The song was notably covered by American soul singer/actress Melba Moore, who scored a moderate hit with it on the US *Billboard* Soul and Club singles charts in 1978. A year later, entertainer Wayne Newton released his version. Nearly identical in rhythm and instrumentation to the original, it only cracked the bottom of the *Billboard* Hot 100. Incidentally, Newton was the first to record and release a Barry Gibb composition in the US, with 'They'll Never Know' from his 1965 album *Red Roses For A Blue Lady*.

'Love So Right' (Barry Gibb, Robin Gibb, Maurice Gibb)
Recorded at Criteria Studios, Miami: 21 and 30 January 1976, and Le Studio, Morin Heights, Québec: 6 May 1976
Chart positions: Brazil: 1, Canada: 2, US: 3, Ireland: 14, Australia: 21, West Germany: 28, UK: 41
Barry's falsetto lead here is a self-proclaimed intentional mimicry of late 1960s and early-1970s ballads recorded by Philadelphia soul pioneers The Delfonics. Demonstrating his incredible vocal range, Barry reaches what's believed to be his highest note on a released recording (G#5) twice in the

song's playout. 'Love So Right' is also distinct as one of the earliest tracks on which the Gibbs attempted a full chorus in falsetto harmony.

A notable change from older Bee Gees ballads is substituting strings for synthesiser, which is instantly audible at the beginning; a decision Albhy said was made for financial reasons. He also played piano on the track, while Blue Weaver played Fender Rhodes.

Released in September 1976 as the album's second single, it was warmly embraced in North America, where it peaked in the US and Canada at numbers 3 and 2, respectively. It was less successful in the UK, where it fell just short of the top 40.

American soul singers Thelma Houston and Jerry Butler covered the song on their 1977 Motown album *Thelma & Jerry*, in a medley with Chicago's 'If You Leave Me Now'. Vocal trio The Lettermen – best known for their 1962 cover of the pop standard 'When I Fall In Love' – released a version of 'Love So Right' on their 1979 *Love Is ...* album.

'Lovers' (Barry Gibb, Robin Gibb, Maurice Gibb)
Recorded at Criteria Studios, Miami: 29 and 30 March 1976, and Le Studio, Morin Heights, Québec: 6 and 26 May 1976
'Lovers' demonstrates the brothers' skill in using vocals to create texture, with alternating lead falsettos by Barry and Robin and an uncharacteristically low counterpoint vocal part on the refrain with Barry doing his best Bobby Womack growl. The subject matter is lightweight, but weaving synths, saxes, and handclaps deliver a rhythmic chug that's difficult to resist. It was the B-side of 'Boogie Child' in most markets.

'Can't Keep A Good Man Down' (Barry Gibb, Robin Gibb, Maurice Gibb)
Recorded at Le Studio, Morin Heights, Québec: 6 May 1976
A solid, straightforward R&B gambol that feeds off Dennis Bryon's thick drums, babbling guitars, and hiccups of Blue Weaver's Hammond B3 organ. The use of varying bridge dynamics – where Barry and Robin each solo – is a great contrast to the refrain.

'Boogie Child' (Barry Gibb, Robin Gibb, Maurice Gibb)
Recorded at Le Studio, Morin Heights, Québec: 6 May 1976
Chart positions: Italy: 5, Canada: 9, US: 12, New Zealand: 13
Released in early 1977, the album's third single is playfully funky, made punchy with a guttural guitar line and chatty horns. New Orleans-born-

and-bred saxophonist Gary Brown solos on the instrumental bridge which – in contrast to the rest of the album – uses real strings. Brown also appears prominently on other Gibb sessions throughout the late 1970s and early 1980s.

The instrumentation might be all feelgood, but the lyrics find the protagonist lusting after a younger woman, and the line 'a man could die for the way I'm thinking', suggests the infatuation might border on the inappropriate. It should probably all be taken with a grain of salt, though – the Gibbs' sense of humour has often been edgy, so it's fair to assume this was orchestrated with tongue rather firmly planted in cheek.

Regardless of the wince-worthy verbiage, 'Boogie Child' provided The Bee Gees with their sixth consecutive top 20 hit since the release of *Main Course*, and another Canadian top ten entry.

'Love Me' (Barry Gibb, Robin Gibb)

Recorded at Criteria Studios, Miami: 30 March 1976, and Le Studio, Morin Heights, Québec: 23 and 25 April 1976

'Love Me' is a ballad that could have been just as at home on *Main Course*, meshing a chorus that feels like vintage Bee Gees with a more-contemporary R&B sound on the verses and bridge. Barry's precisely multi-tracked falsetto is clearly heard on the latter.

While this version has surfaced on multiple greatest hits compilations over the years, the song has had a long shelf life as a hit for other artists. RSO labelmate and friend Yvonne Elliman released her version as a single in September 1976 (it appeared on her album of the same name in 1977). It became a top 20 hit in the US and Canada and reached 4 and 6 in Australia and the UK, respectively. Elliman – who was married to RSO executive Bill Oakes at the time – had first gained attention playing the role of Mary Magdalene in the original 1971 cast of stage musical *Jesus Christ Superstar*, later touring and recording with Eric Clapton in between releasing her own records in the first half 1970s. On 14 February 2022, Elliman issued a new live version of 'Love Me' via social media, which had been recorded at a recent Boston show.

British singer and EastEnders actress Martine McCutcheon, probably better known globally for her role as Natalie in the movie *Love Actually*, recorded the song – sounding nearly identical to Elliman's version – for her 1999 album, *You Me & Us*. The single reached number six in the UK.

'Subway' (Barry Gibb, Robin Gibb, Maurice Gibb)
Recorded at Criteria Studios, Miami: 27 January 1976, and Le Studio, Morin Heights, Québec: 6 May 1976

The *Children Of The World* sessions were clearly a positive experience for everyone involved, and any doubt that might have existed while the group whetted their appetites for R&B/soul on *Mr. Natural* and *Main Course* seemed to disappear. 'Subway' embodies that exploratory spirit, with pure exhilaration for the 'city life' it refers to. You can feel and picture it rather tangibly when you listen. It's almost an antithesis to its darker successor, 'Stayin' Alive', which paints the urban existence as desperate and dangerous.

Barry is heard fully and comfortably in his falsetto voice here. Listen to the places near the end where it's tough to discern where Gary Brown's saxophone solo ends and Barry's high rasp begins.

'The Way It Was' (Barry Gibb, Robin Gibb, Blue Weaver)
Recorded at Criteria Studios, Miami: 23 February 1976, and Le Studio, Morin Heights, Québec: 12 April and 6 May 1976

A beautiful, pensive ballad in the spirit of *Main Course*'s 'Songbird'. Blue Weaver again shares a writing credit for his lovely piano melody.

Barry recorded the track while Robin and Maurice were on hiatus. Gary Brown makes another brief appearance with a late-song saxophone solo.

Soul superstar Gladys Knight recorded a fine version on her 1978 album *Miss Gladys Knight*.

'Children Of The World' (Barry Gibb, Robin Gibb, Maurice Gibb)
Recorded at Le Studio, Morin Heights, Québec: 18 April and 6 May 1976

Released outside North America as the album's fourth and final single, this song is a bit of an oddity compared to the rest of the set. Opening with a three-part harmony a cappella introduction, its foundation is mid-tempo R&B. The syncopated acoustic guitar alongside the drums and bass gives it folk overtones. Midway, the song changes key and breaks into a spacey synthesiser solo before returning to the original key.

The song was reportedly inspired by Maurice's son Adam, who was born in February during the sessions.

British comedian Kenny Everett famously parodied it in the early 1980s on *The Kenny Everett Video Show*.

At the 1979 *UNICEF: A Gift Of Song* gala concert, The Bee Gees performed the song's a cappella introduction, joined by a small multinational children's choir. They also sang a 30-second segment during their *BG2K* concert in Fort Lauderdale, Florida on New Year's Eve 1999 as part of the show's medley section.

While the *Children Of The World* album gave the band a new creative lease, they also took the opportunity to infuse a little bit of humour into the final product, evidenced by the collection of inside jokes in the liner notes. The US released product, however, featured a new addition to the label credits. Blue Weaver remembers:

> Dick Ashby put a blackboard up to put all the credits on. At the end, of course, it always had 'By arrangement with The Robert Stigwood Organisation', and that was always the final thing. Our roadie at the time was Tom Kennedy, so, we added 'and Tom Kennedy', and it got into print, didn't it! Millions of records went out with 'By arrangement with The Robert Stigwood Organisation and Tom Kennedy'. Have a look at the singles of 'Love So Right'. There was a Gold album with the label on it as well, all saying 'and Tom Kennedy'. Robert wasn't too pleased about that!

The funny credit also appeared on copies of the 'Boogie Child' single.

As The Bee Gees' commitments escalated with promoting their increasingly successful new album, they cancelled two live engagements during the month of September: a two-week Las Vegas residency, and a free concert at the historic Palace Lido in Douglas, Isle of Man in support of the island's Olympic athletes.

With more and more music buyers headed to dance clubs to hear current hits, RSO pushed out an EP of special disco versions of 'Boogie Child', 'You Stepped Into My Life', 'You Should Be Dancing', and 'Subway'. A 12" promo of that version of 'You Should Be Dancing' was also issued. None of the songs were actually remixed for these products – portions of the original recordings were simply spliced in to extend their play times.

Whilst the 'You Should Be Dancing' momentum was still high, 'Love So Right' (backed with 'You Stepped Into My Life') was released as the album's second single. The group's evolving sound was taking off in North America, where the song was a top three hit on multiple charts.

But the reception seemed to be growing cooler overseas, with the single making just a minor dent in most countries.

In the thick of the album's upward chart climb, Andy Gibb arrived in Miami to begin work on his first album *Flowing Rivers*, having freshly inked a contract with RSO. Barry, Albhy, and Karl were to produce the record, though Barry would only be present for two new tracks – 'I Just Want To Be Your Everything', which he wrote on his own especially for the project, and '(Love Is) Thicker Than Water', which he co-wrote with Andy. The balance of the songs were Andy's compositions. Over half were new takes of songs he'd previously written and recorded in Australia with Col Joye: 'In The End', 'Come Home For The Winter', 'Let It Be Me', 'Starlight', 'Flowing Rivers', and 'Words And Music'. He wrote two new songs with Albhy Galuten (uncredited on the album): 'Dance To The Light Of The Morning' and 'Too Many Looks In Your Eyes'. Andy had envisioned a country rock record in the vein of The Eagles, who were also recording at Criteria Studios for their forthcoming album *Hotel California*. Their guitarist Joe Walsh visited the *Flowing Rivers* sessions and agreed to play on '(Love Is) Thicker Than Water'. Contrary to popular belief, he does not play the main guitar line on 'I Just Want To Be Your Everything'. That was delivered by veteran player Joey Murcia.

The album sessions were completed in a couple of weeks in October. In 2017, Albhy told *Albumism*: 'Andy was just so full of, just, I don't know, fire and brimstone, or piss and vinegar. He was just so excited and young and fired up about it. It was absolutely fantastic. Certainly, for me, it was a buzz'.

Since The Bee Gees' band was busy preparing for the tour to promote *Children Of The World*, the production team opted for local session players on Andy's album. Since Albhy and Karl had worked extensively in Miami for several years, and had developed a deep network of musicians from which to choose. Drummer Ron 'Tubby' Ziegler, bassist Harold Cowart, guitarists Joey Murcia and George Terry, and pianist/keyboardist Paul Harris were brought on board. Impressed with what they heard during the sessions, the production team employed this basic line-up on a long string of recording projects they were to oversee through to the decade's end.

With Bee Gees' work taking priority over most other RSO projects, it was almost an entire year before *Flowing Rivers* was released, although the first single arrived much sooner. But not everything related to Andy's big career advancement was copacetic. Being folded into the family business – so to speak – under the watchful eye of Robert Stigwood and RSO came with a decent helping of politics, pressure, and excess that began to drive a wedge between Andy and his new bride Kim. While Andy hadn't even released an album yet, his famous family had already given him access to people who were all too happy to let him party with them. He began experimenting with drugs and alcohol, which further troubled his marriage, and it wouldn't be too long before they began to have a negative impact on his path as a musician.

The Bee Gees and their band retreated to the Isle of Man later in September, but only to rehearse for their North American tour to start the following month. Once again, dodging their immigrant labour limitations in America and an 83% tax gouge in the UK (Barry and Maurice were considered exiles), they set up in the then-abandoned Douglas Bay Hotel.

With the *All This And World War II* film forthcoming on 12 November, 20th Century Fox sent the soundtrack to retail on 25 October in the US and UK.

All This And World War II (Soundtrack) (1976)

Personnel:
Barry Gibb, Robin Gibb, Maurice Gibb: vocals
Nicky Hopkins: piano
Les Hurdle: bass
Barry Morgan, Ronnie Verrell: drums
The London Symphony Orchestra
Orchestral arrangements: Wil Malone
Conductors: Harry Rabinowitz, David Measham
Engineer: Keith Grant
Producer: Lou Reizner
Recorded in late 1975 at Olympic Sound Studios, London
Release dates: UK and US: 25 October 1976
Chart positions: Netherlands: 17, UK: 23, New Zealand: 37, US: 48

All This And World War II was a cinematic montage of clips from various sources, including British, American, and German newsreels and Hollywood movies, depicting the war. The soundtrack consists of Beatles songs covered by a variety of big-name acts, including Ambrosia, Leo Sayer, Keith Moon, Rod Stewart, David Essex, Jeff Lynne, The Four Seasons, Helen Reddy, Status Quo, Peter Gabriel, Frankie Valli, Tina Turner, and – of course – The Bee Gees, who had been lifelong Beatles fans.

The film was savaged by critics, and audience turnout was extremely poor. 20th Century Fox sat up and took note by promptly pulling the film from distribution after just two weeks. It's seldom been seen since – usually only at film festivals and on one or two rare occasions on television. It's never been released on home video or DVD in its original form, but a revised edition by original director Tony Palmer, titled *The Beatles And World War II* (using a different soundtrack and footage), was released on DVD with a two-CD set via Gonzo Multimedia in 2016. It only has 22 of the original album's 28 tracks, and, sadly, omits two of The Bee Gees' contributions.

The filmmaker's original intention was to use actual Beatles music in the film. But the producers made the decision to use cover versions after weighing up the cost of licencing the original tracks and the realisation that additional money could be made from a soundtrack album. The decision was a sound one, as the soundtrack generated more revenue than the film.

The soundtrack was produced by American Lou Reizner – also an A&R executive and head of Mercury Records' European operations. In 1971, he'd recorded an eponymous solo album, which included the Barry Gibb song 'The Day Your Eyes Meet Mine'. Reizner didn't hide his love of lush orchestration and allowed arranger Wil Malone a free rein on the soundtrack. It worked well on some tracks, but others – such as Status Quo's 'Getting Better' – suffered because of it. But The Bee Gees' tracks were tastefully done and gave the songs a new dimension.

The Bee Gees originally recorded six songs for the double-album soundtrack in late 1975, though only three would be included. The unused tracks were 'She's Leaving Home' (shelved in favour of Bryan Ferry's version), 'Lovely Rita' (substituted with a take by Roy Wood of The Move, Electric Light Orchestra, and Wizzard fame), and 'Lucy In the Sky With Diamonds', replaced by Elton John's cover, which was almost certainly used because it had been a major hit the previous year.

In the UK, the soundtrack was issued on the Riva label, founded in 1975 by Rod Stewart's manager Billy Gaff. It was attractively packaged in a gatefold cover with lyrics on the inner sleeves, plus a poster with stylised icons of the participating artists. In the US, the album appeared on 20th Century Records and the packaging was far more elaborate. A sturdy slipcase housed the discs in a gatefold sleeve with artwork varying from the UK version. The inner sleeves and poster were replaced by a splendid 36-page booklet with a die-cut cover, containing colourised stills from the film, artist images, and lyrics.

The album proved to be more popular and successful than the movie and even charted in some territories. It was reissued twice in the US as *The Songs Of John Lennon And Paul McCartney Performed By The World's Greatest Rock Artists* on 20th Century Records and Sessions Records. In the UK, the album was simply repackaged as *Top Of The World*, using unsold American 20th Century Records discs. The album was finally released on CD in 2006 on the Hip-O Select label, and again in 2015 as a limited issue release on the Culture Factory label, complete with the original gatefold sleeve.

'Golden Slumbers'/'Carry That Weight' (John Lennon, Paul McCartney)
Recorded at Olympic Sound Studios, London: late 1975

All The Bee Gees songs on the soundtrack were originally in the medley on side two of The Beatles' 1969 album *Abbey Road*. 'Golden Slumbers' was the sixth of the nine-song medley and is based on a poem 'Cradle Song' by dramatist Thomas Dekker, which was first published in 1603. Paul McCartney saw sheet music for 'Cradle Song' on the piano at his father's house. He didn't read music, so he created his own using the poem's first stanza with minor word changes as the chorus. 'Golden Slumbers' gives Barry an opportunity to show off his breathy ballad voice and his full-strength voice within a verse and chorus. While Paul McCartney's original features a gravelly chorus vocal, Barry's wasn't quite forceful enough to mimic that.

'Carry That Weight' immediately follows 'Golden Slumbers' on the *Abbey Road* track list, as it does here, and has been interpreted as The Beatles acknowledging that nothing they would do as individual artists would equal what they had achieved together and they would always carry the weight of their Beatle past. Paul McCartney has said the song was about the Beatles' business difficulties and the atmosphere at Apple at the time. Here the song has the brothers singing in unison – and to very good effect, adding emphasis to the rather bombastic tympani-heavy accompaniment.

'She Came In Through The Bathroom Window' (John Lennon, Paul McCartney)
Recorded at Olympic Sound Studios, London: late 1975

This was the fifth song in the *Abbey Road* medley, but it stands alone here. Paul McCartney said the song was inspired by fans who hung around outside Abbey Road studio, the Apple Corps offices, and The Beatles' homes. Those fans were known as the 'Apple scruffs', and on one occasion, they broke into McCartney's St. John's Wood house. The song's title focuses specifically on a fan named Diane Ashley, who confessed, 'We were bored, he was out, and so we decided to pay him a visit. We found a ladder in his garden and stuck it up at the bathroom window which he'd left slightly open. I was the one who climbed up and got in'.

In contrast to McCartney's smooth lead vocal, Barry's take steps it up a notch by pushing his voice just enough to get that gravelly rasp – sounding more like Joe Cocker (who had covered the song in 1969). Maurice and Robin join in for the chorus, but they're further back in the mix.

'Sun King' (John Lennon, Paul McCartney)
Recorded at Olympic Sound Studios, London: late 1975
The second song in the Beatles' medley was 'Sun King', which, like the previous track, stands alone from its traditional place in the medley here. This is quite different to The Beatles' original, with a sumptuous – if slightly overblown – orchestral arrangement. The song showcases the group's superb harmonies and gives Maurice a brief opportunity to do his best John Lennon imitation in a short solo-vocal section. The faux-Spanish section is nicely accented with Mexican Mariachi band horns and castanets.

Just ahead of The Bee Gees' return to the US to finish preparing for the *Children Of The World* tour, RSO released *Bee Gees Gold, Volume One*, in North America.

Bee Gees Gold, Volume One (1976)
Release date: November 1976
Chart position: US: 50
Side 1: 1. 'How Can You Mend A Broken Heart', 2. 'Holiday', 3. 'To Love Somebody', 4. 'Massachusetts', 5. 'Words', 6. Lonely Days'
Side 2: 1. 'Run To Me', 2. 'I've Gotta Get A Message To You', 3. 'My World', 4. 'I Can't See Nobody', 5. 'I Started A Joke', 6. 'New York Mining Disaster 1941'

This compilation was released in the US and Canada to capitalise on the group's recent chart successes there – making their first batch of international hits freshly available to fans who embraced their earlier sound, while offering something different for their growing base of younger listeners. The record mostly replaces the two previous hits retrospectives *Best Of Bee Gees* and *Best Of Bee Gees, Volume 2*, which likely were a bit harder to come by at the time since they were last available through RSO in 1973. *Bee Gees Gold, Volume One* reached number 50 on the *Billboard* Top LPs and Tapes album chart in the US. In Canada, it surprisingly missed the *RPM* album survey, but was still certified Gold by the Canadian Record Industry Association.

Future *Gold* volumes were never released, but *Bee Gees Greatest* effectively filled the gap by collecting their notable 1975-1979 output. However, it still ignored the singles from *Mr. Natural*, which were not part of a retrospective until Polydor issued the 1990 box set *Tales From The Brothers Gibb: A History In Song 1967-1990*.

In a review dated 30 October 1976, former US trade magazine *Cashbox* said, 'The Bee Gees are one of the few groups who can put out an album of songs that have all gone Gold and call it Volume One. All of these tunes were big hits, and one is staggered by the sheer numbers'.

The album has never been released on CD or via any streaming service, though original copies on LP and cassette are easy to come by on resale and auction sites.

RSO also saw fit to re-release *Odessa* on LP and cassette in North America in November.

Odessa

Release date: November 1976
Side 1: 1. 'Odessa', 2. 'You'll Never See My Face Again', 3. 'Marley Purt Drive', 4. 'Melody Fair'
Side 2: 1. 'Sound Of Love', 2. 'Give Your Best', 3. 'I Laugh In Your Face', 4. 'Never Say Never Again', 5. 'First Of May', 6. 'With All Nations (International Anthem)'

The track list was heavily cropped and rearranged to fit on a single vinyl disc. The decision might have been financial. Pressing and marketing a double-album set for a quick reissue was likely a tough sell – especially if plans were already in the works for a two-disc live album the following year. Why *Odessa* was specifically chosen for a refresh and not their more-popular 1960s albums is curious. Perhaps it was because it was the least readily available of their back catalogue in those markets.

This edition skipped using the expensive red flocking that was used on the original cover. Instead, RSO opted for a plain red cardboard sleeve.

The Canadian cassette release appears to have the original two-LP-length track list intact. Interestingly, RSO offered a Canada-only reissue of *Trafalgar* around the same time – maybe original copies were scarce enough there to justify it.

On 8 November, the brothers flew to New York City for an extended promotional campaign leading up to the fast-approaching *Children Of The World* tour. They announced that all proceeds from the 7 December stop at Madison Square Garden would be donated directly to the Police Athletic League, Inc. – the city's 'largest independent youth development not-for-profit organisation'. American R&B group Tavares – whose version of The Bee Gees' 'More Than A Woman' was to be on the *Saturday Night Fever* soundtrack – were the support act for the show. The concert grossed approximately $31,000 US (the equivalent of about $153,000 in 2022), which was presented to PAL President and Chairman Robert M. Morgenthau a few days later.

The brothers also attended a luncheon with New York mayor Abe Beame at his Gracie Mansion residence in Yorkville, adjacent to the Upper East Side. Mayor Beame presented them with The Key to the City of New York – a prestigious award bestowed to individuals since 1702 in recognition of public service and citizenship.

The Bee Gees' star was unquestionably on the rise again, and the hype building in New York about the tour was palpable. Chris Charlesworth of *Melody Maker* wrote at the time: 'A casual visitor to New York this month could be excused for thinking that The Bee Gees are currently running for elected office. The faces of the Brothers Gibb – serious and studied in their patriotic poses as World War I flying aces – peer down from posters that are firmly fixed to the rear of each and every blue bus that traverses the streets and avenues of Manhattan'. New Yorkers could even drop by a new Bee Gees International Headquarters shop that RSO had opened on Manhattan's 57th Street to purchase concert tickets, albums, and merchandise.

Once the tour commenced at Chicago's Auditorium Theatre on 27 November, the group discovered the heightening wave of public enthusiasm wasn't just limited to New York. Their 12-city road trip (including Toronto and Montréal in Canada) brought them face-to-face with capacity crowds at some of the largest venues they'd played in both countries up to that point. The tour concluded on 20 December at The Forum in Los Angeles. Crews were brought in to record the final show and collect film footage for a potential television special. The 22-song set was soon to be made into a double album, *Here At Last ... Bee Gees ... Live*, released in May 1977. The live set was a condition of a new five-year contract The Bee Gees had signed with RSO, so they began mixing it right after the Christmas holidays – all while writing and recording new songs for their next studio album.

The Gibbs' renewed success seemed to equally surprise and delight them. On the December New York tour stop, Robin told *Melody Maker*: 'We're becoming bigger now than we ever were before. In fact, we are bigger now than we ever were before. No one would ever have thought that it would happen'.

Unbeknownst to The Bee Gees, the big wave of hits and accolades they'd achieved that year was just a small taste of what awaited them in 1977.

1977

After *Children Of The World* cemented the group's contemporary reputation and strengthened the creative relationships with their band and co-producers, they regrouped in early 1977 to start tackling new projects. 'Boogie Child' was issued in January as the album's third and final single – just missing the US top ten, but still adding to their growing hitmaking credibility in North America. The B-side was the equally playful, but slightly less bawdy, 'Lovers'.

The next month, RSO issued the album's title track as a single in the UK, with 'Boogie Child' relegated to the B-side – undoubtedly an attempt at a hit since Britain wasn't responding as well as the US were to their new, funkier material. It was not a success. There must have been some sadness and frustration with the group losing some support back home in this new commercial rebirth. However, things were to turn around for them by the end of the year.

As British citizens living and working in the US, the Gibbs and their band had visa limitations, affording them only so many days of the year to work in the country. To help mitigate this, Robert Stigwood booked them studio time at Château d'Hérouville in the French countryside rather than have them return to Miami.

The 'Château' was constructed in the 1700s and was even painted by Vincent van Gogh in the summer of 1890, shortly before his death. It was also reportedly a temporary residence of composer Frédéric Chopin. Its life as a recording studio began in the early 1970s. Elton John was among the first notable pop musicians to craft an album there, fittingly dubbed *Honky Château*. The Grateful Dead, Uriah Heep, Iggy Pop, Marvin Gaye, Fleetwood Mac, and Cat Stevens would follow suit at different points throughout the decade.

With that rich history and the studio's location in a quaint village not far from cosmopolitan Paris, the property seems like it would be a serene, inspiring setting to make music, no? According to Maurice in the 2000 documentary *This is Where I Came In – The Official Story of The Bee Gees*, the Gibbs and their entourage found it to be rather in a shambles: 'Now, château sounds *[mimicking a French accent]* absolutely *gorgeous*, doesn't it? Beautiful buildings, great grounds and gardens, and ponds and fountains. *No.* It's *nothing* like that. It was a half-built castle, no central heating, nothing, and it was a dump'. Former RSO Records President Bill Oakes remembered the Château in the 2020 *Broken Heart* documentary as 'really kind of decrepit. I think it'd been used to make porn movies'.

Still, everyone seemed to make the best of their less-than-ideal accommodations. The first order of business was to mix and edit the tracks captured on the 20 December 1976 tour stop at the Los Angeles Forum for an album which would soon become *Here At Last ... Bee Gees ... Live*. The show was originally recorded for broadcast on the *King Biscuit Flower Hour* – an American syndicated radio show that featured concert performances by various rock artists. In its prime, the programme was carried by more than 300 radio stations throughout the US. The series had an impressive lifespan, producing shows from 1973 until 2005. The Bee Gees' instalment aired on 30 January 1977, and it used the unabridged raw show recordings, which were broadcast in quadraphonic with stereo-compatible sound.

The production team did the necessary editing to fit the long set onto a double LP. Some performance blemishes were corrected – Barry's falsetto lead, in particular, was touched up on tracks like 'Love So Right', as it had a discernible rasp. Dennis Bryon's drumming was reportedly untouched, but there were some bass fixes made and some percussion was added.

With the live set in the can, the group could focus on recording a new album. By February, they had started demos of four songs: 'If I Can't Have You', 'Night Fever', 'Warm Ride', and 'More Than A Woman'. The success of *Children Of The World* and its two biggest singles affirmed that Barry's falsetto was now their golden ticket, so everyone in the studio found ways to use and stretch it as much as possible.

The timeline for what happened next gets a bit cloudy depending on the individual recollections of those involved. What's certain is that the plans to record a fully-fledged follow-up to *Children Of The World* were halted by a call from Robert Stigwood, during which he announced that he'd bought the rights to make a film adaptation of British journalist Nik Cohn's June 1976 *New York* magazine article 'Tribal Rites of the New Saturday Night' – which had been brought to his attention by then-RSO Records president Bill Oakes. The premise: examining the social behaviours of young people who patronised disco clubs on weekends in New York City. Cohn touted it as an authentic cultural study: 'Over the past few months, much of my time has been spent in watching this new generation. Moving from neighbourhood to neighbourhood, from disco to disco, an explorer out of my depth, I have tried to learn the patterns, the old/new tribal rites ... Everything described in this article is factual and was either witnessed by me or told to me directly by the people involved. Only the names of the main characters have been changed'.

The protagonist in Cohn's article – a 20-something Brooklynite named Vincent – was the model for the eventual *Saturday Night Fever* lead character Tony Manero. 'During the week, Vincent sold paint in a housewares store. All day every day, he stood behind a counter and grinned. He climbed up and down ladders; he made the coffee, and he obeyed. Then came the weekend, and he was cut loose'.

Allegedly, that was about as much as The Bee Gees knew about the project when they were summoned to contribute. Cohn's article might have been a colourful and compelling read, but a vehicle for a blockbuster film? Maurice recounted in 2001's *This Is Where I Came In – The Official Story of The Bee Gees*: 'You know, he told us it was about this guy who works in a paint shop on the other side of the bridge in Brooklyn, and he blows his wages every Saturday night in a club and wins a dance competition. And we thought, [*sarcastically*] 'Nice one, Rob''. Stigwood seemed to feel like he had a hit on his hands – and, well, he hadn't steered the brothers wrong before ...

In Dennis Bryon's book *You Should Be Dancing: My Life With The Bee Gees*, he remembers Barry mentioning the film before he'd left the UK for France: 'Barry called me at my house in Cardiff: 'Hi Den. Robert's making a film in New York. It's a low-budget project called *Tribal Rites of the New Saturday Night*. He wants us to put down a few songs for the film''.

However, Albhy Galuten recalled things a bit differently when he explained the course of events to *Albumism* in 2017: 'My memory is that they had roughly written the outline of 'Stayin' Alive' when they were in Bermuda with Robert before that, and they had the outlines of a lot of the songs'. The most important thing to clarify is that The Bee Gees' contributions to what became *Saturday Night Fever* were not custom vehicles built specifically for the storyline. Some accounts insist that 'Stayin' Alive' was conceived after Stigwood's request. But Albhy said, 'Yeah, we had no idea about the film. We'd never seen it, and we didn't know much about it at all. We weren't writing stuff for a film. We were just writing nice music that happened to work for the film'.

The team stayed in France throughout March and tackled three additional songs: '(Our Love) Don't Throw It All Away' (a Barry and Blue Weaver co-write), 'How Deep Is Your Love', and 'Stayin' Alive'. The

Château was isolated, and the early-spring weather left them with little to do but tinker with the tracks. Albhy said in the 2020 *Broken Heart* documentary: 'We had the demos, and then we went into the process of making real records. Barry and Karl and I lived in that control room, I don't know, 16 hours a day'.

In April, the entire operation was moved back to Miami, where they once again took over Criteria Studios' Studio C for further adjustments and mixing. 'Stayin' Alive', 'How Deep Is Your Love', and 'Night Fever' were firmly designated as the three contributions The Bee Gees would have included on the soundtrack album, while their recordings of 'More Than A Woman' and 'If I Can't Have You' were to be used as demos for final versions recorded by Tavares and Yvonne Elliman, respectively. 'Warm Ride' was never used; most likely because it sounded too much like 'Night Fever'. However, it did surface on several other artists' projects over the next two years.

Meanwhile, Andy's first RSO single, 'I Just Want To Be Your Everything', was released in the US that month (delayed until May in the UK), very quickly making its debut on the *Billboard* Hot 100 the week of 22 April. This was immediate proof that Barry was able to work his songwriting and production magic outside of The Bee Gees. The combination of Andy's fresh young voice, an infectious melody, and Barry's obvious background falsetto presence was irresistible to US radio and retail.

The positive experience the Barry/Albhy/Karl production team had making *Flowing Rivers* with Andy led them to more external projects. The first was in April for New York-based rock band Network. Albhy and Karl were producing their eponymous debut album, but Barry was also involved with assembling the set's first single 'Save Me, Save Me'. Albhy recalled in 2021: 'Barry and I wrote the song, and we thought it was a hit. It was at a time when we were recognising hits and making good hits. The band was brought to us by (future Sony Music CEO) Tommy Mottola, who was their manager ... They asked Barry to write a hit song with a falsetto chorus, so that's what the original version of 'Save Me, Save Me' had. When we got to the studio to record it, Tommy said, 'You know, I think they need to be harder than that. The chorus can't be in falsetto, it has to be in natural voice'. So, when we restructured the song for natural voices, [the released version] it just didn't work. I think, honestly, if Tommy had left it the way it was originally conceived, it would've been a hit record'.

The fact that 'Save Me, Save Me' was a flop makes it bewildering that five other artists released their own versions of it over the next 18 months. The Four Seasons frontman Frankie Valli added it to his July 1978 solo album *Frankie Valli ... Is The Word* – the same month singer Teri DeSario included it on her debut LP *Pleasure Train*, along with its Barry-written lead single 'Ain't Nothing Gonna Keep Me From You'. American rock band Rare Earth and bandleader/arranger Ray Conniff also recorded the song in 1978. Finally, legendary British singer Dusty Springfield covered it for her eleventh studio album *Living Without Your Love,* in January 1979.

One win from the Network sessions was the team meeting keyboardist George Bitzer, whose intuitive ear had impressed Barry, Albhy, and Karl. On numerous occasions over the next decade, Bitzer was hired to play on several tracks for the Gibbs and related artists.

The next project was for Samantha Sang – an Australian singer who had already recorded with Barry in England in summer 1969, resulting in the single 'The Love Of A Woman' and 'Don't Let It Happen Again, (both penned by Barry and Maurice), but with little resulting success. Sang reportedly visited Barry while The Bee Gees were in France, and they agreed to try again after the *Saturday Night Fever* sessions were finished in April. Allegedly, Sang had originally been offered '(Our Love) Don't Throw It All Away', but the production team eventually opted to cut a new track called 'Emotion' – a mid-tempo ballad that had reportedly taken Barry and Robin just ten minutes to write. Albhy remembered the session in a 2021 interview with the authors: 'That's Barry doing all the background parts. One of my favourite things about it – and I'm sure when you've listened to it, you've never noticed it before – is the synthesiser intro at the beginning, which I played. It's a dead steal from [American jazz and blues singer and pianist Dinah Washington's] 'September In The Rain''.

Since The Bee Gees' band was on a break at the time, the producers brought in the players from Andy's *Flowing Rivers* to build the instrumentals for the song: drummer Ron 'Tubby' Ziegler, bassist Harold Cowart, guitarists Joey Murcia and George Terry, and their new associate, George Bitzer. Barry was impressed with how agile they were at creating a custom sound for each record, and, according to Albhy, 'Emotion' might have been the catalyst for changing his studio ethos, and, eventually, the fate of The Bee Gees' relationship with Blue, Alan, and Dennis. Albhy told the authors in 2021:

Being a band is an incredible, wonderful thing. And they'd really sort of become a band. But when you're in a band, it's very much collaborative. Everyone's coming up with their own parts, and you hope it all works out in the end. With session musicians, you kind of explain to them what you want, and they do it. And maybe you said, 'Well, no, I'd like something a little more upbeat', and they say, 'Yes sir!'. And they are creative and they're coming up with the parts, but they're much more 'Do you want blue? Green? Tell me what you want and I'll do it'. You can be much more specific. I think for Barry, the Samantha Sang record kind of showed him, 'Oh, wow! I get to have the final say. I have this unspoken communication with Albhy and Karl. And there's nobody that's not in the room – it's not like, say, Robin's going to come in after five hours and say 'I don't like it'. The three of us were always in the room, and we'd developed this unspoken language. We could just look at each other and go, 'No, that vocal needs to be replaced'. The right person can say it with the right amount of tact, but we were all sort-of firing on the same cylinders. For Barry, it was really fun, and it came out at a time when they were very hot – it was a hit record when there were lots of other hit records.

In contrast with 'Save Me, Save Me', 'Emotion' was a major hit when it was released in December, hitting the charts just in time to nestle itself among the supportive momentum of the *Saturday Night Fever* soundtrack in March 1978; reaching number three in *Billboard* and topping the *Cashbox* chart in the US. It was also a number one hit in Canada and New Zealand, and it reached 11 in the UK. The Gibbs were so omnipresent on the charts and airwaves at the time that many believed Samantha's breathy lead vocal was really Barry's falsetto voice slowed down to disguise it so The Bee Gees could rack up another hit under another moniker.

Barry, Albhy, and Karl also produced the single's B-side 'When Love Is Gone' – a curious decision since the song wasn't written by anyone in the Gibb camp (it was penned by American singer-songwriters Brian Wells and Paul Evans, and French film-score composer Francis Lai). The song has an arrangement like, but slower than, its A-side, and closes with Barry's unmistakable falsetto ad libs. Samantha's *Emotion* album contained two additional Gibb songs: a new take of 'The Love Of A Woman', and a cover of 'Charade'.

Recognising the timelessness of 'Emotion', American pop singer Johnny Mathis rushed to record it (as a duet with soul chanteuse Deniece Williams) for his March 1978 album, *You Light Up My Life*, which also included a cover of 'How Deep Is Your Love'.

'Emotion' has enjoyed a rather lengthy shelf life. In 1994, The Bee Gees finally recorded their own slightly more up-tempo version for a compilation titled *Love Songs*, which ended up being shelved. The recording officially saw the light of day on the 2001 best-of package *Their Greatest Hits: The Record*. That same year, US R&B outfit Destiny's Child released it as the third single from their *Survivor* album, which saw the song return to the US top ten and chart similarly in many European countries, including the UK. Former Spice Girls member Emma Bunton also covered it for her 2019 album, *My Happy Place*.

In May, *Here At Last ... Bee Gees ... Live* was released internationally.

Here At Last ... Bee Gees ... Live (1977)

Personnel:
Barry Gibb: vocals, guitar
Robin Gibb: vocals
Maurice Gibb: vocals, bass
Alan Kendall: guitar
Dennis Bryon: drums
Blue Weaver: keyboards, synthesiser
Geoff Westley: keyboards
Joey Murcia: guitar
Joe Lala: percussion
Horns: The Boneroo Horns – Peter Graves: trombone, Whit Sidener: alto sax, Ken Faulk: trumpet, Peter Ballin: tenor sax, Jeff Kievit: trumpet, Stan Webb: baritone sax
Recorded 20 December 1976 with the Wally Heider Mobile Unit No. 1, at The Forum, Los Angeles
Engineers: Ray Thompson, Paul Sandweis, Mike Caver, Karl Richardson, Michel Marie
Concert Sound by Showco – engineer: John Balsutta
Mixed January-February 1977 at Château d'Hérouville, France
Release date: UK and US: May 1977
Chart positions: New Zealand: 1, Spain: 2, Australia: 8, US: 8
Tracklisting: Side 1: 1. 'I've Gotta Get A Message To You', 2. 'Love So Right',

3. 'Edge Of The Universe', 4. 'Come On Over', 5. 'Can't Keep A Good Man Down'
Side 2: 1. Medley: 'New York Mining Disaster 1941'/2. 'Run To Me'/2b. 'World'/3a. 'Holiday'/3b. 'I Can't See Nobody'/3c. 'I Started A Joke'/3d. 'Massachusetts', 4. 'How Can You Mend A Broken Heart', 5. 'To Love Somebody'
Side 3: 1. 'You Should Be Dancing', 2. 'Boogie Child', 3. 'Down The Road', 4. 'Words'
Side 4: 1. 'Wind Of Change', 2. 'Nights On Broadway', 3. 'Jive Talkin'', 4. 'Lonely Days'

Here At Last ... Bee Gees ... Live captures the group and band in superb form. The original raw tracks on the *King Biscuit Flower Hour* radio show were broadcast before they were remixed for the album. Copies of the *King Biscuit* recordings have circulated for years, so comparisons between those and the final mix can easily be made. To be fair, the live album is quite faithful to the original concert recording. Only one major cut was made from the stage programme – the band introductions, which gave the audience a bit of a breather before the concert climax and encores. Though the intros are good to hear on the *King Biscuit* version, it really does interrupt the flow of the music as a home listening experience.

The album performances show The Bee Gees at what may be their vocal peak, along with their most cohesive and exciting live band. The arrangement and playing feel much more energetic and visceral than on the later concert recordings from the *One For All* and *One Night Only* tours. Even the explosive 1979 *Spirits Having Flown* tour felt shiny and corporate by comparison, and the addition of vocal group The Sweet Inspirations – as legendary as they are – felt unnecessary as a complement to the Gibbs' extraordinary vocals. From start to finish, *Here At Last ...* is a rich listening experience and completely unpretentious.

The songs here were an evolution of the 1975 *Main Course* tour set, but with fewer deep cuts like 'Don't Wanna Live Inside Myself' and 'Road To Alaska'. The only unexpected twist on the 1976 tour was the reintroduction of *Mr. Natural*'s 'Down The Road' to the setlist, which had great stage energy.

The Forum show was filmed for a possible TV special, however, after reviewing the footage, the group was unhappy with the video quality and the idea was canned. It's not known if that video still exists in a vault somewhere.

The album gave The Bee Gees their second consecutive top ten showing in North America, and scored them their second RIAA Platinum disc. It was also a major hit in Australasia, topping the charts in New Zealand and ranking as *Recorded Music New Zealand*'s fifth most-successful album for the year.

The album's US success was largely propelled by an extensive (and certainly expensive) prime-time TV ad campaign – something RSO had never done before. Over three weeks in late August and early September, commercials were run in primetime slots on networks in 15 major centres: New York, Los Angeles, Chicago, Philadelphia, Boston, San Francisco, Washington, D.C., Cleveland, Dallas-Fort Worth, St. Louis, Minneapolis-St. Paul, Miami, Atlanta, Seattle-Tacoma, and Baltimore. *Billboard* estimated the campaign extended the album's retail life well into the fall – to the tune of an extra 450,000 in unit sales.

The album cover image of the brothers performing during the medley portion of the concert was taken by acclaimed American photographer Waring Abbott, as were the individual back cover photographs from the performance. Only one can be pinpointed to a particular song – that being Barry performing 'Words,' for which he has always taken off his guitar and held the microphone in his hand. The gothic-lettered logo on the cover was now synonymous with their brand.

The inner gatefold superimposed three similar full-stage shots at varying angles, making it difficult to interpret at first sight. These appear to have been taken at rehearsal, as the band's attire appears more casual than in the show images. The inner sleeve photos were taken by Andy Kent, Neal Preston, and Ed Caraeff.

The album became available as a two-CD set in 1990 but has not been reprised in that format since. Capitol/UMe did reissue it on black and limited-edition tangerine vinyl on 8 May 2020.

A superb, powerful new arrangement made 'I've Gotta Get A Message to You' an impressive concert opener. A blast of horns on the intro replaces the piano-string-voice combo on the original recording, and the slowed tempo gives the song a more deliberately soulful feel. The key change near the end is a good launching pad for Barry's natural-voiced ad-libs as the track winds down, finishing with all three in harmony on the final chord.

'Love So Right' was still in the US top 30 on the night of the Forum concert, having peaked at number three a few weeks earlier, so the crowd response at the start is proportionally fervent. This live version is very faithful to the arrangement on *Children Of The World*, although Robin's voice is much more prominent on the chorus.

The live version of 'Edge Of The Universe' was released as a single alongside the album in May 1977 (August in the UK), clearly aiming to boost album sales with some radio recognition. 'Words' – with its refreshed live arrangement – was the B-side. The single was a top 20 hit in Canada and New Zealand and reached the top 30 in the US. Its selection is a bit unusual as it wasn't one of the strongest tracks on this album or *Main Course*, but, by association, it was recognisable enough to get them a bit more mileage out of the latter. The single was heavily edited, lopping off over two minutes of its original album length.

'Come On Over' and 'Can't Keep A Good Man Down' are both faithful reproductions of the original versions that only solidify the band's reputation for sounding just as good in the studio as they did on stage.

By the time of the Forum show took place, the group had amassed 26 chart singles in the US alone. So, what do you do when you have so many hits and limited time in your set? Turn them into a crowd-pleasing medley, of course! The Bee Gees had incorporated a medley section in concerts since the November 1968 tour of Germany when they performed the rather bizarre combination of 'In My Own Time', Frankie Valli and the Four Seasons' 'C'mon Marianne', 'I Can't See Nobody', and Cream's 'Strange Brew'. On the 1971 tour, they included a short acoustic medley of their Australian-era songs 'Jingle Jangle' and 'In The Morning', and in 1974 they coupled the latter with 'Alexander's Ragtime Band' – a staple from their cabaret gigs in the days before they even had a recording contract. By 1975, the medley was extended to include many old favourites, much like the one here. But on rare occasions, the audience was treated to portions of more rarely performed picks like 'Don't Forget to Remember', which segued into the chorus of the never-before (or again) performed 'Odessa'.

The Bee Gees' medleys were often played with minimal instrumentation – usually, they involved just the brothers singing around a microphone with Barry's acoustic guitar as a guide. Although here, 'I Started A Joke' and 'Massachusetts' benefit from drums, keyboards, and a bit of sweetening from Alan Kendall's slide guitar-playing.

Barry's natural tenor voice on the 'Run To Me'/'World' portion is probably the most gorgeously clear it's ever sounded, in concert or otherwise.

Their seminal classic 'To Love Somebody' had received a major makeover for the *Main Course* shows, which was kept for this tour. The original's baroque-pop bounce is slowed down significantly, sounding more bluesy and grittier and giving Barry plenty of time to tease out the verses in his full-chest voice. The horns follow suit, buoyed by a bellowing baritone sax, and a Hammond organ replaces the string flourishes at the end of the chorus. After 1979's *Spirits Having Flown* tour, this version of the song was abandoned and future live renditions followed the original arrangement much more closely but without the brass section and live strings.

'You Should Be Dancing' here sounds very much like the prototype. But at 4:15 – where the song would usually end – the band launches into a five-minute jam, straight through to the finish.

The Forum show took place just days before 'Boogie Child' was released as the third single from *Children Of The World*, perhaps explaining why the crowd reaction is fairly reserved. Blue Weaver and Alan Kendall got to have a bit of fun with the extended length.

The Bee Gees needed to rock out more, and on the rare occasions they did, they did it well – as this blistering performance of 'Down The Road' proves. It was an odd tour song choice given it was a *Mr. Natural* deep cut and was likely unknown to their more recent followers. But they sped it up significantly to a near-'You Should Be Dancing' tempo, and Barry belts out the verses in his powerful natural register with considerable gusto. Sadly, they didn't perform it on future tours.

The standard 'Words' was reworked for mid-1970s tastes. Gone was Maurice's simple compressed-piano introduction – this version features Blue Weaver teasing the melody out more intricately in a similar vein to 'Songbird'. Alan Kendall joins midway with a beautifully subtle pedal steel, giving it a distinctive country flavour that develops as the song progresses. It's arguably one of the best arrangements of it they ever performed live.

A brisk-paced version of 'Wind Of Change' steps the performance up gear and is the first of three consecutive numbers from the *Main Course* album. The Boneroo Horns' saxophonists Peter Ballin, Whit Sidener, and Stan Webb interject a few energetic woodwind blasts throughout, and Joe Lala gets a few nice opportunities to flex his conga skills. Robin's solo vocal also pops up unexpectedly at the beginning of each of the verses.

Obviously, the audience would want to hear the falsetto ad-libs at the end of 'Nights On Broadway', but Barry's thick natural voice is integral to the melody's strength. As previously mentioned, Maurice takes on the task – perhaps not achieving the same power, but he matches the range flawlessly to the point where there's still some debate among fans as to whether they are Barry's vocals that were either pre-recorded or added to the mix later.

One of the group's most introspective tracks – 'Lonely Days' – was elevated to a raise-the-rafters affair from its more reserved studio original, especially with the faster choruses. It remained a permanent concert fixture for the rest of their career.

While filming for *Saturday Night Fever* was wrapping up in New York in May, Robert Stigwood was already focused on other projects. Shooting of a movie version of the hit Broadway musical *Grease* was set to start in June – again with John Travolta in the lead role (of Danny Zuko) as part of a three-picture deal he'd signed with RSO. Long-time Gibb family friend Olivia Newton-John was set to star as Sandy Olsson opposite Travolta.

What Stigwood came up with next was perhaps initially inspiring in concept – but as the year wore on, its application became disastrous for nearly everyone involved. In late 1976, he'd approached Beatles producer George Martin with the idea of making a fantasy film based on the band's 1967 opus, *Sgt. Pepper's Lonely Hearts Club Band*, and requested he serve as the project's musical director. Martin was sceptical, even though Stigwood had promised him autonomy and a handsome payment. Martin wrote about his reservations in his 1979 autobiography, *All You Need Is Ears*:

> My first inclination was to say no out of hand. I knew in my heart of hearts that The Beatles would not have approved. And – although I don't need their permission to run my life – I still wondered if it was right to go over old ground. On the other hand, Robert assured me that if I took the job on, I would have complete artistic control over the music, and would be able to dictate exactly what it should sound like. In addition, he was dangling a small fortune under my nose – more than I had ever had for a film before. Then I asked myself whether I was really thinking of doing it because of the money. If you do something for money which otherwise you don't want to do, you are doing it for the wrong reason, and you shouldn't do it at all.

Stigwood had imagined the affair as a spectacular all-star tribute to The Beatles and their music, brought to life on screen and bolstered by new interpretations of songs from the original *Sgt. Pepper* and a script woven around them. He got The Bee Gees on board to front the film along with singer-guitarist Peter Frampton by May, which is when filming was supposed to start. Martin said delays ensued because 'No one was cast in the other roles, and all sorts of names – some plausible, others highly implausible – were being bandied about. Then there was trouble with the director. The first one they hired was a television director, who proved to be unsuitable, and it took some time to find a replacement'.

Fulfilling the ultimate rock-and-roll dream that Dr. Hook & The Medicine Show sang about on their 1972 hit 'The Cover Of *Rolling Stone*', The Bee Gees' resurgent success put them on the front of issue 243 of the magazine on 14 July 1977.

To support his rising career and the continued chart ascension of 'I Just Want To Be Your Everything', Andy Gibb began making the rounds on television – starting with the 14 May episode of *American Bandstand*, performing his rising hit and 'Flowing Rivers', followed by a studio appearance on *Top Of The Pops* in the UK on 16 June.

After a 14-week climb up the *Billboard* Hot 100, 'I Just Want To Be Your Everything' reached number one on 30 July. It displayed incredible chart stamina in the US. After three weeks at the pole position, the single relinquished its peak to American R&B group The Emotions' 'Best Of My Love'. After sitting in the top three for almost a month, Andy's single reclaimed the top spot on 15 September – a very unusual chart feat at the time. It spent a total of 16 weeks in the top ten, becoming US radios' most-played track of 1977, and was named as *Billboard*'s number two single for the year. Those accomplishments have held up strongly over the years. In a 2018 ranking of 60 years of the Hot 100 chart, 'I Just Want To Be Your Everything' was placed at 29. It also topped the charts in Canada, Australia, Brazil, and Chile. In the UK, it stalled at 26. Despite Andy's massive success across the pond, the European response to his music was to remain tepid throughout his career – partially a symptom of RSO focusing its energy on the North American market, but also a product of the Gibbs perhaps being a bit out of touch with non-US tastes.

Andy returned to *American Bandstand* on 6 August to reprise the single, along with '(Love Is) Thicker Than Water', which had been chosen as the second single from the forthcoming *Flowing Rivers* album. He also performed the two songs the day before on NBC's *The Midnight Special*.

The Bee Gees' summer was relatively quiet as they waited to begin work on the *Sgt. Pepper* film and soundtrack. In the meantime, Barry and Linda vacated their Isle of Man home and moved to Miami Beach permanently. Most of the Gibb family soon followed, including Linda and Yvonne's parents and her brother Herbie. Andy and Kim Gibb also relocated to the area, and Hugh, Barbara, and Beri Gibb left Australia to join their brood. Robin and Molly continued to spend most of their time in England, purchasing a new house in Virginia Water, Surrey.

Barry and Linda had transplanted themselves just in time to welcome their second son Ashley Robert Crompton Gibb, born at 9:00 a.m. on 8 September at Miami's Mount Sinai Hospital. Ashley was born with a heart disorder and spent his first month in intensive care.

About a week later, Barry joined the twins at Cherokee Studios in Hollywood to record songs for the *Sgt. Pepper* soundtrack. Filming began a month later at MGM (now Sony Pictures) and Universal City Studios.

On 9 September – nearly a year after it was recorded – Andy Gibb's debut album *Flowing Rivers* was finally released. It reached number 19 in the US, and was certified Gold on 22 November, and Platinum on 4 August 1978. In Canada and Sweden, it peaked at 9 and 4, respectively.

Andy promoted the album by appearing on *The Mike Douglas Show* on 8 September. He was then featured on the 23 September broadcast of the syndicated music show *Don Kirshner's Rock Concert*. He performed an excellent extended set that included half the album's tracks: 'Flowing Rivers', 'Starlight', 'I Just Want To Be Your Everything', '(Love Is) Thicker Than Water', and 'Too Many Looks In Your Eyes'. For this and other TV performances, Andy was backed by American pop/rock band Pages, which consisted of future Mr. Mister members Richard Page and Steve George on background vocals, and keyboardist and guitarist Peter Leinheiser, bassist Jerry Manfredi, and drummer Russ Battelene. The band accompanied Andy on his first North American tour later in the year.

Released alongside *Flowing Rivers* was the set's second single, '(Love Is) Thicker Than Water', which Barry and Andy had worked on the previous year. Albhy Galuten told *Albumism* in 2017: 'I don't know if I'd call it underrated, but it's a really, really unusual song'. Structurally, it was different from much of what Barry had written in recent years, and it certainly deviated from the singer-songwriter vibe Andy had been following in his songs. There isn't a specifically catchy verse/ chorus exchange – which might have been a bit of a risk for RSO after the previous single being such a compelling pop record. Commercially, '(Love Is) Thicker Than Water' was slow burning – but after an 18-week climb, it reached number one on 4 March 1978, replacing The Bee Gees'

'Stayin' Alive' at the top of the *Billboard* Hot 100. Andy's single landed at number two in Canada but failed to chart in the UK.

While *Saturday Night Fever* was still in post-production prior to its release, Robert Stigwood took a major gamble and released a single from it. Not that the stunningly beautiful 'How Deep Is Your Love' needed the context of the movie to be a massive hit, of course, but its success did have implications for the opening of the film. According to RSO President Bill Oakes in the 2020 *Broken Heart* documentary, Robert said:

'Why do we wait for the release of the film? Let's put out a single now'. And then he started with the heads of Paramount, like, 'How many theatres?'. And they told him something like 200. He said, 'I'm releasing the record in every city. Why can't [the movie] be in every city?'. So, they made a deal whereby if the record got to the top 20, they would increase the number of screens. If it got top ten, they'd go more.

Luckily, Stigwood won out. 'How Deep Is Your Love' debuted in the US at number 83 the week of 22 September. The following week it was in the top 50, and two weeks later reached the top 20. Right in time for the soundtrack release in mid-November, the single jumped to nine on its way to number one. Three weeks ahead of the movie's theatrical release, the soundtrack was on store shelves.

Saturday Night Fever (Soundtrack) (1977)
Personnel:
Barry Gibb: vocal, guitar
Robin Gibb: vocal
Maurice Gibb: vocal, bass guitar
Blue Weaver: keyboards
Alan Kendall: guitar
Dennis Bryon: drums
Joe Lala: percussion
Horns: The Boneroo Horns – Peter Graves: trombone, Whit Sidener: alto sax, Ken Faulk: trumpet, Peter Ballin: tenor sax, Jeff Kievit: trumpet, Stan Webb: baritone sax
String arrangements: Wade Marcus
Engineers: Karl Richardson (Criteria), Michel Marie (Château d'Hérouville)
Producers: The Bee Gees, Albhy Galuten, Karl Richardson
Recorded between February and March 1977 at Château d'Hérouville,

France; Circa-April 1977 at Criteria Studios, Miami; September 1977,
Cherokee Studios, Los Angeles ('More Than A Woman', 'If I Can't Have You')
Release dates: US: 15 November 1977, UK: December 1977
Chart positions: Australia: 1, Austria: 1, Canada: 1, France: 1, West
Germany: 1, Italy: 1, Japan: 1, Netherlands: 1, New Zealand: 1, Norway: 1,
Sweden: 1, UK: 1, US: 1
Gold certification: France, Greece, Italy
Platinum certification: West Germany (x3), Netherlands, UK (x7), US (x16)
Diamond certification: Canada

While the early chart performance of 'How Deep Is Your Love' might
have been an indication of the film and soundtrack's hit potential, it's
abundantly clear that nobody involved had anticipated the cultural
landslide they'd be caught up in by the end of the year. Gaining
explosive popularity within a matter of weeks, *Fever* – and by pure
association, The Bee Gees – became the universal representatives of the
disco movement in almost every sense. But neither the film nor The Bee
Gees were the catalyst for it. Former RSO president Bill Oakes counters
that the broad societal disco trend was on a downward slide by 1977,
and even Paramount executives had chided him while it was being
developed. Oakes told *Vanity Fair* in 2013: 'They thought it was rather
silly. Disco had run its course. These days, *Fever* is credited with kicking
off the whole disco thing – it really didn't. Truth is, it breathed new life
into a genre that was actually dying'.

Saturday Night Fever – like the culture it documents – is a complicated
film. It might be propelled by the gloss of its fervent music and energetic
dance sequences, but it also quite bluntly contends with the class
segregation, racism, homophobia, misogyny, sexual violence, and drug
and alcohol abuse that had an impact on real people in real places.
On first viewing, many were shocked by the film's explicit nature.
Perhaps that's why it resonated so deeply – it reflected how people were
frustrated with their enviromental restraints, whether they were cultural,
economic or generational. Albby Galuten explained to *Albumism* in 2017:

The thing that makes music really touch lots of people, is when it gives
some sort of a voice to people who have not had a voice. The Beatles
gave a voice to adolescents, and obviously, Motown and Stax gave a
voice to people who did not have a voice, just like hip hop did. And
so, I always wonder, 'Who did *Saturday Night Fever* give voice to?'.

And then I realised, it was working-class Americans who had no output and nobody representing them. And here was something saying, 'Even though my day-to-day life may be mundane, I can go out on Saturday night and I can resonate. This speaks to me'.

Given that none of The Bee Gees' songs were tailored for the film, it's miraculous how seamlessly and effectively they escalate the narrative. Although 'How Deep Is Your Love' had gained traction before anything else from the film was in the public eye and ear, one wonders if 'Stayin' Alive' or 'Night Fever' would have had quite the same impact had they just been included on The Bee Gees' planned studio album.

The *Saturday Night Fever* soundtrack has sold well over 50,000,000 copies worldwide, and it was the biggest-selling album of all time until Michael Jackson's *Thriller* usurped it in 1983. In the US, *Fever* spent 24 consecutive weeks at number one, and nearly three years in total on the album chart. It's an achievement that's even more impressive given it was a rather expensive double LP with a price of about $12.98 (roughly $61 in 2022 terms, adjusted for inflation). The soundtrack topped charts worldwide. In the UK, it was ranked the fifth top-selling album of the decade.

The *Fever* set has been reissued numerous times since 1977, receiving a 40th anniversary box set commemoration on 17 November 2017 that included a complete remaster, new remixes of 'Stayin' Alive', 'Night Fever', 'How Deep Is Your Love', and 'You Should Be Dancing' by famed Romanian-Canadian DJ and engineer Serban Ghenea, a collector's book, art prints, a movie poster, and a turntable mat.

The rest of the soundtrack contained original score pieces Robert Stigwood commissioned from American composer David Shire – plus a wide slate of mostly familiar tracks, like KC and the Sunshine Band's 'Boogie Shoes', and Walter Murphy's 'A Fifth Of Beethoven', which had been hits within the prior two years. Whilst the artists probably got a boost in exposure by association, it's unlikely they made much from the album's stratospheric sales. Albhy Galuten told *Albumism* in 2017:

In the annals of history, it could be one of the most profitable records ever created because it's a double album, and I don't know how much Robert paid David Shire in royalties, because a lot of the songs like 'Night On Disco Mountain' are just sort of orchestra stuff to fill out the album. I mean, you know, he did a good job and they're all fine and lovely, but they're not pop songs. And songs like 'Boogie Shoes' – it was all in the plan to have a few hits and to have a lot of stuff that was inexpensive. I believe I heard that [Stigwood] has licensed those songs – like the Ralph MacDonald track ['Calypso Breakdown'] – for pennies. I think the only things he was paying full royalties on, were the major artists. I don't even know what the deals were like for Tavares or Yvonne Elliman. They didn't have huge hits at the time, so they probably had really low licensing fees. The person that made out like a bandit with that record – besides The Bee Gees, because writers' royalties are fixed and they're not negotiable – was Robert and RSO Records.

'How Deep Is Your Love', 'Stayin' Alive, and 'Night Fever' all reached the top of the *Billboard* singles chart consecutively, accumulating a total of 15 weeks at the summit between 24 December 1977 and 13 May 1978. Though that run is impressive, it was only one of many staggering commercial achievements The Bee Gees and their associated productions would garner over the next two years.

While the Gibbs' songs were created in a vacuum a continent away from the film's Brooklyn setting, their permanent adhesion to the images of John Travolta as dancing dunce Tony Manero tripping the light fantastic in some ways obfuscated their brilliance as individual pieces of art. The music was to bring The Bee Gees immeasurable fame and success – the otherworldly kind that only a tiny fraction of acts has ever experienced. But becoming a phenomenon comes with a cost, and it was one that was to change the course of their personal and professional lives forever. The Bee Gees spent many following years alternating between completely rejecting *Saturday Night Fever* and gleefully embracing it as part of their legacy as it fell in and out of public favour. But since the late 1990s, the soundtrack has been more widely lauded as a cultural asset. It was added to the US National Recording Registry in the Library of Congress in March 2013 for preservation as a historically important artistic work. Even *Rolling Stone* – which has typically been dismissive of The Bee Gees' catalogue – has consistently ranked the soundtrack among its 500 greatest albums of all time.

The album cover, emblazoned with a striking gold, blue, and silver logo – and, of course, a glittering disco ball – was designed by Susan Herr and Tom Nikosey, the latter of whom had styled the graphics of *Children Of The World*. The imposing Bee Gees portrait looming over an oddly artificial-looking figure of John Travolta on a lit-up dance floor was shot by famed American fashion photographer Francesco Scavullo. It's likely the most well-known image of the Gibbs – posed grinning, standing shoulder-to-shoulder in body-hugging white outfits. It's been copied and parodied many times – even by The Bee Gees themselves.

The movie-set dance floor measured 24 x 16 feet (7.3 x 5 metres) and was made up of 288 coloured light-up squares, which flashed to their own time along with the music. The dance floor was sold at auction for $1.2 million in Calabasas, California, on 27 June 2017 – a world record for a piece of a film set.

'Stayin' Alive' (Barry Gibb, Robin Gibb, Maurice Gibb)

Recorded at Château d'Hérouville, France: February/March 1977and
Criteria Studios, Miami: circa April 1977
Chart positions: Australia: 1, Canada: 1, Italy: 1, Mexico: 1, Netherlands: 1, New Zealand: 1, South Africa: 1, US: 1, Austria: 2, Belgium: 2, Finland: 2, France: 2, Spain: 2, Switzerland: 2, West Germany: 2, Sweden: 3, Ireland: 4, Norway: 4, UK: 4
Gold certification: Denmark, France
Platinum certification: Canada, Italy, UK, US

> Great steaming medallions and disco boots, what do we have here? The most dangerous record of the '70s. Place record on turntable, light fuse and stand well back.
> Barry Gibb, 1990

Barry's quote is acerbic, but appropriate given The Bee Gees' and the public's complicated relationship with 'Stayin' Alive'. It's the most famous song in their catalogue, and likely the most polarising. It's been celebrated for its recording excellence and condemned for its wide association with the perceived gaucheness of 1970s pop culture. Understandably, the Gibbs' affections for it have waxed and waned over the years.

From a writing, production and sonic standpoint, 'Stayin' Alive' is a wonder. Not a second of its nearly five-minute length is wasted as the Gibbs' multitracked vocals, strings, horns, percussion, and keys bounce around its soundscape. Its trademark walking guitar line (allegedly modelled after American R&B singer-songwriter Betty Wright's 1972 hit 'Clean Up Woman') was developed by co-producer Albhy Galuten and taught to guitarist Alan Kendall in the studio. Albhy also credited the brothers with contributing elements of the string and horn arrangement

– Robin, for example, came up with the dramatic string cascades at the end of the breakdowns where Barry sings, 'Life's goin' nowhere/ Somebody help me, yeah'. Underneath it all is the perfect chug of Barry's rhythm guitar.

The film's producers had at one point decided to use 'Stayin' Alive' for John Travolta and Karen Lynn Gorney's mid-film dance scene and requested that a slow section be written into the song. The Gibbs and their producers begrudgingly obliged at first, creating a version that plays through the first two verses as usual, but diverts to a short ballad segment with a key change – sounding melodically like the bridge on 'Love Me'. The section's romantic lyric, 'When you are close to me, I feel no pain/I see rainbows that flow from your hair', is lovely, but did absolutely nothing to support the survivalist grit that gave the track its urgency. In 2017, Albhy told *Albumism* the brothers 'wrote it and we put it in. And we *hated* it. We were like, 'No! This *sucks*! You had a hit song and you just blew it!'". After heated protest, the film's producers conceded and the original uncompromised version, mercifully, prevailed.

Additionally, 'Stayin' Alive' prompted an unexpected studio innovation that was to have a major lasting effect on not only the Gibbs' future recordings but on the work of incalculable other artists and producers. Drummer Dennis Bryon had to leave the sessions to attend to his ailing mother, who was ill with Alzheimer's disease, before his performance could be captured. After toying with the idea of using a drum machine instead, it was decided to fabricate something that sounded more authentic by isolating a small section of Bryon's drums from the recording of 'Night Fever' and creating a loop from it. Employing an intricate system of spliced tape sections and reels strategically placed around the editing room (Albhy and Karl visually recreated the setup for a segment of the 2020 *Broken Heart* documentary), they were able to produce a full drum track that was rhythmically steady without being overtly mechanical. Given a tongue-in-cheek credit as 'Bernard Lupe', the same loop track was used on 'More Than A Woman', and two years later in some variation on songs from Barbra Streisand's *Guilty* album: 'Woman in Love', 'Life Story', and 'What Kind of Fool'. What was intended to be a temporary gap filler in Dennis' absence became the heartbeat of the entire song. When he returned, he agreed the fix had to be kept and added cymbals and hi-hats to give the track texture.

The recording of 'Stayin' Alive' completely changed the way the team made records moving forward. While much of their work to that point had been played live in the studio, the looping process seemed to especially fuel Barry's interest in constructing separate elements of a song to achieve perfect timing and lush complexity and assembling them later. However, Albhy later lamented to *Albumism* about them not continuing to take a more organic approach: 'Stayin' Alive', in particular, was the first time we were really putting things together one at a time, unfortunately. I think now everybody does everything one at a time, and I think we suffer a great loss for that because there's not enough people playing together in a room, which creates a lot of serendipity and interesting stuff that you don't get when it's all pieced out'.

While 'Stayin' Alive' will forever remain a memorable part of cinematic history as the essential pulse of John Travolta's emblematic strut down Brooklyn's 86th Street in the movie's opening scene, the track has also lived a long and diverse life as a pop culture opus, appearing in countless films, TV shows, and commercials over the last 40 years. In recent years, the American Heart Association touted it as an effective rhythmic guide for performing emergency cardiopulmonary resuscitation on victims of cardiac arrest. The track has been covered and sampled by a wide range of artists – from Ozzy Osbourne, to Dweezil Zappa, to Tiny Tim. The most commercially successful cover was in 1995 by British electronic group N-Trance, who revamped the song almost completely (except for the guitar lick and vocal hook) with new verses featuring rapper/DJ Ricardo da Force. It was a huge success, reaching number one in Australia and Canada, and two in the UK, Finland, Iceland and Switzerland. In the still-Bee-Gees-averse US market, the single only climbed to number 62. Foo Fighters also recorded the song for their 2021 *Hail Satin* LP. In 2022, producer DJ Khaled released a track titled 'Staying Alive'', which interpolated almost nothing of the original song except for the use of the line 'Ah, ah, ah, I'm stayin' alive'. The Gibbs were still given a writing credit. The single reached number 5 on the *Billboard* Hot 100 and Hip Hop/R&B survey and charted in the top ten in Canada and South Africa.

Proud of their work on the track, The Bee Gees allegedly sent a pre-release copy to their mentor Arif Mardin, who replied insisting that a dance song in a minor key could never be a hit. After the song became the group's biggest-ever single to that point, Mardin reportedly sent his protégés an apologetic bouquet of flowers.

On 10 February 2017, Capitol Records released a new remix by Serban Ghenea, which previewed a 40th-anniversary *Fever* soundtrack reissue which also included Ghenea's refreshed versions of 'Night Fever', 'How Deep Is Your Love', and 'You Should Be Dancing'. While the remixes didn't result in many earth-shattering arrangement changes, the tracks' dynamic ranges are audibly expanded, and there are points where some of the original vocal and instrumental subtleties are almost mixed out amongst all the noise.

'How Deep is Your Love' (Barry Gibb, Robin Gibb, Maurice Gibb)

Recorded at Château d'Hérouville, France: February/March 1977, and Criteria Studios, Miami: circa April 1977

Chart positions: Brazil: 1, Canada: 1, Chile: 1, Finland: 1, France: 1, US: 1; Ireland: 2, Italy: 2, South Africa: 1, Australia: 3, UK: 3, Sweden: 4, Norway: 5, Belgium: 6, New Zealand: 6, Netherlands: 8, Austria: 13, West Germany: 21

Gold certification: Canada; France; US

Platinum certification: UK

Robin Gibb:

> Personalities are examined in this tune, but female or male aren't even mentioned. It has universal connotations, and it clicks with everyone. Before we cut the song, we knew we could fuse some of our own personalities into the track. Love is the anchor; it's a foundation.

'How Deep Is Your Love' was written mainly by Barry, Robin, and Maurice. Barry worked out the melody with keyboard player Blue Weaver, although he is not credited as a songwriter – he should have been. Albhy Galuten later admitted this was 'one song where Blue had a tremendous amount of input. There [were] a lot of things from his personality. That's one where his contribution was quite significant – not in a songwriting sense, though when you play piano, it's almost like writing the song. Blue had a lot of influence on the piano structure of that song'.

Blue tells his story behind this track, though variations of it have been told over the years:

> One morning, it was just myself and Barry in the studio. He said, 'Play the most beautiful chord you know', and I just played. What happened was, I'd throw chords at him, and he'd say, 'No, not that chord', and I'd keep moving around, and he'd say, 'Yeah, that's a nice one', and we'd go from there. Then I'd play another thing. Sometimes I'd be following

the melody line that he already had, and sometimes I'd most probably lead him somewhere else by doing what I did. I think Robin came in at some point. Albhy also came in at one point, and I was playing an inversion of a chord, and he said, 'Oh no, I don't think it should be that inversion, it should be this', and so we changed it to that, but by the time Albhy had come in, the song was sort of there.

In the 2020 *Broken Heart* documentary, Blue added that the song had been inspired by Frédéric Chopin – a previous resident of the Château. 'So, every time I looked at this piano, I envisaged Chopin sitting down and playing. I sat down at the piano and thought of his 'Prelude in E-flat major', and I knew Barry could sing in E-flat. When we were working like that, I had a cassette player, and I'm sure it happened at that point'. A fuzzy recording exists of the song at a very early stage when the melody and lyrics were still being shaped (it's unknown if it's the specific one Blue is referring to). Even with poor sound quality, it's remarkable to hear the song coming to life so quickly.

A cleaner demo was later made at Château d'Hérouville, with additional recording done at Criteria Studios when they returned Miami. Blue recalled:

We started work about 12 o'clock, maybe one o'clock in the morning, and that demo was done at about three or four o'clock in the morning. Albhy played piano on the demo – I'd drunk too much or gone to bed or something. Then I woke up the next morning and listened to that, and then put some strings on it, and that was it. Then we actually recorded it for real in Criteria Studios. The chords and everything stayed the same. The only thing that changes from that demo is that when we got to Criteria Studios, I worked out the electric piano part which became the basis of the song. It was the sound of the piano that makes the feel of that song.

This demo has the song almost in full form, with an audible click track in the background. Barry adds: 'A lot of the textures you hear in the song were added on later. We didn't change any lyrics mind you, but the way we recorded it was a little different than the way we wrote, in the terms of construction. A little different for the better, I think. The title 'How Deep Is Your Love' we thought was perfect because of all the connotations involved in that sentence, and that was simply it'.

The final product is stunning. Barry and Robin's lead vocals on the verses blend almost seamlessly, and Barry's falsetto is constrained to ad-libs and harmonic sweetening. Buoyed by Blue's honey-rich Fender Rhodes piano, the melody sways between major and minor chords, lifting on the chorus with swells of lush strings. It's certainly among the most beautiful songs The Bee Gees ever recorded. Rightfully, it began to soar up the charts before *Saturday Night Fever* was released and became The Bee Gees' fourth American number one single on 24 December. It stayed in the *Billboard* top ten for 17 consecutive weeks, which set a chart record. On *Billboard*'s 2018 60th anniversary rankings of its top singles throughout the history of the chart, 'How Deep Is Your Love' is listed at number 25.

In 1983, Chicago-based songwriter Ronald Selle sued The Bee Gees for plagiarism, citing evidence of two identical eight-bar passages in both 'How Deep Is Your Love' and his 1975 composition 'Let It End'. The case went to trial and the jury initially returned a verdict in favour of Selle. The Gibbs and their legal team appealed, and the verdict was overturned based on Selle's lack of evidence that the Gibbs would have had reasonable access to his song in order to commit the claimed act of plagiarism. Selle's recording had not been publicly released and had only been shopped to labels that had no association with the Gibbs. The Selle vs. Gibb case was an industry landmark and set an important precedent in the adjudication of musical plagiarism litigation.

'How Deep Is Your Love' has become a pop standard with hundreds of cover versions, including those by Johnny Mathis, Luther Vandross, Lionel Hampton, Donny Osmond, Michael Ball, Cilla Black, and even actor David Hasselhoff. The most commercially significant was by English pop group Take That, fronted by lead singer Gary Barlow. Their version – from their 1996 *Greatest Hits* compilation – became a massive hit, reaching number one in the UK, Denmark, Ireland, Italy, Lithuania, and Spain. It was not released in the US. Take That's version was updated in 2018 for another retrospective, *Odyssey*, with Barry providing a guest vocal.

'How Deep Is Your Love' was an obvious classic song choice for Barry's 2021 *Greenfields* album, for which he collaborated with country quartet Little Big Town and renowned Australian guitarist Tommy Emmanuel. It's probably Barry's best vocal on the album; he's in good form with his breathy lead and falsetto. Little Big Town harmonise beautifully on the choruses, and Emmanuel adds tasteful touches throughout.

'Night Fever' (Barry Gibb, Robin Gibb, Maurice Gibb)

Recorded at Château d'Hérouville, France: February/March 1977, and Criteria Studios, Miami: circa April 1977

Chart positions: Brazil: 1, Canada: 1, Ireland: 1, Spain: 1, UK: 1, US: 1, Mexico: 2, New Zealand: 2, Norway: 2, South Africa: 2, Germany: 2, Belgium: 3, Japan: 3, Netherlands: 3, Switzerland: 3, Austria: 4, Italy: 5, Sweden: 5, Finland: 6, Australia: 7

Gold certification: UK

Platinum certification: Canada, US

Wasting no time capitalising on the movie's unprecedented momentum, RSO released 'Night Fever' as a single in February 1978 just as 'Stayin' Alive' hit number one on the *Billboard* Hot 100. 'Night Fever' spent eight weeks at the top, immediately after 'Stayin' Alive' and Andy's '(Love Is) Thicker Than Water' had logged four and two weeks at the summit, respectively. It also landed in second place on *Billboard*'s list top songs of the year behind Andy's 'Shadow Dancing'. 'Night Fever' sold over 2,500,000 copies in the US alone. It became the group's first UK number one since 'I've Gotta Get A Message To You' in 1968, and ranked at 42 on *Billboard*'s 60th-anniversary list of the most successful singles in Hot 100 chart history.

In the film, 'Night Fever' is played under a scene showing Travolta's character primping before a night out. Apparently, the camerawork – which zeroed in on his bare chest and black briefs – caused much pearl-clutching among studio execs who viewed the scene as gratuitously homoerotic. Film director John Badham told *Vanity Fair* in 2013: 'We got all kinds of hassle. We were letting some man walk around in his underwear, showing his body off'.

The song title apparently inspired the Gibbs' suggestion to Stigwood that the film's early title be changed from the clichéd (or, in their words, 'corny') *Saturday Night* to *Saturday Night Fever*. Robert hesitated at first, saying the phrase 'Night Fever' sounded 'too pornographic'.

The genesis of the song's string-swept melody was credited to keyboardist Blue Weaver. He explains in *The Ultimate Biography of The Bee Gees: Tales of the Brothers Gibb*: "'Night Fever' started off because Barry walked in one morning when I was trying to work out something. I always wanted to do a disco version of 'Theme From *A Summer Place*' by The Percy Faith Orchestra or something; it was a big hit in the '60s. I was playing that, and Barry said, 'What was that?', and I said, 'Theme From *A Summer Place*'. Barry said, 'No, it wasn't'. It was new. Barry heard the idea – I was playing it on a string synthesiser – and sang the riff over it'.

The promotional video for 'Night Fever' remained unseen until it was first issued on VHS tape and made available to members of The Bee Gees *Quarterly* fan club in 1994. It shows the brothers (including a rare-for-the-period beardless Barry) singing the song in a darkened studio layered over B-roll footage filmed while driving along Motel Row on Collins Avenue – a three-mile motel strip in what's now Sunny Isles Beach, Florida. Most of the motels shown are now closed or demolished.

In 1999, the British romantic comedy film *Whatever Happened to Harold Smith?* included the original version of 'Night Fever' with overdubs by experimental British punk rock band Janus Stark. Those with a penchant for a harder edge to their music will appreciate guitarist Gizz Butt's chops. Australian singer Kylie Minogue also released a version in November 2016, which appeared on the compilation *Saturday Night Fever (Music Inspired by the New Musical),* and, curiously, on a French reissue of her holiday album *Kylie Christmas.*

In 2007, Rhino Records made an early demo of the song available for digital download in conjunction with an expanded release of The Bee Gees' 1979 *Greatest* compilation, but the demo wasn't included on any physical release. The prototype is fairly close to the finished product, but Robin's vocal is more audible – particularly in the ad-libs near the end. Real strings had yet to be added to the track as there are some rudimentary synth parts in their place.

'More Than A Woman' (Barry Gibb, Robin Gibb, Maurice Gibb)

Recorded at Château d'Hérouville, France: February/March 1977, and Cherokee Studios, Los Angeles: circa September 1977
Chart positions: Italy: 4, Australia: 31

In 1990, Maurice quipped: 'This is a song we wrote with unimaginable results. Tavares had a big hit with it. One of the songs that made *Saturday Night Fever* such a success, and when the whole world was dancing'.

In the film, 'More Than A Woman' accompanies an iconic scene where Travolta and Gorney's characters glide across the floor elegantly as they compete in a dance contest at the 2001 Odyssey club that served as one of the story's principal settings.

The Bee Gees' recording of the song was not originally intended for the album. It existed for most of 1977 as a demo blueprint for the recording by Tavares – an American R&B group that were the opening act for The Bee Gees on the second half of the *Children Of The World* tour in 1976. It's likely that RSO president Bill Oakes – who would have heard the demo and was overseeing the soundtrack compilation – requested the Gibbs turn in a finished version to round out side one of the first *Fever* disc.

They touched up the track at Cherokee Studios in Los Angeles while the Gibbs were recording music for the *Sgt. Pepper* film in September 1977, so it's plausible that the momentum of the newly released 'How Deep Is Your Love' single encouraged RSO to want another Bee Gees song on the album.

In 1978, Tavares made 'More Than A Woman' a top 40 success in Canada and the US. It fared even better in the UK, where it reached number 7. Despite The Bee Gees' take not being released as a single in North America and the UK, it became the definitive version, receiving massive radio airplay alongside their other *Fever* contributions. Those who are unaware of the song's background are often surprised it wasn't a monster hit like 'Stayin' Alive' or 'Night Fever' because of its omnipresence at the time.

The Bee Gees had never performed 'More Than A Woman' live until their November 1997 *One Night Only* concert in Las Vegas (where it was included in a short medley with 'Night Fever'), which was recorded for an album and video released the following year.

British boy band 911 scored a big hit with 'More Than A Woman' in 1998, debuting and peaking at number two in the UK. In June 2021, British musician and producer SG Lewis widely released a remix (subtitled 'SG's Paradise Edit) on streaming platforms, reaching the top 40 on both the iTunes and Apple Music charts. It's unknown if the Gibb camp officially sanctioned the new version, but it was promoted heavily on The Bee Gees' social media platforms. An animated lyric video featuring the original version of the song was also produced around this time.

'Jive Talkin' (Barry Gibb, Robin Gibb, Maurice Gibb)
'Jive Talkin'' was reportedly used in a film scene that was cut from the final version, but the track was kept on the set anyway. Due to distribution licensing restrictions, later LP and cassette reissues of the *Fever* soundtrack instead contained the version from *Here At Last ... Bee Gees ... Live*, but the original was restored for CD reissues.

'You Should Be Dancing' (Barry Gibb, Robin Gibb, Maurice Gibb)

'You Should Be Dancing' appeared in its unedited form on side two of the second *Fever* disc.

'If I Can't Have You' (Barry Gibb, Robin Gibb, Maurice Gibb)

Recorded at Château d'Hérouville, France: February/March 1977, and Cherokee Studios, Los Angeles: circa September 1977

Rounding out the infamous first side of disc one the soundtrack LP, Yvonne Elliman's recording of 'If I Can't Have You' became the fourth consecutive US number one single in the US from the soundtrack on 13 May 1978. The Bee Gees' original take was not used in the film or included on the soundtrack; instead, it was relegated to the B-side of the 'Stayin' Alive' single, and appeared on 1979's *Greatest* compilation. In 1990, Maurice said the song had originally been written for Swedish pop group ABBA. It was among the first songs they recorded for their planned 1977 studio album. Allegedly, it was offered to Elliman after The Bee Gees had first wanted her to sing 'How Deep Is Your Love', however, at Robert Stigwood's insistence, the Gibbs kept the ballad for themselves.

The group was not involved in Elliman's version, which was produced by Freddie Perren. He – along with Tamla/Motown founder Berry Gordy, Jr., Fonce Mizell, and Deke Richards – was a member of prolific production team The Corporation, who were at the helm of dozens of the Jackson 5's classic songs, including their biggest early-1970s hits 'ABC', 'I Want You Back', and 'The Love You Save'. Consequently, the background singers on 'If I Can't Have You' – Julia and Maxine Waters and Marti McCall – would all work with The Bee Gees on various projects in the future.

'If I Can't Have You' was far-and-away Elliman's biggest hit. On New Year's Eve 2021 – after a long hiatus from recording and performing – she released to social media a live video of the song from a concert in Boston as a duet with her former *Jesus Christ Superstar* co-star Ted Neeley.

British singer Kim Wilde covered the song in 1993 (released on her hits compilation *The Singles Collection 1981-1993*). It was a top three hit in Australia and made the top ten in Belgium and Ireland, and the top 20 in the UK, Iceland, Italy, the Netherlands, and Switzerland. British singer-songwriter Jess Glynne also released a version in 2016 for the

Saturday Night Fever (Music Inspired by the New Musical) covers album that became a minor hit in France.

Back in Los Angeles, The Bee Gees were busy filming *Sgt. Pepper's Lonely Hearts Club Band*, all while the *Saturday Night Fever* soundtrack was beginning to ignite. On 23 November, they appeared on *The Mike Douglas Show* when the host visited the *Sgt. Pepper* movie set to interview them and co-stars Peter Frampton, George Burns, Paul Nicholas, Frankie Howerd, Sandy Farina, and Dianne Steinberg. Filming was apparently not going well, and the brothers grew increasingly unhappy with their involvement as the project took shape. At one point, they allegedly begged Robert Stigwood to axe them from it altogether, to no avail. As always, they were still writing new material while they were working on the film.

Meanwhile, Albhy Galuten and Karl Richardson had set up shop a short distance away at Wally Heider Studios on Cahuenga Boulevard in Hollywood to start work on Andy's second album, *Shadow Dancing*. Karl explained to *Albumism* in 2018:

The band was out, and they stayed at the Chateau Marmont with Andy. And The Bee Gees [*sarcastically*] I think were doing some movie with Robert Stigwood. But we did it at Heider's studios – I think it was near Hollywood and Vine, in the Wooden Room. And I remember that AGHO – the Andy Gibb Hit Orchestra – which was Harold, Tubby on drums, and Joey Murcia was the guitarist. Barry would show up to the studio as an excuse to get away from the movie, and we were in a little Heider room. Albhy would show up to the hotel at night, and Andy was staying upstairs at the Chateau. You would woodshed the band, you know – 'Let's find the groove here'. And Tubby had a practice pad, you know, a drummer's practice pad. Or maybe he was hitting his sticks on the chairs or something. We would hang, and the rhythm tracks came out of that, where everybody was talking to everybody. That was the groove.

All four brothers are credited writers on the album's title track, reportedly in one sitting on the same night Barry, Robin, and Maurice also penned two additional songs, 'Too Much Heaven' and Tragedy', which would be reserved for their next studio album. Contrary to popular belief, all four brothers do not sing background vocals on 'Shadow Dancing'. They were a mix of Barry, Andy, and session singer

Johnne Sambataro. Johnne remembers the significant challenge of having to match Barry and Andy's familial blend. He told *Albumism* in 2018:

> [Barry] told me a story once when we were singing, and I don't even remember during what song this came about. We were singing, and we ran into a little problem locking in, and he started talking to me about background vocals and singing in general and that it's kind of like acting. You've got to find a character and stay with the character, and sometimes you're smiling, and sometimes you're making an angry face. When you create this character with your voice, you create this mental picture, and people see that when they hear the vocal. At the time, it really helped me get into focus with how to blend with Barry and Andy, because they sounded so much alike. And I had to find that place because I didn't sound like them, and I had to find that pitch in the same kind of singing and breath, where there was a lot of breath coming out, to sing in unison and on pitch.

Barry was also the primary producer of four of the album's tracks: 'Shadow Dancing', 'An Everlasting Love' (a song he'd recently written on his own), 'Why' (which he co-wrote with Andy), and '(Our Love) Don't Throw It All Away' – the ballad he and Blue Weaver had composed during the sessions at Château d'Hérouville, to which Barry added a new bridge section for Andy to sing between the song's second chorus and outro. Those songs were eventually earmarked as the album's singles ('Why' was released in limited markets outside North America). If Andy had any hope of one of his own compositions becoming a hit, it was quickly extinguished in favour of maximising Barry's Midas touch as a hitmaker.

As with *Flowing Rivers*, Albhy and Karl co-produced the rest of the album. Andy turned in another solid batch of songs he'd written on his own – 'Fool For A Night', 'Melody', 'I Go For You', 'Good Feeling' and 'Waiting For You', all showed maturity and depth. Andy and Albhy co-wrote 'One More Look At The Night' (though Albhy was again not credited on the album, as had been the case with 'Too Many Looks In Your Eyes' and 'Dance To The Light Of The Morning' on *Flowing Rivers*). It was sadly the last occasion on which Andy would write so prolifically.

Though Andy's front-facing success was growing exponentially, he was struggling behind the scenes and had been regularly using cocaine and drinking heavily to cope with the mounting pressures of his newfound fame. His wife Kim became pregnant in the spring, but as Andy's career began to take off, it became clear to her that he wouldn't be able to escape his addiction and have a healthy enough relationship with his work to commit to her and their baby. After trying unsuccessfully to get him back on track, Kim left Andy and soon returned to Australia.

By all accounts, Andy was focused, happy, and in good professional form while recording *Shadow Dancing*. He would reach even greater heights over the next year, but his personal problems would, unfortunately, also grow.

On 14 December, The Bee Gees attended the premiere of *Saturday Night Fever* at Grauman's (now TCL) Chinese Theatre in Hollywood. It opened throughout North America two days later. Within days, the film's many detractors were silenced, and Robert Stigwood's early confidence in the storyline was justified. By the end of December, the film grossed $25.900,000 in the US alone, making back its budget more than seven times over. Those figures are even more stunning given that it was only available to a limited audience as the Motion Picture Association of America had given the film an 'R' (restricted) rating because of its plentiful profanity and explicit subject matter.

With the film and soundtrack racking up big numbers everywhere, RSO issued 'Stayin' Alive' as the next single in North America (delayed until January in the UK since the film wouldn't open there until spring). Reportedly, RSO hadn't intended to release it at that point, but moviegoers who had heard it play during *Fever*'s opening scene started burning up radio station telephone lines requesting it. RSO obliged and rushed it out. The Bee Gees' version of 'If I Can't Have You' was the B-side, which might have been a bit confusing for some buyers since Yvonne Elliman's take was the one they heard in the film.

On 11 December, The Bee Gees co-hosted the inaugural *Billboard* Music Awards with American actor/singer Kris Kristofferson, which was televised live from the Santa Monica Civic Auditorium. They were nominated for Top Pop Group of the year, while Andy was nominated in the Best New Artist category. The Bee Gees also won a prize for public service from the Don Kirshner Rock Awards – a Grammy Awards alternative celebration developed by the former Monkees manager-turned-TV producer. It was just the second (and the last) year of the ceremony.

Though *Saturday Night Fever*'s rapid boil was just starting, The Bee Gees were characteristically already eyeing their next studio album after their previous attempt had been abruptly snuffed out by Robert Stigwood's passion project. With most of the world quite literally dancing in the aisles to their music (movie theatres had to hire additional staff to keep *Fever* viewers in their seats during screenings), the three brothers were back at Criteria Studios within weeks, ready to move on.

1978

In just a few weeks, *Saturday Night Fever* had evolved from a low-budget box office underdog to an unqualified smash. While 'How Deep Is Your Love' and 'Stayin' Alive' had been making big waves at North American radio and retail, the next few months were to engulf the brothers in a veritable tsunami as the rest of the world began to latch on.

On 2 January, Barry, Robin, and Maurice returned to Los Angeles to resume filming *Sgt. Pepper's Lonely Hearts Club Band*. While the Gibbs had often spoken of a desire to make feature films, Stigwood's fantasy everything-but-the-kitchen-sink musical comedy wasn't what they'd envisaged. Director Michael Schultz and writer Henry Edwards had ensured that not much was expected from the ensemble cast in terms of acting. Only veteran actor George Burns – who also narrated the film – had substantial lines. While the cast was a virtual who's-who of entertainment, the film's bizarre plot played out more like a fatuous children's story than a credible piece of cinema.

While on set, the brothers noticed that during breaks the dancers were all listening to the *Saturday Night Fever* soundtrack. The Bee Gees were somewhat cocooned during filming and had little idea how massively successful the film and album were becoming. In a 2020 interview, Barry joked that when filming started, the brothers were sharing a Winnebago – but by the time filming finished, they had one each. By Hollywood-lot standards, there weren't many greater status symbols to be had.

Filming of *Sgt. Pepper* ended on 15 January, celebrated with a wrap party on 18 January at Culver Studios, just down the street from MGM.

On 16 January, Andy's international debut single 'I Just Want To Be Your Everything' was nominated for Favourite Pop/Rock Song at the American Music Awards, but lost to Debby Boone's 'You Light Up My Life', which had spent ten weeks at number one in the US the previous fall, edging out Andy's single as *Billboard*'s top chart song of the year.

The more prestigious 20th annual Grammy Awards ceremony was held at the Shrine Auditorium in Los Angeles on 23 February and was broadcast live on American television with singer John Denver as host. The Bee Gees received the award for Best Pop Performance by a Group for 'How Deep Is Your Love' – their first-ever win. Andy was nominated in the Best New Artist and Best Pop Vocal Performance, Male categories.

Andy became a father when daughter Peta Jaye Gibb arrived on 25 January. Andy had promised to be in Australia with Kim for the birth, but his professional obligations and escalating addiction interfered. What should have been a joyous occasion for the new parents devolved into a public nightmare, with the scandal-hungry press eager to profit from Andy's fast-rising teen-idol appeal. Andy and Kim divorced in April, followed by a long and harrowing legal battle over financial support, which resulted in a small sum being awarded to Kim, in addition to a money trust for Peta. In the end, sadly Andy would only meet his daughter once during his lifetime.

For the month of January, British-American band (and RSO labelmates) Player had held the *Billboard* Hot 100 number one slot with their ballad 'Baby Come Back', which had immediately followed 'How Deep Is Your Love' to the top after it had finished its three-week run. The Gibbs had no creative involvement with 'Baby Come Back', though there was still a connection. Lead singer Peter Beckett remembers that after a long series of rejections from other record companies, their producers Dennis Lambert and Brian Potter pitched the song to RSO in the hope of landing the band a record deal. Peter told *ClassicBands.com* in 2009: 'They got in touch with [label president] Al Coury at RSO ... they played it to The Bee Gees and Robert Stigwood, and they loved it. Next minute, we were signed'.

After three weeks at number one, 'Baby Come Back' was replaced by 'Stayin' Alive' on 4 February, remaining there for four weeks. Three days later, RSO – hungry to continue the hit streak and keep up with *Fever's* shattering public response – served up the soundtrack's third single, 'Night Fever'. The B-side was a live version of 'Down The Road' from *Here At Last ... Bee Gees ... Live.*

The single wasn't released in the UK until 7 April, and Polydor UK went to great lengths to fulfil the demand for it. They imported 80,000 singles from the US, 96,000 from Spain, 90,000 from Belgium, 20,000 from Ireland, and 85,000 from RCA's UK pressing plant in Durham. The balance was met by Phonodisc as the single topped sales of 650,000. Because of the various sources for the pressings, the single was available with three different catalogue numbers: RSO 002 (UK), RS118 (US), and 2090 272 (Europe).

UK pressings of the *Saturday Night Fever* album remained native, with RCA supplying 15,000 sets a day, and the West Drayton plant produced up to 20,000 a week. Sales of more than 550,000 units as of 12 May were supplemented by sales of 100,000 cassettes. Extra problems created by the double album format and its inserts were solved by using two mailing houses near London and a government rehabilitation centre that employed Securicor vehicles for shop deliveries. The pressing plants at Phonodisc and RCA worked 24 hours a day, seven days a week for over six weeks. As extraordinary as sales were in the UK, the movie didn't open in some parts (including Manchester, Scotland, and the North-East of England) until 15 May, despite opening on 23 March in most other locations. As they were all around the world, advance album sales were a huge boost for the film. Anyone not owning the album when they saw the film quickly corrected the matter as soon as they left the theatre. The album and film promoted each other. To this day, the *Fever* soundtrack is the biggest seller in the Polydor label's long UK history.

Back in the US, Andy's second single from Flowing Rivers, '(Love Is) Thicker Than Water', displaced 'Stayin' Alive' as the *Billboard* number one single the week of 4 March. The Gibbs had landed in unprecedented chart territory. In the weeks of 25 February and 4 March, five singles written and produced by at least one of the brothers were simultaneously in the Hot 100's top ten. 'Night Fever' had jumped into it while 'How Deep Is Your Love' was still clinging to the bottom of the top ten after an already record-breaking run of 17 weeks. 'Stayin' Alive' hung onto the number two position for several weeks, earning RIAA Platinum status in the process. Also, Samantha Sang's 'Emotion' had risen to the top five.

That unbelievable feat matched a similar *Billboard* milestone established by the brothers' idols The Beatles' during the week of 4 April 1964 when five of their songs occupied all top five positions of the Hot 100 chart: 'Can't Buy Me Love' at number one, followed by 'Twist And Shout', 'She Loves You', 'I Want To Hold Your Hand', and 'Please Please Me'. However, The Beatles had written only four of the five tracks. 'Twist And Shout' – a cover of The Top Notes' 1961 original that was successfully revisited by The Isley Brothers in 1962 – was penned by American songwriters Bert Berns and Phil Medley.

RSO grandly lauded the occasion with a *Spectacolor* billboard message on the Allied Chemical Building in New York's Times Square, which flashed every eight minutes. The full text and graphics were spread over ten screens:

RSO congratulates The Bee Gees. For the first time since The Beatles, five hits in the top ten! Bee Gees have the #1 single and #1 album in *Billboard*, *Cashbox*, and *Record World*! Congratulations! RSO congratulates The Bee Gees for the greatest songwriting achievement ever!

At that point, The Bee Gees also tied with Elton John for logging the most 1970s US number one singles, with six apiece. Paul McCartney and Wings and Stevie Wonder were in second place with five, while The Jackson 5, John Denver, Diana Ross, The Eagles, and KC and the Sunshine Band each had four. The Gibbs, of course, were to break the record just a few weeks later.

In March, *Billboard* reported that Chappell Music was warming up The Bee Gees' publishing catalogue with plans to promote their writing talents via a special publisher's album for distribution to artists, producers, and other interested parties. However, the revival of the group's vintage songs had already begun. Singer-songwriter Jackie DeShannon (perhaps best known for her 1965 hit with Burt Bacharach and Hal David's 'What The World Needs Now Is Love') covered 'To Love Somebody' for Amherst Records, while Benny Mardones interpreted 'I Started A Joke' on his debut album for Private Stock, *Thank God For Girls*. American pop singer Rita Coolidge's update of 'Words' was a top 20 hit in the UK, and one-time Drifters member Bill Fredericks released the Polydor album *Love With You*, showcasing a dozen Gibb tunes.

In the American marketplace in particular, The Bee Gees' brand was in high demand, and a myriad of products using their image surfaced on store shelves. The Bic Rock Lighter was introduced at the National Association of Recording Merchandisers (NARM) convention in New Orleans in March. Bic disposable butane lighters were imprinted with the logo of one of 11 popular acts: The Bee Gees, Boston, Doobie Brothers, Commodores, Peter Frampton, Jefferson Starship, The Steve Miller Band, Fleetwood Mac, Foreigner, The Marshall Tucker Band, and Yes. Each of them received a royalty on all lighters sold. The range was expanded to 75 artists by the end of 1978, and as a sign of the concept's success, Bic maintains the line to this day. This was but the tip of the iceberg, as all manner of merchandising companies wanted to get in on the act. Thermos created a Bee Gees backpack and metal lunch boxes showing images of the brothers individually, and another with a group photo. Carnival Toys, Inc. made a Bee Gees toy guitar, and Vanity Fair made two different Bee Gees record players (one with a pulsing disco light), an AM transistor radio, record cases, a wireless microphone, and a sing-along radio and microphone. Mattel created a Bee Gees Rhythm Machine – famously used by German electronic music group Kraftwerk on their single 'Pocket Calculator' from their 1981 album *Computer World*.

Andy's image was also exploited, most notably in the form of an 8" 'disco dancing' doll that only vaguely resembled him, made by Ideal. There were also jigsaw puzzles, posters, trading cards (complete with bubble gum), iron-on patches and t-shirts. RSO included order forms for various Gibb-branded trinkets inside their LP sleeves. As kitsch as these items were, there was obviously a market for them, and they sold quite well. These days, they're desirable collectables.

On the chart front, 'Night Fever' ascended to number one in the US on 18 March, five weeks after its release, unseating Andy's '(Love Is) Thicker Than Water'. It clung to the summit for eight weeks, longer than any other single that year.

Another single with Bee Gees connections that climbed the charts in early 1978 was 'Too Much, Too Little, Too Late' by Johnny Mathis and Deniece Williams. The US number one was written by Steve Kipner's old Tin Tin bandmate John Vallins, and Steve's father and former Bee Gees manager Nat Kipner, who had mentored the group in Australia when they transitioned to his Spin label from Festival Records. On the B-side was the duo's cover of 'Emotion'. Coincidentally, Barry had recorded Mathis' 1957 hit 'The Twelfth Of Never' in 1966, which was released on the 1970 Bee Gees compilation *Inception/Nostalgia*.

With *Saturday Night Fever* working overtime as fuel for The Bee Gees' commercial explosion, the brothers were able to be somewhat reluctant about their celebrity – at least for the time being. Rather than thrust themselves into the limelight with personal appearances, interviews and concerts, they opted to retreat to Criteria Studios in March and begin work on a proper follow-up album to *Children Of The World*. They'd been writing songs since late 1977 and were to spend almost all of 1978 recording them. Sessions lasted through November, and within less than a year, they were to emerge with their fifteenth studio album, *Spirits Having Flown*.

In April, RSO Records' Australian arm released The Bee Gees' original recording of 'More Than A Woman' as a single, which was also issued in Chile, Portugal, and Italy. In most other territories, Tavares' cover of the song was the only available single of the song. The Bee Gees' version peaked at 33 in Australia, while Tavares' single didn't chart there at all.

RSO pushed out the title track from Andy's forthcoming *Shadow Dancing* album as a single, which debuted at 69 on the *Billboard* Hot 100 on 15 April, adding to the inescapable flood of Gibb songs in chart circulation. 'Night Fever' was still at number one (halfway through its run at the top), and 'Stayin' Alive' was at number two, where it had been for four weeks since it vacated the pole position. Yvonne Elliman's 'If I Can't Have You' made its way to number five, Samantha Sang's 'Emotion' was at 11, '(Love Is) Thicker Than Water' was at 17, and 'How Deep Is Your Love' claimed its thirtieth chart week at number 49.

With the main lobby of New York's United Nations General Assembly building as a backdrop for a high-profile May press conference, Robert Stigwood, The Bee Gees, television personality David Frost, and United Nations International Children's Fund executive director Henry R. Labouisse launched the Music for UNICEF campaign. The highlight of the project was to be a star-studded concert broadcast from the General Assembly in January 1979. 'We have made a lot of money in the last two years, and now we want to give some of it back', Barry explained of their involvement in the charity. The Bee Gees pledged to donate all royalties from an upcoming song to UNICEF. Robert Stigwood added, 'It is planned that every penny raised by Music for UNICEF will go to UNICEF. The music itself will be administrated without fee for the benefit of UNICEF, by Chappell Music. All the worldwide legal and financial ramifications are being ironed out with the relevant authorities'.

The gala concert was to be hosted by David Frost and broadcast live on the NBC network in the US, and simultaneously by satellite around the world. An album of the event's performances was to follow. 'Our objective is to have other writers join us in this as well', Barry continued, urging other composers to donate music and participate in the gala. A final list of 'founder composers' was expected to be finalised by June.

The idea for the benefit came two months earlier at a Miami meeting between The Bee Gees, Robert Stigwood, and David Frost. Frost – who became executive producer of the telecast along with Stigwood – then took the idea to UN Secretary-General Kurt Waldheim, who gave his approval for the project. The year 1979 was earmarked as 'International Year Of The Child'.

At the press conference, Frost announced that the combined revenue from the telecast, the donated songs, and the accompanying album might yield up to $100,000,000 for UNICEF. Artists who committed early to the cause were Elton John and American progressive rock band

Kansas, who at that time were riding high with their hit single 'Dust In The Wind'. Ultimately, neither donated a song or appeared at the concert. Tickets to the event were rumoured to cost $5,000 each (the equivalent of almost $20,000 in 2022, adjusted for inflation), but this ended up not being the case as tickets never went on general sale. They were instead all given to members of the UN diplomatic corps.

Having purchased the screen rights for the Broadway musical *Grease*, Robert Stigwood enlisted Barry to write the title song for the screen adaptation. The stage show already had an opening song – 'Alma Mater' – written by its creators Jim Jacobs and Warren Casey, who apparently had also written a title song that was dropped from the production before it made it to Broadway. But the ever-astute Stigwood believed Barry could write a better one.

According to legend, Barry was struggling to write a song to fit the unusual title and had phoned Stigwood to seek advice. Barry told *Entertainment Weekly* in 2018: 'I said, 'How do you write a song called 'Grease'? I don't understand what direction I would take to do that'. And Robert said, 'Just 'Grease duh-duh-duh-duh-duh, Grease duh-duh-duh-duh-duh'. Just do it'. So, he wasn't very helpful. But I understood that they really wanted something that was positive and sunny'. However, Stigwood did drop one key phrase during their conversation: 'Grease is the word'. Hence, a classic song was written.

Albhy Galuten has recalled with feigned horror that an unimportant business meeting had prevented him from having a writing credit with Barry on the multi-million-selling song. Barry – who was reportedly rather generous in including others in his process and giving them credit – had asked Albhy to join him in the studio to write it. Alas, when Albhy arrived late due to the meeting, Barry had already written most of 'Grease' by himself.

Released on 6 May in the US – with a lead vocal by Frankie Valli, who had fronted American vocal group The Four Seasons since the 1950s – the single was to sell over 7,000,000 copies worldwide. The song was featured twice in the film – over the opening animated sequence (created by British artist John David Wilson) and reprised during the closing credits. The session musicians included Barry's *Sgt. Pepper* co-star Peter Frampton on guitar, and frequent players Tubby Ziegler, George Terry, and Harold Cowart. Barry's falsetto can be heard popping up at different points in the background; reportedly, his natural voice was also mixed in to fill out Valli's lead in a few places.

Intriguingly, when Valli recorded 'Grease', he didn't have a recording contract. But following the single's release on RSO – which also issued the soundtrack – he was quickly signed to Warner Bros., which also held Valli's group The Four Seasons under contract.

Grease starred John Travolta – per the three-picture deal he signed with Stigwood in 1976 – in the lead role of Danny Zuko, alongside Olivia Newton-John as Sandy Olsson. The film followed in the footsteps of *Saturday Night Fever* as a gigantic hit for Stigwood and Paramount. To date, it's grossed nearly $400,000,000 worldwide. For 34 years, it was the most successful live-action musical film in history until it was usurped by the film production of *Les Misérables* in 2012.

'Grease' was one of four new songs in the film which were not part of the original stage show. The others were 'Sandy', 'Hopelessly Devoted To You', and 'You're The One That I Want' – the latter two written by John Farrar, Olivia Newton-John's long-time collaborator who had known The Bee Gees since their Australian days. 'Grease' was the album's only song not performed by a film cast member. The film's director Randal Kleiser did not like the new songs because they didn't suit the film's late-1950s/early-1960s-era storyline. Demonstrating his savvy business mind once again, Stigwood's insistence on their inclusion was proven to have been the right thing to do when all four songs were massive hits around the world. The 'Grease' single was certified Platinum and topped the charts in the US and Canada, also reaching the top ten in Australia, the Netherlands, New Zealand, the UK, Ireland, Belgium, France, Norway, and Sweden. The B-side was an instrumental version, and in the US only, it had a saxophone solo by Gary Brown.

'Grease' was also on Valli's next album *Frankie Valli ... Is the Word*, which included his next single: another version of 'Save Me, Save Me', the song originally written by Barry and Albhy in 1977 for Network. The album was released in September in the US, and in November in the UK. 'Save Me, Save Me'. was produced by Bob Gaudio of The Four Seasons, and to his credit, of all the versions of the song, Valli's was by far the most dynamic and commercial – though it didn't replicate the chart success of 'Grease'. It deserved better.

While The Bee Gees never recorded their own version of 'Grease', they performed the song on their *One Night Only* concert tour between 1997 and 1999. On one of the verses, Valli's vocal from the original recording was piped in while footage from the film was screened behind the brothers on stage. It was included on the 1998 *One Night Only* live album and DVD.

In 2018, accompanying a 40th-anniversary reissue of *Grease* on DVD and digital platforms, Universal/Capitol released Barry's original demo of the song online. Albhy Galuten is heard playing the piano while Barry claps his hands to keep the tempo. When *Entertainment Weekly* asked if he was excited about the demo being made available, Barry responded flatly: 'No, not particularly. I'd just rather people enjoy the film as a whole. It was a small thing on my part to come up with that song'.

In 1993, Australian actor and singer Craig McLachlan – then playing the lead role of Danny in a UK stage production of the show alongside American singer-songwriter Debbie Gibson as Sandy – released his cover of 'Grease', which peaked at number 44 in the UK.

On 13 January 2016, Fox Broadcasting Company in the US produced a live television remake of *Grease*, which fused together scenes and songs from both the original stage and film productions. British singer Jessie J, staying quite faithful to Valli's take, performed the film's title track as the show's opening act. It was also included – with the altered title 'Grease (Is The Word)' – on a companion soundtrack album issued by Paramount Pictures on 31 January.

On 13 May, Yvonne Elliman's 'If I Can't Have You' became the fourth and final *Fever* single to reach number one in the US, dethroning 'Night Fever'. The soundtrack was in its seventeenth consecutive week at the top of the *Billboard* Top LPs & Tape chart and persisted there for another seven weeks before finally relinquishing the crown to Scottish singer-songwriter Gerry Rafferty's *City To City*. Elliman's achievement also marked a huge RSO milestone: the label's singles accumulated 21 uninterrupted weeks at the top of the Hot 100.

On 9 June, Andy Gibb performed 'Shadow Dancing' on NBC's *The Midnight Special* – just over a week away from the single becoming his third consecutive US chart-topper. When it began an extraordinary seven-week sojourn at number one on 17 June, Andy became the first solo artist in US chart history to have his first three singles reach the summit. The Platinum-selling single was also named *Billboard*'s number one song of 1978, edging out 'Night Fever'. 'Stayin' Alive' ranked at number four. 'Shadow Dancing' was also number one in Canada and Brazil, and reached the top five in New Zealand, Sweden, and Norway. The Brits responded less enthusiastically to their native son; the single reaching a disappointing number 42.

The *Shadow Dancing* album was also released the same month (delayed until September in the UK), propelling Andy to number 7 on the

Billboard album chart. It reached number one on Canada's *RPM* survey the week of 29 July. The album was a minor hit in most other markets. It joined *Flowing Rivers* in being certified Platinum by the RIAA.

Shadow Dancing's release was accompanied by a second single: Barry's 'An Everlasting Love'. It contrasted the title track's funky, laid-back groove with a cantering tempo enveloped by vocal-layer countermelodies at the song's climax. It was certainly different from anything Andy had yet recorded, but perhaps mirrored some of the same structural ideas The Bee Gees had used on songs like 'Fanny (Be Tender With My Love)'. Johnne Sambataro recalled the song was a taxing vocal when he spoke to *Albumism* in 2018: 'The only thing I remember about 'An Everlasting Love' was almost hyperventilating singing that song *[laughs]*. I'm tellin' ya, it was a mouthful to sing that chorus and it goes on forever!'. In October, the single peaked at 5 in the US. In the UK, it became Andy's sole top ten single.

Sparing no expense, Robert Stigwood held a lavish premiere for the *Sgt. Pepper's Lonely Hearts Club Band* film at the Palladium on Sunset Boulevard in Los Angeles on 18 July, followed by a party with over 1000 guests at the Beverly Hills Hilton. On 20 July, the East Coast premiere took place at Radio City Music Hall in New York City, with mayor Ed Koch declaring it 'Sgt. Pepper Day'. All proceeds went to the New York Police Athletic League, which The Bee Gees had supported back in 1976. The star-studded after-party was a gala supper at the Roseland Dance Hall. While The Bee Gees and other stars of the film were at both premieres, the film's other major star Peter Frampton was absent due to being in a serious car accident in The Bahamas three weeks earlier.

Sgt. Pepper's Lonely Hearts Club Band (Soundtrack) (1978)

Personnel:
Barry Gibb, Robin Gibb, Maurice Gibb: vocals
Cast vocals: Peter Frampton, Sandy Farina, Paul Nicholas, Diane Steinberg, Frankie Howerd, Steve Martin, Alice Cooper, Billy Preston, George Burns, John Wheeler, Jay MacIntosh
George Martin: piano
Max Middleton: keyboards, synthesiser
Robert Ahwai: guitar
Wilbur Boscomb: bass
Bernard Purdie: drums
Peter Frampton: guitar

Tower of Power Horns: horns
Producer, Orchestral arrangements: George Martin
Engineer: Geoff Emerick
Recorded in May 1977 and September 1977 at Cherokee Studios, Los
Angeles
Release date: UK and US: July 1978
Chart positions: US: 5, Australia: 13, UK: 38

The Beatles' landmark album *Sgt. Pepper's Lonely Hearts Club Band* was
released in May 1967. It not only defined the year in music but created
a massive cultural shift, causing pop music to be embraced as an art
form and as a vehicle for social and political expression of the decade's
younger generation. Its impact has been long-lasting, and nearly six
decades later, it's still regarded as one of the most important recordings
in music history.

Sgt. Pepper's fantasy imagery inspired several spin-off interpretations
and re-imaginings, including The Beatles' 1968 animated film *Yellow
Submarine*. In 1974, American theatre director Tom O'Horgan – who
had mounted the hit Broadway musicals *Hair* and *Jesus Christ Superstar*
– assembled his own reading in the form of a rock spectacle for the
stage: *Sgt. Pepper's Lonely Hearts Club Band on the Road*. It played at
the Beacon Theatre In New York City for 66 performances, closing in
early 1975 after it was panned by critics. Coincidentally, the show was
produced by the Robert Stigwood Organisation, who had bought the
rights to nearly 30 Beatles songs for the production.

Stigwood must have believed there was more life in the *Sgt. Pepper*
concept after O'Horgan's off-Broadway calamity. He commissioned
writer Henry Edwards to fashion a film script loosely based on the play,
with his leased bundle of Beatles songs leveraged to provide much of
the character narrative in the style of a rock opera. If that sounds like a
recipe for disaster, it was.

Though Stigwood didn't have The Beatles to sing the songs, he did
have at his disposal a group that could tackle the Fab Four's intricate
melodies and tight harmonies. Enter The Bee Gees. When Beatles'
producer George Martin signed on to the project, Stigwood was likely
assured he had a formula that couldn't miss.

But then there was the matter of making the entire affair translate
to film. The Bee Gees – with singer-songwriter and guitarist Peter
Frampton and comedian and actor Steve Martin – were the stars. While

Stigwood had struck box office gold with *Saturday Night Fever*, even his savoir-faire couldn't save *Sgt. Pepper* from itself – marred by poor acting, an incoherent storyline, and on-set tensions. It recouped its costs at the cinema, but the film and soundtrack received a steady stream of scathe from nearly everyone who saw and heard them.

Decades after its release, the criticism that followed the *Sgt. Pepper* soundtrack seems but an innocuous blip in The Bee Gees' long trajectory. But at the time, it threatened to cause significant career damage. Reconstituting what is arguably The Beatles' most historic contribution to modern music within a dizzily silly film that had little semblance of a reasonable storyline was already a risky venture. Taking more Beatles songs from their other albums and tacking them onto the *Sgt. Pepper* moniker could be construed as sacrilege. All told, the entire project was an experience everyone involved regretted completely. Hindsight is 20/20, but The Bee Gees should have run away from any involvement in this project the moment it was offered to them. The fact that the movie was a Robert Stigwood production and that they had immeasurable faith in him as their long-standing manager still only makes it slightly more understandable.

Early in their career – even in their Australian days – The Bee Gees fought off accusations of being mere Beatles imitators. Debuting in the London music scene in 1967 with their similar nasal harmonies, they were dismissed for the same reason. Only through their sheer ability to prolifically write and produce high-quality songs did they overturn that notion. In 1978, well-established and at their commercial and artistic peak, they agreed to be involved with this project. One possible reason they accepted the offer – apart from management pressure – was that the brothers were unabashed Beatles fans. The opportunity to work with George Martin must have also been terribly tempting.

In a case of what might have been extreme posturing given their eventual deep unhappiness with the project, Robin didn't help endear The Bee Gees to their detractors when he said prior to the film's release, 'There is no such thing as The Beatles now. They don't exist as a band, and never performed *Sgt. Pepper* live in any case. When ours comes out, it will be – in effect – as if theirs never existed'. Whilst George Martin was brought into the project to ensure its 'Beatles integrity', his determination to ensure the recordings were faithful to the originals – as Barry has said – may have inhibited the album and the artists from applying their talents and making their individual mark on these classics.

Regardless of the film's mauling by the critics, the album bounced immediately into the *Billboard* album chart in the US at number 5. However, this was based on advance orders only, and sales quickly dropped off afterwards. Feeling overly confident about the film and the power of The Bee Gees' name, RSO in the US had manufactured 2,000,000 copies of the expensive two-LP set. Because of plummeting retail numbers, record stores were allowed to return unsold albums for credit. The joke in the record industry at the time was that it was the first album to 'return Platinum'.

The album also reached a respectable 38 in the UK and 13 in Australia. Regardless of the film's reputation, the soundtrack achieved Platinum certification in the US, and Silver in the UK. Stigwood, at least, must have been laughing all the way to the bank.

In the long run, the poor reviews mercifully had little impact on The Bee Gees' and co-star Peter Frampton's careers. The eventual backlash against the Gibbs, which began in earnest in July 1979 and continued to be an albatross for their commercial viability for at least a decade, had more to do with overexposure than anything else.

Despite some of the venomously unkind statements made about their work on these songs, The Bee Gees turned in some solid performances on *Sgt. Pepper*. George Martin – who later admitted he wished he hadn't signed on for the project – said working with The Bee Gees was a highlight. He wrote in *All You Need Is Ears*: '[They] are very professional, and in a curious way, there was a sense of déjà vu for me. Although I had never thought of them being like The Beatles, they do have the same irreverent sense of humour, and it was strange how certain situations and experiences could be revived ten years on. When it came to harmony singing, they were incredibly facile'.

Revisiting The Beatles' music was one thing but reinterpreting the album artwork was another. A copy of Peter Blake's iconic *Sgt Pepper* cover would never have been an option – they left that for the final scene of the movie! So, what to do?

Designer and illustrator Tom Nikosey, who had also created the logo used on Andy's *Flowing Rivers* and *Shadow Dancing* albums, was recruited to design a logo worthy of the project. Nikosey had also worked for Crosby, Stills & Nash, Bob Seger & the Silver Bullet Band, The Commodores, and Canadian band Stonebolt. Obviously, the job was in good hands.

He came up with a fabulous design which included the 'Sgt. Pepper' name in a bold and beautiful cursive script arcing over 'Lonely Hearts

Club' on a gilded ribbon. The pièce de résistance: a trumpet in the shape of a heart, and the word 'Band' created from the lead-pipe. In what was possibly a cheeky homage to the original Beatles album cover logo, the graphic elements are placed on (though overlapping) what could be intended as a bass drum rim and skin.

There is a very subtle difference to the front cover of the UK edition of the album and those released in all other territories. The UK and Canadian editions were on the A&M label, while it was on RSO elsewhere, so this could be the only reasoning for the variation – a pattern of extremely light-coloured sepia hearts on the white background. The inner gatefold featured several movie stills and a centrepiece of the 'SP' trumpet, which was an important prop in some scenes, including Steve Martin's performance of 'Maxwell's Silver Hammer' and Billy Preston's 'Get Back'. The back cover included all the song titles, but in an order that curiously corresponded to neither the album running order nor their placement in the movie. An important design element appears at the top of the back cover: a heart with three stripes, which was a recurring motif in the film.

The two records were housed in identical inner sleeves, which had track listings and credits on one side and a still from the film's finale and a list of the cast and production crew on the other. A 20"-by-60" poster was also included, featuring notable artist Birney Lettick's illustration of The Bee Gees and Peter Frampton wearing brightly coloured outfits, including flying helmets, goggles, and white silk scarves while standing on a tuba with strawberries growing out of the bell.

A limited-edition pressing on shocking-pink vinyl was released in the UK.

'Sgt. Pepper's Lonely Hearts Club Band' (John Lennon, Paul McCartney)

Recorded at Cherokee Studios, Los Angeles: May (music) and September (vocals) 1977
Performed by The Bee Gees and Paul Nicholas

The title track introduces the band, with Paul Nicholas in the role of Dougie Shears initially taking the lead vocal, and The Bee Gees taking the chorus. Robin takes the introduction of Peter Frampton on his own, joined by his brothers to announce his character as Billy Shears.

The instruments The Bee Gees mime with during the film are not ones they're normally associated with – Barry plays bass, Robin is on guitar, and Maurice is on drums. While it might have made more sense – in terms of constructing a convincing appearance, anyway – to have

Barry on guitar and Maurice on bass, it was never considered an option to have Robin on drums, as Maurice recalled: 'Robin knew that he wouldn't be good as a drummer, because he'd be very stiff – where I'm very loose, and I could follow a beat, because being a bass player, you always follow the drums a lot'.

In addition to the royalties accumulated from the use of their songs in the film, The Beatles also experienced a quick singles chart resurgence because of it. EMI – whose contract with The Beatles had ended two years earlier and gave them wide clearance to reissue their material – capitalised on the film by issuing the original version of the song paired with 'With A Little Help From My Friends' as a two-track A-side single (backed with 'A Day In The Life'), via Capitol Records. It was released on 14 August in the US and reached 71 on the *Billboard* Hot 100 the week of 30 September.

A UK release followed in September on Parlophone, eventually peaking at number 63.

'With A Little Help from My Friends' (John Lennon, Paul McCartney)
Recorded at Cherokee Studios, Los Angeles: May (music) and September (vocals) 1977
Performed by Peter Frampton and The Bee Gees
Written as Ringo Starr's track for The Beatles' *Sgt. Pepper's* album, Lennon and McCartney deliberately composed a melody with limited range – except for the last note, which McCartney worked closely with Starr to achieve. When first presented with the song, Ringo insisted on changing the first lines – 'What would you think if I sang out of tune?/ Would you throw ripe tomatoes at me?' – so fans wouldn't be inspired to actually throw tomatoes at him should he perform it live. Unfortunately for Robin, this had actually happened to him during a solo concert at the Redwood Festival in New Zealand on 31 January 1970, though not while singing this particular song.

In the movie, Frampton takes on Ringo Starr's vocal, while The Bee Gees sing the questions in the call-and-answer part. It's pretty faithful to the original version, and it's carried off very well.

'Getting Better' (John Lennon, Paul McCartney)
Recorded at Cherokee Studios, Los Angeles: May (music) and September (vocals) 1977
Performed by Peter Frampton and The Bee Gees

Another song from The Beatles' *Sgt. Pepper* album. Interestingly, the title didn't spring from the imaginations of either Lennon or McCartney. 'It's getting better' was a favourite saying of British drummer Jimmie Nicol. He substituted for Ringo Starr, who was ill for eight days on The Beatles' 1964 Australian tour before disappearing back into anonymity. The phrase reportedly popped into McCartney's head while walking his sheepdog one day in 1967.

The movie scene setting for this song is outside a barn with cows and chickens all around while a small audience watches them. Paul Nicholas records them to send a demo tape to the record company, B.D. Records.

It's a good version, with Frampton taking McCartney's original lead vocal and The Bee Gees emulating Lennon and Harrison's harmonies.

'I Want You (She's So Heavy)' (John Lennon, Paul McCartney)

Recorded at Cherokee Studios, Los Angeles: May (music) and September (vocals) 1977

Performed by The Bee Gees, Dianne Steinberg, Paul Nicholas, Donald Pleasence, and Stargard

This was the closing track on side one of The Beatles' 1969 album *Abbey Road*, written by John Lennon about his love for Yoko Ono.

It's quite long and drawn-out, but it's ideal as a scene-setter as the band is greeted from a private jet by B.D. Records' owner (played by Donald Pleasence) as they ride in his open-top stretch limo. They are driven through sleazy parts of town and meet a bevy of beautiful women at the swimming pool at B. D.'s house. They later have what's described as a 'typical record business dinner', where they sign a contract under the influence of one thing or another – Barry's character is being plied with cocaine by his newfound lady friends. As each group member signs the contract, their attire changes to a B. D. Records t-shirt, implying that he's taking the shirts off their backs. Maurice – with a huge glass – slumps on the table, so B. D. puts the pen in his hand and signs for him. Maurice revives and grabs the contract as B. D. walks away, pulling him off his chair as he collapses on the floor. It's one of the movie's few genuinely funny moments.

While Donald Pleasence, Dianne Steinberg, and Paul Nicholas take on various parts of the lead vocal, The Bee Gees don't get much of a look in. But when they do the 'She's so heavy' parts, it's so good.

'Good Morning, Good Morning' (John Lennon, Paul McCartney)

Recorded at Cherokee Studios, Los Angeles: May (music) and September (vocals) 1977

Performed by Paul Nicholas, Peter Frampton, and The Bee Gees

Another song from the original *Sgt. Pepper* album. John Lennon was apparently inspired to write the song having seen a television advertisement for Kellogg's Corn Flakes breakfast cereal.

The song suits the scene perfectly, with a sprightly Paul Nicholas ushering the hungover band into a limousine waiting outside their hotel. They start to sober up when they see a bill poster plastering their image everywhere. The scene cuts to a recording studio, where they are by now bright-eyed and bushy-tailed. Further scenes show footage from a record pressing plant where the actual soundtrack album was being manufactured, and the band's arrival at a Tower Records store where they are mobbed by fans.

Nicholas takes the opening lead vocal with Frampton, and the Gibbs' vocals come in on the titular accents. The following verse is Barry and Robin singing in unison, then they alternate lines on the bridge. It's an effective combination, and though the blend was employed frequently on their own songs, it was never done quite like this.

'She's Leaving Home' (John Lennon, Paul McCartney)

Recorded at Cherokee Studios, Los Angeles: May (music) and September (vocals) 1977

Performed by The Bee Gees, Jay MacIntosh, and John Wheeler

Another track from the original *Sgt. Pepper*, 'She's Leaving Home' was inspired by a story printed in Britain's *Daily Mirror* on 27 February 1967. It told of a 17-year-old girl named Melanie Coe, who had run away from home with her boyfriend, leaving behind a cushy lifestyle and a couple of confused parents who were at work when she departed.

The Bee Gees aren't seen at all in this scene where Strawberry Fields (played by actress Sandy Farina) leaves home to be with her boyfriend Billy Shears (played by Peter Frampton).

Very unusually on this song, the lead vocal and extra vocal harmony are partly processed through a vocoder as the voices of Mr. Mustard's robots. They also provide high harmonies backing Jay MacIntosh and John Wheeler, who play Strawberry's parents. Robin picks up the narrative beautifully before MacIntosh and Wheeler take it back with Broadway-esque singing.

'Oh! Darling' (John Lennon, Paul McCartney)

Recorded at Cherokee Studios, Los Angeles: May (music) and September (vocals) 1977
Performed by Robin Gibb
Chart positions: US: 15, New Zealand: 40, Norway: 40

'Oh! Darling' was the fourth song on The Beatles' 1969 album *Abbey Road*. Sung by Paul McCartney, its laid-back rhythm-and-blues feel and bass line are reminiscent of Fats Domino's classic 'Blueberry Hill'. McCartney's vocal escalated to a frantic screamed plea as the track progressed.

In the movie, the band is seen in the studio with Robin playing electric piano and singing. Sandy Farina enters the control room and Peter Frampton leaves, followed quickly by Barry and Maurice, while an oblivious Robin plays on.

Most songs on the album garnered criticism, although Earth, Wind & Fire's 'Got To Get You Into My Life' and Aerosmith's 'Come Together' were almost always excepted. 'Oh! Darling' should also have been included, as this was startlingly different to The Beatles' original. Robin turns in an extremely powerful and emotive vocal.

It was released as a single and in October, peaked respectably at number 15 on the *Billboard* Hot 100. To date, it remains Robin's highest-charting solo single in America.

Medley: 'Polythene Pam'/'She Came In Through The Bathroom Window'/'Nowhere Man'/'Sgt. Pepper's Lonely Hearts Club Band (Reprise)' (John Lennon, Paul McCartney)

Recorded at Cherokee Studios, Los Angeles: May (music) and September (vocals) 1977

'Polythene Pam' (John Lennon, Paul McCartney)

Performed by The Bee Gees
Written by John Lennon but credited to Lennon/McCartney, 'Polythene Pam' appeared in the medley on *Abbey Road*. It's a bizarre song about a kinky sexual encounter Lennon had with a girl who dressed in polythene whilst in Jersey. He admitted, 'She didn't wear jack boots and kilts, I just sort of elaborated. Perverted sex in a polythene bag. Just looking for something to write about'.

The movie performance is in a full-blown concert scene, and Barry gets mobbed on stage. It's a good rocking song, performed confidently with Barry evidently enjoying taking the lead vocal.

'She Came In Through The Bathroom Window' (John Lennon, Paul McCartney)

Performed by Peter Frampton and The Bee Gees

This was the second time The Bee Gees recorded this song: their first was for the *All This and World War II* film soundtrack two years earlier.

In the movie, the visual shows newspaper articles proclaiming the band's success combined with a concert setting.

The track appears as the second song in the medley here, in a similar manner to the original by The Beatles on their *Abbey Road* album, following 'Polythene Pam'. Peter Frampton takes the lead vocal with The Bee Gees on supporting harmonies. Unlike their earlier version, this is a funkier jazz-hued arrangement.

'Nowhere Man' (John Lennon, Paul McCartney)

Performed by The Bee Gees

This is the oldest Beatles song on the soundtrack. From their 1965 *Rubber Soul* album, it's a song John Lennon wrote about himself after racking his brain in desperation for five hours trying to come up with another song.

The medley's third song, the scene is backlit to show silhouettes of the band. Barry sings the verse as a spotlight shines on him. The chorus is the whole band, and they are also illuminated.

It's a perfect song for The Bee Gees. The verses are a cinch for Barry to sing, and the chorus beautifully demonstrates the brothers' consummate grasp on harmonising. It's all so effortlessly natural.

Released – in Italy only – as the B-side to Barry's 'A Day In The Life' single, it became an extremely interesting collectable. It was lengthened by editing in a repeat section, whereas the medley version is a very short 1:24.

'Sgt. Pepper's Lonely Hearts Club Band (Reprise)' (John Lennon, Paul McCartney)

Performed by Peter Frampton and The Bee Gees

This reprise of the title song is the medley's final piece and is faster than the first version and has heavier instrumentation. In the movie, it's introduced as a programme on BDTV called *The Sgt. Pepper Special*. It's performed on an elaborate stage set with a studio audience. The scene is intercut with clips of their families and friends watching the show on TV back home in Heartland.

But the scene belongs to Maurice for his drumming. He'd practised for nearly two months with session drummer Bernard Purdie, who played on the recording. Maurice admitted it was very difficult, but he was extremely flattered when 'Bernie told me, 'I'm glad they picked you, because in that last filming, you didn't miss one beat, and you hit every drum I hit when I recorded it'. I was very knocked out from his compliments'.

This is the soundtrack's only song where Barry gets to fully exercise his falsetto voice.

'Because' (John Lennon, Paul McCartney)

Recorded at Cherokee Studios, Los Angeles: May (music) and September (vocals) 1977 Performed by Alice Cooper and The Bee Gees

From The Beatles' *Abbey Road* album, 'Because' is notable for its prominent three-part-harmony vocals by Lennon, McCartney, and Harrison – recorded three times to make nine voices in all.

In the movie, bad-guy Father Sun's brainwashed followers put on headphones and watch him on screens while the band break into his domain and steal the Sgt. Pepper band's tuba. Father Sun – played by shock rock legend Alice Cooper – discovers the intrusion, and in a fight with Robin, he strangles him before Barry comes to the rescue and sucker-punches him and he lands face-first in a pie.

The unlikely combination of Alice Cooper and The Bee Gees works quite well here. Alice was well-known for his theatrical stage act, therefore, getting into character as a villain was never going to be a challenge. His sinister vocal performance contrasts superbly with The Bee Gees' gloriously pure and wholesome harmonies. Alice frequently complimented The Bee Gees' music in subsequent interviews.

'Carry That Weight' (John Lennon, Paul McCartney)

Recorded at Cherokee Studios, Los Angeles: May (music) and September (vocals) 1977

Performed by The Bee Gees

Another song The Bee Gees had recorded previously for the *All This and World War II* soundtrack. This features in the funeral scene, where they, Peter Frampton, Paul Nicholas, and an unknown cast member carry Strawberry Fields' glass coffin and place it on a horse-drawn hearse.

It's a solid arrangement that supports the brothers' strong unison chorus well.

'Being For The Benefit Of Mr. Kite' (John Lennon, Paul McCartney)

Recorded at Cherokee Studios, Los Angeles: May (music) and September (vocals) 1977

Performed by Maurice Gibb, Peter Frampton, George Burns and The Bee Gees

From The Beatles' *Sgt. Pepper* album, this song drew influence from a 19th-century poster of Pablo Fanque's Circus that John Lennon bought at an antique shop during the filming of The Beatles' 'Strawberry Fields Forever' and 'Penny Lane' promos in Sevenoaks, Kent. He explained, 'Everything from the song is from that poster, except the horse wasn't called Henry'.

In the movie, the band leads a procession of circus performers into Heartland for a benefit concert, while they perform on top of a bus.

Maurice gets to sing the lead vocal on the introductory verse, while The Bee Gees and Peter Frampton take the second. After a waltz interlude for the dancing horse, Barry takes the first two lines of the final verse, and George Burns the next two. Frampton and the Gibbs then assume the verse's second half to close the track.

'A Day In The Life' (John Lennon, Paul McCartney)

Recorded at Cherokee Studios, Los Angeles: May (music) and September (vocals) 1977

Performed by Barry Gibb and The Bee Gees

This Beatles epic was the final song on their *Sgt. Pepper* album. It came after the title-track reprise, which would have been the logical closing song, but 'A Day In The Life' was one of those songs you quite simply couldn't follow.

The scene where the song appears follows Strawberry's funeral, so it maintains a sombre feel with Barry sitting alone by a lake. He walks over to Robin and Maurice outside a derelict house before the middle eight kicks in, and there are several scene changes in quick succession: the band getting into a limo outside a hotel; Barry smoking marijuana with B. D.; recording in the studio; and finally, concert footage, before returning to the derelict house. The climactic ending coincides with Billy – so consumed with grief at Strawberry's death – jumping from a window to end it all. The Sgt. Pepper weathervane on top of the city hall spins and takes on human form in the shape of Billy Preston, then zapping Billy with a lightning bolt and saving him from certain death.

It's a definite album highlight, and Barry performs it impeccably. Appropriately, it was a single A-side in France and Italy, where the B-sides were 'Sgt. Pepper's Lonely Hearts Club Band' and 'Nowhere Man', respectively.

'Sgt, Pepper's Lonely Hearts Club Band (Finale)' (John Lennon, Paul McCartney)

Recorded at Cherokee Studios, Los Angeles: May (music) and September (vocals) 1977

Performed by The Cast

The movie's final scene was filmed at MGM Studios on 16 December 1977. It was a spectacular star-studded reprise of the title song, where the cast were joined by 'Our Guests at Heartland' – an invited list of celebrities who formed a chorus standing in formation, somewhat imitating the image on The Beatles' *Sgt. Pepper* album cover. The arrangement is patently disco, with thumping drums, string and horn flourishes, and wah-wah guitar sweetening throughout.

The guests were: Peter Allen, Keith Allison, George Benson, Elvin Bishop, Stephen Bishop, Jack Bruce, Keith Carradine, Carol Channing, Jim Dandy, Sarah Dash, Rick Derringer, Barbara Dickson, Donovan, Dr. John, Randy Edelman, Yvonne Elliman, José Feliciano, Leif Garrett, Adrian Gurvitz, The Harlettes, Billy Harper, Eddie Harris, Heart, Nona Hendryx, Barry Humphries as Dame Edna Everage, Etta James, Bruce Johnston, Joe Lala, D.C. LaRue, Jo Leb, Marcy Levy, Mark Lindsay, Nils Lofgren, John Mayall, Curtis Mayfield, Bruce Morrow, Peter Noone, Alan O'Day, Lee Oskar, The Paley Brothers, Robert Palmer, Wilson Pickett, Anita Pointer, Bonnie Raitt, Helen Reddy, Minnie Riperton, Chita Rivera, Johnny Rivers, Monte Rock III, Danielle Rowe, Seals and Crofts, Sha Na Na, Del Shannon, Joe Simon, Connie Stevens, Al Stewart, John Stewart, Tina Turner, Frankie Valli, Gwen Verdon, Diane Vincent, Grover Washington Jr., Johnny Winter, Wolfman Jack, Bobby Womack, and Gary Wright.

Returning to Miami on 24 July after a frantic week of *Sgt. Pepper* movie premieres and parties, The Bee Gees were back at work on their forthcoming album.

In retrospect, it might appear as though anytime Barry put pen to paper in 1978 it resulted in a hit of epic proportions. However, the song

'Ain't Nothing Gonna Keep Me From You' was an exception. Released on the Casablanca label in July and sung by Teri DeSario, the single only reached number 43 in the US the week of 2 September.

DeSario was the spouse of Boneroo Horns player Bill Purse, who had been involved in several Gibb projects over the past few years. Albhy Galuten recalled DeSario's performance at a Miami nightclub to the authors in 2021: 'I went to see her with Barry, and we thought she was a great singer. So we said, 'Well, let's do something''. Barry wrote the song specifically for her and sang background vocals on the track, which was included on her debut album *Pleasure Train* (featuring yet *another* version of the now persistent 'Save Me, Save Me'). Albhy pondered, 'I don't know why it wasn't a hit. It was a good record. We thought it was a hit, but maybe it wasn't promoted well'.

As 1978 wore on, an incalculable number of clones and send-ups of the *Saturday Night Fever* soundtrack surfaced on store shelves, all undoubtedly hoping to cash in on its massive appeal. Some were infinitely better than others. One of the most enjoyable had to be that by the producers and cast of the popular children's TV show *Sesame Street*.

They released the album *Sesame Street Fever* in July. Theirs also had something most other derivatives didn't: an actual Bee Gee!

Sesame Street Fever (1978)

Personnel:
Robin Gibb: vocals
Frank Oz (Cookie Monster, Grover, Oscar the Grouch): vocals
Jerry Nelson (The Count): vocals
Caroll Spinney (Big Bird): vocals
Jim Henson (Ernie): vocals
Recorded in May 1978 (possibly at CBS 30th Street and Mediasound Studios, New York)
Release date: UK and US: August 1978
Chart position: US: 75

Featuring characters from *Sesame Street*, the album cover parodies that of the *Saturday Night Fever* soundtrack, with a white-suited Grover à la John Travolta posing on the dance floor, and Ernie, Bert, and Cookie Monster in the image of The Bee Gees. However, the real interest is Robin's involvement. His children were big fans of the show, and the LP's liner notes state that 'Robin Gibb appears courtesy of his children, Melissa and

Spencer Gibb'. Robin's wife Molly and the children joined him in New York City to visit the *Sesame Street* studio to promote the release.

The album was not a stellar chart performer, peaking at 75 on the *Billboard* Top LPs & Tape survey (unsurprising as it was primarily intended for children), but it was a sleeper seller and ended up being a surprise commercial success, notching up sales of over 500,000 copies and earning a Gold record certification. In November, Robin, Molly, Spencer, and Melissa again travelled to New York to receive the award, which was presented to them by the *Sesame Street* character Big Bird.

There is no Gibb involvement in the writing of these songs, which were all penned by *Sesame Street's* resident composer Joe Raposo.

Of interest to collectors is the Canadian Special Disco Remix edition of the album, which has extended versions of some songs: most notably 'Trash', which is lengthened from 4:18 to 6:06. The album in its original form has only been released on CD in Japan, though it is available on streaming platforms.

'Sesame Street Fever' (Joe Raposo)
Recorded in May 1978 in New York
Incorrectly credited to Robin Gibb, The Count, Grover, Ernie, and Cookie Monster on the album cover, Grover's credit belonged to Big Bird. It was released as a single in Norway, Germany, the UK, and Japan, backed with the non-Gibb-related song 'Has Anybody Seen My Dog?', which featured the voices of the Grover and Marty characters. It was also a single in North America, with the abbreviated title 'Fever', featuring 'Trash' on the B-side. The characters were voiced by Jerry Nelson (The Count), Caroll Spinney (Big Bird), Jim Henson (Ernie), and Frank Oz (Cookie Monster).

'Trash' (Joe Raposo)
Recorded in May 1978 in New York
This is a Robin solo track: though Oscar the Grouch and Grover are credited on the single, they do not appear. Robin turns in a strong and beautifully warm vocal on a song with rather strange subject matter (well, maybe for anyone except Oscar) – extolling the virtues of people's garbage.

'C Is For Cookie' (Joe Raposo)
Recorded in May 1978 in New York
The song is performed by Cookie Monster but includes a brief, endearing introductory dialogue from Robin.

The cover of the 2 September issue of *Billboard* magazine proclaimed it was a 'Special Showcase Tribute'. Inside, the news articles included a photograph of the brothers at Criteria Studios being presented with an Ampex Golden Reel Award for *Saturday Night Fever*. They were also presented with a $1,000 cheque to give to the Bertha Abess Children's Center, their selected beneficiary.

However, two other articles called attention to the beginning of a Bee Gees backlash, fuelled by their omnipresence on radio. The first was about the National Association of Broadcasters' first Radio Programming Conference in Chicago, where comedian and social commentator Dick Gregory opened proceedings with a sometimes-biting keynote address in which he warned broadcasters that their future depended on how they used what he referred to as their 'enormous power'. Later in a section on playlists, WNBC New York programme director Bob Pittman suggested that radio stations must look at 'the total sound, the total image of a station', and avoid programming too much of one artist, 'like we did with The Bee Gees and Andy Gibb'.

The second article referred to the British disco scene, which was seen to be developing as a separatist movement. Steve Allen – who ran a business operating ten mobile discos – had recently opened a shop in Peterborough called Discoasis, which sold soul, jazz, funk, back-catalogue, and import items – designed, said Allen, 'to cater for our large clientele of disco-goers and fashion-conscious kids who don't all want The Bee Gees ad infinitum'.

By contrast, the supplement '*Billboard* Salutes The Bee Gees' was an enormous 170-page tribute magazine heaping praise on the Gibbs. Apart from the glowing editorial section, 118 pages were tributes and thank-you messages from record companies, music publishers, concert promoters, recording studios, and many others with business links to The Bee Gees, alongside more personal salutes from the likes of Neil Sedaka, Frankie Valli, Samantha Sang, Marvin Hamlisch, The Osmonds, Karl Richardson, Albhy Galuten, and – on the back page – Robert Stigwood.

On 6 September, Barry and Robin appeared on the high-rating US talk show *The Merv Griffin Show*, recorded in July while they were in Los Angeles for the *Sgt. Pepper* premiere. They talked about the success of *Saturday Night Fever* and the *Sgt. Pepper* film. Amidst the 17-minute interview, Barry deflected Griffin's question on the possibility of Andy joining The Bee Gees and instead spoke about plans for The Bee Gees to perform in Russia.

It should come as no surprise, therefore, that the group were taking no chances with the risky international money market when it came to guarding their fast-growing fortunes, and as early as May, *Billboard* reported that The Bee Gees attempted to negotiate a barter agreement with Iron Curtain countries (at the time including Poland, East Germany, Czechoslovakia, Hungary, Yugoslavia, Romania, Bulgaria, Albania, and the Soviet Union), whereby their revenues would be calculated and paid off in commodities such as grain and oil. However, the deal fizzled out when it became too diplomatically complex. However, ABBA did manage to close successfully on a similar agreement around the same time.

The Bee Gees' voices were heard on American band Chicago's tenth studio album *Hot Streets*, released in October. The brothers sang background vocals on the Peter Cetera-led song 'Little Miss Lovin''. This came about when both bands were recording albums at Criteria Studios. Chicago's engineer Mike Stahl recalled hearing the brothers' 'amazing harmonies – it was just astounding! I was in the control room, and there are no words to describe the feelings of hearing those soaring harmonies on one of Chicago's songs. I was seeing and hearing true talent'. Blue Weaver also appeared on the album, playing synthesiser on the tracks 'No Tell Lover' and 'Show Me The Way'.

In return, Chicago's horn section – Lee Loughnane (trumpet), Walt Parazaider (woodwinds), and James Pankow (trombone) – played on a handful of tracks for The Bee Gees' album in progress. On music site *ProSoundWeb* in 2019, Mike Stahl recounted in detail their experience as guests at the brothers' session:

I brought the brass section over to the main studios at Criteria Studios, to begin rehearsing. When we arrived, to everyone's complete surprise, we discovered that no brass charts had been written. I could tell the guys were upset, because Jimmy Pankow always spent long hours writing the brass charts, getting them perfect for all three instruments. Since the charts weren't done, we all assumed we'd have to come back another day. When Barry came into the studio and introduced himself to everyone, he asked his engineer to run the rhythm tracks they'd recorded the day before. When Jimmy asked him about the brass charts, he said, 'I'm going to write them now'. As the music started, he sat down at the piano and began singing and hitting single keys on the piano, to signify which notes he wanted the brass to play.

His transcriber sitting next to him furiously wrote down what Barry was playing, and then charted it for all three of the brass instruments. None of us had ever seen anything like it! When they ran the track the second time, Barry started singing and hitting the notes on the piano the way he wanted the brass to accent them, with his voice: 'Da-Da-Da-Dot Da-Da-Da-Dot Dot-Dot-Dot'. And then again, 'Da-Da-Da-Dot Da-Da-Da-Dot Dot-Dot-Dot'. The Chicago guys were staring at me and I was staring at them – we were all overwhelmed. No one could play the notes, have them written down and transcribed for sax, trombone and trumpet, and then have them ready to record within 30 minutes. That just can't happen! And yet it did.

But not everyone was convinced of Barry's prodigiousness. Stahl recalled:

Jimmy pulled me aside and said Barry must be doing this for show – 'This can't be real'. I told him I thought he was wrong, because on many of my trips to The Bee Gees' studios, I'd talked with their engineer Albhy Galuten, and he'd told me what a genius Barry Gibb was. I knew that we'd just witnessed a true phenomenon. After the charts had been duplicated for all the brass players, the guys were then thinking this was going to take a long time to record, because, again, simply, the charts couldn't be correct. No one was that good … there were going to be too many wrong notes and too many bad accents and everything. These mistakes would then take a lot of time to correct, and then they would have to be re-recorded.

But once the musicians started sinking their teeth into the arrangements, their tune quickly changed. Stahl continued:

The level of scepticism was at an all-time high as the brass players took their seats in the studio until they started reading the charts and playing the parts. The sound was full, and the stabs and staccatos were tight and bright. They were literally perfect. No bad accents, no bad notes, nothing. The song was completed in under an hour, and we were out of there. When we listened to the playback after the brass was finished, the brass charts were nothing short of amazing and had a totally fresh feel which gave the song a new meaning. Barry was tapping his pencil on the console, and was very pleased.

Despite the session's harmonious outcome, according to Stahl, Barry's sharp ear and quick writing skills left at least one musician a bit overwhelmed by what they'd experienced:

> As we were leaving, everyone thanked them profusely for the experience, and we got into our car for the drive back to the house. The ride back was very depressing, especially for Jimmy, who always agonised over his charts to get them perfect, sometimes taking days to perfect them. Since he was the only one who wrote the brass parts for the group, this tour-de-force he'd just witnessed seemed to affect him the most, knocking him for a loop. It wasn't that his charts weren't good, it was just that he, and the rest of us, had never witnessed anything like that. Even superstar writers and performers need to get out of their own bubble sometimes, and this was a huge revelation.

The Bee Gees completed their new studio album on 10 November. It had been given the working title *Spirits* early on in a few different publications, though they'd gone in a different direction in between and considered calling it *Reachin' Out* after one of the songs on the tracklist. They finally arrived at *Spirits Having Flown*.

With their *Fever* songs still in heavy rotation almost everywhere, they pushed out a new single in advance of the album's scheduled arrival of February 1979. 'Too Much Heaven' – a lush R&B ballad with layers upon layers of falsetto harmonies – was released in North America on 21 November (it had arrived almost a month earlier in the UK). While the song was an evolution of the group's contemporary sonic trademark, its lush orchestration hearkened back to their late 1960s/early 1970s Bill Shepherd arrangements, where swirls of strings and horns were wrapped thickly around the vocals. While little was known about what the rest of the album would sound like, it was evident that 'Too Much Heaven' was a big, carefully planned diversion from anything related to *Saturday Night Fever*. The single entered the *Billboard* Hot 100 immediately at number 35, the highest debut of any song that year. Within four weeks, it was in the top three.

Andy logged his third consecutive American top ten single from *Shadow Dancing* (his fifth overall) during the week of 16 December with his version of '(Our Love) Don't Throw It All Away'. It clung to the number nine spot for four weeks through to 6 January 1979 – the same week it became his fourth certified Gold single. Unfortunately for Andy, his best career year ever was becoming overrun by his personal turmoil. Within just a few months, things would be incredibly different for him on many fronts.

As they had during The Bee Gees' first wave of global fame in the late 1960s, their former Australian record label Festival Records stepped in at the year's end to capitalise on the group's recent stratospheric success by offering their 1963-1966 output on the new compilation *Birth of Brilliance*.

Birth Of Brilliance

Release date: December 1978

Side 1: 1. 'Wine And Woman', 2. 'I Was A Lover, A Leader Of Men', 3. 'Timber', 4. 'Claustrophobia', 5. 'Could It Be', 6. 'Peace Of Mind', 7. 'To Be Or Not To Be', 8. 'I Don't Think It's Funny'

Side 2: 1. 'Three Kisses Of Love', 2. 'The Battle Of The Blue And The Grey', 3.' Theme From Jaimie McPheeters', 4. 'Turn Around, Look At Me', 5. 'Every Day I Have To Cry', 6. 'How Love Was True', 7. 'You Won't See Me', 8. 'Lonely Winter'

Side 3: 1. 'In The Morning', 2. 'Like Nobody Else', 3. 'All By Myself', 4. 'Storm', 5. 'Butterfly', 6. 'Terrible Way To Treat Your Baby', 7. 'Exit, Stage Right', 8. 'Coalman'

Side 4: 1. 'I Am The World', 2. 'Cherry Red', 3. 'I Want Home', 4. 'Monday's Rain', 5. 'How Many Birds', 6. 'Secondhand People', 7. 'Born A Man', 8. 'Spicks And Specks'

In the ten years since The Bee Gees had left Australia, Festival Records had licenced an innumerable number of albums (usually to obscure labels) containing the group's earliest material. Usually shoddily put together with no semblance of song chronology, these budget (or drugstore) compilations – often under various grand titles – flooded the market. Earlier in 1978, a series of them – with names like – *Turn Around, Look At Me, Monday's Rain, Take Hold Of That Star, Peace Of Mind*, and two double album volumes called *The Bee Gees Bonanza* – were issued by the Pickwick International label in North America. There are no details available regarding how well these sold, but they're still rather plentiful on the used record market.

However, Festival saved a more ambitious retrospective for its local Australian audience. *Birth Of Brilliance* is a 32-track double album encompassing a wide swathe of The Bee Gees' Festival-released recordings, along with a few more obscure tracks – many of which hadn't been available to Australian fans previously. It was the most comprehensive compilation of the trio's Australian catalogue to that point. For the occasion, some effort was made for the collection to be significant. Noted Australian music historian Glenn A. Baker wrote the liner notes for the project. All the tracks are in their original mono format. The package included early Bee Gees photos, and some of the Australian artists who had covered their songs in that era.

Curiously, *Birth Of Brilliance* was released on the Infinity label – a Festival subsidiary initially established in January 1971 to market newly-emerging rock acts.

Ten songs – to this point available only on the rare 1970 European compilation album *Inception/Nostalgia* – made their Australian début on this collection. For serious collectors, 'Monday's Rain' has the vocal track from the original single (appearing here on LP for the first time), which differed from the one on the 1966 *Spicks And Specks* album.

The lack of chronological track sequencing is disappointing. 'The Three Kisses Of Love' and 'The Battle Of The Blue and Grey' – the group's earliest-released songs – are buried on side two, while the first two songs on side one are from 1965. On the positive side, both sides of the second disc are truer to the timeline, with all of them having originated in 1966.

The compilation's limited release almost assured its status as a collector's item. It was reissued in 1994 as a two-CD set.

Given The Bee Gees had essentially commandeered most of the *Billboard* pop charts in 1978, it's no surprise they finished the year by sweeping the magazine's annual Talent-in-Action Awards, which was recognised in the 23 December issue. They took away prizes for Group of the Year (for the Hot 100 and Top LPs & Tape charts combined); Album, Pop Album, and Soundtrack of the Year for *Saturday Night Fever*; Pop Singles and Pop Albums Artist of the Year; and Pop Singles and Pop Albums Group of the Year. Also, Barry, Albhy, and Karl were awarded Producers of the Year.

With what can only be described as an explosive year for The Bee Gees now in the rear-view mirror, they looked to turn the page in 1979 with music made completely on their terms. But the good and – as they would discover – the bad outcomes of their association with *Saturday Night Fever* would be inescapable.

1979

In early January, the Music For UNICEF concert that had been several months in the making finally came to fruition. The Bee Gees arrived in New York City shortly after the new year to receive a mix of accolades and attend conferences prior to the benefit.

On 6 January, 'Too Much Heaven' – the single from which The Bee Gees had committed all royalties to the cause – reached number one in the US, seven weeks after its début. It was their fourth consecutive chart-topper in both the US and Canada, all but guaranteeing the imminent release of *Spirits Having Flown* would be a momentous occasion.

In recognition of their previous work for the Police Athletic League charity, the group received their annual Superstars of the Year award at the Americana Hotel (now the Sheraton New York Times Square Hotel) in Midtown Manhattan. They were the first-ever music group to be honoured. Among the award's past recipients were New York/San Francisco Giants centre-fielder Willie Mays, and New York Knicks point guard Walter 'Clyde' Frazier.

The following day, the Music For UNICEF Concert: A Gift Of Song was held at the United Nations General Assembly. The concert marked the beginning of the International Year of the Child and raised money for UNICEF's world hunger programmes. The host was David Frost, with American actors Henry Fonda, Gilda Radner, and Henry Winkler serving as co-hosts introducing many of the acts. The concert opened with The Bee Gees performing the first verse of 'Children Of The World' twice – on their own first, and then accompanied by a multinational children's choir. All the other artists then sang short portions of one of their own songs before congregating onstage to perform ABBA's 'He's Your Brother'.

David Frost then explained:

At the beginning of the International Year of the Child, each artist here who you've seen tonight has made a lifetime commitment to the world's children. Some of them have written one special song for the occasion tonight, some of them have chosen one of their most popular previous compositions, but all ten – brand new or standards – will tonight become the property of the children of the world, as each of our founder composers turns over the copyright and the future income from the song to Music For UNICEF.

The concert featured some of the biggest names in pop music at the time, performing a mix of major hits and lesser-known songs: Kris Kristofferson and Rita Coolidge ('Fallen Angels'), Olivia Newton-John ('The Key' and an excerpt of 'Let Me Be There'), Andy Gibb ('I Go For You' and a portion of '(Our Love) Don't Throw It All Away'), Earth, Wind & Fire ('September'/'That's the Way Of The World'), Rod Stewart ('Da Ya Think I'm Sexy?' and a short version of 'I Was Only Joking'), Donna Summer ('Mimi's Song'), Andy Gibb and Olivia Newton-John ('Rest Your Love On Me'), ABBA ('Chiquitita'), John Denver ('Rhymes And Reasons'), and The Bee Gees ('Too Much Heaven'). Not all the performances were live, notably ABBA and The Bee Gees turned in lip-synced takes – but the brothers at least went to the trouble of staging a full band and orchestra behind them for 'Too Much Heaven' to at least give the illusion that they weren't miming. Everybody appeared for the closing song: Jackie DeShannon's 'Put A Little Love In Your Heart'. At the end of each performance, the artist signed a large parchment, deeding their gift of a song and declaring support for UNICEF's goals. Some artists only released the royalties for a limited time, but The Bee Gees' contribution of 'Too Much Heaven' was granted in perpetuity. By 2003, it had reportedly earned more than $7,000,000 for UNICEF.

NBC broadcast the concert in the US on 10 January, with full-page press advertisements declaring it to be 'The TV Special of the Year'. The ad showed Elton John amongst the list of participants, however, he did not appear. Media statistics show the viewing audience was over 52,000,000. Airing in the UK on 13 January, it was also taken up by broadcasters in over 70 other countries.

A few days later, The Bee Gees jetted to the West Coast to receive a star on the Hollywood Walk of Fame at a ceremony on 12 January. Their star is located on the western end of the 1.3-mile-long Walk, at 6845 Hollywood Boulevard – close to Grauman's (now TCL) Chinese Theatre and the Hard Rock Café. The Bee Gees had generally been hidden away from the public for much of 1978, but the outing became a rather intense and personal reminder of just how enormously popular they'd become. Fans turned up in droves at the unveiling and crowded the Gibbs and their families. Robin remembered: 'There were about 5000 people there – the largest crowd they'd ever had for one of those ceremonies. Before I knew it, I barely had room to breathe, and I was scared to death because I had my kids with me. When we finally got back to the limousines, fans were climbing all over them, and they followed our cars for miles. We almost didn't get away'.

At the American Music Awards held later the same day at the Santa Monica Civic Auditorium, the group were victorious in two categories: Favourite Pop/Rock Group and Favourite Soul/R&B Album. Barry Manilow – who pipped Andy in the Favourite Pop/Rock Male Artist category – presented them with the former award. Barry's acceptance speech was short but to the point: 'We'd like to thank Al Coury, Bob Edson, Robert Fitzgerald, all the people at RSO Records, and Robert Stigwood, our manager'. Johnny Paycheck and Chuck Berry handed the brothers the Favourite Soul Album prize for *Saturday Night Fever*. Robin thanked the same people as he accepted the award, while Barry hastily chipped in with 'and the public!'.

Adding to the hype of the *Spirits Having Flown* launch was the advent of *The Official Bee Gees Fan Club*, which was contracted to Entertainers Merchandise Management Corporation in North Hollywood, California. A four-dollar-per-year membership fee bought the recipient a 23-piece welcome kit, which included a glossy folder, an assortment of posters, photo prints, a newsletter, and – of course – order forms to buy even more merchandise! Of special interest was a 7" 33-RPM record, with the first side containing 'A Personal Message from The Bee Gees', much of which was the brothers bantering and briefly discussing the just-finished album and a proposed tour for the summer. The chatter was interrupted by an acoustic rendition of 'Silent Night'. On the B-side was 'The Rescue Of Bonnie Prince Wally': a vocal comedy skit they recorded with help from their friend David English. Most casual fans were probably unaware the brothers had been creating silly bits like this for most of their lives, so the Goons-esque voices and dialogue might have been a head-scratcher among all the sleek imagery of the Gibbs as dance-floor gods and sex symbols of the moment.

The Gibbs' stunning track record as hitmakers prompted artists from all genres to flock to Criteria Studios to record music – certainly in the hope of capturing whatever magic The Bee Gees had harnessed during their sessions. Lacking in space, plans were reportedly in the works between the brothers and Criteria Studios founder Mack Emerman to build Studio E – a new addition to the main facility constructed especially for The Bee Gees. The new space would be primarily reserved for their projects, customised to their specifications with brand new state-of-the-art recording equipment. It would also give them more flexibility to mentor other artists without having to compete with others for studio time. But by late in the year, the project had fallen through.

The brothers were renting a warehouse about nine miles away at 1801 Bay Road in Miami Beach to store their growing equipment inventory. From this came the decision to purchase the building and convert it into a studio, which was closer to their homes and which would afford them more privacy away from the busy mainland. The Bee Gees began using the studio, christened Middle Ear, the following year.

At the end of January, The Bee Gees' 15th studio album *Spirits Having Flown* was released in the US.

Spirits Having Flown (1979)

Personnel:
Barry Gibb: vocals, guitar
Robin Gibb: vocals
Maurice Gibb: vocals, bass
Alan Kendall: guitar
Blue Weaver: pianos, ARP synthesiser, vibraphone
Dennis Bryon: drums
Gary Brown: saxophone
Harold Cowart: bass
Joe Lala: congas, percussion
Herbie Mann: flute
George Terry: guitar
Daniel Ben Zebulon: congas
Horns: The Boneroo Horns – Peter Graves, Whit Sidener, Kenny Faulk, Neil Bonsanti, Bill Purse, Stan Webb; The Chicago Horns: Lee Loughnane, James Pankow, Walter Parazaider
Conductor: Albhy Galuten
Engineers: Karl Richardson, Dennis Hetzendorfer, John Blanche
Producers: The Bee Gees, Karl Richardson and Albhy Galuten
Recorded between March and November 1978 at Criteria Studios, Miami
Release dates: UK: 24 January 1979, US: 5 February 1979
Chart positions: Australia: 1, Canada: 1, France: 1, Italy: 1, New Zealand: 1, Norway: 1, Sweden: 1, UK: 1, US: 1, West Germany: 1, Austria: 2, Japan: 2, Netherlands: 3
Gold certification: Finland, France, UK, US
Platinum certification: Canada (5x), Hong Kong, New Zealand, US

While *Saturday Night Fever* helped The Bee Gees conquer radio and retail with tremendous force, they spent almost the entirety of 1978 encapsulated at Criteria Studios writing and recording. While *Fever* had brought them an unprecedented level of success, the songs they contributed to it became affixed to a vision that simply had not been theirs. Afterwards, the brothers frequently commented that they felt rather detached from all of it.

What eventually became *Spirits Having Flown* was a reclaiming of creative control, using their fast-rising worth to make an album on their own terms and timeline. Armed with the confidence, time, and funds needed to experiment and push boundaries, they crafted their most innovative and ambitious effort, leaving almost no studio gadget or method unexplored. Its precise, expert production – even by 21st-century standards – was stunningly complex and layered.

If the energy in the Gibb camp to make *Spirits* was high, so were the expectations to build on the strength of its predecessor. Karl Richardson told *Albumism* in 2019:

We had to live up to this standard, this bar we'd set. There was some talk about, 'Okay, we just can't let anything go out that isn't higher than this bar', and that was the dedication of the project. Nothing went out the door without the complete approval of everybody all the way around. Only after the mixes were in the can did we feel like, 'Oh, we finally got [there]. We raised the bar high enough'. We didn't talk about it that much, because it was so fun doing it, but we knew there was that thing of … not pressure, so much, but we weren't going to let it go until it was right.

Spirits was a deliberate departure from the sound of *Saturday Night Fever*. Karl recalled:

We knew it wasn't going to be dance music so much. It was more like a direction, a consciousness. The R&B was always there, and that was Barry's right hand. He'd pick up the acoustic guitar and made those rhythms from the get-go. We had drifted away from the dark side of discotheque, because that whole era – and we'd had great success with 'You Should Be Dancing' and things like that – it became a little bit more of an art form to make records rather than just a groove. It was a conscious decision by all of us in the control room.

Barry had become the most recognisable and profitable voice in pop music, and his ubiquitous falsetto was used to its fullest extent on this album. Some have wondered whether Robin and Maurice are even on the recordings. Of course they are, but their voices are further back in the mix – on repeated listens, and with a bit of focus, you can hear how their tone differs from Barry's. But everyone involved have insisted adamantly that this was by consensual design to maintain the momentum the *Fever* songs had established. Though they achieved that goal, there is some question as to whether his vocal pervasiveness obfuscated *Spirits*' stylistic diversity. In hindsight, even Barry admitted they may have overindulged with his falsetto.

Maurice was also less present as a co-producer and instrumentalist during the album's making. His ongoing relationship with alcohol was progressively worsening, exacerbated by severe back pain that would eventually be resolved with surgery the following year.

The Chicago horn section were credited on the tracks 'Too Much Heaven' and 'Search, Find'. But some accounts indicate they might have also played on 'Tragedy'. Harold Cowart – who played bass on the production team's external projects and on Andy's records – is also on the album (perhaps as a substitute for Maurice), as are veteran percussionist Daniel Ben Zebulon (who had previously worked with Richie Havens, Isaac Hayes and Stevie Wonder, among others) and legendary jazz flautist Herbie Mann.

In 1978, the Gibbs wrote several songs in addition to those on *Spirits Having Flown*, but the exact order and dates are unknown. They penned at least two with Andy ('Where Do I Go' and 'The Love Inside') that may, at some point, have been intended for his next solo record, but they ended up on Jimmy Ruffin's *Sunrise* and Barbra Streisand's *Guilty* projects that Robin and Barry produced, respectively. Other titles floated from the period were 'Nobody' (which evolved into 'Forever, Forever', eventually finished by Robin with Jimmy Ruffin), 'This Could Be Goodbye', 'Castles', 'Ecstasy', and 'Feelings'. The Gibbs tended to recycle parts of songs, so it's possible these evolved into other finished tracks somewhere down the line.

One completed song, 'Desire' (which initially had the working title of 'Midnight'), was recorded and mixed for the album, but was dropped before release, likely because it had similar melodic traits to other songs on the record – especially 'Spirits (Having Flown)'. Instead, 'Desire' was preserved for Andy's 1980 album, *After Dark*. A demo exists with Barry singing the song in his natural voice on the verses, so it's presumed the version The Bee Gees had finalised for *Spirits Having Flown* followed suit. The finished product heard on *After Dark* is the exact take from the Spirits sessions, except Barry's lead vocal was scrubbed out and Andy's was laid on top of the intact instrumentation by The Bee Gees' band and Barry, Robin, and Maurice's harmony vocals on the choruses. 'Desire' became a US top five for Andy in March 1980. It's also one of only three known released recordings to include all four brothers' voices.

Spirits Having Flown was an expertly produced mélange of genres, capitalising on The Bee Gees' burgeoning R&B/soul acumen and seasoned with rock, funk, blues, and folk. Shortly after its release, the album quickly vaulted to number one in the US and the UK – their only studio album to do so. Demonstrating their ability to appeal across identity boundaries, the album also made the top ten on the *Billboard* Top R&B Albums chart. Globally, *Spirits* is estimated to have sold over 30,000,000 copies, though it's been alleged its US single-Platinum certification is wildly inaccurate because RSO/Polydor failed to properly track and report its sales over the years. Likely, its sales in America alone are probably closer to six or seven million by now; perhaps more if digital streams and downloads are added. Regardless, it's indisputably The Bee Gees' most commercially successful studio effort. 'Too Much Heaven', 'Tragedy', and 'Love You Inside Out' all topped the *Billboard* Hot 100 in the first half of 1979. Combined with the *Saturday Night Fever* singles, this accumulated an uninterrupted run of six US number one hits. This put The Bee Gees on par yet again with another Beatles chart record – 'I Feel Fine', 'Eight Days A Week', 'Ticket To Ride', 'Help!', 'Yesterday', and 'We Can Work It Out' all took a turn at the Hot 100 summit over a shorter 54-week period between 26 December 1964 and 8 January 1966.

As statistically important as *Spirits* was to The Bee Gees' commercial legacy, it seemed to have equally contributed to their overexposure. They later acknowledged the album's arrival while the embers from *Saturday Night Fever* were still burning hot might have been mistake. Robin reflected in the 2001 documentary *This Is Where I Came In – The Official Story of The Bee Gees*: 'When we brought out *Spirits Having Flown*, it did phenomenally well. At the same time, *Fever* was still in the top ten. You know, we could have left it another year, and it still probably would have been a little too soon with what was going on'.

The album's complicated arrangements made the tracks rather difficult to replicate live, so only two songs from the album were played on the ensuing *Spirits Having Flown* Tour later in the year: 'Tragedy', and an acoustic version of 'Too Much Heaven'. Both songs remained fixtures of their live shows for decades. No other *Spirits* songs ever appeared in a Bee Gees concert, but Barry did unexpectedly include 'Spirits (Having Flown)' in the set list for his *Mythology* solo tour in 2013 and 2014.

While *Spirits Having Flown* marked the start of the end of the group's unprecedented halcyon days and the decade they helped to define musically, its influence on 1980s artists is left largely unexplored and underappreciated; U2 and Michael Jackson are among many artists who have credited songs like 'Tragedy' and 'Love You Inside Out' as sources of inspiration. In hindsight, the album remains essential listening as a master class in modern pop production and recording.

Though it was re-released on both black and limited-edition 'blood-red' vinyl by Capitol/UMe on 8 May 2020 (along with a selection of other seminal Bee Gees albums), it's odd that *Spirits* has eluded any kind of major ceremonial reissue. What's been made available in physical product and on streaming services could use some remastering, and there seem to be enough interesting demos and outtakes available to make an extended revamp worth the effort – maybe for its 50th anniversary in 2029?

The design concept and images for the album are attributed to American photographer and art director Ed Caraeff, who had worked with the group on and off since 1972 – furnishing cover photos for *Life In A Tin Can, Best Of Bee Gees, Volume 2,* and *Children Of The World.* The photos of the brothers on the rear cover and gatefold, and the shot of them on the boat on the inner sleeve, were most likely taken on Biscayne Bay near their homes. The inner sleeve flipside also features photos of Blue Weaver, Dennis Bryon, and Alan Kendall, superimposed on a collage of black and white photos of the brothers.

The front cover of the album contains an italicised, orange-neon-lit variant of Ernie Cefalu's original classic logo.

'Tragedy' (Barry Gibb, Robin Gibb, Maurice Gibb)

Recorded at Criteria Studios, Miami: between March and November 1978
Chart positions: Australia: 1, Canada: 1, France: 1, Ireland: 1, Italy: 1, New Zealand: 1, Spain: 1, UK: 1 US: 1, Austria: 2, South Africa: 2, Switzerland: 2, West Germany: 2, Belgium: 3, Netherlands: 4, Norway: 4, Sweden: 6, Finland: 7, Japan: 32
Gold certification: France, UK
Platinum certification: Canada, US

In 1990, Robin said of 'Tragedy': 'I've always loved singles, and to me this represents the classic single – high urgency, one-word-statement chorus line with an equally contagious verse. I love this record'.

In 1979, *Rolling Stone* accurately described the album's opening track and second single as a 'mini melodrama that gallops along a bed of synthesized lava'. The production team used an impressive amount of technology to generate and manipulate the intricate web of sounds that propel the track. Albhy Galuten explained to *Albumism* in 2019:

[*Spirits*] was our first real flexibility to have multiple tracks that we could plan on and put together. And we had a click that we could use to drive a sequencer. I remember on 'Tragedy', the bass drum was a noise generator from the sequencer, and we had all these sequenced parts from an ARP [synthesiser]. It was a little box that had 16 sort of de-tented faders – one for each 16th note. And you could set the pitch on each note and then program the sound, and it would play them following the click, and then we'd delay the click so it would come out on time. So, if you listen to 'Tragedy', there's all these sequenced things, and the bass drum part was a synthesiser that might've been the first thing we laid down.

In the same interview, Karl Richardson recalled creating the song's attention-grabbing intro:

'I remember the big [synth] pads ... 'dah-daahh-daaahhh, dah-daahh-daaahhh ', you know, all those'.

Albhy interjects:

'That was a sawtooth. Three waveforms slightly out of tune so they would beat nicely. It was sort of one of my classic sounds that I used to use'.

It's patently confusing that anyone would call 'Tragedy' a disco song. If anything, its dramatic pulse and melodic histrionics borrowed more obviously from progressive or arena rock.

'Tragedy' is the musical equivalent of a panic attack, and every note builds on the intensity of the last, mirroring the lyrical narrative of its protagonist being in absolute misery. Barry's verse vocal and the collective chorus harmonies pierce through the noise like razors, achieving a tonal clarity and sharpness that hadn't been heard on previous tracks. And then – three and a half minutes in – the energy peaks with a staticky explosion which is repeated throughout the outro, each preceded by Barry's shocking operatic scream.

That same explosion was the subject of footage filmed at Criteria Studios that aired in a Bee Gees special on the US TV network NBC later in 1979. It showed a recording session with Barry in front of a microphone blowing through his cupped hands to achieve the effect. Although that exact moment on film was staged, they did incorporate the sound of Barry's breath in the boom heard on the track, with some time-intensive technical enhancements. Karl affirmed in his *Albumism* interview:

It was a thing called a product generator. It was a new toy that someone … you know, we were in tune with all the [Audio Engineering Society] shows – you know, 'What's the new stuff coming out?'. And I guess we just got a sample of it. It was a box, and you put two inputs in it, and it generates all these harmonics and products. So, the two things that went into it were Albhy, or maybe Blue, holding the notes on the bottom end of a piano across multiple keys – maybe as many keys as you could mash down on a grand piano – and then Barry's voice going 'Pbbhhhh!' into a dynamic microphone, blowing air through the diaphragm to distort it. And then you mix these two signals through the generator, and whatever came out sounded like dynamite [*laughs*]. It was very technological – nobody had that sound, I know that for a fact.

Of course, today it's easy to drop an authentic sound effect into a mix, but in those days, they often had to improvise.

Shortly after its February 1979 release, 'Tragedy' reached number one in the US (their fifth consecutive), the UK, Australia, Canada, Spain, Ireland, Italy, France, and New Zealand.

In 1998, British dance/pop outfit Steps released a modernised version that was included on their second album *Steptacular*, which also topped the UK and New Zealand charts. Foo Fighters also created a take for their 2021 album, *Hail Satin*.

'Too Much Heaven' (Barry Gibb, Robin Gibb, Maurice Gibb)
Recorded at Criteria Studios, Miami: between March and November 1978
Chart positions: Argentina: 1, Brazil: 1, Canada: 1, Chile: 1, Italy: 1,

New Zealand: 1, Norway: 1, South Africa: 1, Spain: 1, Sweden: 1, Switzerland: 1, US: 1, France: 2, Ireland: 2, Netherlands: 2, UK: 2, Finland: 4, Australia: 5, Belgium: 8, West Germany: 10, Austria: 13
Gold certification: France, UK
Platinum certification: Canada, US

'I received an invitation/Come to the United Nations'.

These lines The Bee Gees wrote in 1967 for the *Bee Gees' 1st* album track 'In My Own Time', proved prophetic on 9 January 1979 when they performed 'Too Much Heaven' at New York's UN headquarters during the Music For UNICEF Concert.

'Too Much Heaven' was released as a single almost three months in advance of the album. It's an R&B ballad enveloped in strings, horns, and woodwinds; a stunning piece of music. Its lush opulence and spiritual lyric have afforded it a significant post-1970s shelf life. It's likely the most widely remembered of the album's tracks.

Many of the voices heard on the song are Barry's, which he multitracked with stunning precision without listening to any other vocals, according to Albhy Galuten's 2019 *Albumism* interview:

I remember Barry never listened to other vocals when he was singing his background tracks. I don't think he had to do a second take on any of them. And then we put them up, and they were all absolutely on time together, every breath together, every vibrato, everything in tune. There were three tracks of Barry on each of three parts in two octaves, so that's eighteen tracks of Barry. Then, three tracks of the three brothers singing together. I remember we did three of the tracks – since we were tripling everything – with the three of them singing, just to sort of add the rougher edge because Barry's were almost too perfect.

The recording's complexity made it next to impossible to reproduce on stage. On the *Spirits Having Flown* tour, they sang a shortened version in their natural voices with just Barry's guitar as accompaniment and performed an identical arrangement in most of their live shows moving forward. Barry sang a slightly extended version on his 2014 *Mythology* solo tour.

The group's vocal instincts had evolved to the point of being almost otherworldly. Spencer Gibb illustrated a first-hand example in a 2019 conversation with *Albumism*:

If you listen to ['Too Much Heaven'] as an arrangement – especially from a producer's perspective – what is unique is that because you have the orchestra underneath and minimal other instrumentation, the vocals might as well be a choir with the orchestra. It's so lush and textured together. I had the opportunity to be in the studio with them many, many times, and the way they knew each other was just fucking creepy. My dad would be doing a vocal take, and Barry would be sitting at the console, and what I'd hear was something magical. And Barry was like, 'Ahh … no. You're flat'. And I'm like, 'No, he fucking *wasn't!*', and I have a good ear. My dad would say, 'Okay', and then he'd sing again, and it would be just slightly more perfect. Not much, to my ear, but then Barry would say, 'Okay, perfect. You've got it'. And then Barry would go in, and my dad would produce him, and it'd be the same thing. They could just hear shit in each other's voices that nobody else could, and that was just a part of being brothers and growing up together. My dad and Barry would often sing a lead vocal together, and it would sound like one voice.

Two notable cover versions of the song each had a Bee Gee involved. Barry sang background vocals on US singer Jordan Hill's take on her eponymous David Foster-produced début in 1996, and Robin guested on German pop group US5's replica in 2007.

The Bee Gees' version appeared in Kevin Smith's 2001 film *Jay and Silent Bob Strike Back*.

When The Beach Boys' Brian Wilson inducted The Bee Gees into the Rock and Roll Hall of Fame in 1997, he said in his introductory speech, 'I remember when I heard 'Too Much Heaven' for the first time. I thought, 'It's not a song, it's not a record. It's a place where people sing. And I love going to that place'.

The Gibbs have often spoken of 'Too Much Heaven' being one of their finest and favourite compositions. Barry recorded a new version in 2019 with singer Alison Krauss for his solo album *Greenfields*. Barry sings it in his natural voice as opposed to the falsetto that we'd become so accustomed to, and Krauss' feathery soprano complements him beautifully. However, while Barry touted this as a country and bluegrass album, this is well wide of the mark and must surely be looked upon as a missed opportunity for Krauss to showcase her bluegrass fiddle skills.

In the 2020s, 'Too Much Heaven' is enjoying yet another revival as a frequent subject of the recent music 'reaction video' trend, where

YouTube content creators listen to and comment on vintage songs, supposedly for the first time. Though some of them are certainly contrived, the new generation of listeners' enthusiasm for The Bee Gees' vocal skills is heartening.

'Love You Inside Out' (Barry Gibb, Robin Gibb, Maurice Gibb)

Recorded at Criteria Studios, Miami: between March and November 1978
Chart positions: Canada: 1, US: 1, Ireland: 6; UK: 13, Italy: 17, New Zealand: 17, West Germany: 21, Belgium: 22, Netherlands: 35, France: 39, Australia: 77

The release of 'Love You Inside Out' as *Spirits*' third single was a double-edged sword. On the one hand, it was statistically significant as their sixth consecutive US number one, granting them the prestige of matching The Beatles' previous chart record established between 1964 and 1966. On the other, it was the final Bee Gees single to top the *Billboard* survey, and their last top ten hit in America for a decade.

The song's slow funk introduction is anchored by Blue Weaver playing grand piano filtered through a Leslie speaker that modulates its pitch to give it a warbled reverb effect.

The track is unusual for a Gibb song at the time, employing two distinct rhythms between the laid-back verses and the slightly more intense choruses, and a third on the startlingly frantic bridge. Robin's vocal is especially audible in the chorus, which was not the norm on *Spirits Having Flown*.

In 2019, Karl Richardson said of the song for *Albumism*: 'That was a great R&B feel too; the rhythm and blues on that record, just when you think about how the groove worked ... I remember Michael Jackson came back to us and said, 'You know, that's one of my favourite records to play''.

The song is one of just a handful of The Bee Gees' hits they never performed live.

'Love You Inside Out' has been called out in some media circles over the years as an alleged example of the American record industry's payola scheming – a pervasive insider phenomenon where record companies paid or exchanged favours with radio executives and trade publications to raise a record's chart position or get airplay. Reportedly, RSO Records' president Al Coury was a frequent instigator. Some observers believed the song was only a number two hit based on its sales and airplay, but Coury had coaxed *Billboard* higher-ups to nudge it into the pole position to round out The Bee Gees' six-single run at the top. None of this has been proven, and likely won't ever be.

Canadian singer-songwriter Feist recorded a jazz-infused cover titled 'Inside And Out' on her 2004 album *Let It Die*, which landed her a top 30 adult contemporary chart hit there. It was also sampled by American rapper Jay-Z and R&B singer R. Kelly on their 2002 single 'Honey', and by Snoop Dogg on his 2005 'Ups & Downs' single. Both were minor *Billboard* Hot R&B/Hip-Hop hits.

'Reaching Out' (Barry Gibb, Robin Gibb, Maurice Gibb)
Recorded at Criteria Studios, Miami: between March and November 1978
The album's almost-title track is a beautiful ballad that begins with dreamy synths, rim snare drum, and picked acoustic and electric guitars. Structurally like 'Too Much Heaven', it escalates in intensity through a key change, and plays out through to the end with harmonies and falsetto ad libs. Albhy Galuten suggested to *Albumism* that it 'sounds like one of those classic Philadelphia R&B tracks. It's like, 'Oh, this could've been a Spinners hit''.

'Spirits (Having Flown)' (Barry Gibb, Robin Gibb, Maurice Gibb)
Recorded at Criteria Studios, Miami: between March and November 1978
Chart positions: Ireland: 14, UK: 16, Netherlands: 36
The title track (which began with the title 'Passing Thought') is arguably one of the album's finest moments, eschewing R&B in favour of a lilting samba rhythm propelled by acoustic guitars, brushed snare, congas, and woodwinds. Barry's natural voice barely rises above a whisper in the verses, conceding to big, bright falsetto harmonies on the chorus. The lengthy outro continues the instrumental break melody from between the first chorus and second verse, building in layers of synths and strings that Barry developed with Albhy Galuten.

Two early demos of the song illustrate its development. The first is a slower, rudimentary run-through with an unfinished lyric, with Barry's lead vocal and acoustic guitar to the fore supported by basic backing from the band. The other is a take with almost everything in place, save for vocal harmonies and orchestral sweetening. Albhy told *Albumism*:

I'm really happy with a lot of the orchestration on that song. We did the strings in Miami, and so it was a fair amount of work because they're not like the New York or L.A. string players – not the same kind of experience. But we had time, so we spent more time with them and got all the pieces really right. And the Boneroo Horns and all of the parts were just well put together around the vocals and the arrangements for the song. I was just very pleased with how it came out. It was, again, where Barry and I were kind of firing on all cylinders. I would go to his house, and we would play a cassette, and we would sing the parts to each other, and I'd write them down and then orchestrate them.

'Spirits (Having Flown)' was released as a single outside North America to promote the *Greatest* compilation that arrived in late 1979, though some argue it would have been wise to issue it there as its vocal style and Latin influence could have helped the public and media away from typecasting The Bee Gees as disco loyalists.

It also appeared on a few future compilations, often, sadly, with Barry's count-in chopped from the front end. In early 1980, it became The Bee Gees' seventh consecutive UK top 20 hit – the last one they would have there until 1987.

'Search, Find' (Barry Gibb, Robin Gibb, Maurice Gibb)
Recorded at Criteria Studios, Miami: between March and November 1978
A track that could have easily been a single, the bright, punchy 'Search, Find' hearkens back to the looser R&B approach The Bee Gees took on *Children Of The World*. Shiny horns, breezy strings, and session player Harold Cowart's exquisite jumpy bass line chase each other as the song sprints forward – appropriate, as the protagonist seems to be in breathless pursuit of an object of desire.

Some listeners have pointed out that the title track from Michael Jackson's 1987 album, *Bad*, bears a striking similarity to 'Search, Find' in its chord structure and vocal styling – albeit with a different tempo. It's certainly not impossible that Jackson could have used it as inspiration given his affection for the Gibbs and their music.

American singer Eloise Laws recorded a version for her self-titled 1980 album.

'Stop (Think Again)' (Barry Gibb, Robin Gibb, Maurice Gibb)
Recorded at Criteria Studios, Miami: between March and November 1978
While the entire album challenged Barry's vocal capabilities, this slow-burning ballad found him also navigating a tricky 12/8 time signature

while delivering a lead in his uppermost register. By Albhy Galuten's account, it might have also been the most technically arduous track on the album to assemble, given the amount of manual editing co-producer Karl Richardson had to do to get the timing and atmosphere just right. Albhy told *Albumism*:

> It's like a B.B. King song – just a great slow blues ballad and a fantastic song that should be covered by somebody. But I remember it was the most tape edits I think ever done on one track in the world. It was a very slow tempo and it was very hard to play, and we finally got a take that we thought had all the right dynamics and the right feel. It sort of moved around a lot in time, so Karl would … I don't know, I remember there must've been a hundred, hundred-and-fifty splices in it. Taking time out was easy. Putting time in, meant that it needed the ambience, so he had little bits of tape all over the wall with markings on them – like, that this [piece] had the 'right overhead at minus twenty'. And when we needed, he'd find the right piece with the tape on it, and splice it in.

Karl added:

> What was interesting was that it was two-inch-wide tape, so when you put it in the splicing block, you're slicing it at an angle. And some of the slices were about three-eighths of an inch, so basically, you're taking out a very, very small amount of time – hand-splicing tape, which was a very physical process. The master – because it was two inches wide – I played it and recorded it on another machine, and I called it a dumb master, because you weren't going to overdub with all these splices flying through the heads. It was a mechanical marvel. And the song wasn't in 4/4, it was in 12/8 or something, which was funny. But we got through it.

Session player Gary Brown – who had played on tracks like 'Subway' and 'The Way It Was' – furnished the wailing saxophone solos throughout.

'Living Together' (Barry Gibb, Robin Gibb, Maurice Gibb)
Recorded at Criteria Studios, Miami: between March and November 1978
Certainly one of the quirkiest pieces of music from The Bee Gees' latter-1970s output, 'Living Together' doesn't open with the guitar-and-keys

combo that was typical of their up-tempo tracks of the period – instead, it fades in on a full-tilt symphonic overture that could easily be mistaken for the work of a Romantic-era composer. 20 seconds in, the mini-opus releases into a flurry of strings and ends abruptly with a low clavinet note. Then it's back-to-funk with a wall of vocals and the rhythm section on the first chorus.

The lyric is more playful than poignant, relying mostly on the repeating key phrase: 'Why ain't we living, living together/Instead of being so, so far apart?'. The simplicity is of great benefit to the flow. The chorus then breaks into a middle section where Barry's falsetto and natural voice engage in a call-and-answer exchange on the lines, 'Why ain't we living together?/Living together instead of bein' alone?'. It's the two verses that yield more sophisticated verbiage, delivered in a distinctive, full Robin falsetto – a welcome respite from the sameness of Barry's voice to this point. Once you hear Robin's vocal tone in front, it's easier to pick it out in other tracks on the album.

Spencer Gibb spoke of the track in 2019:

[It] really showcases my dad's crazy falsetto. It's nuts. *Spirits* was one of the first Bee Gees records that didn't feature my dad heavily on lead vocals, and I wish there had been more of that. It's my only real criticism of it. If you take a look at the '60s, in many respects – or even most respects – my dad was the voice of The Bee Gees. In the '70s, Barry became the voice. And by the time they got to *Spirits* – my dad had sung lead on a lot of tracks on *Children Of The World*, and *Saturday Night Fever* wasn't backing away from that specifically – there were other songs he sang on that they didn't get to finish before they submitted stuff for the film. There was a big preoccupation with having hits, there was a big preoccupation with having a cohesive sound, and I think that my dad kind of took a back seat vocally in terms of leads because they wanted that cohesive sound, they wanted the hits.

'I'm Satisfied' (Barry Gibb, Robin Gibb, Maurice Gibb)
Recorded at Criteria Studios, Miami: between March and November 1978
Similar to 'Living Together', the chorus on 'I'm Satisfied' is front-loaded, allowing the verses to carry more of the nuanced vocals and lyric. In between Barry's singing during the intro, there are audible hollow puffs of Herbie Mann's flute.

The closing refrains are a neat collage of Barry vocals, with each line offering a different texture and tone. Interestingly, the original demo had a pronounced shared lead vocal by Barry and Robin.

'I'm Satisfied' was the B-side of the 'Love You Inside Out' single.

'Until' (Barry Gibb, Robin Gibb, Maurice Gibb)
Recorded at Criteria Studios, Miami: between March and November 1978

In 2019, Blue Weaver recalled the creation of 'Until': 'I was programming the Yamaha CS-80 [synthesiser] for another song when I started playing around with that sound. Barry came in and started to sing, and within about 30 minutes, we had put down the synth and most of the vocal ideas. It was a perfect track to end the album with, and such an emotional performance'. A recording exists of the two working out the track in the studio, with Barry venting his frustration when he and Blue fall out of sync for a few moments during one of the verses. Nonetheless, it's purely enjoyable to listen to their creative process and hear evidence of how much Blue contributed to the melodic development of their songs in this period.

The short, spacious ballad is starkly different from the rest of the album having no discernible chorus, and Barry's natural and falsetto voices have a distinctly unusual timbre. The song served as the B-side of the 'Tragedy' single.

Related Song:
Rest Your Love On Me (Barry Gibb)
Recorded at Le Studio, Morin Heights, Québec: 2 May 1976

This was written and recorded during the *Children Of The World* sessions in 1976, but seems most pertinent to mention here due to it being the 'Too Much Heaven' B-side and for its own notable chart achievement in January 1979.

While 'Too Much Heaven' raced up the US singles charts in late 1978 ahead of *Spirits*, 'Rest Your Love On Me' caught the attention of country music station programmers, who began playlisting it. The song soon surfaced on *Billboard*'s Hot Country Songs chart. The week of 13 January 1979 – as 'Too Much Heaven' spent its second week at number one on the Hot 100 – 'Rest Your Love On Me' peaked at number 39.

Singer-songwriter Stephen Stills – who had also appeared as a percussionist on 'You Should Be Dancing' – is confirmed to have played bass on the earliest version of 'Rest Your Love On Me'. There is some debate as to whether or not his bass line was preserved on the completed take, or if it was replaced by George 'Chocolate' Perry or Maurice. Albhy Galuten recalls the song started as a jam, with Barry making up the lyrics and melody on the fly. It was finished later in the *Children Of The World* sessions. The song didn't appear on any issue of *Spirits Having Flown*, instead making its album debut later in the year as part of the *Greatest* compilation.

The track is unusual in that it uses female backing vocalists in place of the brothers, but that is far more prominent on the demo than on the final version.

The song was recorded four more times between 1979 and 1981. Two versions were duets between Andy Gibb and Olivia Newton-John – a live performance from the Music For UNICEF Concert, and a studio take from later in the year, which appeared on Andy's *After Dark* album. Maurice was enlisted to co-produce The Osmonds' 1979 album *Steppin' Out*, which had a version of the song that very closely followed the original.

American country singer Conway Twitty's 1981 cover topped the US country charts. The Gibbs were not involved in that production.

Barry revisited the song on *Greenfields* in 2021, with Olivia Newton-John returning to her role as guest vocalist. That rendition is interesting in that it starts out sounding a lot like The Bee Gees' version but begins to sound like Andy and Olivia's reading about halfway through. Sadly it would be one of Olivia's final recordings before her untimely death in August 2022.

On 13 February, The Bee Gees appeared on the BBC 2 music show *The Old Grey Whistle Test*, hosted by 'Whispering' Bob Harris, who interviewed the brothers at Criteria Studios. They discussed writing and producing for other artists, and, briefly, their 'enjoyable' involvement with the *Sgt. Pepper* film.

Two days later, The Bee Gees were the big winners at the 21st annual Grammy Awards, collecting four trophies for their work associated with *Saturday Night Fever* from a total of six nominations – Album of the Year, Best Arrangement for Voices ('Stayin' Alive'), Best Pop Vocal Performance by a Duo or Group, and Producer of the Year which they shared with Albhy Galuten and Karl Richardson. 'Stayin' Alive' missed out on Record of the Year and Song of the Year honours – both were awarded to Billy Joel for 'Just The Way You Are', the lead single from his landmark 1977 album, *The Stranger*.

In the UK, the 'Tragedy' single had debuted at number seven the week of 11 February and vaulted to the summit two weeks later. It appeared twice on *Top Of The Pops* that month, first in the 15 February chart rundown and then on 22 February, accompanying a performance by dance troupe Legs & Co, who staged another routine to 'Tragedy' on the 9 March episode.

Maurice had begun work as co-producer of The Osmonds' *Steppin' Out* album in late 1978. It was released in March 1979 on PolyGram's Mercury Records subsidiary. Senior Criteria Studios engineer Steve Klein served as Maurice's counterpart, although he likely did most of the work in the booth. Details of the sessions are scant, though, by all accounts Maurice's drinking limited whatever expertise and handiwork The Osmonds might have hoped he would contribute to the project. Maurice doesn't play or sing on any part of the album. Among the tracks (chiefly written by sundry Osmond brothers) was Barry's 'Rest Your Love On Me' – a song the Gibbs (or at least Barry) must have strongly believed had more potential mileage given how many times it surfaced that year. Several familiar Gibb-related players also appeared on the project: Blue Weaver, George Bitzer, George Terry, Joey Murcia, George 'Chocolate' Perry, Joe Lala, and the Boneroo Horns – though it's not known specifically where or when they appear on any of the songs.

Neither the album nor any of its singles were hits. Osmond siblings Donny and Marie seemed to have more of the public's attention at the time – their weekly US variety show was still on the air at that point. Marie was also romantically linked to Andy for a short period.

The 24 March issue of *Billboard* (the same one in which 'Tragedy' hit number one on its Hot 100 chart) featured an article identifying a major piracy issue involving the *Spirits Having Flown* album in Taiwan. Michael Kwang – head of RSO/Polydor licensor Kolin Records – identified at least five pirate entities responsible for nearly 150,000 unauthorised pressings. A similar problem had occurred with the *Saturday Night Fever* soundtrack, of which nearly 1,000,000 pirated units had been sold, versus 8,000 authorised copies.

In April, Polydor issued the Music For UNICEF concert album, *A Gift Of Song*.

A Gift Of Song: Music for UNICEF (1979)
Release date: US and UK: April 1979
A Gift Of Song packaged the ten primary stage performances from the 9 January concert event, adding to the royalties the charity would

accumulate from the project. The songs were in a different sequence to the broadcast, and the two ensemble songs were omitted. The Bee Gees' 'Too Much Heaven' was essentially redundant, as it had been lip-synched to the record. Andy turned in a notably energetic performance of 'I Go For You' – a rocking track from *Shadow Dancing* that he must have chosen to show his range and perhaps to give one of his own songs wider exposure. It was never released as a single, but it was used the B-side of his last major US hit, 'Time Is Time', over a year later. It also seems his tender acoustic take on 'Rest Your Love On Me' with Olivia Newton-John inspired her eventual appearance on his next studio album *After Dark* to sing it, but it's possible Barry already had them in mind to cover the song.

The album liner notes state transparently that some of the recordings had been 'studio enhanced', but it's unclear if that referred to the lip-synched tracks, or just that touch-ups had been made to others in post-production.

A Gift Of Song was not a major hit, reaching only 171 on the *Billboard* Top LPs & Tape chart the week of 1 September – most likely because most of the songs were recent releases from other well-known albums. The album cover featured cartoonish caricatures of the musicians illustrated by Bill Utterback, an American artist best known for his mid-century work for *Playboy* magazine.

In April, the third *Spirits Having Flown* single 'Love You Inside Out' was issued, debuting at 37 on the *Billboard* Hot 100 the week of 20 April (while 'Tragedy' was still in the top ten). It entered the UK chart at 28 the following week.

While it seemed like The Bee Gees' winning streak was impenetrable, a sweeping shift in the pop music landscape – particularly in North America – was soon to change everything. In their post-*Saturday Night Fever* careers, the brothers defiantly and repeatedly rejected being labelled as a disco group, insisting they'd been doing nothing more than constructing music inspired by the R&B and soul veterans that had influenced them for years. Even as a musical construct, the true origin of disco is a bit fuzzy, but its emergence as an underground form of expression and escape among oppressed communities – especially ones in which Black, brown and gay identities intersected – is widely acknowledged. In its earliest iterations as a movement, it also gave voice to diverse artists who wouldn't have been accepted in the mainstream reaches of the music industry.

But by 1979, disco was no longer in the recesses of society – it had evolved into a powerful, pervasive global commodity driven by corporations rather than by musicians. 'It all goes back to one thing and the same thing that's happening now: greed', former Studio 54 DJ Nicky Siano asserts in the 2020 *Broken Heart* documentary. 'Greed is the thing that happens in people, that really ruins a lot of shit. In the beginning, you would buy a disco-bannered record, and it would be a great song, no matter which one you picked out. But then some executive in diapers decided, 'Let's put 'disco' on all these records we wanna sell', and it wasn't good music anymore, it was garbage. So that was, I think, the straw that broke the camel's back'.

However, it wasn't just the music industry that was eager to glom on to the trend. Nearly every corner of the consumer market – from fast food restaurants to exercise equipment – was saturated with disco-themed imagery and terminology. The tide first began to turn on American radio, where station staff had grown weary of the format, and the omnipresent Gibbs had become a major source of contention. 'I'm working at a top 40 station in New York – a big one, WXLO, but it was known as 99X', the station's former newscaster Charley Steiner explained in the 2020 *Broken Heart* documentary. 'Most radio stations had a very small playlist, and The Bee Gees probably had the top four, top five hits any given week. And for those of us at the radio station, we're ... we're gonna take hostages! And then Andy Gibb too. He was like the caboose on this musical train. It was like waves in the sea'.

But for the time being, The Bee Gees continued to prosper. On 22 April, they received the *Daily Mirror's* British Rock & Pop Award for Best Group, which Robin accepted on their behalf. Other nominees in the category were Irish rock band The Boomtown Rats and Electric Light Orchestra.

In support of *Spirits Having Flown*, The Bee Gees spent much of the spring mounting a 38-city, 41-date North American tour – their first since 1976, and certainly their most ambitious to date. The plans were big, audacious, and expensive, with state-of-the-art lighting, sound, and stage construction, certainly befitting one of the biggest bands in the world. Added to the list of amenities was a leased Boeing 720 aircraft that privately ushered the Gibbs and their entourage between stops – to the tune of more than a $1,000,000. The livery? A black, red and gold colour scheme with the *Spirits Having Flown* tour logo and title emblazoned on either side. A stylised likeness of the brothers' faces adorned the tail.

Rehearsals began on 28 May in the storage space the group had leased on Bay Road in Miami Beach. With their rigorous schedule, they sent their mother Barbara and niece Berri as their representatives to the Broadcast Music, Inc. (BMI) awards banquet at the Beverly Wilshire Hotel in Los Angeles on 5 June. The ceremony celebrated the top 100 most-played songs of 1978. 'Night Fever' took top honours among 11 other songwriting prizes that were bestowed upon at least one of The Bee Gees (Barry had a hand in writing all 11 winning songs, while Robin had seven, and Maurice, six). Andy Gibb received two nods – for 'Shadow Dancing' and '(Love Is) Thicker Than Water'. Stigwood Music swept the ceremony with 16 awards – the most collected in a single year in the ceremony's history.

Four days later, 'Love You Inside Out' climbed to number one in America, staying for just one week as it interrupted Donna Summer's run at the summit with 'Hot Stuff'. In the UK, 'Love You Inside Out' peaked at 13. It was to be the last Bee Gees song to top the *Billboard* Hot 100 in the US.

On 28 June, the *Spirits Having Flown* Tour kicked off in Fort Worth, Texas, at the 14,000-seat arena inside the Tarrant County (now Fort Worth) Convention Center. The approximately 90-minute setlist contained 'Tragedy', 'Edge Of The Universe', 'Night Fever', 'Love So Right', 'Stayin' Alive', a medley of 'New York Mining Disaster 1941'/'Run To Me'/'Too Much Heaven'/'Holiday'/'I Can't See Nobody', 'Lonely Days', 'I Started A Joke', 'Massachusetts', 'How Can You Mend A Broken Heart', 'Nights On Broadway', 'To Love Somebody', 'Words', 'Wind Of Change', 'How Deep Is Your Love', 'Jive Talkin'', and 'You Should Be Dancing'. The background vocalists were The Sweet Inspirations – the American gospel/soul group founded in the late-1950s by Emily 'Cissy' Houston – mother of singer Whitney Houston and aunt of future Bee Gees beneficiary, Dionne Warwick. By 1979, their line-up consisted of Sylvia Shemwell, Estelle Brown, Myrna Smith, and Gloria Brown. They had been signed to RSO and released one album – *Hot Butterfly* – before disbanding later in 1979 and remaining inactive until 1994.

The public response to the tour was, unsurprisingly, fanatical. It was quickly and fully sold out at every stop, which benefited ticket scalpers; some allegedly snatching up to $700 for seats with $15 face values. The tour grossed over $10,000,000 (nearly $40,000,000 in 2022 terms, adjusted for inflation).

A film crew had been hired to follow the tour, capturing footage to be included in an upcoming prime-time NBC special. Four dates were cancelled – including 2 and 3 August in Kansas City, due to a roof collapse at Kemper (now Hy-Vee) Arena in a powerful storm that had rolled through the area on 4 June.

Regular fans weren't the only ones rushing to arenas and stadiums to see the Gibbs in the flesh. A parade of celebrities surfaced at multiple venues on the tour. John Travolta appeared on stage with the brothers in Houston on 30 June – taking a break from filming his third Stigwood feature *Urban Cowboy* – and surprised the crowd with some of his now infamous *Fever* choreography. At Los Angeles' Dodger Stadium on 7 July, Rod Stewart, Olivia Newton-John, Karen Carpenter, Harry Wayne Casey (frontman of KC and the Sunshine Band), Barbra Streisand, and actors Cary Grant and Jack Nicholson were in the audience. Streisand's visit with The Bee Gees backstage that evening was at least a partial catalyst for an album project which was to begin with the Gibb/Galuten/ Richardson production team in a few months' time. When the tour stopped in Oakland, California, Andy sang with his brothers during the encore of 'You Should Be Dancing'; footage of which has been regularly shown in various Bee Gees documentaries and specials.

But while the *Spirits* tour generated jaw-dropping profits (many stops were making around half a million dollars each), the disco backlash began to bubble over outside the venues. Perhaps no single instance was as vitriolic as the 'Disco Demolition Night' baseball promotion at Comiskey Park in Chicago on 12 July, during which local radio station WLUP-FM offered 98-cent tickets to a Chicago White Sox/Detroit Tigers game in exchange for fans bringing their disco records to the stadium to be destroyed in an on-field explosion. The now-historic event was spearheaded by disgruntled radio DJ Steve Dahl, who had been fired from his job at Chicago's WDAI-FM when it switched formats from rock to disco the previous year. The White Sox organisation engaged Dahl, who had amassed a significant following as he regularly panned artists (including The Bee Gees) and records associated with disco on air, as it seemed like a good way to sell tickets. In the end, they were right – more than 50,000 attendees packed the stands that night – exponentially more than had been showing up to regular games at the time. Once Dahl had orchestrated his planned spectacle, thousands rushed the field. The Chicago police, wearing riot gear, chased them off about an hour later. Severe playing-field damage and excess debris (including an incalculable number of records tossed from the stands) prevented the night's second game from proceeding. It was eventually forfeited, as the Sox's facility wasn't in a playable state according to the league regulations.

While many (including Dahl) have defended Disco Demolition Night as strictly serving as a protest of disco's pervasive silencing of rock music, others (including many academics) insist it was an audacious condemnation of cultural groups by a majority white, straight, cisgender male population that had begun to feel threatened by the elevation of under-represented people. 'I was an usher at Comiskey Park – that was my first job', producer Vince Lawrence remembers in the 2020 *Broken Heart* documentary. 'We were letting people in, and I pointed out to my chief usher, 'That record ... that record ... that record ... that record ... that record ... that record – those aren't disco records. Those are just ... those are R&B records. And the thing that I noticed more than anything was it was mostly Black records. When I got older, I recognised that this was actually the end of an era. It was a book-burning. It was a racist, homophobic book burning. And The Bee Gees got caught up in that. They were part of that culture that was lifting people up'.

While The Bee Gees were somewhat isolated from the chaos for a time, it began to seep into their lives as they continued to tour. Maurice recalled in 2001: 'We had FBI and Secret Service around the airplane every time we landed in a certain place, because of the bomb threats. It was scary stuff'. Robin: 'The backlash was a very frightening experience. When things get to that point, you're out of control of the whole thing'.

From 5 to 28 August, there was a break in the tour. The brothers publicly began to signal they were thinking about what would happen once the tour was finished – and it seemed to involve potentially putting the group to rest. Even if they hadn't begun to fall out of favour amidst the backlash, the breakneck pace of the past few years was clearly taking a toll on them. Robin told *People* magazine: 'We don't want to be an old group again. No lasting images, like Nixon standing on the White House lawn with the chopper behind him, waving goodbye. We came into this world to work together, but we can't be Bee Gees forever. We want to go out on top'.

The ongoing stress of everything – coupled with his back issues – allegedly made Maurice increasingly dependent on alcohol as the tour progressed, to the point where he would often be too intoxicated to play. Several fail-safes were reportedly in place during each of the shows, including muting his guitar and vocal mic, and having off-stage players performing his parts. The adoring public, by design, remained blissfully unaware that there was a problem.

Once the *Spirits* tour picked back up again, the group played five straight shows at New York City's Madison Square Garden between 7 and 12 September. They were awarded MSG's Gold Ticket award, which had been initiated two years earlier for performers who attracted more than 100,000 ticket buyers to the venue, which the Gibbs accomplished in the first three shows there. Musicians Billy Joel, Diana Ross, Kiss' Gene Simmons and Paul Stanley, and actor Al Pacino were reportedly among the attendees.

Before their 24 September show in Landover, Maryland, then-US President Jimmy Carter invited the group to the White House in recognition of their charitable efforts for UNICEF.

The tour's final stop – on 6 October – landed the Gibbs back in their adopted hometown, where they played Miami Stadium. It would be their last tour date for an entire decade, and they would not perform at another Miami venue until 1992.

While The Bee Gees didn't definitively come to a halt as they'd been suggesting in the press, the brothers quickly got to work on outside projects in the last quarter of the year. Barry returned to the studio with Albhy and Karl to produce Andy's third album, *After Dark*. What should have been a victorious follow-up to the massively successful *Shadow Dancing* turned into a rather sombre affair, instead revealing the reality of Andy's downward slide into drug addiction and paralysing anxiety. Albhy recalled the sessions several years later: 'By the time we got to that last Andy album, he [was] in such bad shape that we were just doing something to put on it. It wasn't an Andy album anymore; it was a big contractual obligation'. Some preliminary recording had apparently been done in May, but much of *After Dark* was recorded in October and November. The production team did their best to patch up Andy's faltering voice, often by pairing it with a Barry vocal, or in some cases, substituting it completely. Barry reportedly could muster a rather accurate impersonation of his little brother, so even in spots where it might seem obvious that Andy was singing, he wasn't. Allegedly there were many other occasions when Andy didn't show up in the studio at all, leaving his producers to essentially push forward with what was more realistically a Barry Gibb album than anything else.

Andy wrote two songs on his own for *After Dark* – 'Back To The Wind' and 'Warm'. Neither ended up on the album, but the recordings do exist. His only writing credits were two Barry co-pens – the ballads 'Someone I Ain't' and 'One Love'. They're fair songs, but a far cry from the solid writing contributions Andy had made to *Shadow Dancing* and *Flowing Rivers*. The rest of the record was buoyed by four very good Barry-written songs: 'After Dark', 'Wherever You Are', 'Dreamin' On', and 'I Can't Help It', one of two duets with Olivia Newton-John. Andy and Olivia also reimagined Barry's 'Rest Your Love On Me', which they'd performed at the Music For UNICEF concert. Barry and Albhy supplied the ballad 'Falling In Love With You', which they'd written about two years earlier, and the two Bee Gees songs 'Warm Ride' and 'Desire' were recycled, completing the tracklist.

Despite all the glue and tape holding *After Dark* together, it's a cohesive and well-produced album. Andy's personal and professional struggles were to remain under wraps, at least for now, and his new record arrived early in 1980 with his still-enthusiastic fan base unenlightened about what was happening behind the scenes.

As Barry, Albhy, and Karl worked to save Andy's career from disaster, they were also spending a significant amount of time on a project they hoped would be an unqualified smash. After Barbra Streisand had met The Bee Gees during the *Spirits* tour that summer, her manager Charles Koppelman approached Barry to write songs for one side of her next album, which would eventually become the landmark *Guilty*. Barry told *Billboard*'s Paul Grein in 1980: 'It started off with them suggesting a few songs, which we listened to. We then submitted five of our own songs, and Barbra liked them and asked us to write five more'. Barry and Robin co-wrote five songs for the album: 'Woman In Love', 'Run Wild', 'Promises', 'Life Story', and 'Secrets', the last of which wasn't used. The three Bee Gees wrote 'Guilty' – a mid-tempo romp that transformed nicely into a Barry and Barbra duet. Barry and Albhy composed four additional songs: 'What Kind of Fool' (another future duet), 'Never Give Up', 'Make It Like A Memory', and the eventually-shelved ballad 'Carried Away'. One more song that did make the final cut was 'The Love Inside' – a gorgeous, emotive ballad that all four brothers wrote in 1978 (though by the time the album was released, it was credited to Barry only). It's possible it had been intended for Andy (Barry's initial demo was sung in a style that seemed to purposely emulate Andy's caramel-smooth voice), though Streisand's mesmerising take proves the production team found its rightful interpreter.

Demos were recorded in October at Criteria Studios – many of which Barry sang in falsetto to match Streisand's register. Albhy recalled to *Albumism* in 2020: 'We went into Studio A and we just put [them down]. I think we had maybe the LinnDrum machine, and I played piano and Barry played acoustic on some of the songs. On some he didn't play, because I think [they] were musically different than what he'd usually play on the guitar'.

Work on *Guilty* was then paused until early 1980, when the production team moved their base to California. Karl remembers:

We cut the first versions of the tracks at Criteria Studios, to take them to Los Angeles so we could capture Barbra singing there, because I believe she was filming a movie at the time. Recording was sort of like a hobby for her at that moment, and we could only get her for so many hours of so many days, originally. So, the decision was to cut the music in Miami, then produce her vocals, then come back to do the mix.

As if Barry didn't already have enough on his plate, he announced that he and former RSO President and long-time family friend David English would be making a film titled *Whirlpool*, which would focus on drug smugglers in Miami. It's unknown how much work was done on the project, but it certainly was never finished.

Meanwhile, Robin and Blue Weaver paired off to write and produce an album for American R&B/soul singer Jimmy Ruffin at Kingdom Sound on Long Island, New York, where Robin had recently purchased a home. Ruffin was best known for his 1966 US and UK Tamla/Motown top ten hit 'What Becomes Of The Broken Hearted'. He'd released albums for Polydor in the early 1970s and signed to RSO to record what eventually became his seventh studio effort, *Sunrise*. Four of the album's songs were written by Robin and Blue and were completed by year's end: 'Hold On (To My Love)', 'Night Of Love', 'Searchin'', and 'Two People'. The rest were finished the following January at Criteria Studios. Alan Kendall and Dennis Bryon played on the set, as did the regular Gibb session players George 'Chocolate' Perry, Joe Lala, George Terry, and the Boneroo Horns.

While the brothers were otherwise occupied, RSO released the two-disc retrospective *Bee Gees Greatest*, which paid appropriate homage to their staggering latter 70s run of hits, plus other notable compositions.

Bee Gees Greatest

Release date: UK and US: October 1979
Chart positions: Australia: 1, US: 1, New Zealand: 2, Canada: 4, UK: 6, West Germany: 43
2007 Reissue
Chart positions: Austria: 4, Ireland: 4, France: 5, Spain: 5, Sweden: 24, Denmark: 25, Netherlands: 35, Switzerland: 60, Belgium: 65, Italy: 92
Side 1: 1. 'Jive Talkin'', 2. 'Night Fever', 3. 'Tragedy', 4. 'You Should Be Dancing', 5. 'Stayin' Alive'
Side 2: 1. 'How Deep Is Your Love', 2. 'Love So Right', 3. 'Too Much Heaven', 4. '(Our Love) Don't Throw It All Away', 4. 'Fanny (Be Tender with My Love)'
Side 3: 1. 'If I Can't Have You', 2. 'You Stepped Into My Life', 3. 'Love Me', 4. 'More Than A Woman', 5. 'Rest Your Love on Me'
Side 4: 1. 'Nights On Broadway', 2. 'Spirits (Having Flown)', 3. 'Love You Inside Out', 4. 'Wind Of Change', 5. 'Children Of The World'

Released in October, *Greatest* was perfectly timed for the Christmas market, capitalising on the group's astronomical success between 1975 and 1979 – and undoubtedly the enthusiasm of the hundreds of thousands of North American fans who had sold out the freshly wrapped *Spirits Having Flown* tour. For some time, it seemed there was a real possibility *Greatest* might be The Bee Gees' final release, given how adamantly they insisted on needing a break from being a group. Nonetheless, it served as a firm bookend to a wildly prosperous and creative period they seemed quite ready to leave in the past.

Knowing the climate in North America would be inhospitable to a new Bee Gees single, RSO released 'Spirits (Having Flown)' to promote *Greatest* elsewhere in the world.

The first issue of *Greatest* was a double LP and spread the songs over the four sides with some vague theme about their placement, though this was not explained anywhere. The album would have benefitted from liner notes or a little annotation justifying the inclusion of the songs. It appears, however, that side one of the first disc is dedicated to the faster songs, and side two is focused on ballads. Side three (on disc two) appears to be songs that became hits for others. Side four gathered up four reasonably successful singles with the *Main Course* track 'Wind Of Change' thrown in for good measure – though, in keeping with the hit-singles theme, 'Boogie Child' or the live version of 'Edge Of The Universe' would have been more appropriate choices.

In the UK, RSO issued a promotional collection titled *Short Cuts* ahead of the album. Packaged in a plain white sleeve with a four-inch-square sticker in the top left-hand corner bearing the title and a scaled-down version of the yet-to-be-revealed *Greatest* album art, it featured a 'Fast Side' – with 'Jive Talkin', 'Stayin' Alive', Night Fever', 'Tragedy', and 'Wind Of Change' – and a 'Slow Side' that featured 'How Deep Is Your Love', 'Fanny (Be Tender with My Love)', 'Spirits (Having Flown)', 'Love So Right', and 'Too Much Heaven'. All tracks were significantly truncated and segued, but this is far from being a megamix as was becoming popular at the time.

A remastered and expanded edition of *Greatest* was released on a double-CD package by Reprise Records in 2007. It contained the welcome addition of a rare, lengthy mix of 'Stayin' Alive' with added horn interludes (previously only available on a 12" promo version), and the previously unreleased *Fever* sessions product 'Warm Ride'. The remixes on the second CD seem wasteful as they don't improve on or innovate the original tracks.

The album artwork was a beautiful visual masterpiece created by Tom Nikosey, incorporating the classic gothic Bee Gees logo expanded into an embossed roundel format with the addition of a golden bird and intertwined ribbon spelling out the legend 'Greatest'. The sleeve was a lavish triple gatefold featuring Ed Caraeff's stunning portraits of the brothers on the interior panels. Each brother was assigned a picture label on the records too – Side one: Barry; Side two: Maurice; Side three: Robin; and Side four: all three Bee Gees. The US issued the album with special anti-static inner sleeves adorned with The Bee Gees logo in red, with RSO's famous red cow logo at the bottom.

As The Bee Gees were now highly commoditised, the label included a now-obligatory merchandise flyer inside the sleeve. One side promoted a new book *The Legend – The Illustrated Story of The Bee Gees* – written by friend and RSO executive David English with illustrations by Alex Brychta – featuring the Gibbs and many of their friends and family members as zoomorphic cartoon characters. The flipside seemed like a good place to shift the surplus 1979 tour merchandise and to give the short-lived *Official Bee Gees Fan Club* a plug.

The *Greatest* packaging was the first RSO release to be treated with a new special chemical process, which reportedly allowed the label to detect counterfeit copies – a costly problem that had been associated with their most popular records over the previous year. According to a 1980 *Billboard* article, the FBI and the RIAA estimated pirated records had cost RSO between $30 and $50 million in lost profits. The innovative fix appeared to work as subsequent RSO releases seemed to not have been affected by counterfeiters to any great extent.

'(Our Love) Don't Throw it All Away' (Barry Gibb, Blue Weaver)
Recorded at Château d'Hérouville, France: February/March 1977, and Criteria Studios, Miami: circa April 1977

This was the most interesting track on the album's original issue – up to that point, it had only been known to the public as an Andy Gibb song. Blue came up with the melody, while Barry furnished the lyric. Blue Weaver: 'That was me playing around again. It wasn't done for *Saturday Night Fever*, it was just something that we did'.

This version is in a higher key than the take Andy recorded for *Shadow Dancing*. As mentioned previously, this original version is missing the middle eight Barry wrote specifically for that project. While The Bee Gees' version was never an official single, at least two 7" promo discs of the song were minted. In Canada, the B-side was 'If I Can't Have You', printed with the catalogue number 'DJ 24'. The typical RSO label is emblazoned with a line drawing of the Greatest cover image. An Australian issue with the catalogue number 'POL 56' was paired with 'Spirits (Having Flown)'.

The Bee Gees introduced the song into their concert setlist for the *One Night Only* tour starting in 1997, where they performed it live with Andy's vocal piped in on the second verse while film footage of him was projected on a large screen in the background.

Singer and actress Jennifer Love Hewitt (a cast member of the US children's music show *Kids Incorporated* in the late 1980s and early 1990s) recorded a version for her self-titled 1996 album. Her take omits the bridge, replacing it with a repeat of part of the first verse.

Barbra Streisand covered '(Our Love) Don't Throw It All Away' on her 2005 *Guilty Too* album (*Guilty Pleasures* in North America), which Barry produced and appeared on. Though not a duet with Barry, he reprised the call-and-answer background vocals as he did with Andy on *Shadow Dancing*.

2007 Reissue
'Warm Ride' (Barry Gibb, Robin Gibb, Maurice Gibb)
Recorded at Château d'Hérouville, France, February/March 1977; Criteria Studios, Miami, circa April 1977

'Warm Ride' was originally written and recorded during the *Saturday Night Fever* sessions. But it was never completed and remained as a demo which was offered to other artists – including The Who's Roger Daltrey, who declined to record it. Barry's lead vocal and choruses on the demo were all sung in falsetto.

The first to record the song was old friend and ex-Marbles member Graham Bonnet, who released it as a single in March 1978 and achieved a number one hit with it in Australia. Next was the single by American soul band Rare Earth, which peaked at 39 on the *Billboard* Hot 100 that year. It followed Bonnet's version into the Australian charts but stalled at 68.

Finally, Andy included 'Warm Ride' on his 1980 album *After Dark*. His version was slower and in his natural, breathy voice, with Barry's characteristic rhythm guitar chugging in the background.

While it was good to see The Bee Gees' version finally surface, it seemed rather out of place on a greatest hits package. It utilised the same drum loop they had manufactured for 'Stayin' Alive' that had been extracted from Dennis Bryon's drumming on 'Night Fever' – a song to which 'Warm Ride' was markedly similar. It's likely the reason it hadn't been developed further for *Fever*.

'Stayin' Alive' (Promo 12") (Barry Gibb, Robin Gibb, Maurice Gibb)

A very worthy inclusion, this stretched-out version of 'Stayin' Alive" was otherwise only available on a highly sought-after Special Disco Version 12" promo single issued just in the US in 1978. This extended mix included horn parts normally obscured by other instrumentation on the familiar version.

Remixes

Perhaps the hope of these remixes was to generate some radio and club play upon the release of the 2007 reissue, but the various remixes of already classic tracks like these seemed like unnecessary filler. Apart from the previously unheard vocal count-in by Barry at the start of the Teddybears Remix of 'Stayin' Alive', these revamps don't add much new or valuable to the album.

'You Should Be Dancing' (Jason Bentley/Philip Steir remix)
'If I Can't Have You' (Count Da Money remix)
'Night Fever' (GRN remix)

'How Deep Is Your Love' (Supreme Beings of Leisure remix)
'Stayin' Alive' (Teddybears remix)
'If I Can't Have You' (The Disco Boys remix)

On 21 November, NBC broadcast *The Bee Gees Special* – the 90-minute production for which parts of the *Spirits Having Flown* tour had been specially filmed. It was produced by Ken Ehrlich – a US producer and director who had created the PBS *Soundstage* series on which The Bee Gees appeared in 1975. Concert performances of 'Stayin' Alive', 'New York Mining Disaster 1941', 'How Can You Mend A Broken Heart', 'Wind Of Change', 'I Started A Joke', 'Nights On Broadway', 'Words', 'Jive Talkin'', 'You Should Be Dancing' (with Andy on 10 July in Oakland). and 'I've Gotta Get A Message To You' comprised the bulk of the programme, interspersed with interview segments, vintage video clips, and behind-the-scenes footage shot during the tour and at Criteria Studios.

Perhaps the most interesting of the special's diversions was a jam with American country singers Willie Nelson and Glen Campbell, who joined The Bee Gees backstage to sing impromptu versions of The Everly Brothers' 'Bye Bye Love' and 'All I Have To Do Is Dream', Buddy Knox's 'Party Doll', Don Gibson's 'I Can't Stop Loving You' (made popular by Ray Charles), and the Gibbs' own 'To Love Somebody'.

Despite the large quantity of vibrant, high-quality footage that exists from the *Spirits* tour, neither the special nor the unedited concert performances have ever been made available for sale or streaming to the public; something fans have hoped would happen over the years. A portion of the concert film was used for the opening credits of the 2020 *The Bee Gees: How Can You Mend A Broken Heart* documentary, and displayed beautifully in high definition.

Near the end of 1979, it was reported that Barry (which he has publicly denied on a few occasions) had been offered the leading role of Che Guevara in a planned film adaptation of Tim Rice and Andrew Lloyd Webber's *Evita* based on the life of actress/politician/activist and First Lady of Argentina Eva Perón. This began life as a standalone album of songs, released in 1976, and evolved into a successful West End musical two years later with Robert Stigwood attached as a producer. The film was slated to start production in 1980, but a series of directorial and casting issues delayed the process for nearly 15 years. It was finally in theatres in 1996, with singer Madonna cast as Perón and Spanish actor Antonio Banderas as Guevara.

Maurice was also allegedly writing music for another upcoming RSO film, *The Fan*. The psychological thriller was released in a timelier fashion than *Evita*, landing in theatres in May 1981, but Maurice was nowhere to be found in the credits. Instead, Italian composer Pino Donaggio supplied the score.

The final Bee Gees release of the 1970s was the 'Spirits (Having Flown)' single on 28 December in the UK. It eventually peaked at number 16 early in 1980.

The group began and ended the decade with an exceptional level of uncertainty about their future, albeit under disparate circumstances. They entered 1970 personally and professionally fractured, gradually sifting through the rubble of their breakup to find common ground and resuscitate their love for making music together. By the end of 1979, the brothers had realised a magnitude of commercial and artistic success that surely exceeded even their wildest fantasies. But the public and media recoil from their association with *Saturday Night Fever* forced them to rethink how they approached their craft. While their output as the de facto Bee Gees waxed and waned over the better part of the 1980s under the weight of the blowback, they remained a powerful force in the industry as eminent songwriters and producers. Despite the best efforts of their detractors, they were to survive – and thrive.

Epilogue

Barry, Robin, and Maurice have often remarked they were songwriters first – a mantra that became somewhat of an occupational necessity as they temporarily adjourned themselves from The Bee Gees at the close of 1979. The disco backlash wasn't just swift, it was severe – dragging out into a nearly decade-long grudge the American media especially seemed unwilling to recant. What was perhaps most baffling about the brothers' ouster was that they continued to champion a string of major hit singles and albums for other artists as writers and producers in the first half of the 1980s – most of which had all the unmistakable sonic earmarks that radio and retail allegedly despised about them.

Still, The Bee Gees had enough status and capital to push ahead. While being ostracised certainly hurt them, the most tragic victims of the deluge were the diverse artists who had been amplified by the disco movement who no longer had the resources or support to continue. Many careers were extinguished in the aftermath.

As the new decade drew breath, the Gibbs demonstrated how quickly and adeptly they could navigate and – in some cases – conquer uncharted territory. Andy Gibb's *After Dark* was released in February. Its lead single 'Desire' reached number four in the US and number ten in Canada, while the Andy and Olivia Newton-John duet, 'I Can't Help It', peaked at 12 on the *Billboard* Hot 100 later in the year. In May, RSO issued Jimmy Ruffin's *Sunrise*, with its first single 'Hold On To My Love' breaking into the US and UK top ten.

However, it was Barbra Streisand's *Guilty* that affirmed the Gibbs had pursued a righteous artistic path out of their 1970s heyday. Released in September 1980 after Barry, Albhy, and Karl invested months of studio time to precisely calibrate the recordings to their liking, it was a global smash, becoming – and remaining – the most successful studio set of Streisand's career. In the US, it had a three-week reign at number one, and was nominated in five categories at the 24th Annual Grammy Awards in 1981. Barry and Barbra took home the trophies for Best Pop Performance by a Duo or Group with Vocal for 'Guilty', which peaked at three in the US. The album's first single 'Woman In Love' is Streisand's most successful single ever, and reached the pole position in over 20 countries, including the US, the UK, Germany, Canada, and Australia.

The Bee Gees' story across the rest of the 1980s is less of an arc as it is a complicated mosaic of exceptional wins and heartbreaking losses. Through it all, the Gibbs continued to write, record, and produce compelling music that added to their already distinctive catalogue – remaining steadfastly determined to regain the popular and critical ground they lost from the worst of the disco blowback. In between the illustrious collaborations, hit records, and accolades came unprecedented tests of their professional fortitude and of their family bond and personal relationships – worthy of detailed discussion in the next volume of this series.

Bibliography

Books

Arnold, P.P., *Soul Survivor: The Autobiography* (Nine Eight Books, 2022)

Bilyeu, M., Cook, H., Hughes, A.M., Brennan, J., Crohan, M., *The Ultimate Biography Of The Bee Gees Tales of the Brothers Gibb:* (Omnibus Press, 2000, 2001, 2003 and 2012)

Brahms, C., Sherrin, N., *Too Dirty For The Windmill: A Memoir of Caryl Brahms* (Constable, 1986)

Bryon, D., *My Life With The Bee Gees* (ECW Press, 2015)

Holland, R., *As I Heard It: In The UK Music Industry 1969 To 1979. Part 1: In the Recording Studio* (Ebook, 2019)

Leaf, D., *Bee Gees: The Authorized Biography* (Octopus Books, 1979)

Sandoval, A., *Bee Gees: The Day-By-Day Story, 1945-1972* (Retrofuture, 2012)

Wright, S., *Graham Bonnet: The Story Behind The Shades* (Easy On The Eye, 2017)

Newspapers and Magazines

UK
Fab 208
Melody Maker
New Musical Express
Record Mirror

US
Billboard
Cashbox
Goldmine
Guitar Player
Record World
Rolling Stone

Websites
Joseph Brennan's *Gibb Songs*
Albumism.com
BeeGeesDays.com
45cat.com

BMI.com
Discogs.com
Newspapers.com
OfficialCharts.com
TVPopDiaries.co.uk

Sleeve Notes

Arnold, P. P., *The Turning Tide* (Kundalini Music, 2017)
Stanley, B., Sandoval, A., *Saved By The Bell: The Collected Works Of Robin Gibb 1968 – 1970* (Reprise, 2015)
Tales From The Brothers Gibb – A History In Song 1967-1990 box set liner notes (Polydor, 1990)

The Bee Gees in the 1960s
Decades

The Bee Gees in the 1960s
Decades
Andrew Môn Hughes, Grant
Walters & Mark Crohan
Foreword by Spencer Gibb &
Vince Melouney
Paperback
256 pages
57 colour photographs
978-1-78952-148-1
£16.99 / $24.95

**The formative
decade in the
history of this
hugely successful
group.**

the
Wishing Shelf
book awards
FINALIST

The Bee Gees
in the 1960s

Andrew Môn Hughes, Grant Walters & Mark Crohan
Foreword by Spencer Gibb & Vince Melouney

In April 1967, the Bee Gees launched themselves onto the international music scene with the release of 'New York Mining Disaster 1941'. Whilst that haunting classic would be the first of many hits, the Bee Gees – consisting of brothers Barry, Robin and Maurice Gibb – had been releasing records since 1963. As extraordinary as it sounds, with more than ten years of performing and four years of recording behind them, the Gibb twins, Robin and Maurice, were just 17, while elder brother Barry was only 20.

In an incredible career, the Bee Gees would go on to sell over 200 million records, making them among the best-selling music artists of all time. They would be inducted into the Rock and Roll Hall of Fame, the Australian Recording Industry's Hall of Fame, and the Songwriters Hall of Fame and receive lifetime achievement awards from the British Phonographic Industry, the American Music Awards, World Music Awards and the Grammys. According to Billboard magazine, the Bee Gees are one of the top three most successful bands in their charts' history.

Few musical groups have provided the soundtrack to our lives like the Bee Gees, and it all started in the fascinating decade that was the 1960s.

On Track series

Alan Parsons Project – Steve Swift 978-1-78952-154-2
Tori Amos – Lisa Torem 978-1-78952-142-9
Asia – Peter Braidis 978-1-78952-099-6
Badfinger – Robert Day-Webb 978-1-878952-176-4
Barclay James Harvest – Keith and Monica Domone 978-1-78952-067-5
The Beatles – Andrew Wild 978-1-78952-009-5
The Beatles Solo 1969-1980 – Andrew Wild 978-1-78952-030-9
Blue Oyster Cult – Jacob Holm-Lupo 978-1-78952-007-1
Blur – Matt Bishop – 978-178952-164-1
Marc Bolan and T.Rex – Peter Gallagher 978-1-78952-124-5
Kate Bush – Bill Thomas 978-1-78952-097-2
Camel – Hamish Kuzminski 978-1-78952-040-8
Caravan – Andy Boot 978-1-78952-127-6
Cardiacs – Eric Benac 978-1-78952-131-3
Eric Clapton Solo – Andrew Wild 978-1-78952-141-2
The Clash – Nick Assirati 978-1-78952-077-4
Crosby, Stills and Nash – Andrew Wild 978-1-78952-039-2
The Damned – Morgan Brown 978-1-78952-136-8
Deep Purple and Rainbow 1968-79 – Steve Pilkington 978-1-78952-002-6
Dire Straits – Andrew Wild 978-1-78952-044-6
The Doors – Tony Thompson 978-1-78952-137-5
Dream Theater – Jordan Blum 978-1-78952-050-7
Electric Light Orchestra – Barry Delve 978-1-78952-152-8
Elvis Costello and The Attractions – Georg Purvis 978-1-78952-129-0
Emerson Lake and Palmer – Mike Goode 978-1-78952-000-2
Fairport Convention – Kevan Furbank 978-1-78952-051-4
Peter Gabriel – Graeme Scarfe 978-1-78952-138-2
Genesis – Stuart MacFarlane 978-1-78952-005-7
Gentle Giant – Gary Steel 978-1-78952-058-3
Gong – Kevan Furbank 978-1-78952-082-8
Hall and Oates – Ian Abrahams 978-1-78952-167-2
Hawkwind – Duncan Harris 978-1-78952-052-1
Peter Hammill – Richard Rees Jones 978-1-78952-163-4
Roy Harper – Opher Goodwin 978-1-78952-130-6
Jimi Hendrix – Emma Stott 978-1-78952-175-7
The Hollies – Andrew Darlington 978-1-78952-159-7
Iron Maiden – Steve Pilkington 978-1-78952-061-3
Jefferson Airplane – Richard Butterworth 978-1-78952-143-6

Jethro Tull – Jordan Blum 978-1-78952-016-3

Elton John in the 1970s – Peter Kearns 978-1-78952-034-7

The Incredible String Band – Tim Moon 978-1-78952-107-8

Iron Maiden – Steve Pilkington 978-1-78952-061-3

Judas Priest – John Tucker 978-1-78952-018-7

Kansas – Kevin Cummings 978-1-78952-057-6

The Kinks – Martin Hutchinson 978-1-78952-172-6

Korn – Matt Karpe 978-1-78952-153-5

Led Zeppelin – Steve Pilkington 978-1-78952-151-1

Level 42 – Matt Philips 978-1-78952-102-3

Little Feat – 978-1-78952-168-9

Aimee Mann – Jez Rowden 978-1-78952-036-1

Joni Mitchell – Peter Kearns 978-1-78952-081-1

The Moody Blues – Geoffrey Feakes 978-1-78952-042-2

Motorhead – Duncan Harris 978-1-78952-173-3

Mike Oldfield – Ryan Yard 978-1-78952-060-6

Opeth – Jordan Blum 978-1-78-952-166-5

Tom Petty – Richard James 978-1-78952-128-3

Porcupine Tree – Nick Holmes 978-1-78952-144-3

Queen – Andrew Wild 978-1-78952-003-3

Radiohead – William Allen 978-1-78952-149-8

Renaissance – David Detmer 978-1-78952-062-0

The Rolling Stones 1963-80 – Steve Pilkington 978-1-78952-017-0

The Smiths and Morrissey – Tommy Gunnarsson 978-1-78952-140-5

Status Quo the Frantic Four Years – Richard James 978-1-78952-160-3

Steely Dan – Jez Rowden 978-1-78952-043-9

Steve Hackett – Geoffrey Feakes 978-1-78952-098-9

Thin Lizzy – Graeme Stroud 978-1-78952-064-4

Toto – Jacob Holm-Lupo 978-1-78952-019-4

U2 – Eoghan Lyng 978-1-78952-078-1

UFO – Richard James 978-1-78952-073-6

The Who – Geoffrey Feakes 978-1-78952-076-7

Roy Wood and the Move – James R Turner 978-1-78952-008-8

Van Der Graaf Generator – Dan Coffey 978-1-78952-031-6

Yes – Stephen Lambe 978-1-78952-001-9

Frank Zappa 1966 to 1979 – Eric Benac 978-1-78952-033-0

Warren Zevon – Peter Gallagher 978-1-78952-170-2

10CC – Peter Kearns 978-1-78952-054-5

Decades Series

The Bee Gees in the 1960s – Andrew Môn Hughes et al
978-1-78952-148-1
The Bee Gees in the 1970s – Andrew Môn Hughes et al
978-1-78952-179-5
Black Sabbath in the 1970s – Chris Sutton 978-1-78952-171-9
Britpop – Peter Richard Adams and Matt Pooler 978-1-78952-169-6
Alice Cooper in the 1970s – Chris Sutton 978-1-78952-104-7
Curved Air in the 1970s – Laura Shenton 978-1-78952-069-9
Bob Dylan in the 1980s – Don Klees 978-1-78952-157-3
Fleetwood Mac in the 1970s – Andrew Wild 978-1-78952-105-4
Focus in the 1970s – Stephen Lambe 978-1-78952-079-8
Free and Bad Company in the 1970s – John Van der Kiste 978-1-78952-178-8
Genesis in the 1970s – Bill Thomas 978178952-146-7
George Harrison in the 1970s – Eoghan Lyng 978-1-78952-174-0
Marillion in the 1980s – Nathaniel Webb 978-1-78952-065-1
Mott the Hoople and Ian Hunter in the 1970s – John Van der Kiste
978-1-78-952-162-7
Pink Floyd In The 1970s – Georg Purvis 978-1-78952-072-9
Tangerine Dream in the 1970s – Stephen Palmer 978-1-78952-161-0
The Sweet in the 1970s – Darren Johnson from Gary Cosby collection
978-1-78952-139-9
Uriah Heep in the 1970s – Steve Pilkington 978-1-78952-103-0
Yes in the 1980s – Stephen Lambe with David Watkinson
978-1-78952-125-2

On Screen series

Carry On... – Stephen Lambe 978-1-78952-004-0
David Cronenberg – Patrick Chapman 978-1-78952-071-2
Doctor Who: The David Tennant Years – Jamie Hailstone 978-1-78952-066-8
James Bond – Andrew Wild – 978-1-78952-010-1
Monty Python – Steve Pilkington 978-1-78952-047-7
Seinfeld Seasons 1 to 5 – Stephen Lambe 978-1-78952-012-5

Other Books

1967: A Year In Psychedelic Rock – Kevan Furbank 978-1-78952-155-9
1970: A Year In Rock – John Van der Kiste 978-1-78952-147-4
1973: The Golden Year of Progressive Rock 978-1-78952-165-8

Babysitting A Band On The Rocks – G.D. Praetorius 978-1-78952-106-1

Eric Clapton Sessions – Andrew Wild 978-1-78952-177-1

Derek Taylor: For Your Radioactive Children – Andrew Darlington 978-1-78952-038-5

The Golden Road: The Recording History of The Grateful Dead – John Kilbride 978-1-78952-156-6

Iggy and The Stooges On Stage 1967-1974 – Per Nilsen 978-1-78952-101-6

Jon Anderson and the Warriors – the road to Yes – David Watkinson 978-1-78952-059-0

Nu Metal: A Definitive Guide – Matt Karpe 978-1-78952-063-7

Tommy Bolin: In and Out of Deep Purple – Laura Shenton 978-1-78952-070-5

Maximum Darkness – Deke Leonard 978-1-78952-048-4

Maybe I Should've Stayed In Bed – Deke Leonard 978-1-78952-053-8

The Twang Dynasty – Deke Leonard 978-1-78952-049-1

and many more to come!

Would you like to write for Sonicbond Publishing?

At Sonicbond Publishing we are always on the look-out for authors, particularly for our two main series:

On Track. Mixing fact with in depth analysis, the On Track series examines the work of a particular musical artist or group. All genres are considered from easy listening and jazz to 60s soul to 90s pop, via rock and metal.

On Screen. This series looks at the world of film and television. Subjects considered include directors, actors and writers, as well as entire television and film series. As with the On Track series, we balance fact with analysis.

While professional writing experience would, of course, be an advantage the most important qualification is to have real enthusiasm and knowledge of your subject. First-time authors are welcomed, but the ability to write well in English is essential.

Sonicbond Publishing has distribution throughout Europe and North America, and all books are also published in E-book form. Authors will be paid a royalty based on sales of their book.

Further details are available from www.sonicbondpublishing.co.uk. To contact us, complete the contact form there or email info@sonicbondpublishing.co.uk